AT WORK IN THE
ECONOMY O

# JAN BREMAN

# AT WORK IN THE INFORMAL ECONOMY OF INDIA

*A Perspective from the Bottom Up*

OXFORD
UNIVERSITY PRESS

# OXFORD
UNIVERSITY PRESS

Oxford University Press is a department of the University of Oxford.
It furthers the University's objective of excellence in research, scholarship,
and education by publishing worldwide. Oxford is a registered trademark of
Oxford University Press in the UK and in certain other countries

Published in India by
Oxford University Press
YMCA Library Building, 1 Jai Singh Road, New Delhi 110 001, India

© Oxford University Press 2013

The moral rights of the author have been asserted

First Edition published in 2013
Oxford India Paperbacks 2016

ISBN-13: 978-0-19-946771-6
ISBN-10: 0-19-946771-4

Typeset in Adobe Garamond Pro 10.5/12.5
at MAP Systems, Bengaluru 560 082, India
Printed in India by Avantika Printers Pvt Ltd, New Delhi 110 065

# Contents

AT WORK IN THE INFORMAL ECONOMY OF INDIA

*List of Tables*                                             ix
*Preface*                                                    xi
*List of Abbreviations*                                      xv

Introduction                                                 1

1. The Political Economy of Dualism                          12
2. A Short History of the Informal Sector                    26
3. At Work                                                   44
4. Circulation and Immobilization of Labour                  64
5. Social Profile and Locale                                 87
6. Resistance to Exclusion and Coping with Insecurity        112

Conclusion                                                   137

*Bibliography*                                               144
*Index*                                                      153

## SELECTED READINGS

*Publisher's Acknowledgements*                                                163

1. The Market for Non-agrarian Labour: The Formal versus
   Informal Sector                                                           165
2. The Study of Industrial Labour in Post-colonial India:
   The Formal Sector—An Introductory Review                                  211
3. A Question of Poverty                                                     247
4. Quality of the Labour Process                                            268
5. The Expulsion of Labour from the Formal Sector
   of the Economy                                                           302
6. Neo-bondage: A Fieldwork-based Account                                   329
7. Proletarian Life and Social Consciousness                               346
8. Informality as a Regime of Exploitation and
   Marginalization                                                          392
9. Myths of the Global Safety Net                                           425
10. The Eventual Return of Social Darwinism                                 432

*Bibliography*                                                              441
*About the Author*                                                          459

# At Work in the Informal Economy of India

# Tables

1.1 Sectoral Distribution of All Workers, 1999–2000
and 2004–5                                                      24

1.2 Percentage Distribution of Workers in the Informal
Economy and Formal Economy at Three Different
Levels, 2004–5                                                  24

3.1 Daily Wages Paid to Rural and Urban Informal Sector
Workers in South Gujarat, Early 1991                            57

5.1 Percentage Distribution of Population and Informal
Workers by Poverty Status and Social Groups, 2004–5            96

5.2 Percentage Distribution of Informal Workers by
Socio-Religious Groups Within Different Categories
of the Poverty Status, 2004–5                                  97

6.1 Inspections in Gujarat under Labour Laws Applying
to the Informal Economy, 2008                                 127

# Preface

This book is in the nature of a case study. A long one since it covers the outcome of the empirical research I have been engaged in for more than four decades. A case study also because the settings of my investigations from beginning to end have been either rural or urban locations in Gujarat. This state stands out in India for its impressive record of economic growth, which started already in the early 1970s, and for its acceptance lock, stock, and barrel of the neoliberal credo. Gujarat is held up by the corporate bosses of globalized business as a model of successful capitalist enterprise and as a roadmap that needs to be emulated for the good of the world at large. That is not the perspective, however, that can be foregrounded in an analysis which has the workforce in the lower echelons of the economy as its focal point. Behind the facade of the middle to higher classes and their ever-increasing prosperity, so adored in the lore on shining India, lies the vast terrain in which the labouring poor masses are made to squat and toil in squalor. The economy that organizes the interaction between the *haves* and the *have-nots* has been the focus of my investigations all along. It was the theme on which I delivered in 1976 my inaugural address at the Erasmus University in Rotterdam (Breman 1976a). In those years the informal sector, as it became known, was supposed to be a catchment zone for land-poor and landless labour thrown out of agriculture and the countryside. Torn loose from the village but without social capital and having no appropriate skills, they were yet unable to gain access to industrial jobs in the big cities. In the rosy line of thinking which then prevailed the upward mobility of the workforce on-the-move between sites and sectors was just a matter of time. When a quarter of a century later I delivered my valedictory address at the University of Amsterdam, it was clear that the dynamics were in the opposite direction. The outcome still labelled as development was not a clear-cut process of urbanization and industrialization which would have allowed the swelling tide of migrants

from the rural hinterland to settle down in their new habitat and find
a regular job. Rather ongoing circulation and casualization became the
hallmark of their life and work. A turn for the worse was how I wrote up
in 2001 the withering away of secure employment and the changeover
by vested interests to a strategy of informalization that has kept labour
footloose (Breman 2001a).

I have backed up the main body of text with selected readings, added
to discuss in more detail the substance of the successive chapters. The
series of back-up papers are all from my earlier writings on the subject.
Underlying this choice is not an avid impulse for self-reference but stems
from the motif to highlight consistency as well as inconsistency in the
arguments put forward, to comment in a time frame on continuities versus
ruptures in the debate waged on origin, meaning, magnitude, shape,
composition, or classification, and to question why and when changes
in opinion on how to appraise the unwieldy concept of informality came
about. While the core study is written in the style of a textbook and also
has that format, the selected readings elaborate on a variety of issues
raised. They may be referred to for illustrating other points of view or
reflecting on contrasts in perception. While the rapidly growing body of
literature on the informal economy is accounted for in the main treatise,
I would like to draw the attention of readers in particular to the sets of
data brought together by the National Commission for Enterprises in the
Unorganized Sector (NCEUS). I consider the series of reports produced
by this panel of experts between 2004 and 2009 to be a landmark in the
documentation on work, employment, and labour relations for the large
majority of India's workforce, a digest of information on the appalling
condition of the working classes. And more than that, the NCEUS
has added a critical note of dissent to the glowing tribute with which
Indian politicians and policymakers have welcomed the booming of a
thoroughly informalized economy which has kept the price of labour
fixed at the lowest possible level.

The drawback of my retreat into a case study is that it does not allow
me to generalize on the findings of my fieldwork of long standing.
Having been engaged in research on the informal economy elsewhere
in Asia, my contention is that the drift of change reported—a further
widening of the gap between rich and poor—is anything but exceptional.
The economic success of Gujarat has a high human cost, the naked
exploitation and subordination of the labouring classes. Again, what
goes on at the sites of my investigations now and in the recent past has to
be contextualized in a much wider setting. While earlier on development

was the catchword for comprehending the transformation of economy and society within the frame of the nation state, the focus of analysis has resolutely shifted to the transnational realm. The progression in scale to globalization appears to culminate in a reversal of the direction of transformation as earlier assumed. The plausibility of a development trajectory in line with the popular adage of the Rest following the West, that is, going from an informalized to a formalized economy and thus taming the forces of capitalism, has become contentious. A fundamental reappraisal suggests that by switching from state to market and allowing for a hegemony of private over public, informality as the organizing principle of economic activity would seem to indicate that the West follows the Rest rather than the other way around. Time and again I have put on record my critical views on the alacrity with which vested interests are determined to push the gospel of a globalized economy benefiting all and sundry. Those voices do not speak up on behalf of the suffering classes of mankind. To end, I am grateful to all those who have enabled me, especially so during the last 10 years, to continue the research to which I feel a lasting commitment: the ongoing struggle for welfare and emancipation of the labouring poor in the world at large.

AMSTERDAM
SEPTEMBER 2012

# Abbreviations

| | |
|---|---|
| BPL | Below the Poverty Line |
| GDP | Gross Domestic Product |
| GoI | Government of India |
| ILO | International Labour Organization |
| IMF | International Monetary Fund |
| JNNURM | Jawaharlal Nehru National Urban Renewal Mission |
| MGNREGS | Mahatma Gandhi National Rural Employment Guarantee Scheme |
| NCAER | National Council for Applied Economic Research |
| NCEUS | National Commission on Enterprises in the Unorganized Sector |
| NCRL | National Commission on Rural Labour |
| NSSO | National Sample Survey Organisation |
| NTUI | New Trade Union Initiative |
| OBC | Other Backward Caste |
| PL | Poverty Line |
| PPP | Purchasing Power Parity |
| SC | Scheduled Caste |
| SEWA | Self Employed Women's Association |
| SEZ | Special Economic Zone |
| ST | Scheduled Tribe |
| TLA | Textile Labour Association |
| UPA | United Progressive Alliance |
| *WSJ* | *Wall Street Journal* |

# Introduction

The informal economy is described and analysed in this publication as a regime to cheapen the cost of labour in order to raise the profit of capital. My assessment of the hugely distorted balance between the interests of labour and those of capital is highlighted in the text that follows, and upon which I have further elucidated in 10 *Selected Readings*. These are chapters or articles taken from my earlier work on the subject and highlight specific features more briefly discussed in the successive chapters of the main text. Is informality a new regime? Not at all. I found it already in full shape when I started my local-level anthropological research in west India at the beginning of the 1960s.

Agriculture was then the mainstay of livelihood in the countryside of south Gujarat. The large majority of the people in the villages of my fieldwork, four-fifth of them, were either land-poor (self-)cultivators or landless labourers. The latter were employed by the larger landowners who abstained from working on the land themselves. The agrarian economy had become monetized from the late colonial period onwards and wages were not any longer paid in kind but in a mix of cash—less than one rupee per day—plus some food, tea, and other perquisites. My investigations took place at the tail end of what had been a system of agrarian bondage. It was a relationship in which landless households remained attached to those of landlords from generation to generation. Although the terms of engagement were extremely exploitative, a survival guarantee—that I characterized as patronage—had a moderating impact on the interaction between master and servant. It essentially boiled down to the question of how many clients the providers of livelihood were able to maintain rather than how many labourers they needed for farming their land. I attributed the fading away of bondage to the rise of capitalism as the dominant mode of production. The change in agrarian employment towards casualization and contractualization indicated that labour was being thoroughly commodified.

On my return to the sites of my fieldwork a decade later, this trend had become more apparent. The increased marginality of the rural proletariat was not counteracted by state-sponsored relief to compensate for the loss of security and protection benefits that the landlords used to provide to their clientele at the bottom of the village hierarchy. The rising pressure on agrarian resources due to demographic growth resulted in a deterioration of the land–man ratio that added to the already abundant supply of labour in the primary sector of the economy. More significant, however, was the drop in demand for landless labour induced by capitalism as the organizing principle of production. Labour had degraded into a commodity that could be hired and fired at will, without the guarantee of continued employment to which the erstwhile farm servants were entitled. The farming employers did not consider it to be their duty to engage local labour for the work to be done. When outside labourers turned out to be cheaper and easier to control, they were given preference over and above the landless waiting for recruitment in the same village. Moreover, the seasonality of the cash crops cultivated encouraged the influx of migrants at the time of harvesting and planting as well as the need to move out in order to find other employment during the slack in the prolonged interval between the peak periods. No doubt, the rural labour market had never been a closed one. In one of the villages of my fieldwork, I found land-poor and landless households going off to brickyards all the way to Mumbai because of lack of employment at home. Since long, seasonal migration is a familiar pattern of mobility for landless and land-poor households, but the transition to capitalism has accelerated both the influx and exodus of labour redundant in their place of origin.

High unemployment rates spread over major parts of the agrarian cycle, in combination with extremely low wages, explained the pauperized state in which I found the inhabitants of the land-poor and landless colonies when I came back for a new spell of fieldwork in 1971–2. Suffocated with poor households—for the low-productivity labour power of which there was no adequate local demand—the only way to end a life of chronic misery was to get out of employment in agriculture and to search for work away from home. Under the new mode of profit maximization, labour was massively redundant and more than willing to become footloose, but the problem was lack of access to regular jobs elsewhere and in other branches of activity. There was still no electricity supply in the first village of my fieldwork and the country track leading to it flooded off and on during the monsoons.

Construction of concrete roads and mechanized traction, replacing draught animals, did not take off until the mid-1970s. Together with the improved physical infrastructure, the state transport bus service which then began to operate made the locality easier to reach as well as to leave. What had not changed, however, was the lack of connectivity of the subaltern classes with the non-agrarian economy. How could that barrier be broken down? The sub-district town was nearby and it did not take more than half an hour of cycling or an even shorter bus ride to go there. But there were still no bicycles to be found in the landless colonies, a bus ride was too expensive, and anyway, how to get qualified for whatever employment was available outside agriculture?

A life of acute poverty is a life spent at the margins of mainstream activity. The condition of isolation applied, in particular, to the landless labourers in the village. They had no exposure to, let alone experience with, work beyond agriculture. Having no property whatsoever and being fully illiterate, they were also ill equipped to qualify for alternative employment. The land-poor households were somewhat better placed for finding more promising avenues to the future. The small piece of land they owned or sharecropped yielded foodgrains which saw them through at least part of the year, and irrigation made their land more productive than it had been in the past. But all the arable land held by them was parcelled out in tiny plots that could not be further fragmented among the next generation. Still, they were somewhat better prepared when the push out of agriculture started to accelerate. They had sent their children at least to primary school, and backed up by that social capital, these youngsters found their way to and around in the wider economy. The most successful among them were appointed to jobs in the lower grades of government service: as office clerk, bus conductor, mailman, hospital nurse, primary school teacher, etc. Most of these postings were in the public sector managed by the state and open to candidates who, because of their membership of Scheduled Castes (SCs) or Scheduled Tribes (STs), benefited from the policy of positive discrimination. The quota system introduced helped to create more space for qualified candidates hailing from the backward segments of the workforce. This was the period from the mid-1970s until the end of the 1980s when the public sector further expanded and was able to accommodate a small forward section of the backward communities that, while opting out of agriculture, did so equipped with some property as well as other forms of social capital. The vanguard, mainly consisting of the offspring of petty peasant households, provided mediation in support of kinsmen and neighbours who wanted to follow in their footsteps and who needed to be recommended for their suitability in applying for outside employment. The subsequent shrinkage of the public sector also brought to a halt the selection of job seekers from the milieu of the underprivileged, but the network established by the first batch in the non-agrarian labour market was by now strong enough to pave the way for people coming later in the search for work away from the village.

This was the backdrop to my next round of investigations in their milieu with a clear focus on the workforce dependent on the informal economy. Who were they, how did they find employment, what kind of work did they do, which were their further prospects, did they manage to get skilled in their job career, what were their wages and how were these settled, and above all, were they now better off than working on the land in the village? In order to get an answer to these questions, I had decided to shift my research basis to the district town, situated along the main railway line running in the southern direction to Bombay (now Mumbai) and in the northern direction via Surat–Vadodara to Ahmedabad. The district headquarters was also the location for a variety of government agencies, while for the promotion of industrial economy, the Gujarat Industrial Development Corporation had set up a fairly large park at the urban outskirts which attracted capital and entrepreneurs to open small- and medium-scale workshops. Thus, Valsad town became the new site of my fieldwork conducted in 1971–2. Pivotal in reporting on my investigations was the distinction made between work and employment in the informal versus the formal sector of the economy. The assumption of a dual order was the substance of my inaugural address that I delivered at the Erasmus University in 1976.[1]

The informal sector was supposed to function as a waiting room for labour that could not be instantly incorporated in the formal economy. It was to be a training ground for migrants pushed out of the rural–agrarian hinterland who had to adjust to the urban setting and to the different kinds of work available there. Becoming more skilled and engaging themselves in collective action, they were going to increase their bargaining strength and aspire for higher wages. Their upward mobility would result in crossing the boundary that separated them from employment in the formal sector. It was a long and winding trajectory, passed through in leaps and bounds, but in the end rewarded by the gain of secure and protected jobs and all the labour rights going together with it. What the progress hoped for entailed requires an exposure of the employment conditions enjoyed by an urban-based industrial working class and a discussion of the concomitant lifestyle that marked the status and dignity they had gained. It set them apart from the much larger multitude of workers that continued to drift around in the lower circuits of the urban economy. But in a reappraisal of the pace and direction of the ongoing economic transformation, a new wisdom came up in the early 1990s suggesting that redemption from poverty had to be sought by formalizing capital instead of labour. This idea found strong support in the milieu of policymakers who had now openly sided with the neoliberal credo that did not tolerate any intervention in the market and wanted to do away both with the government-run public sector and with the broad range of labour rights. The remedy was not taming the excesses of capitalism, but instead allowing it to get more firmly embedded in the milieu of the poor by regulating, securing, and protecting property rights. The hype on microcredit to make petty capital more productive was a natural sequence to this line of thought.

Right from the beginning of the debate in the early 1990s, I had pointed out that it would be misconceived to portray the informal economy as an urban phenomenon. In my subsequent research, I drew attention to labour mobility in the countryside and the recruitment of seasonal migrants, both incoming and outgoing, for employment in agribusiness and rural industries. My findings, reported in a monograph on footloose labour (Breman 1996), brought together the informality of both the rural and urban economy in south Gujarat. The main focus in the study was on Surat, a city doubling its population every 10 years and where informality has boomed for decades as nowhere else in the country. The industrial work regime I found in this urban growth pole brought out the stark contrast with employer–employee relationship supposed to be standard fare in the formal economy. Initially, the informal sector was looked upon as a buffer for the landless and land-poor classes pushed out in ever-greater numbers from the nearby or faraway hinterland to the urban economy. In town or city, they would find, for the time being, refuge in a kind of intermediate zone where they could scratch around for bare livelihood until their eventual incorporation into an industrial mode of production. Industrialization did indeed occur, but at a much lower pace of expansion than earlier anticipated. It became quite clear that the transformation from an agrarian to an industrialized society was not going to materialize. The absorption of the new arrivals mainly took place in building, transport, and above all, trade and services. Together these sectors far outweighed the absorption of labour in industry. The economic policy radically changed course and formalization of employment was not any longer the awaited outcome. The drift had to be in the opposite direction and informalization was now considered to be the solution rather than the problem. The recipe with which the new policy was sold suggested that total casualization and contractualization would generate more and higher paid jobs. By a sleight of hand, irregular, insecure, and unprotected work was now proclaimed to be in the best interest of the labourers themselves. The closure of mills in the city of Ahmedabad towards the end of the twentieth century motivated me to find out about the impact on the massive workforce that lost, together with their regular jobs, all labour rights they enjoyed as well as their decent and dignified existence.[2]

Informality and mobility of labour are closely intertwined phenomena. Migration is usually understood as leaving the place of origin in order to resettle at the site of destination. In that frame, departure from the village is the beginning of a route that is supposed to end in the city, and this shift from rural to urban is foregrounded in much of the literature on migration. The assumption ignores, in the first place, that a lot of movement for work goes on within the countryside. But an even more important oversight is that many people go off only to return home some time later. Even if these migrants might want to settle down at the place of arrival, they are often unable to establish a firm foothold and have no option but to go back or drift on to another halt, no less temporary than the last one. Remaining on the move is a consequence of their inability to qualify for regular, secure, and protected jobs. Floating around a large number of informal worksites keeps them entrapped in ongoing footlooseness. It is a type of labour nomadism that should be addressed as circulation instead of migration, and this is how I have put it on record (Breman 1996). Economic necessity drives people out of their rural habitat but for quite a lot of them, departure is also a way to escape from a mode of agrarian employment which they experience as demeaning. Does it mean that as a genuine proletariat they are not only free from means of production but also free in their choice of employment? No, because many are mobilized in a state of immobility. The large contingent of seasonal migrants, in particular, is recruited for work far away from home in the dry months of the annual cycle. In the lean period, deep poverty forces them to sell their labour power in advance. The agrestic serfdom in which they used to work and live in the past has been replaced by a new kind of more contractual bondage that shows how these labourers become attached to temporary worksites far away from home.

In my discussion of the social identities that go together with life at the bottom of the urban and rural economy (see Chapter 5), I have emphasized the diverse composition of this huge workforce. A consistent outcome in my long-standing fieldwork is that the social and economic backgrounds in the milieu of origin—that is, having some property or none at all together with ranking low in the social hierarchy as members of SC or ST, coming from an intermediate caste or belonging to a religious minority—are important markers for finding access to work outside agriculture and the village. What further stands out is that the enormous heterogeneity and the concurrent fragmentation, as crucial features of informality, act as major obstacles in attempts at collective action. Still, I do not hesitate to speak of a proletarian consciousness as a shared identity of the subaltern classes working and living in the lower echelons of the informal economy. Next comes Chapter 6 reiterating the point made before that rather than generating more work of higher quality, as the proponents of unrestrained flexibilization would have it, informality is a mode of employment meant to exploit and marginalize labour. The promise of inclusion notwithstanding, the informal workforce is used as a reserve army of labour floating around between town and countryside and sectors of the economy in search of a meagre livelihood. Policymakers have been reluctant to take into account the social and political cost of a workforce segmented along communal lines and have engaged in fierce competition with each other for securing access to the scarce employment available, a rivalry bolstered by mutual antagonism. The overnight dismissal of a workforce of more than 125.000 mill hands from the corporate textile industry in Ahmedabad led to attacks on the religious minority in the city. No doubt, the pogrom was instigated and supervised by the leadership and cadre of a mainstream political party, but the dirty work was done by *lumpenized* elements who, only a few years before, had stood in the mills next to mates who were now hunted in the streets while their property was sacked and burnt down. The ghettoization that followed in the aftermath destroyed the civic fabric of this metropole. Giving a free hand to the market forces and doing away with public space, public institutions, and public agency is paving the way for a climate of social Darwinism, a situation in which the most vulnerable classes at the bottom of the economy do not stand together but are made to fight each other.

The main purpose of this introduction is to give a rationale and provide a handle to the text that follows, backed up by selected readings in which I elaborate on the issues discussed in the successive chapters. However, I still need to explain the subtitle, 'A Perspective from the Bottom Up'.

While the regime of informality is worldwide, this publication is in the nature of a case study drawn out over a period of four decades. It is based on anthropological fieldwork from 1971–2 onwards in Gujarat, a state with the highest rate of economic growth in the country and which has been my anchor point for research since the early 1960s. The rural as well as urban terrain covered is essentially from the bottom up, and I have tried to come as close as possible, for as long as possible, to the people engaged in non-agrarian work. The huge size of the informal economy, in which more than nine out of every 10 workers in India are stuck, suggests that it would be preposterous to try and make statements valid for all of them. My bias in the local-level research carried out has been consistently in favour of the subaltern classes that constitute the large majority of the total workforce. I readily admit that not all forms and levels of informality imply working and living in poverty. No, informality can even be a device to escape from poverty, as exemplified in the figures of labour brokers and slumlords, but also in the profiles of petty owners–entrepreneurs who grow prosperous in the exploitation of the underdogs. Micro-studies tend to come closer to the people engaged in the informal economy. A major reason why large-scale sample surveys fail to capture the pitiable condition and inferior status of the underclasses in economy and society fairly and fully is that the structure and culture of informality continues to be monitored through the eyes of formality. In several of my recent publications (see Introduction, 'The Great Transformation in the Setting of Asia', in Breman 2010a), I have commented on the methodological bias caused by the kind of telescopic view that is the hallmark of investigations having their origin in the formal domain. As I pointed out in a symposium held on how to 'measure' poverty, the distant view cannot but remain incomplete as well as opaque.

This distortion is partly induced by the maxim that what is illegal can also not be put on official record. A clear example is the spiriting away of booze in accounts on the lifestyle of the poor. As I found and highlighted in my fieldwork narratives, addiction to drinks or drugs is at the bottom of the rural economy, a way to escape from the daily drudgery and misery. But the beholders of the Gandhian heritage have seen to it that prohibition remains the undiluted public dogma in Gujarat, as a result of which drinking is claimed not to exist and cannot be reported in official surveys and censuses. Thus, in the statistical data poured out by the NSSO [National Sample Survey Organisation], expenses under the heading of intoxicants are shown as negligible, while in reality, the consumption of moonshine often takes a quarter or even more of the dismally low budget of the landless households. The problem of real expenses that remain hidden is not restricted to consumption on the sinful side of life. There is no lack of case studies proving that the poor pay a lot of money for keeping or regaining a modicum of health. It is fortunately not necessary any longer to point out that in the last couple of decades, they have been forced to shift from public to private healthcare. Still understated, however, is the amount of cash they spent on healers, quacks and self-medication, while trying to avoid the more costly services of professionals. The old adage that the poor pay more for what they buy has also to be understood in terms of their vulnerability—caused by denigration and discrimination—to extortion from the higher-ups: spurious and whimsical cuts in their wages by employers or their agents, bribes handed over to petty officials, and levies raised by the strong arm of the state for giving the poor access to the public arena. All such transactions are, of course, far beyond the purview of the investigators of poverty operating from the formal side of the economy. (Breman 2010a: 137–8)[3]

It is not the view from outside that should prevail but the view from within and at close quarters. Finding out what the labouring poor do—why they do it and how they do it—is bound to fail if the lens used in the collection of data remains remote and alien to the terrain under scrutiny. It would require much more than just complementing quantitative with qualitative methods and techniques of investigation or macro-level studies with micro-level ones.

There is one more disciplinary difference in the methodology practiced. Anthropologists by and large tend to collect the data themselves and also process and report their own findings. In contrast, economists often have a less direct contact with the research setting. They make use of surveys conducted by field investigators and do not necessarily process the data they report. It means that their analyses are based on mediated investigations and demonstrate a more remote relationship to empirical reality rather than when observed from close-by. The difference is, of course, a gradual one. There are anthropologists who never go to 'the field', while on the other hand there are economists who do engage themselves in first-hand studies and handle the set of data they have brought together from the beginning to the end of their research. All said and done, the plight of people in the lower echelons of economy and society is not duly accounted for in our reporting. It is as if their condition and problems are not meant to be put on record.

What I consider to be the strength of this volume, the unwavering focus from beginning to end on one region in India, is at the same time, a source of apprehension because my description and analysis are not presented in a comparative frame. I have investigated informality also elsewhere in Asia, but my findings in Indonesia, China, and Pakistan stand on their own and are not incorporated in this publication.[4] It means that I have desisted from contextualizing the outcome of my research in a wider setting. The need to do this is clear because, although the regime of informality is a global phenomenon, it stands to reason that it differs much in magnitude, shape, composition, and dynamics throughout the world at large. A single-country study cannot do justice to the diversity that exists. Having put on record that a broader perspective is required, I would also like to deny that my findings are atypical. Rather than making a case for exceptionalism, the underlying assumption in my argumentation is that the informality regime, as presented in the following chapters, has a wider relevance and validity. Coined in the early 1970s, the concept of the informal sector was firmly associated with the global South, that is, a phenomenon which had its origin in the economies and societies that had just come out of their agrarian past. The received wisdom was of a transition process, suggesting that the Southern hemisphere would follow the trajectory through which the Northern hemisphere had been transformed earlier on, that is, the passage from agrarian–rural to industrial–urban. According to this development paradigm, which became universally accepted, the 'Rest' would eventually follow in the footsteps of the West. In that line of thought, the regime of informality was considered to be a stage in the civilizational switch that was going on, an intermediate and time-bound break in the long traverse from tradition to modernity. Now, it seems that the pace is in the opposite direction, that is, the West following in the pathway of the Rest. It means driving back large segments of the workforce once again to the wall from which they started to bounce back with the emergence of the welfare state in the Atlantic region a century ago. My basic argument is that in view of the disembeddedment of capitalism at the transnational level, informality tends to become the overarching structure of the global labour market. The economic recession going on presently is portrayed as a crisis of financial capitalism, but an alternative reading of the global meltdown is bound to emphasize the rapidly changing capital–labour balance in the Western economies, a shift that bails out capital while fiercely cutting down on the fundamentals of the welfare state wherever that trend towards a social order based on equity and a fair deal for all and sundry had managed to tame the excesses of predatory capitalism. Informality is now upfront worldwide and has led to a further widening of the gap between the haves and the have-nots. It is an outcome which demands an agonizing reappraisal of the earlier route to emancipation for the working classes of mankind at large.

## NOTES

1. This was on the occasion of my nomination to the Chair of Comparative Sociology in the Faculty of Social Sciences. The lecture was published in English a few months later as 'A Dualistic Labour System? Critique of the "Informal Sector" Concept', *Economic and Political Weekly*, vol. 11, no. 50, part 1, November 1976, pp. 1870–6; and parts 2 and 3, December 1976, 1905–8 and 1939–43.

2. It was the theme of my valedictory address in 2001 at the University of Amsterdam where I had gone to set up the Centre for Asian Studies Amsterdam in 1987. See Breman (2001b).

3. See, on the same issue, Breman (2008).

4. For my reporting on the regimen of informality in Indonesia, see Breman and Wiradi (2002); for China, see Chapter 9, 'Labour Migration from Rural to Urban China', in Breman (2010a), and for Pakistan, see Chapter 11, 'The Political Economy of Unfree Labour in South Asia: Determining the Nature and Magnitude of Debt Bondage', in Breman (2010a). See, further, Breman (2012).

# 1

# The Political Economy of Dualism

DUALISM AS AN ONGOING STORY

The informal economy consists of all activity generating work and employment that is not registered and administered by public regulation. The concept owes its name to clubbing together what it is not, that is, the gainful pursuits belonging to the domain of the formal economy, summed up as all market transactions monitored by and subjected to state inference. The backdrop to the construed divide was the idea that the latter belonged to the realm of modernity which came to the fore in the late colonial and post-independence era, while the former supposedly lingered on as the traditional or *bazar* economy which continued to provide livelihood for the large majority of the workforce. The new sector, the formal one, took the shape of enterprises based on more advanced techniques of production and more complex forms of business management in contrast to the amorphous segment lagging behind in scale of operation, size of manpower, productivity, and capital intensity, but dominant by far in terms of employment. The dichotomy that arose was also written up as the organized versus the unorganized circuit of the economy.

The formal–informal binary can be classified as a late version of the dualism theory which began to dominate, first, the study of colonial economics and was next proclaimed as the hallmark of development economics. In the early twentieth century, the Dutch economist-sociologist, J.H. Boeke (1910), argued that the economic behaviour of Western man was founded on capitalist principles which did not apply to the peoples of the colonized Orient. The 'natives' represented the human species not driven by the tenets of the *homo economicus*—who strove to gratify their unlimited wants ceaselessly and efficiently on the basis of profit maximization—but were content as *homo socialis* to restrict their material wants and obstinately refused to exert themselves to work more than was necessary for a modest living. It essentially meant that they prioritized other requirements than purely material ones. Where the two cultures clashed, which occurred in the Netherlands Indies when Western enterprises began to mobilize native labour—as in agro-industry and mines—the mismatch in economic rationality between the non-capitalist and capitalist code of conduct did not take long to surface. Boeke (1953) formulated what became known as the law of inverse wage elasticity, which maintained that when the price of labour went up, the supply of workers fell. In his view, the gap between the Western and Oriental economic culture was not time bound but a lasting one, the first dynamic and the latter inherently static (ibid.).[1]

A variant of the dualism theory came back in the thesis postulated by Lewis (1954). In his more nuanced version, the contrast in economic behaviour between the West and the 'Rest' was reduced to a matter of phasing. Lewis explained how a capitalist sector emerged in the backward economies of the world by drawing on unlimited supplies of labour locked up in the subsistence economy. The huge reservoir of structurally underutilized manpower available in the rural hinterland of the world became, in this view, the driving force for a development process which saw the gradual expansion of a capitalist sector not propelled, at least not initially, by the urge to increase the labour price (ibid.). This economist predicted that industrial wages in the developing countries would only start to rise once the supply of surplus labour from the countryside tapers off. In his argumentation, capitalism is not immanently Western in nature, and having entered the non-Western world, manifests itself as bifurcating as well as connecting the urban–industrial and the rural–agrarian economy. The process identified as development would expand the high-productivity sector, that is, industry, by the absorption of increasing quantities of labour from the low-productivity subsistence sector, that is, agriculture.

In its final formulation, or at least for the moment so, the theory of dualism is seen as demarcating a formal versus an informal sector *within* the urban economy, the former shaped along capitalist lines and the latter remaining grounded in a traditional or backward and subsistence-oriented logic. This dualism paradigm of fairly recent coinage is the focus of my treatise. An early report which I published on the informal–formal sector binary was based on anthropological fieldwork carried out in a district town situated along the main railway line in south Gujarat in 1971–2. It is added to this volume as the first of a series of

*Selected Readings*, 'The Market for Non-agrarian Labour: The Formal versus Informal Sector'. I have elaborated in the subsequent decades on various features of the informal economy in India where I have located most of my fieldwork-based research.

In all the three instances just mentioned, the wider frame of reference for analysing the concept of dualism is the process of capitalist globalization which has accelerated in the recent past, during the nineteenth and twentieth century in particular. Having its origin in the West, the transformation towards capitalism in this part of the world was thought to precede a similar process of change in non-Western countries, a rupture in an age-old peasant civilization which boiled down to the restructuring of the agrarian–rural order by an industrial–urban one. The drastic turnaround in the dominant sphere of production, which Polanyi (1944) described and analysed for Great Britain and Europe from the mid-nineteenth century onwards,[2] became identified as the route through which the underdeveloped nations would have to pass in their endeavour to catch up with the developed Western countries. It is against this background that the discovery of the informal sector in the Third World in the early 1970s should be understood. On becoming redundant in agriculture and the rural economy at large, land-poor and landless segments started to drift to the cities in search of work and income. Since the formal sector of the urban economy was still too small to accommodate the rapidly growing army of migrants torn loose from their habitat in the hinterland, the newcomers to the city had no option but to accept employment modalities which were clubbed together and labelled as informal sector activity. Thus, dualism emerged as a prominent theme of studies on urban work and life in the globalizing South during the second half of the twentieth century.

## THE PATH OF DEVELOPMENT

In the trajectory of development in the post-colonial world, as outlined by Lewis (1954), capitalism was shown to be a circuit which would begin with industrial production and expand over the urban economy. This was, after all, the way in which the transformation had come about in the Western hemisphere, as documented in the work of Polanyi as well as of many other economic and social historians. However, the assumption of parallel paths to capitalist development in the process of globalization lacks plausibility if we consider the record of Western enterprise in the colonial era. Rather than mills and other urban worksites, agribusiness and mines spearheaded the new mode of production and gave the early manifestation of capitalism in the colonies a distinctly rural flavour. Does it mean that the massive workforce recruited by plantations and mines, required to produce commodities for the global market, was engaged on formal sector conditions of employment? Most definitely not. As a matter of fact, labour was mobilized in bondage and kept in this state of dependency for the duration of the work contract. The labour regime in such enclaves of Western business consisted of a blending of capitalist and non-capitalist traits. The coolie became the archetype of the Asian labourer in the service of colonial capitalism (Breman 1989, 1990).

In the transition to an urban–industrial order which became the dominant development model in the globalizing heartland of capitalism, the plight of labour started to improve from the end of the nineteenth century onwards. Why? One explanation attributed this progress to the social struggle waged by the industrial proletariat against mill owners and other employers. Having initially written off a residue of the *have-nots* as the undeserving poor, it now turned out that even the insertion of this pauperized section was required in a process of industrialization which was still more labour than capital intensive. The collective action of the workforce fuelled by trade unionism led to a shift in the balance between capital and labour. Political parties were established and suffrage had to be conceded to give voice to the working classes in the new economy that lacked formal representation until then.

Another interpretation of the same process was prone to ascribe the restructuring of social and political space to the enlightened self-interest among the bourgeoisie that incorporating the lower strata in mainstream society made good sense (de Swaan 1988). It would dampen the risk of political upheaval provoked by the frustration and anger of *les classes dangereuses* about the skewed distribution of the wealth created. Moreover, raising the purchasing power of the proletariat would benefit both poor and non-poor classes because of the stimulus given to further market expansion. The *social question*, which had become a major issue articulated in fierce debates inside as well as outside the parliamentary arena in Europe towards the end of the nineteenth century, was defused with the emancipation of labour, made manifest in the concomitant rise of the early welfare state. In a steady flow labour laws were promulgated, first and foremost, for the industrial workforce, regulating the conditions of employment: fixing minimum and maximum age for recruitment and retirement; wage levels; mode and frequency of payment; restriction in hours of work; protection against health hazards; etc.

Another major step forward in making work decent and dignified was the inclusion in the work contract of social security benefits such as sick leave, medical insurance, pension on retirement, and dearness allowance to cope with price rise. Of similar importance in shoring up labour rights were the clauses to allow for bargaining for a better deal or register protest against premature discontinuity of employment and to settle industrial disputes by arbitrage. An extensive government machinery was set up charged with the implementation and surveillance of the legislation on industrial relations. The tripartite formula, an institutional setting in which representatives of employers, employees, and government officials were nominated as stakeholders, laid the foundation for the progressive formalization of labour arrangements. The state became an arbitrator with the role to mediate between the conflicting interests of labour and capital.

The transformation which led to the capitalist development of Europe also became accepted as the blueprint for restructuring the economy once India would have been liberated from alien rule. Developmentalism became a policy manual, a feat of social engineering which changed the mould of all post-colonial societies and economies now clubbed together as the Third World. Modernity was the hallmark of this planned and controlled process of transformation in a trajectory which suggested duplication of the trail as it had emerged and matured already one century earlier in the Atlantic basin of the Western world. It was a path breaker–follower kind of syndrome which was meant to last. In the words of Cohn (1980: 212), 'these theories say to Asians, Africans or Latin Americans: what you are today we have been in the past; you may become what we are today, but by that time we, of course, will be something else because we will have gone on'.

In the late colonial era, a bridgehead of modern industry had already sprung up in the main cities of the colonized world. The factorized workforce, a tiny minority and predominantly of rural origin, was regarded as the vanguard of a proletarian class which would rapidly grow in size. The pressure on agrarian sources was much higher than it had been in pre-industrial Europe. The leadership of the struggle for national independence decided that the inclusion of the landless households as beneficiaries of the land reforms to be carried out was counterproductive since redistribution of the surplus in this manner would further increase the percentage of farms too small for a viable holding. The wishful thinking presumed that the agrarian underclasses, bereft from means of production, were going to face a much better future in the industrial enterprises of the urban economy to come. Policies concerning labour came to be closely associated with industrial work. The agrarian–rural mode of production, although still the mainstay for the majority of the population, would come to an end soon and be replaced by large-scale enterprises making use of advanced technology and situated in urban localities. The trek out of the countryside seemed to herald the approaching transition towards the type of society that had evolved in the Western part of the world.

Employment in the formal sector of the economy, the terrain in which trade unions flourished, became the main focus in studies on work and labour, as I have detailed in the second of the *Selected Readings*, 'The Study of Industrial Labour in Post-colonial India: The Formal Sector', included in this volume. The identification of industry as the leading sector resulted in a corpus of labour ordinances which, modelled on the development route in the West, labelled relations between employers and employees as industrial ones. Formalizing labour, rather sooner than later, had become an article of faith on the eve of independence, and the National Planning Committee set up by the All India Congress Committee, chaired by Jawaharlal Nehru, gave the government-in-waiting considerable power on how to attain this worthy objective in the decades of central planning that followed. A public sector was built up, paid for, and directly managed by government. The multitude of jobs generated under this policy, meant to lay the foundation of an industrial infrastructure, was given the firm imprint of formal employment conditions. The writ of the state loomed large in the economic sphere but only in compartments subjected to regulation.

The received wisdom at that moment in time was that Indian capitalism would differ little from the mode of production that had shaped economy and society in the Western world. No doubt, it was not going to happen overnight but as a phased evolution, with a modern circuit surging ahead at high speed and a more traditional one lagging behind. In other words, a formal sector paving the way and an informal sector slowly following in the footsteps of the more dynamic segment. The imbalance between both signalled a trend towards a new dualism made manifest in a setting of urbanization. In this portrait, workers in the formal sector of the economy, in industry above all, are set apart as belonging to a privileged and protected enclave. They are identified as a class of skilled factory hands permanently engaged in technologically advanced enterprises and supervised with modern management techniques. Because of their tenured employment and relatively decent pay, they constitute a labouring 'aristocracy' with a high social standing enjoying a comfortable lifestyle. Indeed, those who belong to the upper bracket of the industrial workforce lay claim to a dignity that derives from their status as organized and legally protected employees. The moment one tries to specify all these features, however, it becomes clear that they add up to an *ideal type* as understood by M. Weber: a compilation of traits which provides a stereotyped image in which the work and lives of only a small section of mill labourers, or for that matter office workers, can be recognized [for clarification of the term coined by Weber in 1904, see the translation published as 'Objectivity in Social Science and Social Policy' in *The Methodology of the Social Sciences* (see Weber 1949)]. To put it in another way, it is almost impossible to demarcate the average worker in the informal economy. The differences among them are too great. Just as progressive variations predominate among the players in the superior league, there is no question of a clear and rigid rupture with a homogenized mass of labour outside.

## THE FALLACY OF A BINARY DIVISION

The structure of the economy does not allow itself to be split in two sectors, one formal and the other informal. As a matter of fact, I have been critical of the formal–informal sectoral divide from the moment this duality started to be discussed. The different segments of the workforce are cross-cut by broader social relationships and operate in structures which cannot be reduced to a simple dichotomy. Neither can a neat fault line be detected between an organized and an unorganized sector, although the National Commission on Labour ventured to do so in its report published in 1969 (GoI 1969). Unorganized was defined in this document as 'those who have not been able to organize in pursuit of a common objective' (ibid.: 417). An irrefutable statement, but the opposite is more difficult to uphold since even in modern factories, only a tiny portion of the employees have ever become members of trade unions. The same authoritative source referred to the category of unprotected labour, synonymous with employment on informal or unorganized terms, with the added remark that this segment was mainly found in larger cities. The only further information provided was that 'very little is known about it and much less has been done to ameliorate its conditions of work' (ibid.: 434). No attempt was made to estimate the magnitude of the working class beyond the boundaries of state action. The lack of any attempt at quantification is an illustration of the indifference that prevailed about labour arrangements and conditions beyond the pale of formality.

At first sight, the idea of dualism is persuasive and the contrast can be summed up as follows. In the formal sector, security characterizes the lives of workers in regular employment. They are paid reasonably well, are properly skilled, protected by labour laws, and duly organized for collective action. Their style of life and work provides them with prestige and respect. In the lower echelons of the economy, labourers are not in regular employment but hired and fired according to the need of the moment. Work is irregular; its rhythm is subjected to sudden and unexpected fluctuations. Long hours of ceaseless toil are followed by days or weeks of forced inactivity. The state of flux is aggravated by the practice of employers of giving preference to outsiders over and above local labourers. Occupational variability then becomes a must for survival, and income is so low that all household members have to work. The misery they have to face finds reflection in endemic life crises. Such divergence, however, pertains to the polar extremes on both sides. The various labels used—formal, protected, and organized versus their opposite counterparts—do not run parallel in a coherent and consistent pattern articulated in straightforward binary.

One of the definitional problems arises precisely due to the lack of concordance between the different dimensions of the dualism concept. It is simply not true, for instance, that informal sector workers manufacture goods and produce services only, or even principally, for clients in their own circuit. Just as, the other way around, many formal sector commodities find their way to informal sector customers. Furthermore, formal sector regulations are often avoided by outsourcing and subcontracting, that is, transferring some or even all business activities and industrial production to the informal sector. These are only some arbitrarily chosen examples, amongst many, of the interdependence and interpenetration of both sectors. The line of demarcation between the higher and the lower circuit is not transparent and sharp but nebulous and fluid. Instead of accepting the existence of a regime falling apart into two sectors, I have opted in my analysis, for a fractured, differentiated, and varied model which illustrates the enormous diversity of modes of employment in both sectors. It is more than saying that the propensities of the one can be understood only in relation to those of the other. Rather than harping on their mutual exclusion, I have gone on record articulating their interconnectedness. At the top of the range is guaranteed job security, and at the bottom, the multiple vulnerabilities are easy to discern. A unidimensional hierarchical stratification does not exist. Confusing heterogeneity characterizes the intermediate zones. The dignity inherent in formal sector jobs retrogrades into infamy down below. At this tail end are the people who can be designated as 'coolies'.

Though the term is banned from official use, due to the denigration it is said to imply (GoI 1969: 31, fn 2), it seems appropriate to the degrading treatment which labour nomads are forced to endure, constantly on the move and sent off with wages barely enough to survive. The focus in the successive chapters will be on the kind of people who are poor and constitute the broad underclasses of society. In addition to intense poverty, 'coolie' life is characterized by arduous manual work, physical exhaustion, and the stigma of uncleanliness. Exposed to appalling work conditions polluted by fumes, noise, stench, and filth, they are rapidly worn out in the labouring process and drained from the vitality needed to pull on.

## MODERNITY VERSUS TRADITIONALISM

In my rejection of the dualism concept, I also refuse to accept the proposition that a modern–capitalist sector is juxtaposed to a traditional and backward circuit in which a subsistence ethos is lingering on. According to the National Council for Applied Economic Research (NCAER), the contribution of the informal economy was more than half to two-third of gross domestic product (GDP) at the end of the twentieth century (Sinha et al. 1999). The stance taken in this volume expresses the view that the spirit of capitalism is the driving force of the Indian economy at large, and pervades relations of production from top to bottom. Among the enormous variety of activities labelled informal or pre-capitalist, there are many which have been created by the capitalist transformation of the economy. Instead of postulating a rupture between 'modern' and 'traditional', or capitalist versus non-capitalist, what should be emphasized is the drastic restructuring of the entire economic system and the interdependence between the constituent parts.

Some scholars, however, do believe that the formal–informal divide is a type of dualism of which the composite parts operate on the basis of different and mutually opposed economic rationales. A major proponent of this school of thought is Sanyal (2007), who has theorized on the political economy of post-colonial capitalism. In his treatise, he makes a distinction between a circuit of capitalism driven by accumulation versus a second circuit labelled by him as a need-based economy, that is, an ensemble of economic activities undertaken for the purpose of meeting needs. While both are commodified and monetized, thus essentially capitalist in nature, the higher circuit rests on primitive accumulation which leads to large-scale dispossession and displacement. Sanyal (2007) argues that the victims of these politics of exclusion retreat in a space of their own, a circuit of informality in which they are engaged as petty commodity producers in a wide range of subsistence activities that are beyond the legal norms regarding minimum wage, labour standards, and social protection. This lower domain testifies to the resilience, agency, and tenacious ability for self-help of the labouring poor who have failed to become absorbed in the formal economy. But this sub-economy at the margins of livelihood is also the result of what Sanyal calls welfarist governmentality in an effort by international organizations and the development state to rehabilitate the dispossessed and castaways by providing them with minimal resources to survive. Underlying that regenerative thrust is the need to seek legitimacy for the capitalist order and to create its broader politico-ideological code of existence. No doubt, the two segments are locked in an asymmetric relationship of dominance and subordination but jointly structured in a larger whole, of which dualism is the organizing principle made manifest in the formal–informal divide. This then is, in his assessment, the type of post-colonial capitalism that has developed in the era of globalization (ibid.).

Although I concur with Sanyal that the informal sector is the product of a brand of capitalism that has refused to acknowledge the right of labour in the Third World to decent and dignified terms of employment, I do not share his view that the formal–informal contrast has solidified in a clear-cut and lasting dichotomy. State regulation has indeed been the criterion that marked the road to emancipation for labour in the process of industrialization as it transformed Western economies and societies more than a century ago. The predatory nature of capitalism became tamed in the transition to a welfare regime. The turnaround meant that the state was activated to bring about economic, social, and political democratization, to become a stakeholder in its own right, in that role promote the expansion of public space and public institutions, and last but not least, to introduce and implement labour laws which would strike a judicious balance between the interests of capital and labour. In the first few decades after independence, the Indian state makers were all set to follow in the footsteps of the development model as it had progressed in the Western hemisphere. The policy resulted in the construction of a bridgehead founded on formalized employment and, by default, in the mapping of an informal segment as containing all labour arrangements that did not fall under the rubric of the lead sector. The construction of a duality, consisting of congruent parts, gave a distinctly tautological twist to the contrast made between the two sectors. Once 'discovered', the informal sector was initially assumed to slowly dissipate in the ongoing process of economic growth that would boost the accumulation of capital and also, induced by increasing state regulation, raise the price of labour and improve conditions of work. In short, the trajectory would be one of formalization.

As discussed in the next section, this premise became falsified with the rise to domination of neoliberal ideology that gave short thrift to the role of the state in the public domain and as arbitrator settling the conflicting interests of capital and labour. Far from being a feature of a backward economy, informality should be understood as an expression of the state's inability or unwillingness to regulate capital and control those who own it. In my perception, the change in policy, which was forcefully carried through towards the end of the twentieth century, signalled that India had opted to speed up the transition to a capitalist economy and society on the basis of cheap labour producing about two-third of the GDP. This is how I understand the logic of dismantling the formal sector of employment and the decision to go uncompromisingly and all-out for a course of informalization.

## A REGIME OF UNREGULATED CAPITALISM

Finally, in this analysis of the formal–informal construction of dualism, the rationale of the concept of informality is located in the labour order underpinning the Indian economy in the era of globalization. Here, we see the contours of a new type of dualism where a formal sector is juxtaposed to an informal one. It is actually a reduction to absurdity since it singles out one factor of production, that is, labour, without querying if and how it pervades the working of capital and vice versa. The supposition that capital firmly belongs to the domain of formality can be questioned on many counts. To begin with, capital owners often resort to the informalization of their businesses in order to avoid appropriation of the surplus value generated by labour through taxation by the state.[3] Accumulation of capital takes the shape of reducing the cost of labour and to make that happen, the writ of the state needs to be circumvented. My argument boils down to saying that if the informal–formal divide makes any sense at all, there is ample reason to explore the binary in the realm of both factors of production. The issue then goes beyond the question of pure and simple labour and should be reformulated to ask why much economic transaction is not monitored, administered, and regulated by the government. It is worth noticing that the accumulation and circulation of capital beyond the reach of the state is a question much less raised and researched than the origin, composition, flow, and control of labour. We are living in an era of unregulated capitalism and that regime, as documented in the subsequent chapters, has dire consequences for the plight of labour. The interrelationship between the progress in well-being made higher up and the sustained deprivation down below should be articulated instead of remaining mystified in analyses that understate, or even deny, the intricate connection between winners and losers on opposite sides of the poverty line. The workforce in the informal economy accounted for roughly half of the national output in 2005. Squeezing labour has become the driving force of India's high growth rate, and the profits made do not trickle down but are siphoned off to higher echelons in the chain of economic activity. In this route, capital but not labour is transacted to formality.

From a somewhat different perspective, what has been said on labour and capital can also be extended to the sphere of governance at all levels of operation. The informalization of the government machinery is a sad spectacle but difficult to ignore. Scams, fraud, corruption on a scale that seems larger than ever before, and the criminalization of politics seem to go hand in hand, rightfully undermining public faith in the rule of law. However, having monitored the changing parameters of work and labour on the basis of anthropological fieldwork, mainly in Gujarat, I shall restrict myself in this treatise on the informal economy to commenting on the condition of the rural as well as urban underclasses and their precarious inclusion in mainstream society. In other words, the emphasis in my analysis will be on the lower circuits of the informal economy.

## IN THE CONTEXT OF TODAY'S SHINING INDIA

What is the total strength of India's workforce and how is it distributed on both sides of the formal–informal divide? The figures, summarized in Table 1.1, on which the NCEUS has based its findings and views are my point of departure.

The population of India has further increased to 1.21 billion in 2011, of which 833 million belong to the rural population, while the urban segment has gone up to 377 million. In the last decade, urban India's growth has been greater than that of rural India, which is a major shift from the earlier trend and is caused by flight away from the land and agriculture. As we shall see, however, it does not mean that, after a slow start, India is now on a fast track of becoming an urbanized

TABLE 1.1    Sectoral Distribution of All Workers, 1999–2000 and 2004–5

| Year | Informal* | | Formal | | Total | |
|---|---|---|---|---|---|---|
| | Million | Percentage | Million | Percentage | Million | Percentage |
| 1999–2000 | 362.8 | 91.5 | 33.6 | 8.5 | 396.4 | 100 |
| 2004–5 | 420.7 | 92.3 | 35.0 | 7.7 | 455.7 | 100 |

*Source*: NCEUS (2009: Main Report I, p. 13).
*Note*: * Included in the informal category are workers employed in the formal sector but on informal conditions.

society with an industrial economy and workforce. With a workforce of close to half a billion—if we accept that, as in 2001, 41 per cent are somehow involved in the labour process—the question on how they make a living takes precedence over all other ones. Of these, roughly 460.5 million people, a meagre 7 per cent, find employment in the formal economy. The 'rest', a staggering 93 per cent, constitute the workforce of the informal economy. Already this distorted distribution shows the problematic nature of a dual construction.

Kannan, one of the NCEUS panellists has, in a follow-up essay (2009), broken up the formal–informal dichotomy into three levels: urban (non-agrarian); urban plus rural (non-agrarian); and total (urban plus rural plus agrarian) respectively. Urban and urban plus rural includes all industry (also construction) and all services (also trade and transport). In line with what we would expect, the percentage distribution of workers in the formal economy is highest in the urban setting and lowest in agriculture, while the reverse sequence is true for workers in the informal economy, as Table 1.2 illustrates. Although a prominent feature in all economic sectors and dominating in both rural and urban areas, informal employment is highest of all in agriculture.

TABLE 1.2    Percentage Distribution of Workers in the Informal Economy and Formal Economy at Three Different Levels, 2004–5

| Sector | Informal Employment | Formal Employment |
|---|---|---|
| Urban (non-agriculture) | 78.9 | 21.1 |
| Urban and rural (non-agriculture) | 83.9 | 16.1 |
| Total economy (incl. agriculture) | 92.3 | 7.7 |

*Source*: Kannan (2009: 7).

However, the need for nuances, changes in distribution over time, and a more differentiated perspective in general, does not detract from what remains a basic cleavage. Insecurity is how the NCEUS has operationalized this divide. In contrast to employees in the formal sector, the rapporteurs argue that workers with informal jobs do not enjoy *employment* security (no protection against arbitrary dismissal), *work* security (no protection against accidents and other risks to well-being), and also have no access to *social* security (maternity and health care benefits, pension, etc.). This set of criteria demonstrates the bifurcation of India's workforce and will be further elaborated in the subsequent chapters.

## NOTES

1. Boeke formulated his thesis in his dissertation in 1910 and stuck to his initial position throughout his career (see Boeke 1953). For a critical assessment and an extensive bibliography of Boeke's work, see Wertheim (1961). In a recent study (Breman 2010d) on the forced system of coffee cultivation in Java from the beginning of the eighteenth century until the end of the nineteenth century, I have argued that Boeke's thesis was inspired by an apology of unfree labour. The peasantry was forced to produce the new crop for the world market without receiving a reasonable wage for their labour or having a say in the quota set for production.

2. Polanyi focused his study on the transformation which took place in Europe. His sketchy and Eurocentric analysis of the processes of change in other parts of the world, mainly restricted to the semi-periphery of Europe, is left aside.

3. In her magnificent book, *India Working: Essays on Society and Economy*, Barbara Harriss–White (2003) has elaborated on the role of capital.

# 2

# A Short History of the Informal Sector

## AN URBAN PHENOMENON?

The informality concept owes its origin to K. Hart who wrote a pioneering paper, inspired by what he found in his anthropological research during the late 1960s, on the economic activity of footloose labour in the urban economy of Accra, Ghana. In his essay, first presented in 1971, he listed the assortment of livelihoods one comes across while walking through the streets of the Third World cities and which did not appear in official statistics or economic censuses.[1] Included in this open-air parade were vendors of food and drink, lottery ticket sellers, parking attendants, market stall holders, shoe polishers, housemaids, newspaper boys, scavengers, transporters of men and commodities, construction workers and navvies, messengers and porters, ambulant artisans, and handymen. In other words, an extensive collection of petty tradesmen, loose and unskilled workers, and other categories with low incomes who lead a laborious but shady existence on the margins of the urban economy beyond the purview of the state. Since the inception of informality concept, the focus has been on the lack of regulation which gives much economic activity an extra-legal twist. The absence of registration is not only the result of an inadequate reach on the part of government agencies but also arises out of an indifference to take cognizance of them.

Quite erroneously, the Wikipedia encyclopaedia defines the informal sector as the part of the economy that is not taxed. Not taxed by the state, so much is clear, but not without levies being imposed. Seen in this way, the use of informal labour has its origin in a desire to keep production or trade outside the confines of the 'formalized' order. The reverse is also true: to remain outside the system of bookkeeping as ordained by the government and excluded from official records and statistics to the extent possible, the employment of labour must remain invisible. This means that, far from being a specific feature of a faulty and 'backward' organizational regimen, informality is an expression of the state's inability and/or unwillingness to control capital and those who own it. An underground economy was one more label that found currency for the motley crowd of operators that includes many figures on the seamy side of life. Hart had a special slot in his portrait for these illicit pursuits which he split in services and transfers. Under the first heading were 'spivvery' in general, receiving stolen goods, usury and pawnbroking (at illegal interest rates), drug pushing, prostitution, poncing ('pilot boy'), smuggling, bribery, political corruption Tammany Hall style, and protection rackets. Under transfers came petty theft (pickpockets, etc.), larceny (burglary and armed robbery), peculation and embezzlement, confidence tricksters (money doubling, etc.), and gambling (Hart 1973: 67).

Not surprisingly, the International Labour Organization (ILO) did not take long to get into the act. The agency decided to launch a World Employment Programme and sent out teams to examine work and labour arrangements outside the modern–organized, large-scale, and capital-intensive sectors of the economy. The first of these reports, routinely written by economists, investigated these modalities of employment in Kenya (ILO 1972) and in the Philippines (ILO 1974). These missions were followed up by a spate of case studies, a fair number of them commissioned to anthropologists, to make an inventory of 'the informal sector' in African, Latin American, and Asian metropoles (among them were Dakar, Abidjan, Kolkata, Jakarta, and Sao Paulo). The choice of sites brought the message home that informality was a feature of the Third World at large. Also, a number of more analytical essays were solicited (see, for example, Kanappan 1980 and Sethuraman 1976).

The research promoted on the informal sector of developing countries from the early 1970s onwards is hampered by the virtual lack of comparison with the profound restructuring from an agrarian–rural to an industrial–urban workforce that went on in the Western part of the world at an earlier stage. The lack of historical perspective coincides with the disciplinary background of many researchers, predominantly development economists and policymakers, who have little affinity with the need to understand this transformation in a protracted time span, highlighting instead of obfuscating the continuity and discontinuity from past to present. It is striking that publications on the subject did not originate among the conventional brand of students on labour, who were mainly interested in formal sector employment. The contents of leading professional journals, such as *The Indian Journal of Industrial Relations* and *The Indian Journal of Labour Economics,* show that their one-sided interest did not change until recently. This neglect was due both to lack of curiosity regarding the lower levels of the urban economy and to lack of affinity with methods of how to promote this kind of investigations. The informal sector included a ragbag of activities for which no statistics were available and to which customary measuring and counting techniques were inapplicable. This is why the landscape of informal sector employment has been charted mostly by anthropologists who were more versed in qualitative rather than quantitative research and engaged in micro-level instead of macro-level investigations.

The definitional yardstick of informal is not the type of activity but the way it is practised. In slightly different wordings and supplemented with new suggestions, the indicators are discussed in a myriad of later studies. The inclusion of several of these characteristics can be questioned. Highly trained formal sector professionals, such as lawyers or accountants, run their business in a manner that does not satisfy the criterion of large-scale operation. It is just as misleading to presume that in the bottom echelons of the urban economy, newcomers are able to establish themselves without any trouble as hawkers, shoeshine boys, or beggars on every street corner. Furthermore, features that were initially accorded great importance—such as the foreign origin of capital and technology, the use of mainly waged labour or not, and the length of the chain between supply of and demand for commodities and services— appear, on closer inspection, not to constitute the watershed between formal and informal operations. The easy answer to this kind of criticism is that urban dualism must be understood not by assuming the validity of each and every separate trait but rather building up to the total fabric in an ideal type of construction. Informal would then be the whole gamut of economic activity consisting of small-scale business with quick returns, low capital intensity, low productivity, inferior technology, mainly family labour and property, no skill formation or merely training 'on the job', easy entry, and finally, a small and poor clientele.

Another way to conceptualize the formal–informal contrast derives from the distinction made between activities that are officially registered and sanctioned and those that are not. Thus operationalized, informal relates to transactions kept out of the sight and control of the government. It explains why it is referred to as the 'parallel', 'underground', or 'shadow' economy. The legal recognition on which the formal sector can rely is not only expressed in the levying of taxes but also in the promulgation of various promotional schemes. The much easier access to the state apparatus enjoyed by the owners or managers of corporate business leads to disproportionate advantages in the granting of various facilities, such as credit and licences, as well as the selective use of official ordinances of what is permitted and what is not. The preferential treatment claimed by formal sector interests disadvantages or even criminalizes informal sector operators when they are seen as making street traffic cumbersome—as, for instance, the sale of vegetables on the pavement and the plying of bicycle rickshaws—or as a threat to 'public order'. The association of informal with subversive or illegal is partly the result of an unwillingness to recognize the economic value generated by the providers of these goods and services. It should also be realized that the exclusion of people living in extreme poverty from access to space, water, and electricity only encourages them to make clandestine use of these utilities considered to be in the public domain and to contravene the official health instructions. Yet, the authorities are prone to conduct fierce campaigns against such violations of the law. In any case, it is clear that the government is not absent in the milieu of informality but actively concerns itself with disciplining the sector.

While looking into the notion of urban dualism as it was proclaimed, I agreed that the concept of informality had drawn attention to the nebulous range of activities, fragmented, divergent, and unorganized, in the lower circuits of the economy that provide a strenuous and precarious livelihood for many people. Highlighting how they scratch around for a living under adverse circumstances has brought an end to the obstinately held belief that those who do not acquire their incomes in a regular and standardized manner, as is customary in the formal sector, have to be regarded as non- or unemployed. However, in my appraisal of the concept, published in 1976 (see Introduction, note 1), I went on to say that the idea of an informal sector gives rise to more questions than it solves. To begin with, the practice of outsourcing and subcontracting production or services has led to the presence of workers employed on informal conditions within the formal economy. Further, the case studies published in the wake of Hart's paper seemed to accept that the formal–informal duality proposed is an urban phenomenon. But it is next to impossible to insist that there is a clear divide in the urban order, while in contrast, the countryside would be characterized by homogeneity. As a matter of fact, the peasant economy *in toto* demonstrates a number of features that are very similar to activity in the informal economy. This is true both for the way production takes place as well as reflected in the patterns of employment. At the same time, it is not so far-fetched to classify plantations, mines, or agro-industries (for example, cotton gins, paper factories, and sugar mills) in the rural area as formal sector enclaves since these enterprises possess most of the dominant features such as large-scale of operation, use of advanced technology, capital intensity, modern management, a composite and hierarchical work organization, as well as a large number of government regulations on how to shape industrial relations. In my anthropological research in south Gujarat, I have paid close attention to the high, although fluctuating, demand for labour in modern agribusiness. One of its pertinent features is that the massive army of harvesters, hired each year by cooperative sugar factories for the duration of the campaign, remains strongly characterized by informal work conditions. The incipient introduction of formalized labour relations in the countryside, both in and out of agriculture, ricocheted on sabotage by employers and subsequently, on the half-hearted, reluctant willingness on the part of government to take a strong stand against such opposition. The resulting absence of a fair balance in bargaining power between capital and labour was a major reason why studies on formal sector employment retained a strong urban flavour. I insisted, however, that if the informal sector concept is of any use at all, it should be applicable to both the urban and the rural economy.

## THE FALLACY OF SELF-EMPLOYMENT

I also expressed my disagreement with the idea, going back to Hart, that the formal–informal sector dichotomy coincides with the distinction between waged labour and self-employment. This is also how the Wikipedia encyclopaedia has conceptualized the divide, stating that informal is the only way to make a living for people who are self-employed, outside the formal economy, and not on anyone's payroll. Falling prey to populist rhetoric, Sanyal (2007) sings the praise of microcredit and in doing so, ignores the critical literature which shows that these small loans, in many cases, do not redeem petty producers from poverty but instead tend to aggravate their misery.[2] In similar vein is his suggestion that the owner–employer of a small-scale workshop is involved in production for consumption and teams up with his employees and seeks to protect them for the predatory practices of big capital in the accumulation–economy (ibid.: 239, 260). This incorrect perception is, of course, in line with the well-known image of an army of odd jobbers and jacks-of-all-trades roaming around in the open air or surviving on put-out-work at home. Engaged in a wide range of full-time or a mixture of part-time activities, they are supposed to do this on their own account and their own risk. Such descriptions usually tend to emphasize the resilience, the ingenuity, and the alertness to new opportunities shown by this multitude of self-employed operators and are apt to highlight the pride they demonstrate in being their own boss. It explains how these workers have earned their reputation as micro-entrepreneurs and why the informal sector is suggested to be a breeding ground for the handling of more sophisticated business which, since it is on a larger scale and capitalist, can only reach maturity in the formal sector. Trained in practice and hardened in the tough struggle for daily existence, one can recognize here the profile of self-made men who start small but, on their way up the ladder, are able to attain the status of true captains of industry.

Another and more critical school of thought is represented by authors who describe and analyse the informal sector as petty commodity production (see, for example, Kahn 1982 and Bernstein 1988). In these writings, the emphasis is on the limited room for manoeuvre in which the invisible bunch of self-employed have to operate, their dependence on suppliers who fob them off with poor quality or overpriced goods, moneylenders who charge extortionate rates of interest for short-term loans, street vendors who are easy prey for the police, sex workers shopped around by their pimps, slumlords who demand protection money, home-based workers unable to fight free from wholesale contractors or their agents who supply them with the raw material, etc. Highlighting their vulnerability due to the lack of institutional protection, the NCEUS has also opted for a definition of the informal sector as framed by a wide diversity of firm-like microenterprises: 'The informal sector consists of all unincorporated private enterprises owned by individuals or households engaged in the same and production of goods and services operated on a proprietary or partnership basis and with less than ten workers' (NCEUS 2009: 12).

What is portrayed as own-account work carried out at the risk of the petty producer is, in fact, very frequently a more or less disguised form of waged labour. There is a wide diversity of arrangements that actually resemble tenancy or sharecropping relations in agriculture, where the principle of self-employment is so undermined in practice that the dependency on the landowner is not much different from that of a hired hand. This is true for many actors operating in the informal sector as the 'hirers' of a bicycle or motor rickshaw who must hand over a considerable proportion of their daily earnings to the owner of the vehicle, or for the street vendors who are provided their wares early in the morning on credit or commission from a wholesale dealer and then in the evening, after returning the unsold remainder, learn if and what they have retained from their transactions. The façade of self-employment is further reinforced by modes of payment that are often associated with informal sector dealings. For example, the subcontracting of manufacture to home-based workers is common occurrence. Piece rate and job work do suggest a degree of work autonomy that is different to the relation between daily wage earners and employers. In the latter case, the time worked is the unit of calculation for the pay made, while it is also paid more regularly: per day, week, or month. The actual mode of payment of this time-rated wage confirms the status of the worker as a regular employee. Putting out and one-off jobs, on the other hand, are in this respect already closer to self-employment.

Last but not least, there is no valid reason to assume that waged labour is a phenomenon inextricably bound with the formal economy. The landscape of informality is covered with small-scale enterprises which not only make use of unpaid labour, requisitioned from the household or family of the owner, but even more with outside hands hired casually or regularly. However, this does not always take the shape of an unequivocal and direct employer–employee relationship. There can be different intermediaries—middle-men who provide raw materials and then collect semi-finished or finished products from home-based workers, or jobbers who recruit and supervise labour gangs—who function as agents for the ultimate boss. In all these cases, it would be incorrect to draw a sharp contrast between self-employment and waged labour corresponding to the informal–formal sector dichotomy. In contrast to the glorification of microfinance and petty entrepreneurship as a defining feature of the informal economy, a point of view strongly propagated by de Soto (1989, 2000) and in various World Bank publications. I suggested in the third of the *Selected Readings*, 'A Question of Poverty', that the promotion of labour rights should be the course to be followed.

## GRASPING AT THE SIZE OF THE INFORMAL ECONOMY

Initial estimates of the size occupied by the informal sector were difficult to come by. It was said to contain a substantial part of the urban workforce, vaguely narrowed down to about half of the total in the major cities and possibly even more in smaller towns. The very broad range indicated the serious lack of terminological clarity as well as indifference towards administrative rigour. The opinion generally held was that, contrary to most inhabitants who had settled down in the city long ago and because of their familiarity with the milieu managed to find their way to the formal sector, recent migrants had to make do with whatever unregulated work and income might be found in the informal economy. Hart focused his seminal paper on these newcomers to the urban milieu. A major conceptual problem, not always acknowledged, is that the formal and informal sectors of the economy are very differently constituted. Use of the term 'economically active' does not have the same meaning on both sides of the dividing line. In the informal sector, women and children but also the old aged as well as handicapped minors and adults of both sexes are involved in the work at hand, although the limited and erratic labour power of these vulnerable categories is not always and fully utilized. This restriction applies to the labour power of able-bodied males at the peak of their physical strength as well. As a matter of fact, one may be employed in both the formal and informal sectors at different moments in time and households cannot be neatly classified as 'formal' or 'informal' on the basis of their occupational profiles. Still, the ratio of earners to non-earners in informal sector households is higher than in pure formal sector households.

The working members of formal sector households, on the other hand, tend to have more permanent employment. It gets even more complicated when some members of the units of cohabitation are employed in the formal economy while other members search for occasional work in the informal economy (Harriss–White 2003: 5). On the basis of his empirical research in Ahmedabad, Papola (1981: 122) calculated that in informal sector households, only one in eight workers is a female. His finding seems to indicate a significant under-registration in terms of gender. Similarly and until recently, the number of children at work has been systematically underestimated. The same can be said for the old-aged women and men who have no alternative but to go on working to the best of their abilities. Usually, they do not withdraw from the labour process themselves but are refused employment when and where they turn up. I may add here that I have little confidence in the completeness and reliability of the figures on which these various estimates are based. This is also because the informal economy tends to be looked at through formal sector eyes, using methods and techniques of investigation that are at variance with styles of work and life which diverge from the perceptions and logic which are taken for granted.

## A WAITING ROOM

The first batch of the informal sector studies created the impression that this segment of the urban economy functioned as a waiting room for a rapidly increasing influx of migrants, the large majority of them land-poor and landless, made redundant in the agrarian economy. On becoming street savvy and more skilled, these footloose labourers would qualify for regular jobs as mill hands and receive higher pay. In their claim for a better deal, they were going to be backed up by the collective action in which they would engage as members of trade unions and in that upward route, cross the gap which separated them from the formal sector. However, the promise of social mobility expressed in this optimistic scenario appeared, in practice, to be only accomplished by a tiny minority. Numerous case studies showed, time and again, that a very considerable part of informal sector workers are born and raised in the city and, at the end of their working lives, have failed to progress much further than where they started—at the bottom of the heap. Similarly untenable was the assumption that informality is merely a transitory phase in the process of development, caused by a slower growth of formal sector employment than required to instantly accommodate the massive influx of labour pushed out of a stagnating and labour-redundant rural–agrarian economy. As economic growth accelerates, concomitant with the transformation to an urban–industrial order, the need for and significance of employment in the informal sector would decline and eventually, little or nothing of this 'buffer zone' would remain.

This piece of wishful thinking had to be reconsidered when the realization came that informality of employment was not a feature of the urban scene only, but had to be extended to the rural economy as well. The agonizing reappraisal led to a drastic increase in estimates on the size of the total workforce employed on informal conditions. But that reconfiguration was even more necessitated by a fundamental change in the development strategy. In the new policy regime that came to dominate in the last decade of the twentieth century, the informal economy was turned around from analysing it as a reservoir of surplus labour to discussing on how to remove all obstacles restraining the free flow of capital. What had been posed as a problem of employability was now found to be the solution to poverty: not less but more informality. The political swing to a doctrine of neoliberalism encouraged free market enterprise, unfettered by government interference, and put an end to the role of the state as a tripartite stakeholder brokering the interests of both factors of production in the economy.

The World Bank took a leading role in lobbying for a major shift in labour policies. In its annual report of 1995 entitled, *Workers in an Integrating World*, the Bank spoke out against formalization of employment (World Bank 1995). The good old argument of a pampered labour aristocracy now came back in a guideline showing that flexibilization of employer–employee relations would be in the best interest of the labouring poor. The basic argument was that, by dismantling the entrenched position of a small but privileged segment of the workforce, more jobs could be created. Labour market dualism, resulting from a misconceived progressive formalization of work arrangements at the wrong time and place, would have to go for the sake of a better future for all.

In many Latin American, South Asian and Middle Eastern countries, labor laws establish *onerous* job security regulations, rendering hiring decisions practically irreversible; and the system of worker representation and dispute solution is subject to often unpredictable government decision making, adding uncertainty to firms' estimates of future labor cost.... Policies that favor the formation of small groups of workers in high-productivity activities lead to dualism (segmentation of the labor force into privileged and underprivileged groups) and tends to close the formal sector off from broader influences from the labor market, at the cost of job growth. (World Bank 1995: 34; emphasis added)[3]

## FROM PROBLEM TO SOLUTION

Government as tripartite stakeholder was blamed for having been party to a deal which raised the price of labour to a level far beyond the competitive capacity of capitalist enterprises and came under pressure to stop interfering in the employer–employee relationship. In rejecting labour market dualism as harmful, the World Bank's retinue of neoclassical economists has wilfully ignored another policy option, that is, a gradual extension of security and protection to the working masses adrift in the rural and urban informal sector economy. The verdict has gone the other way round. Minimum wages are said to be both dysfunctional and inoperative, and most other labour regulations that aim to stifle the free flow of market forces are equally ill-advised. Has not painful experience taught that capital, forced by the need for continuous adaptability in the process of economic globalization, is only interested in flexible work contracts? This implies that labour should be willing to go where it is needed and to work for as long or as short as there is a demand for it. Under these conditions, it is in the enlightened self-interest of workers not to insist on secondary labour rights, asking for a fair price for labour power, let alone to expect the early enforcement of health and safety standards. The free-for-all climate that should reign, according to the recommended scenario, is first and foremost, the freedom of capital not to accept binding restrictions on how to deal with labour. Capital must remain footloose, and that is how it operates most successfully. On the other hand, labour has to obey capital's whimsical commands and has to submit unconditionally to its erratic flows around the global economy. This present course of informalization clarifies that economic growth in the former colonial domains will not boil down to a repeat of the model of urbanization and industrialization that laid the foundation of the Western welfare state. A critical review of the assumption of a parallel development process also has consequences for the policy frame. It means that the informal sector is not going to shrink in size but will continue to expand. In the words of Lubell (1991: 111), the informal sector is here to stay (see also Bangasser 2000).

The high-level policymakers in India did not lose much time to head into the direction that the commanding heights at the transnational level had shown. Private enterprise would be the organizing principle of the economy and the public sector lost its favoured role. In his presentation of the budget for the year to come, Finance Minister Y. Singh announced in 2001, a radical redrafting of the Industrial Disputes Act of 1947. He justified the changes by blaming the rigidity of the existing labour laws. His proposal was to allow companies with fewer than 1,000 employees to close without prior permission from the government. Until then, my anthropological investigations had remained concentrated on rural and urban labour in the informal economy of south Gujarat. The forced exit of large number of workers from the composite textile mills in Ahmedabad around the turn of the twentieth to twenty-first century struck me as a dramatic instance of the turning of the tide between capital and labour, and I decided to study the impact of that upheaval. Altogether around 125,000 regular mill hands in the city lost their formal sector jobs and they had no choice but to try and survive in the informal sector of the urban economy. Once labelled as the vanguard of the working class in the industrial society to come, the workforce made redundant in the mills joined the ranks of the fragmented and unorganized proletariat. They now belonged to an underclass, many times more numerous in size, which has always lacked the bargaining strength to increase the extremely low price paid for their labour power.

My fieldwork revolved around issues highlighting the fall in living standards that were the immediate result of mill closure. To begin with, incomes dropped to less than half the wages earned before. To overcome this setback, other household members were forced to engage in gainful employment. Labour rights fought for by past generations of mill workers disappeared overnight and terms of employment, for example, regulating modes of hiring and firing or wage payment stipulations, were no longer protected by legal codes binding employers to fair practices. The victims also forfeited a number of social security provisions, such as family health insurance and provident fund allowance, which were part and parcel of their formal labour contract. The loss of such secondary benefits further aggravated their vulnerability. Last but not least, as members of a powerful trade union, founded by Mahatma Gandhi at the end of a successful strike in 1917–18, the workers in the textile industry had a proud record of promoting and protecting their class-based interests. They now lacked the kind of collective strength which had helped them to harness the uncontrolled operations of free enterprise. My investigations not only focused on documenting the deterioration in material conditions and the reduction of skill levels but also aimed to find out how the progressive loss of regular and regulated mill jobs has affected the social consciousness of people who used to be identified as standing in the forefront of working-class politics (Breman 2004).

How plausible is the argument that it is necessary to weaken employment security to restrict overprotection of formal sector labour? There is a tendency to attribute this acquired right to the benevolent attitude adopted by the post-colonial state in respect of a vanguard of the emerging industrial society. According to this interpretation, labour welfare was promoted in the first decades following independence to secure employees' interests and to curtail the power of private enterprise through government control of the economic order. Yet, this view can be contradicted by the argument that it was the industrial employers who insisted on job security in the first instance, to ensure that their employees complied with the stipulations of the labour contract. The Workmen Breach of Contract Act (1859) can be seen as an early expression of the desire to tie the employees to their contractual obligations. The colonial government ruled that refusal to work would be regarded a cognizable offence to be punished with detention for three months (Karnik 1967: 25). The reluctance of the first generations of migrant workers from the rural hinterland to bind themselves unconditionally to the rhythm of industrial work gave rise to complaints from employers in later years about the lack of commitment of their workforce. When the expulsion of labour from agriculture and from the village economy increased dramatically during the first half of the twentieth century, it was the turn of the labourers to realize the benefits of a permanent job. At the same time, employers increasingly experienced job security as a burden. Their earlier complaint about a lack of commitment was turned around and interpreted by them as a problem of overcommitment on the part of their employees (Parry *et al.* 1999: 4–17). Industrialists now responded angrily to the workers' inclination to treat their jobs as more or less their personal property. This even extended to employees claiming the right to designate a son or other close relative as the primary candidate to take over their position when they reached the end of their working life. The second one of the *Selected Readings*, 'The Study of Industrial Labour in Post-colonial India' provides an overview of studies on the regulation of industrial relations in post-colonial India at the period when labour came to be closely associated with industrial work and state planning was geared to laying the foundation of industrial society.

The World Bank, in particular, has been a fervent supporter of a policy aimed at ending the dualism in the labour market, not by formalizing but by informalizing the employer–employee relationship. The argument for abolishing 'onerous job security regulations' and other labour laws, such as fixing a minimum wage under the pretext that it hampers the free interplay of supply and demand, has now acquired the status of political correctness. Overruled by more powerful agencies—the World Bank in particular—the weakened position of the ILO in the globalized economy can be adduced by the disappearance of the once so fashionable tripartite formula with the nation state as a prominent stakeholder in the business of regulating and implementing labour rights. Changing tack and in low key, the ILO concentrates now on what it calls decent work deficit 'along the entire continuum from the informal to the formal end of the economy, and in development-oriented, poverty-reduction-focused and gender-equitable ways' (ILO 2002: 4). The South Asian regional office of the ILO in Delhi accepts the rationale for abolishing employment security, but notes that the refusal of workers to agree to such measures is also understandable. Their adamant resistance against further erosion of their employment status is caused by the lack of any system of compensation to alleviate the consequences of involuntary unemployment. These comments led to a recommendation in a prior ILO report that the reforms aimed at doing away with labour market dualism should include a social safety net and the fixation of a minimum wage to ensure an income above the poverty line (ILO 1996; see also Ghose 1999). The rearguard fight is still on, as, for example, in the recommendation to extend the scope of application of labour laws to the informal economy. The minimal stance, formulated in the early days of the neoliberal doctrine, is that there are certain core standards so fundamental that their non-observance should not be tolerated (ILO 1991: 39). The latest report still talks about the tripartite constituents and aims at the protection of workers in the informal economy 'in order to facilitate the transition to formality' (ILO 2010: 7). Whistling in the dark is how I would label such statements that are completely out of tune with what is going on in the circuits which have remained outside the purview of the state.

## USHERING IN THE NEW ECONOMIC REGIME

In Gujarat, the recurrent arena of my fieldwork-based research, the new economic policy of neoliberalism had already started towards the end of the 1970s. The drastic reappraisal which then began insisted on phasing out enterprises and institutions run by the government. I have commented on what this shift from public to private meant for labour in several earlier publications. The politicians and policymakers in charge of this vibrant state on India's west coast, with the highest growth rate in the country, are all set to model its economy on Singapore's success story, while the latest reference point is the river basin of Guangzhou in China. It is a kind of unharnessed capitalism that is strongly backed by the government. The economic freedom propagated tolerates no interference in the free display of market forces from either public agency or civil society (Sud 2012). The shift from public to private, which was one of the tenets of neoliberalism, did not remain limited to the phasing out of enterprises and institutions run by the government. From the last decade of the twentieth century onwards, the neoliberal scenario became a nationwide one, and was also demonstrated in the establishment of Special Economic Zones (SEZs) promoted to lure private capital investment, both foreign and local, to states that wanted to profile themselves in the forefront of the new economy. In addition to straightforward subsidies, very cheap rates for the amount of land required, a holiday on tax, the waving of restrictions on environmental degradation, and last but not the least, the non-application of whatever labour laws had remained statutory were part of the deal that the government offered to the magnates of big business. Under the authoritarian leadership of Chief Minister N. Modi, more SEZs are planned in Gujarat than in any other state, and development has become defined as doing away with all public control on capitalism in its most predatory manifestation, characterized by the absence of even minimal forms of labour protection and security (see also Sood 2012). 'Dispute free' was how the policy consultants marketed their product, which does not allow for trade unionism and collective action. The profound change in economic policy led to jubilation over what came to be labelled as 'Shining India', a slogan that attested to the increasing well-being of the middle classes, expanding in size, and the consumerism which comforted their lifestyle. The good news on the sunny side of the economy overruled voices that spoke of widespread misery and a further widening of the gap between the rich and the poor.

The ugly side of this growth model, that is, the dismal plight of the informalized masses, did not remain unnoticed, not even in official reports. In 2004, the NCEUS was set up with the mandate to review the status of the unorganized/informal sector in India that contained an awesome 92 per cent of the total workforce. Actually, the Commission was constituted not only to study the problems arising from India's vast informal economy but also to recommend solutions. As is clear from the official designation given to the Commission, the nominated members were expected to address issues that the initiators had in mind and that boiled down to the question of how to turn this huge workforce into self-employed petty businessmen. Instead of complying with the cryptic brief they had received, the Commission decided to investigate not how these people should run their microenterprises but what their labouring lives looked like. In the next five years, the NCEUS managed to produce nine reports. The last one, *The Challenge of Employment in India: An Informal Economy Perspective*,[4] summed up its main findings and elaborated on what is identified as the overarching problem: lack of adequate and decent employment yielding a fair wage for the large segments of the workforce hovering at or close to the bottom of the informal economy. The urgency of such a plan of action was underscored by the outcome that in 2004–5, 77 per cent of the population had to make do with, on an average, no more than 20 rupees per day per capita. The Commission's considered opinion of these people as being deprived of a subsistence income stemmed from the observation that the official poverty line, fixed at 12 rupees per day for consumption, was much too low and needed to be doubled in order to meet with international standards.

The Commission's tenure came to an end in early 2009. What happened next? Nothing at all. Receipt of the final report was not even acknowledged by the powers that be, let alone taken up for further action (see Breman 2010b).[5] The stony silence with which the findings and recommendations were met has much to do with the evidence substantiated, which is that a very large chunk of India's informal sector workforce is mired in deep poverty. Their deprivation has not become much less between 1993–4 and 2004–5. In the decade that the neoliberal reforms of the early 1990s started to take off, the rate of employment growth declined significantly, and whatever increase took place was nearly exclusively in the informal economy. There was a similar fall in the growth of real wage rates. As worrisome as the drop in the quantitative growth of jobs was the fact that no improvement occurred in the quality of employment. The reported increase in output per worker means that the higher productivity is the result of squeeze, that is, a further intensification of the labour process. More and more formal workers could hold on to their job only by accepting informalization of their secure and respectable labour standards. Sliding down from what in the doctrine of the free market is looked upon as unduly privileged and protected terms of engagement, these people have come to share the plight of the informal workforce.

## INFORMALITY AS A SAFETY NET
The enthusiasm of the proponents of capital for the recipe of informalization has not waned when taking stock of the alarming findings reported by the NCEUS. As a matter of fact, the World Bank has assigned a new role to the informal economy: to take care of the problem of survival for the unfortunate victims of the global recession unleashed in 2008. The formal sector has drastically reduced employment. The cutting down of jobs, also in companies still making high profits, is enormous, and governments are at a loss for ways to handle the social and political fallout of this downward swing. The pro-free market media have hit upon the informal sector as being free from the sphere of doom and gloom that prevails all around. It is, according to the *Wall Street Journal* (*WSJ*) of 14 March 2009, 'one of the last safe havens in a darkening financial climate' and 'a critical safety net as the economic crisis spreads'. The spokesman for the International Monetary Fund (IMF) is quoted in the same article as saying that 'the situation in desperately poor countries isn't as bad as you'd think' (see Barta 2009). In this view, an admirable spirit of self-reliance enables people to survive in the subterranean circuits of the economy, unencumbered by the tax and security systems that operate in the formal sector. Again, in the same article, a World Bank economist assures the *WSJ* readership that over the next year, the informal sector 'will absorb a lot of people and offer them a source of income' (ibid.). Thus, according to this latest interpretation, the

informal economy is attributed with the role of acting as a safety net and becomes a time-out for the unfortunate people being deported from the formal circuit of the economy.

'Bad luck!' maybe, but no reason to come to their rescue with unemployment benefits and social provisions because they can hold on in the underground circuit. This is one more myth, of course, as I found out on my return to the sites of my earlier fieldwork in early 2009 (Breman 2009).

Another unduly optimistic notion was the suggestion that the informal economy is able to accommodate any number of newcomers. Even if the city is already flooded with shoeshine boys, rickshaw drivers, head loaders, street vendors, construction workers, beggars, and so on, the wishful thinking is 'no problem', more can enter these trades and find a ready supply of customers willing to buy their services. It is the myth of the infinite absorption capacity of the informal economy, and it is just that: a myth. Unemployment and underemployment of the footloose workforce are highly neglected issues which require focused and detailed investigation to shed light on this side of life at the urban and rural bottom which, so far, has remained in the shadow. Why? Because these redundant people can go nowhere to ask for unemployment benefits. In my last round of fieldwork in south Gujarat in late 2010 and early 2011, I found that both intra-rural and rural–urban circulation had gone down at the sites of my current research. This was not because more and better employment opportunities had become available in the village or at a short distance away, but, as I was told, because migrants found themselves crowded out of the job markets with which they were familiar. The same trend has been reported not only on the basis of field-level studies, but is also confirmed by large-scale surveys (see, for example, de Haan 2011: 399). Corroborating the congestion in the labour market is the fact that overall employment has only marginally increased since 2004–5. Estimated at 475.5 million in 2004–5, the figure was scaled down, five years later, to 460.5 million workers in the formal and informal economy together (Kannan 2012: 21). While population growth went on unabated—the 2011 census reported an awesome total of 1.21 billion—employment seems to have stagnated at the level already reached in 2004–5. It would seem that many men, and women even more, are stuck in shorter or longer bouts of unemployment. I am inclined to read this as a signal that the informal economy is getting saturated with an oversupply of labour that is already in a state of reserve. Redundant people, indeed!

## CONTINUITY AND CHANGE

Mine is a short history of the informal sector, going back not further than to the beginning of the 1970s. It was then that the concept was coined and juxtaposed to the formal sector of the economy. After independence, the formal sector became the object of policy and research on which all attention focused. However, as I have already pointed out in the Introduction, it would be misconceived to think of informality as a new regime of work and employment. In a thoughtful and well-documented study on small town capitalism in western India between 1870 and 1960, Haynes has rightly challenged the idea that the informal sector in the way it is presently discussed is a straightforward continuation of economic activity as it used to be organized in 'the past'. I readily accept his statement that the merchant capitalism of the 1990s is very different from the merchant capitalism associated with the *sahukar*s of the late nineteenth century. His closing call, apt and timely, is worth citing: '[T]he task of exploring the condition of informal industry should ultimately become as critical to the discipline of history in the future as the study of large scale organizational forms have been in the past' (Haynes 2012: 313).

## NOTES

1. Hart's essay is an extract from the original paper presented in a conference on urban unemployment in Africa, held at the Institute of Development Studies, University of Sussex, Sussex, 12–16 September 1971. It was subsequently included in a volume published in 1973 (see Hart 1973).
2. On how the developmentalist hype of micro-credit failed to achive what it promised to do, see Arunachalam (2011).
3. For my critical appraisal of the World Bank's views on labour as published in its annual development report 1995, see my paper 'Labour Get Lost: A Late-Capitalist Manifesto' republished in Breman (2003: 167–93).
4. This report as well as the preceding ones are accessible on the website www.nceus. gov.in.
5. In my opinion, the Commission's work should be regarded as a landmark in highlighting the state of the informal economy. In view of the antagonistic attitude with which top-level politicians and policymakers reacted to the way in which the members of the NCEUS operationalized the mandate entrusted to them, I suggest that this episode is not allowed to fade away unnoticed and should be carefully investigated and documented.

# 3

# At Work

## DIVERSIFICATION OF THE RURAL ECONOMY

How do people in the informal economy manage to get access to whatever employment opportunities are available? Mostly, by making use of the social networks in which they are embedded. The village has remained the focal point for the large part of the workforce still engaged in agriculture. Those among them who own some land are predominantly self-employed but are also available for working on larger farms as daily wage earners. Landless labourers are either working as regular farm hands for one of the bigger landowners or have a loose relationship with farmers in the same or neighbouring villages. The trend has been towards a casualized pattern of employment and farm servants nowadays make up only a tiny fraction of the workforce in the primary sector of the economy. Increasing pressure on agrarian resources, caused by land fragmentation in tandem with the progressive mechanization of production, has made off-farm employment a must, especially for those with little or no landholdings. For many households, working on the land is not anymore the prime livelihood as it has been for the generations preceding them. Farmers have become cost conscious and may engage labourers for half a day only. Agricultural labour remains important, but often as a subsidiary activity for youngsters in particular. While males and females in the older age brackets still tend to hang on to what has been or still is their main occupation—working in the fields—their sons and daughters only do so if no other employment is available. Occupational multiplicity is characteristic for the inhabitants of the land-poor and landless hamlets with seasonality as a major determinant.

In the busy period, working on the land is still common practice but in the slack season, the need to find other sources of income becomes imperative. Work is not necessarily apportioned individually and may be assigned to a group of labourers (age mates and living in the same locality) who jointly enter into a contract with a landowner for a specific job—harvesting paddy or any other crop, making embankments, taking out roots, repairing an access road or digging field channels, planting or weeding, etc.—for a lump sum which is divided among them at the end of the day. Search for work outside agriculture is mainly a male prerogative since they can afford to be more mobile than women who have to take care of children and are burdened with the usual household chores. Consequently, agricultural work has become feminized. Local demand for the labour power of men and women is far smaller than the available supply. For the land-poor and landless in particular, survival is only possible if all available household members are mobilized, irrespective of age and gender, when the occasion to earn arises. Access to outside venues of employment has been facilitated by a modernization of the physical infrastructure—all-weather roads and motorized transport—which has intensified the connectivity of the village with the wider economy. This is also how the increasing frequency of off-farm employment has to be understood. Within the village, occupational diversity has remained quite limited and usually takes the shape of self-employment serving a local clientele as petty vendors or craftsmen.

The reduced absorption of labour in agriculture has led to a chronic lack of employment in households for which this is still the main source of income. Working in another sector of the economy, by and large, means going off to search for income in a nearby town or in one of the small-scale enterprises on an industrial estate which can be reached on foot or bike. The desirable status of permanent worker under secure and protected terms of employment conditions, a formal sector job in other words, is rarely available for people with no, or hardly any, assets. A fixed weekly or monthly wage paid without fail to which secondary benefits are added, is a resource that goes a long way in improving one's chances for a decent life. The value attributed to *pagar* (a regular salary) resembles the significance attached to landownership in the agrarian way of life. From the perception down below, hard work alone does not promise access to any form of property. It is, above all, a question of good fortune, getting or being denied support from people higher up, which is of decisive importance in efforts made to influence fate.

The work done by labourers pushed out of agriculture shows a noticeable lack of specificity and regularity. They are expected, above all, to endure heavy physical strain and to work long and erratic hours.

Forced to remain footloose, they drift along a large number of worksites without undergoing the steady rotation of employment as a drastic change. To their mind, all those instances are concerned with *majuri kam*, that is, unspecified, unskilled, and occasional jobs that tax the body and sap the energy to exhaustion. Within the course of a few weeks, or even days, they will pass through numerous sites, located nearer or further away from their habitat, to do the same or a different job, as helpers on a construction site, loading–unloading trucks, as navvy or road worker, cutting down trees, digging a well, or as agricultural day labourer, either on their own or teaming up in small gangs. The meeting of demand and supply is institutionalized in the urban casual labour markets held in the early morning. At the intersection of crossroads or near the bus stations, spread around towns and cities, a floating army of job seekers which includes men, women, and children, bargains with employers or their agents for the sale of their labour power. Many such workers hail from neighbouring villages and are put to work in the urban or rural economy for the duration of the odd job that can end the same day but also may last longer. People flocking daily to the early morning labour market seldom travel by foot more than five to six miles. Those from further away come for a longer period, varying from some weeks to months. Such sojourners bivouac in the town, making their night halt close to the market, in open spaces or along the roadside. They are often men, whether alone or clustered in small groups, but entire families will also undertake the journey. Those who have come for a whole season will punctuate their stay with short absences during which they visit their homes. These urban *nakas* experience the largest number of job seekers between Divali (October–November) and Holi (March). With the approach of the rainy season, they go home to become involved in agricultural operations.

Daily commuting implies that workers have to leave their habitat early in the morning and return close to nightfall or even later. The work rhythm during the annual cycle signals that outside agriculture also, a lot of economic activity takes place in the open air and is marked by exposure to heat, cold, rain, and drought. It does not mean that work carried out between walls and under a roof is performed by labour that is more skilled and enjoys better terms of employment. Females from the village are engaged as domestic servants in the nearby town for cleaning and washing chores in middle-class households. The males with a fixed job belong to the younger age group and are shop assistants or employees in various petty trades and crafts. However, others remain street based as helpers in tea stalls or garages, pedicab operators, ambulant vendors, or porters. A larger contingent, mostly males again, finds employment in small-scale industrial workshops, often clubbed together on estates specially set up for this purpose on the urban fringe. Each workshop rarely has more than 10–20 workers. They are hired as *temperwalas*, temporary hands, and charged with unskilled or low-skilled manufacture as, for instance, assembling parts into final products. Industrial work demands a certain amount of discipline and a sense of time that are difficult to adjust to for a landless boy accustomed to grazing the cattle of a local farmer. Even a few years of schooling will teach, in addition to a modicum of literacy, a feeling for order and regularity, acclimatization to a rhythm based on the division of the day, week, and month into reiterative time slots. To work under a roof, to find shelter from the elements among four walls, in itself gives a higher status to the work that has to be done. But not all those who manage to find access to such a worksite are able to adapt to the demands that go with it. Landowners in the villages of my fieldwork used to tell me, not without gloating, how landless youths from the locality had tried their luck on the industrial estates in the nearby town but soon came back again to work as agricultural labourers because they were unable to stand the rigour of industrial discipline. Such failure encourages the local elite in their conviction that those who belong to the rural proletariat do not have the aptitude for anything else than work on the land.

Non-agrarian work in the immediate vicinity of the village is so scarce that labour is pushed out to faraway destinations as seasonal migrants. It is a two-way traffic of men, women, and children, with contingents arriving from remote hinterlands at the same time that local workers are recruited to go off for many months. This is how large armies of cane cutters, construction workers, quarrymen, road builders, brick makers, and salt pan workers descend each year at the end of the rainy season on the plains of south Gujarat or, conversely, leave for similar destinations elsewhere. The circulation of labour, both intra-rural and rural–urban, will be discussed in detail in Chapter 4. The exodus of labour redundant in agriculture and the village economy is widespread as well as voluminous and their influx into other sectors of the informal economy is taken for granted. However, the absorptive capacity of such employment of the last resort is not unrestricted. This observation refutes the argument that anyone who becomes footloose can easily find something to do elsewhere in the countryside or set up business in the urban streets. Competition is fierce, and those who have secured a niche for themselves will fight tooth and nail to keep latecomers out. Occupational multiplicity suggests flexibility but, quite frequently, this strategy fails to be successful. I have often found respondents in the villages of my fieldwork sitting at home in the middle of the day. 'Waiting for work', was the answer when I asked why. Short or prolonged spells of unemployment is an issue much neglected in studies on the informal economy.

## THE LABOUR CONTRACT

What is the nature of the labour contract? The agreement between the provider of work and the labourer is not spelled out in great detail. It does not stipulate terms and conditions but gets established verbally and casually. Permission to start the job at hand is often mediated by employees who are kinsmen or caste mates of the newcomers and are prepared to vouch for their suitability and appropriate behaviour. Workshop owners prefer to rely for selection and recruitment on primordial contacts. It is not merely a favour granted to 'capable' and 'loyal' workers—who are allowed to bring along a brother, nephew, or friend—but a conscious strategy on the part of employers for keeping control over their workforce, notwithstanding a considerable and rapid turnover. The need for bargaining does not arise since newcomers are supposed to accept what they get paid and abide with the hours of work. The boss is under no obligation to continue the arrangement made and is free to end or interrupt it at any given moment.[1] Termination may be due to seasonal fluctuations, lack of raw material, a fall in sales, or change of ownership of the business, but also when a worker falls out of grace because of sloppy performance, is absent without permission, or lacks in deference to the boss. There is no redress against the practice of instant hire and fire. In a typical enterprise, a core set of more experienced and trusted employees is surrounded by a fringe of temperwalas who may come and go. Flexibilization basically means that a major entrepreneurial risk is rolled down to a workforce that remains casualized.

I have found no sharp bifurcation of the industrial labour market between the formal and informal sector. No doubt, the polar ends are easy to demarcate. In the formal sector, security characterizes the lives of those factory workers who have landed a permanent job. They are paid reasonably well, are adequately skilled, are protected by labour legislation, and enjoy collective agency. Conditions of employment in the lower echelons of the industrial economy amount to almost a total reversal of labour relations in the formal sector. Here, workers do not have permanent jobs and can be dismissed arbitrarily. Production is irregular. Its rhythm is subjected to unexpected fluctuations, with the consequence that the size of workforce varies. Excessively long hours of work are followed by days or weeks of inactivity. This instability gives rise to a continuous drift of labour among the numerous small enterprises. However, it is misleading to focus only on the contrast between the two sides. Instead, it is the enormous diversity within both sectors that should be stressed. At the top of the range is guaranteed job security, at the bottom multiple vulnerabilities predominate. A telling indication of the drawn-out employment stratification, bridging the informal–formal 'watershed', is the progressive informalization of jobs in the higher circuit. Kannan provides quantitative data showing that slightly more than half of the workforce in the shrinking formal economy is now being employed on informal conditions. They may work at higher wages and also more regularly, but their terms of engagement are otherwise similar to those of the informal workforce (Kannan 2012: 12). In other words, a monodimensional hierarchy does not exist. Confusing heterogeneity characterizes the broad middle range where the two sides meet and interact.

The manufactures discussed so far are based in sheds and ateliers in which the production takes place with hired hands employed in these small-scale workshops. Their total number far exceeds the industrial workforce in the formal economy. Home-based workers constitute a third category of industrial labour and represent the least visible but most vulnerable part of this workforce. The dearth of reliable quantitative research means that their magnitude cannot accurately be estimated. Our knowledge of what goes on in this branch of industry is mainly based on case studies. One problem is that home-based work is rarely a full-time activity; rather it is a form of production that occupies more than one household member to varying degrees of frequency and intensity. Consequently, far more women and children than men are involved in home-based work. Since domestic chores are the sole responsibility of women, they are often willing to accept such employment even if it is badly paid. Because they have to combine manufacture with housekeeping, these women carry a double burden. The house is turned into a microenterprise and becomes a worksite with hardly any space or time left for family life. Or rather, both family and household are commodified. Taking care of children, preparing and eating meals, washing and repairing clothes, let alone leisure, are subordinated to the first priority: work to earn money that the household requires for making a living. Most members of the household have to make their labour power available, if not full-time than part-time, for the manufacture of cheap cigarettes (bidis), toys, incense sticks, garments or hosiery, etc.

Under the putting-out system, a work arrangement that dates back to pre-capitalist times, raw materials are brought to the home of the manufacturer and finished products are returned to the supplier or his agent. As discussed in the preceding chapter (Chapter 2), contracting out of production helps to create the illusion that labour is performed under conditions of self-employment. Outsourcing is an organization of the labour process that sets entrepreneurs free from the bother of dealing with labour and from any possible claim on their responsibility as employers. The other way around, the relationship home-based workers have with the contractors force them into extreme self-exploitation. The payment of wages on time rates was a major step forward in the emancipation struggle that marked the progressive formalization of labour in the process of Western industrialization. The standard mode of payment in the informal economy is on piece rate or what is called job work, methods of remuneration that suggest that the workers are free to continue or not with what they are paid to do. It leads to the classification of work as self-employment but behind that façade, a clear employer–employee relationship can be discerned. The manufacturers may also subcontract the work at hand by compelling the women and children of their household to join them in the labour process. During the last few decades, such modalities have become the dominant form of employment in and outside agriculture in the countryside as well as in the urban economy. In the fourth *Selected Reading*, 'Quality of the Labour Process', I have elaborated on these issues.

## RHYTHM OF WORK

The working day in the informal economy is not standardized and that, again, has to do with the pretension of self-employment. Generally, it is more than 10–12 hours per day. At the same time, the length is subject to fluctuations that cut down working time to less than what is required for daily life. The contrast with the formal sector is huge, as I found out when investigating what had happened to workers who lost their jobs with the collapse of the textile industry of Ahmedabad. The work in the mills had a daily rhythm of eight hours, leaving enough time to spend with the family, do a variety of household tasks, and engage in activities outside the home. Such *timepass* has become completely impossible. On paper, the power-loom workshops that now employ many of them on informal sector conditions operate on a three-shift roster, but the working hours are split up in a day shift and a night shift, each lasting 10–12 hours. The boss will not take anyone on for less. More is, of course, no problem. If someone does not turn up for work, a member of the previous shift is eager to step in. Home-based workers can decide for themselves how many hours they work, but the pressure to earn more by starting early in the morning and going on late in the evening is great. Others who work in the open air on their own account are free to determine the length of their working day. Street vendors offer their wares long after night has fallen and have to be up and ready to replenish their stocks at the break of day. Lastly, there are the not inconsiderable numbers who have to spend part of the day or night doing a second job to supplement their low income. The former mill workers have to cope not only with much longer but also much more irregular working hours. Although they used to work in three eight-hour shifts, the shift roster was drawn up in advance and they were paid extra for overtime. Such windfalls are a thing of the past and the regular cycle of their working lives has been replaced by erratic and unpredictable interruptions and long periods of idleness during which they are not paid. The fact that they show up for work is no guarantee that they will actually be employed on any particular day. It is often uncertain whether the working day will begin at all and when it is going to end, while the workers are expected to adapt themselves to these spasmodic and unpredictable fluctuations. In the landscape of the informal economy, waiting and hanging around for work is a common sight. On the other hand, free days and leave have become a luxury and are never paid for.

One of the main features in the lifestyle of mill workers was regularity. Their days were determined by a fixed and rhythmic routine. Although the shift system meant that this routine revolved around a day and a night schedule, it was still a regular and repetitive pattern. To allow the workers to meet all kind of personal obligations, there was a leave system. Their days, weeks, and months were determined by the work at the mill, but they had become familiar with the notion of free time. While in the informal economy leisure is an alien concept, mill workers had become accustomed to spend time 'doing nothing' or to maintain their social contacts outside the home. The factory whistle would announce the change of shift but the mill workers were also equipped with clocks and watches which enabled them to make the distinction between mill time and time spent on a wide range of off-work activities. As a result of this regularity and stability, life had become more dignified. On the other hand, the mass of unskilled workers in the informal economy has no other choice but to subject themselves to the dictates of the production process in which they have to earn their livelihood. Their submission is so complete that outside the work sphere, they have almost no say even over their private life.

In agro-industry, the cane cutters' long working day is extended into the night by another three or four hours when they have to return to the fields to load, on to the lorries, the cane they have cut during the day. The story of suffering is not different for labourers in the brickfields. Their work starts between two and four o'clock at night and continues until the end of the morning. They then have a break, when the women prepare a meal and do other household chores. In the afternoon, it is time to clear the worksite for the ensuing night. Bricks that have been laid out to dry are stacked in rows a little further away. In the evening, the water-soaked earth is taken out of the pits into which it has been dumped the day before and heaped up in lumps close to the spot where the brick maker will sit or squat a few hours later. Altogether, the result is a working day lasting 14–16 hours, but that length does not sufficiently illustrate the burden of the job. Unconditional surrender by labour is manifested in the complete subjection of life to the demands of the job. The smooth and efficient management of agro-industry forces cane cutters to load, at night, the amount of cane they have cut during the day, because the mills' machines run continuously. But why is it necessary that the purely manual production of bricks should start at night? Shrugging off my queries, many brickworks' owners said that this was customary in the branch of industry. Some employers said that drying is a very gradual process. If wet bricks are immediately exposed to the glaring sun, they would break easily even before being put into the kiln. Others argued that workers are less distracted when it is dark, that they work harder in winter to keep warm, and that in summer they prefer to work at night to avoid the day's heat.

A common complaint is that members of the lower castes who come straight from the countryside into an industrial milieu are not able to work attentively and regularly for hours at a time. Fresh migrants are reputed for not yet being spoilt by the comforts of urbanity, but already, earlier generations of employers have expressed their doubts about the working zeal of the newcomers from the rural hinterland. 'Although the vast majority of the workforce is unskilled, urban employment may require certain patterns of coordination and motor responses which differ from traditional agriculture and thus influence the possibilities of commitment.... There may be need for more rhythm and monotonous repetition, coordination, careful timing, and higher levels of spatial, verbal or logical conception' (Kanappan 1970: 321). This stereotype is further articulated in the case of labour from a tribal background. It is said that, as carefree children of nature, they lack the self-discipline that is the basis of any successful performance when becoming engaged in modern methods of production. A more sensible explanation, however, is the lack of regularity inherent to the labour process of the informal economy. Characteristic for the employment regime of the informal economy is the sudden and unexpected alteration of high and low tides, not only per season but even in daily activity. Hours and days of almost unbroken drudgery make way for shorter or longer periods of forced idleness. This contrast between maximum efforts and imposed inactivity reflects the logic of informal sector business and is not the manifestation of an internalized uneconomic idiosyncrasy that disqualifies the worker from a better existence. These men, women, and children have to be present wherever, whenever, and to the extent that there is a need for their services. What seems, at first sight, a disjointed and irregular schedule is not due to unwillingness or lack of discipline. Such an opinion does not do justice to behaviour that shows utmost flexibility in systematically attuning labour supply to the strongly fluctuating demand. Of relevance here is the point Thompson (1993 [1967]: 398) made about the problem of 'disciplining a labour force that is only partially and temporarily "committed" to an industrial way of life'.[2] But time-thrift and a clear demarcation between 'work' and 'life' seem to presuppose an industrial milieu in tune with the factorized urban capitalism that emerged and became dominant in the Atlantic world from the end of the nineteenth century onwards. It does not mean that lack of time consciousness is a feature of the urban and rural proletariat that I have researched in India in the past decades. The daily rhythm of the working classes in the informal economy is conditioned by the need to surrender completely to the unreserved claim on their availability at all hours of the day or night, in all seasons of the year. That this potential demand is only partially and temporarily actualized has to do not so much with their faulty time-thrift, but with the low and capricious demand that is made on their labour power. Taking stock of the quality of the labour process in the informal economy, the next section elaborates on the make-do skilling that takes place, the limited use of technology, the excessive length of the working day, and the awful, debilitating conditions of employment.

## SCHOOLING, SKILLING, AND DE-SKILLING

Nowadays, children from landless households also tend to go to school, although most of them do not study beyond the primary level at best. It means that they remain stuck at a very low level of literacy and numeracy. Parents prepared to send their sons, and even daughters, to secondary school have to bear all kind of expenses. The handful that persevere and go for vocational training are made to pay even more. Due to lack of social capital, the children from poor households are in need of recommendation from the better-off to break out of their milieu. Investment in education is not only costly but also risky because even qualified as skilled workers with a certificate from an Industrial Training Institute, candidates have to face a lot of problem in their search for work. Jobs in the formal sector are so scarce that they have to be bought, and the land-poor and landless do not have the kind of money asked as an entrance fee to the formal economy. Under such adverse circumstances, a better choice for somewhat skilled workers is to go for self-employment. Actually, in the World Bank's standard way of thinking, this is the route to be followed when self-employed peasants opt out of agriculture. In this perception, they first tend to become wage labourers in the informal sector, earn some money, pick up skills, and ultimately, with the savings made, set up an independent business. Labour market flexibility is, in this benign scenario, a winner's and not a loser's game. The myth helps to explain why the Bank so fulsomely praises maximal adaptability as the principal talent required for making one's way up in the labour hierarchy. The trajectory outlined is different from the ground practice in the large majority of cases.

For the labouring poor, only the meanest and most arduous of jobs are accessible. Such work is, by definition, unskilled and does not require much prior experience. Learning by doing is the way newcomers pick up what to do and how to do it. But that training also does not come free of cost. Cuts made in the going wage rate at the time of apprenticeship explain why those who belong to landless castes seldom qualify for skilled jobs. The cash needed for becoming a craftsman prevents youngsters belonging to households without any means of production from joining the somewhat better paid ranks of the informal workforce. Moreover, even at the tail end of the economy, not all jobs, however menial and strenuous they may be, are open to each and every one. Specific branches of trade and industry, as also urban or rural slum habitats, are broken up in distinct social clusters to which people belong with a shared identity along caste, ethnic, religious, or other fault lines. The fences they have erected around their niches to keep out 'outsiders' conflict with the notion of a total state of flux and an unstructured pell-mell in the lower circuits of the informal economy. The dignity inherent in formal sector work changes into disrespect in the lower circuits of the economy. At the bottom is the mass of people who may be termed 'coolies', although, as was pointed out earlier, that term is considered to be so derogatory that it is banned from official use. The disrespect is due to its association with physical exhaustion, the odium of untouchability, and subhuman working conditions characterized by exposure to fumes, noise, stench, and filth. Such workers are made to endure a living hell.

No doubt, skilling upgrades the work status and the other way around, deskilling leads to a loss of dignity. The latter is what happened to the erstwhile mill hands in Ahmedabad. Their informal sector work no longer requires any skill and I regard the stories about the machines they used to operate—telling me the way their bodies shook with the vibrations of the loom—less as nostalgia for what they miss than a complaint that whatever they are doing now no longer has any value. The pride of skill shows on the face of the perambulatory craftsmen who assemble at the early morning labour market. Squatting on the ground, carpenters, masons, painters, and plumbers have their tools in front of them to convey that their labour power is for sale, but customers have to pay a higher price for it than for the hire of the much more numerous unskilled job seekers standing by who have just their labour power on offer. The NCEUS (2009) observed in its final report that the proportion of skilled workers in the labour force was very low in the last decade of the twentieth century. In rural areas, only about 10 per cent of the men and 6.3 per cent of the women possessed specific marketable (formal or non-formal) skills. It was somewhat higher in the urban economy, but still less than 20 per cent for men and about half of that for women. The Commission concluded that skill formation should be at the core of efforts to improve the living standards of the masses working in the informal economy and that formal education would have to be the lever for accomplishing this objective. It is rather unlikely that this ambition is going to be fulfilled in the current political and policy climate.

## CAPITAL IN THE INFORMAL ECONOMY

In south Gujarat, the rise of Surat as a focal point of informal sector activity is a direct consequence of the employment crisis in the formal economy. While in Ahmedabad, the city which used to be called the Manchester of India, more than 50 corporate textile mills closed down in the final decades of the twentieth century, Surat's population increased from less than 500,000 in 1971 to nearly 1,700.000 in 1991 and again, doubling that number in the next two decades to reach more than 4,500.000 million inhabitants in 2011. An increase of 76 per cent means that Surat is possibly the fastest growing city in India during the last decade.[3] The boom of the informal economy located in this urban agglomeration was facilitated by the Government of Gujarat which promised subsidies, tax holidays, 'easy' labour laws, and other bonuses to out-of-state capital. The result, however, is that the public policymakers lost whatever control they had over the industrial climate. As a matter of fact, Surat has paved the way for the wave of liberalization that swept through the county, endorsed and promoted by the World Bank, and it cannot be denied, with enormous success as far as the growth in value and volume of production is concerned. But can these dynamics be framed as development? Of the total money circulation in the city, 60 per cent is *kalu* or *number be*, going around in the black circuit. Informal capital is abundantly available and its owners do not mind spending it casually and conspicuously. From *lakhpati*s (with more than Rs 100,000), many have become *crorepati*s (having above Rs 10,000,000).

Imitating the leisurely lifestyle of the mercantile lords in the feudal past, the capitalist class of the nouveaux riches has built posh bungalows and skyscrapers. These *haves* and *have-more* are, however, tiny enclaves in the landscape of industrial workshops intermixed with slums. From the jerry-built sheds sprawled around, a deafening noise erupts, the ceaseless humming of power looms, and in addition to that, the piercing shrill of the crimping machines that, even at a distance, produce noise debilitating to healthy ears. Adjacent to these workshops are the labourers' hutments and dormitories owned and given out on rent by slumlords. The worksites and sleeping places are not far apart, sometimes even coinciding. The workforce employed in the power looms is split up in two shifts that alternate with each other every 12 hours. The capitalist regime of Surat is an industrial jungle. In order to understand the work and life pattern of the lumpen proletariat in this big cesspool, I have to add that it is made up of migrants. They do not come from the immediate hinterland of the city but hail from places at far greater distance: Saurashtra, Rajasthan, Uttar Pradesh, Orissa, Maharashtra, and Andhra Pradesh. The large majority consists of young males between 15–25 years of age. Those who are married have usually left home without their family. A distinct feature of Surat is the gender distortion in its demographic profile. The balance has become more uneven over the past few decades and is as low as 500–600 women per 1,000 men in some of the most congested localities. In the streets and workshops, the dominated sex is noticeable for its sparse presence. Most migrants are temporary and underpaid hands, constantly rotating along the enterprises in their line of work. These men are hired and fired according to the needs of their industrial bosses until they are worn out. Wages are paid on the basis of piece rate and once productivity falls, because of age or failing health, the workers are rejected and driven back to their place of origin. Sucked oranges, is how these rejects are called.

## WAGES

What are the daily earnings of workers in the informal economy? In the early 1990s, I made a list of the going wage rate for different categories in south Gujarat, the area of my research that is reproduced here (Table 3.1). It is still relevant in the sense that the distance between the various groups of workers is presently, two decades later, about the same as it was then. Of course, the level is higher by a factor five nowadays, but that increase is no indication of any substantial progress made because inflation and rising prices of food, clothes, transport, health care, etc., have led to a stagnation of real wages, particularly in the lowest income brackets.

With a daily wage of 50 rupees in my fieldwork villages in early 2011, agricultural labourers have firmly remained at the bottom of the heap.

TABLE 3.1   Daily Wages Paid to Rural and Urban Informal Sector Workers in South Gujarat, Early 1991

| Kind of Work | Amount (in Rs) |
| --- | --- |
| Agricultural labour in the villages of my fieldwork | 10–12 |
| Seasonal work in rural industries (cane cutting, stone quarries, road construction, brickworks, salt pans) | 10–15 |
| Casual labour in and near small towns | 15–20 |
| 'Helpers' on industrial estates within commuting distance from the village | 16–20 |
| Casual workers in Surat's urban labour markets | 25–30 |
| Semi-skilled workers, regular employees of urban workshops | 35–45 |
| Skilled power-loom operators | 50–60 |
| All-round diamond cutters–polishers | 55–70 |

*Source*: Breman (1996: 142).

This finding is backed up by what the NCEUS wrote about this class of workers: 'Overall wage levels of agricultural labourers have been very low and further the wage rates have registered a low growth rate particularly through the nineties' (NCEUS 2009: 241). Apart from the wage rate, the income gained by various sorts of labour is determined by the total number of days worked per year. In this respect, too, the informal sector shows great variation, not only among different types of activity but even within the same branch of industry or occupational skill. That diversity makes it even more difficult to estimate the annual income of the workers and the households to which they belong. The cyclical character of activity that is said to be characteristic of agriculture also applies to a large part of the informal economy. In the monsoon, for example, work in the open air has to cease completely or is drastically cut down. Such peaks and slacks in production do not only occur in agriculture and the countryside, but also on industrial sites and in urban workshops operating under a roof. This may be due to temporary shortage of raw materials, fall or rise in sales, etc. As pointed out earlier, small-scale employers use such fluctuations to justify their decision for not increasing the capital intensity of their business and for keeping their workforce 'flexible', that is, not in permanent employ. In fact, the capricious and often unpredictable alternation between work and idleness illustrates the unregulated and insecure nature of labour in the informal economy. *Akashi roji*, what work the day will bring, is as unpredictable as the weather, is how casual workers speak about their daily struggle for livelihood.

The obvious solution of combining various sorts of employment, occupational multiplicity in other words, is feasible only to a limited extent. Rather than contrasting with one another, the peaks and falls in various branches of rural and urban industry show a similar pattern of inclusion and exclusion. Agricultural work in the village can, to some extent, be alternated with unskilled work as day labourer elsewhere. However, any more skilled specialization that implies a higher income almost excludes the possibility of temporarily seeking another source of income. The various worksites providing more or less regular jobs are almost shut to one another. With the exception of footloose workers at the bottom of the rural and urban economy, roaming around individually or teaming up in small clusters in search of work, the informal sector is broken down in various circuits of labour which, notwithstanding the low degree of skill required, have little linkage with one another. The travel costs involved, the lack of contacts, inexperience, and barriers thrown up by workers already occupying those niches, all play an important role.

This segmentation allowed me to calculate, in the course of my local-level investigations, that the lowest paid informal sector workers who remain stuck in agriculture could not survive unless they earned wages for at least 120–50 days per year. The majority manage somehow to find employment for 150–240 days. The proportion that can count on work for up to 270 or more days per year is much smaller. The more skilled among them, who even in the eyes of their employers rank as regular, represent an elite among the informal sector proletariat. Finally, there are all kinds of wage variations, not only among enterprises in the same branch of activity but even among workers who happen to be engaged by an employer for the same work. These differences are sometimes due to seniority or skill. However, an employer in the informal economy may also decide to pay a slightly higher wage to workers who have gained his favour, for whatever reason, than to the rest of the workforce, without giving any explanation for such preferential treatment.

It is not arbitrary but structural discrimination that women suffer from in all labour markets which belong to the informal economy. For example, there are no female power-loom operators. They are only hired in these workshops for non-mechanized jobs that do not require any skill. There are also a lot of women around on construction sites but again, invariably, as 'helpers' to males who are considered to be more skilled. Sharp gender differentiation is a major feature of the wage hierarchy even when male and female workers perform the same tasks. It will hardly be necessary to add that women and children are also exposed to practices of exploitation and subordination at the hands of employers and labour contractors. Their commodification is carried over into the sphere of the household. The domination of adult males over wives and minors is taken for granted. It is a mode of control backed up by domestic violence against these most vulnerable members of the informal workforce.

## EXIT FROM THE FORMAL ECONOMY
Mahatma Gandhi's struggle to improve the condition of the mill workers in Ahmedabad began when he took the initiative to launch the Textile Labour Association (TLA) in 1917–18, at the end of a successful strike. The father of the nation presented the working class with a code of good conduct. This catechism, which had to be strictly followed, was at the top of the union's agenda and became a determining factor in the regulation of industrial relations for the next half century. One of the articles of faith was that women workers would have to be expelled from the mills. If wives go out to work, Gandhi admonished, our social life

will be ruined and our moral standards will decline. In his view, the man was the breadwinner who, as a caring husband, used his wages to exempt his wife from paid work, to allow her to take good care of her husband, bring up her children, and be busy with other domestic tasks. The working class should arrange their lives in accordance with the standards of a petit bourgeois lifestyle. The flipside of the workman's ethos Gandhi preached was, of course, payment of a family wage. The (male) worker's pay should be enough to cover the basic needs of the man, his wife, and two children. The TLA saw to the phasing out of women from the textile mills in Ahmedabad in the early 1930s, as part of a rationalization drive in the midst of the economic recession, and their expulsion from formal sector employment did not abate in subsequent decades. On their part, the captains of industry had to concede, not overnight but slowly, to the demand for a living wage for the male workforce that included more than bare survival (Breman 2004: 109–16). The gradual formalization of industrial relations ended with the collapse of the textile industry towards the end of the twentieth century. The fifth of the *Selected Readings*, 'The Expulsion of Labour from the Formal Sector of the Economy', deals with what happened in Ahmedabad when the corporate mills in this city started to close down one after the other. The huge workforce was dismissed overnight and their households had to vie for their livelihood in the informal economy. It also meant that wages forthwith were paid according to the labour power rendered without any overhead added for taking care of dependent members of the household.

A fall from paradise was how the dismissed mill workers experienced their deportation to the informal economy. I have already mentioned earlier in the chapter that the mill workers were able to afford more than the gratification of their most basic needs. Protection against illness or disability contributed to the security and stability of the workers' lives. The insurance was not too expensive and the coverage extended to other household members. The employment contract provided for a lump-sum payment on reaching retirement age, a benefit financed on the basis of a provident fund to which the workers contributed through a savings scheme. The wage level and regularity of payment meant that the workers could buy whatever they needed on credit. The dignity and quality of life that mill work permitted was much more than just the security of allowing for a little more financial breathing space. The capacity to build a modest reserve also expanded the workers' social space and enabled them to view their livelihood from a long-term perspective. The decisive moment came when they were given a permanent employment contract.

One worker told me that in the evening of the day on which he heard that he no longer had to work as a *badli* (stand-in), the parents of the woman who is now his wife came to make him a proposal of marriage. The security of a job 'for life', and the wide range of rights that went with it, encouraged investment in the future. The education of children was given a higher priority than before, as was the arrangement of marriages that would enhance family's standing in the community. The status of mill worker gave those who were previously nameless a much clearer social visibility and identity.

However, with the loss of their formal sector job, all that has changed now. Free time is a luxury that no longer can be enjoyed. Days, weeks, and months are spent trying to earn money to survive and time that is not devoted to that is not leisure time but unemployed time. The propensity to save—building up a reserve that could be used when the occasion arises—is a thing of the past and instead, debts have to be incurred to cover even everyday expenses. The uncertainty of existence has led to a loss of creditworthiness. The struggle to survive demands so much alertness and energy that there is no material or mental room left to invest in the future. Children have to leave school at the end of their primary education, a level that is far too low to give them a favourable start in the labour market. The economy does not really need the child labour, of course, but many children, egged on by their parents, cannot afford to remain unemployed. The former mill workers also worry a great deal about their children's marriage and the cost of this life cycle event. Looking around for suitable candidates is time consuming and assumes that the parents can afford to deliberate at length and carefully on their choice. In the absence of a reasonable dowry, girls, in particular, are forced to accept partners who would never have been eligible before.

With all the variability and fluctuations inherent to employment in the informal economy, what these workers have in common is their exclusion from the manner in which work is arranged in the formal sector. To begin with, the large majority of households cannot survive on the earnings of a single member. In this milieu, a family wage is a notion unheard of. Irrespective of gender and age, the capacity to work of more than one member has to be mobilized, either continuously or off and on, to add to the household income. Not everybody shares to the same extent in the work at hand, but exemption from the obligation to add to the joint budget can only sparingly be given. Children at work are not a rare sight in the informal economy and the practice of payment on piece rate has a lot to do with the utilization of whatever labour power they have.

In the same way, men and women of old age, pressed by need, still pull on in order to earn their minimal keep. Wages are not only much lower in the informal economy, but they are also paid more irregularly. What is termed a daily wage does not necessarily mean that the workers get paid or paid in full at the end of the day. They may have asked for an advance earlier on or, the other way around, the providers of work tell them to come back the next day and then receive the cash outstanding to them. On both sides, there is a strategy to keep the relationship going. Work and payment for it are not necessarily closely connected. When the latter comes before the former, it is because employment is not always available and the proletarian households are not able to build up a reserve that sees them through the lean days and seasons. Landless workers are often not able to accept jobs for which they will be paid only at the end of the month. The household to which they belong simply does not have the carrying capacity to forego the day-to-day wages for such a long time. A way to deal with the problem of deficiency is to sell the labour power in advance, to ask an employer for a loan, *karchi* (literally to eat), with the promise to come for work whenever required with the implied condition that the wage will be lower than the going market rate. Much bigger loans are required to finance life cycle events, cost of marriage above all. Employers are only willing to help out workers with whom they have more than an occasional relationship and whom they feel can be trusted to honour their obligation. The payment of a substantial advance for future work may be the beginning of a relationship that I have qualified as neo-bondage. Since this is a mode of recruitment particularly prevalent in the case of seasonal migration, I shall return to it in the next chapter.

## MORE WORK?

Having discussed, in this chapter, the kind of work available in the lower echelons of the informal economy, the modalities and conditions of employment offered, as well as the wages paid to the workforce concerned, the question that remains is: whether the policy of informalization has indeed generated more and better paid jobs? Dismantling the labour legislation that existed and insisting on flexibilization of the relationship between employers and employees would not only stimulate economic growth but were also propagated to be in the best interest of the working classes themselves. The swing to free enterprise had a low-key start but accelerated in the last decade of the twentieth century. Has the doctrine of neoliberalism, which saw the collapse of the public sector and the fading away of the state in its mediating role between the interests of capital and labour, indeed resulted in a better deal for the huge proletariat which has to rely on the sale of its labour power for making a living? Members and consultants associated with the Planning Commission reported that the growth in employment would have to be generated in the informal economy (Gupta 2002: 4). Coming to the end of a series of detailed surveys on the informal sector landscape, the NCEUS has critically commented on the policies that have been followed and their outcome. In its final report, the Commission pointed out that instead of going up, the rate of growth of employment went down significantly between 1993–4 and 2004–5 (NCEUS 2009). In comparison to the previous decade, the growth rate of wages and average earnings saw a similar decline in the subsequent 10 years. To the extent that employment has gone up, it seems to have been almost entirely in the informal sector of casual, contract, and regular low-wage workers. Indications are that in later years, the labour force participation rate has gone down, a trend discussed as jobless growth (see, for example, Chowdhury 2011: 23). As disconcerting as this stagnation has been the growing informalization of employment in the formal economy. In the earlier discussed analysis of Sanyal (2007), the formal–informal paradigm as construed by him is founded on the dualism between an accumulation and a need-based economy. How do we conceptualize the phenomenon of informalization in this way of thinking? His opaque answer is to distinguish between a need economy which is brutalized and eroded by the higher circuit of accumulation and a lower circuit in which the workforce is able to resist this invasion and to assert its demand for resources minimally required for reproduction. This argumentation seems to assume a differentiated logic which I find a fairly implausible proposition, even one with a tautological slant.

## NOTES

1. In June 2011, I was shown around a factory in Vapi town engaged in the manufacture of plastic buckets, thermos flasks, and ballpoint pens. The market must have been flooded with the last item since the female workers in that section—a gang of 20 women, daily brought from a nearby village by a contractor who pocketed 20 rupees from their daily wage for their 12-hour shift of 120 rupees—were all sent off 'on holiday' until further notice.

2. His observation is from an essay included in the volume referred to; it was earlier published as with the same title in December 1967.

3. Sourced from www.census2011.co.in/census/city/343-surat (accessed on 28 July 2012).

# 4

# Circulation and Immobilization of Labour

## LABOUR NOMADISM

In their search for work, people have to move far away from home and for a long time in order to secure a livelihood. In most regions of India, going off to find employment elsewhere is not a new phenomenon but the scale on which this happens has accelerated much during the last half century or so. The exodus of labour out of Europe's countryside began in the early nineteenth century and led to a major restructuring of the economy and society. The rural–agrarian order disintegrated to be replaced by an urban–industrial way of life. The transformation that took place in the Western world from the middle of the twentieth century onwards was supposed to be the trajectory of transition that the Third World countries would follow. However, this assumption of parallel development is not the received wisdom any longer. Redundant labour, mainly belonging to land-poor and landless households, is pushed out of the primary sector of the economy because of a progressive decline in agrarian employment. Their departure is facilitated by much better connectivity to the outside world. Road building and motorized transport have played a major role in making labour mobile over vast distances. However, in contrast to the masses in nineteenth-century Europe that could leave for underpopulated continents of the planet, migration to foreign destinations has become very cumbersome, in particular for job seekers without assets, skills, and other social capital. Consequently, the large majority of the people pushed out of agriculture have to be absorbed within the same country somewhere and somehow. A sizable part of them do not even leave the countryside but drift around sites of employment that are seasonal in nature. To the extent their mobility is intra-rural in nature, it is usually only for the duration of a season. They have to return to their places of origin again when their presence is no longer required.

During the last half of the twentieth century, I have investigated the coming and going of these people in south Gujarat, a region marked by high economic growth on the western coast of India. Those who belong to this nomadic workforce remain outsiders in the area to which they have been recruited on a temporary and casual basis, and are treated as transients by those who make use of their labour power. While intra-rural labour mobility has remained an under-studied theme in the literature, also in India, the trek of the footloose workforce has been mainly to urban destinations. But is India being transformed into an urbanized society? That remains to be seen. No doubt, many of those who arrive in the city would like to settle down, but find it difficult to do so because of lack of regular work. Their presence is required to build the metropoles, as a transient workforce employed on construction sites, but they are not supposed to stay on once the buildings are erected. The large majority of migrants belong to the labouring poor and are excluded from steady jobs in factories, mills, or even small-scale sweatshops. As a matter of fact, for the rapidly growing workforce at large, urbanization does not take the shape of industrialization. Instead, they find a niche in the service sector as self-employed or waged workers but invariably in the informal economy. Such working profiles dominate in the slums on the urban fringe where newcomers from faraway rural hinterlands congregate. At least, for as long as they succeed in earning enough to stay on. Digesting the monographs in which researchers have reported on slum life, one is struck by the problems these squatters have in establishing a firm foothold in the urban habitat and economy. Many of the residents seem to be passing through, moving on again after some time or going back to where they came from. Although in the Western world, the exodus from agriculture and the countryside was a process that kept labour footloose for some time, most of the migrants who left, sooner or later, managed to become urban citizens and industrial workers. This does not seem to be the trajectory that marks the pattern of change in India and most other developing economies. Informalized employment, usually non-industrial in nature, in tandem with circular mobility, seems to be the prominent features of the transformation presently going on.

Circulation is work related. As dependent members of the household, women and children can come along or are even required to come along in order to take part in the labour process. Those who are not fit to work, because they are too young or too old to earn at least their own keep, are discouraged from accompanying members of the household who move off. It means that labour power, not the unit of cohabitation of which it is part, is made mobile. Recruitment, once started, is both locality and community based. The pattern of segmentation in the labour market that has emerged, rather haphazardly, tends to become reiterative over time in the sense that other factors than a particular aptitude seem to be the main trigger and driving force. Labour circulation has a chain effect and cannot be explained in terms of the supply/demand mechanism operating in the formal labour market. Labour contractors, acting on behalf of employers, form another link in the chain of circulation for the workforce kept footloose. These mediators see to it that their catch has seldom access to other jobs wherever they go, even in the informal economy. Opting out of the circuit with the aim of staying on and settling down at the new worksite is next to impossible. Drifting in and out is not necessarily caused by a local shortage, a lack of hands available, or an unwillingness to work on the terms offered. The preference for outsiders is often part of a strategy resorted to by employers to command pliable and vulnerable labour contingents which, by their status as aliens and transients, have forfeited their bargaining power. Consequently, because of migrants moving in, local labour is rendered superfluous to demand and has to go out in search of alternative employment. They fall victim to the same process of failing to get access to steady work and, in turn, are made to join the reserve army of labour. Thus, influx and exodus are intricately related to each other in a perpetual pattern of circulation.

What is the magnitude of people in India who have left home to work elsewhere for shorter or longer periods of time? Estimates differ widely because the phenomenon of labour remaining footloose is hugely understated in census statistics and macro-level surveys biased by formal sector methods and techniques of data collection. Moreover, there is a lack of consensus on the definition of migration, operationalized in terms of distance (demarcated by the boundaries of district or state) as well as length of absence. Workers commuting on a daily basis between the village and a nearby town are not considered to be migrants. Do sojourners become migrants if they stay on at the worksite for more than a day, a week, or a month? At the opposite end, there are long-distance migrants who go off at a young age to towns or cities in south Gujarat, go home for brief visits, but who settle down again in their place of origin in Orissa or Andhra Pradesh when they are worn out after 10 or 20 years. As semi-permanent migrants, they spend the major part of their working life in loneliness until economic compulsions, due to job loss or old age, ultimately drive them back to 'where they belong', that is, back to the household they have left behind. At both ends, the migratory scale is fluid rather than fixed, difficult to capture in a statistical jargon grounded in formal sector concepts.

Based on the 1991 *Report of the National Commission on Rural Labour*, a migrant is a person who migrates temporarily from his place of residence to some other locality, either rural or urban, with a view to getting waged employment (GoI 1991). A special study group elaborated on this information by stating that a migrant labourer is one who works as part of a temporary workforce in different sectors and returns to his/her place of origin. Rather arbitrarily, that is, on the basis of debatable indicators, the National Commission on Rural Labour (NCRL) calculated in its 1991 report that about 10 million rural migrants went out in search of work. The shift in the composition of the national economy, both sector-wise and in the balance of the rural–urban workforce, accelerated dramatically after the report was published. But it is quite clear that the magnitude of circulation in the preceding decades had not been covered adequately. In addition to heavily underestimating the participation rate of females and children in the seasonal trek out of the villages, both the rural–urban and the intra-rural mobility must have been at least double the reported size. Many who belong to the agrarian workforce have seen their status rapidly changing from self-cultivating peasants to land-poor households. In the preceding generation, there were three cultivators to each landless labourer, a ratio that has since come down to an almost equal one. While it is a matter of dispute whether in south Gujarat the short-distance sojourners on the one hand, and the long-stay migrants on the other hand, should be included in the figure of labour circulation, even when narrowing down the score to seasonal migrants, the stated figures has been much too low in the past decades. Do recent statistics show a higher degree of accuracy? I am afraid not, and once again, even that observation has no foundation in factual and reliable data.

In 2009, the commission charged with reporting on the size and composition of the informal sector workforce drew attention to the vulnerable plight of seasonal migrants in particular, and increased their number significantly. 'Temporary and short duration migrants need special attention because they face instability in employment and are extremely poor. They are engaged in the agricultural sector, seasonal industries or in the urban sector as the self-employed. Some estimates suggest that the total number of seasonal migrants in India could be in the range of 30 million' (NCEUS 2009: 145). Another recent study put the figure of temporary migrants at 100 million without backing up that figure with empirical data (Deshingkar and Farrington 2009: 16). The gap between both tallies, reported for the same year, is illustrative for the poor quality of the empirical evidence. The figures are constantly being upgraded, although more on the basis of guesstimates than firm data. According to Srivastava (2011: 375–7), the figure for short-duration migration—that is, going off for up to six months—is roughly three times higher than enumerated in official statistics.

## IN NEED OF SHELTER

The people pushed out of agriculture do not easily give up the habitat that keeps them embedded in the village of their origin. This is because, mainly, they may have been accepted in the urban space as temporary workers but not as residents. It means, of course, that they simply cannot afford to vacate whatever abode they have left behind in the hinterland. This is in addition to the fact that dependent members of their household do not join them on departure. Here, we notice a major contrast with the transformation that went on in the Western world when the rural exodus escalated one-and-half century ago. When the working classes in Europe started to move out of the countryside, they brought their families along to the cities where they settled down. Public housing was sponsored by state and municipal agencies or by cooperatives set up by the newly arrived citizens themselves. In India, housing societies for the industrial workforce did not become a prominent part of the urban expansion in most regions of the country. Unlike in Europe, where housing cooperatives are a familiar sight in working-class neighbourhoods, in India, this term invariably signals the presence of middle-class owners who have bought their bungalows and apartments from private contractors. Working-class colonies used to be built by employers as coolie lines on the plantations in Assam and the Nilgiris and in the mine belt of Bengal and Bihar. Or as chawls, dead-end alleys filled with one-room tenements, that came up around the textile mills in, for example, Calcutta, Kanpur, Bombay, and Ahmedabad. Due to the relentless informalization of the economy, of which casualized employment is a major feature, the need to keep a stable workforce and to provide at least a modicum of shelter for them has gone.

Informal sector workers who have reached the city with the intent to try and find a more permanent niche in the urban economy have to make their own arrangements. This they manage to do by squatting on unoccupied land or by establishing a foothold in one of the settlements that have sprung up, usually on the outskirts. Davis (2006) has given a vivid portrait of these colonies in his book, *Planet of Slums*. The habitat of self-built shelters fabricated from recycled material lacks all kinds of amenities such as tap water, sanitation, electricity, proper access roads, and a school, and is difficult to reach by public transport. But colonies inhabited by the low castes and classes in the villages are not of a much better quality. For no good reason at all, the word slum has an urban connotation, while the much more numerous shanties spread out in the countryside are similarly populated by residents living in utter degradation. Still, on both sides of the rural–urban axis, the labouring poor have at least a fixed abode, however ramshackle it may be. It is a space in which they can retreat from the harshness of their daily work, from the bullying of the employer or his agent, and from the nagging of neighbours.

However, migrants who remain circulating are often forced to live without a proper shelter and do not enjoy the comforts of privacy. This goes for the power-loom workers who sleep in a packed room in the company of workmates; construction workers who arrange a sort of bivouac at the building site; brick makers who erect a makeshift hut of broken and rejected bricks; gangs of paddy harvesters allowed to cook their meal and pass the night in the farmer's courtyard; and the army of cane cutters who camp along the roadside or in the open field in a tent of canvas sheets. For the duration of the working season, they have to make do without drinking water and toilet facilities. One of these nomads, recruited to harvest cane for the duration of the campaign, had the courage to tell a group of officials who had come to find out about the way they were treated by the mill management that 'even dogs are better off'. I wrote down his exclamation of anger and frustration nearly 30 years ago, but nothing has changed since then (see Breman 1994: 253). The resentment with which these labour nomads react to their plight of exploitation and subordination shows that they are not only after regular jobs but also in search of decency and dignity.

One wonders what the prospects are in the current policy climate of neoliberalism for realizing these ambitions that are fuelled by the rightful demand for a better quality of life. The degradation and dehumanizing work conditions that characterized the initial stage of the great transformation in the West made way for a decisive improvement in the further transition to an urban–industrial way of life. The advance made in that direction in South Asia so far does not seem to give ground for a turn for the better for the much larger land-poor and landless classes on the subcontinent. In the fifth of the

*Selected Readings*, 'The Expulsion of Labour from the Formal Sector of the Economy', I have elaborated on the quality of the labour process.

## INTERDEPENDENCE BETWEEN CASUALIZATION AND MOBILITY

What needs to be emphasized is the strong interdependence that exists between the ongoing practice of wage labour circulation and the preponderance of employment in the informal economies of the globalized Southern hemisphere. Recruitment of labour for a limited time period, lasting no more than one season, is in line with the time-bound nature of many operations on an informal footing: the harvesting of various crops (such as paddy, sugarcane, tobacco, cotton, and mangoes); the quarrying of stones; the moulding of bricks; or the manufacture of sea salt, all take place during the dry months of the year. The same applies to other industries, rural and urban, carried out under fair weather conditions in the open air. Also, on construction sites, all work comes to a halt before the onset of the monsoon. Labour circulation facilitates informal sector activity and also, the other way round, the progressive informalization of the economy puts a premium on movement to and fro by a highly casualized workforce. Conducive to the ongoing rhythm of migration/circulation is an improved spatial infrastructure: transport by motorized vehicles and communication available at both the beginning and the end of the route. The result is that distance can be bridged in a relatively short time by train, bus, or truck, while at the same time, travel costs have gone down. Having said this, I would also like to point out that it is usually not the employer or his agent who bears the cost of the journey made, but the migrants themselves. Ferrying labour gangs from the village to the worksite when they are hired, and back again when they are fired, involves expenses that are charged to their account, adding to the debt which is the start of the contract. The poor resource base of the massive army of males and females, adults and minors, forced to participate in the annual trek to far away destinations to work long hours at low pay rates is a direct consequence of their inability to qualify back at home for better type of jobs yielding higher incomes.

For the large majority of these people, poorly educated or totally illiterate, labour circulation is not a free choice. It is a strenuous and tiresome expedition that has to be repeated again and again, rarely rewarded by getting skilled or bringing back savings that can be used for productive investment leading to a more secure way of life. Circulation is, at best, a survival strategy, a route taken to cope with the threat of unemployment and the lack of means needed to keep the household going. The enormous increase in urban informal jobs has given urban streets a strongly masculine appearance. The lack of adequate and affordable housing forces married men to leave their families behind in the village. The bachelor existence that characterizes the lives of many migrants causes them to congregate in small groups in hired accommodation where they also share meals. Ultimately—but that can be only after many years when their labour power is exhausted—they go back home again.

## A JUNGLE OF VIOLENCE AND ABUSE

It is in this economic and social setting of Surat that I came to observe an orgy of violence that broke out late 1992 in the wake of the Babri Masjid demolition in Ayodhya. What took place was an urban carnage, of which the Muslim minority living in the city became the target. The identity of the hunted was known—of those who got killed, 95 per cent were Muslims. There cannot be the slightest doubt that most of the hunters came from among the hordes of labour migrants who had flocked to the city from far away. The victims, the next of kin of those who did not survive, and other eyewitnesses were unanimous in naming the Kathiawadi diamond cutters, the Uttar Pradesh *bhaiya*s, and the Oriya *mali*s operating the power looms as the main culprits. It was intriguing to witness from close by how this underclass of outsiders, so convincingly portrayed as the victims of the brutal economic regime that reigns in the city, were, by a mere sleight of hand, transformed from sufferers into sinners and became singled out as 'the ones who did it'. The lumpen gangs that committed the bestialities to which members of the Muslim minority fell prone were identified as outsiders who worked in but did not belong to the city. It seems that any other explanation than just to refer to the lumpen behaviour of an alien mass not rooted in the polished *surthi* tradition is held to be superfluous. Still, I am inclined to look back on what happened from a slightly different perspective.

It is not a coincidence that many victims, who escaped with their lives, emphasized in their statements of the bachelors among the migrants who were the perpetrators of the atrocities. This motley collection of young males earns its pay under miserable conditions far away from home and detached from family life. Accommodated in densely packed tenements and sheds during their off-hours, they lead a beastly existence in *jhopadpatis*, such a gay name for their overcrowded and filthy slum habitat scattered in numerous pockets all over the city. The gangs working on day shifts go to sleep in 'beds' still warm from the bodies of their mates whose turn it is to operate the power looms for the duration of the night shift. Part of the same domestic order is that the teams that rotate are supposed to prepare each other's food.[1] My ongoing research on informal sector labour in Gujarat, has shown that violence of all shades and gradations is endemic to this agglomeration's underbelly. It is a macho milieu dominated by drunkenness, hetero- and homo-sexual abuse, gambling, fights and other ills that boggles the sane mind. These are all practices of aggression in which the powerful seek out and discriminate the weak and vulnerable. Such an age and gender distorted atmosphere reduces not only women to targets of rape, often repeatedly so, but explains why also young boys are sodomized. (Breman 2003: 274–5)

Surat is basically one big transit camp of labour coming and going away again. The place is swamped with a floating mass that remains outside the law and beyond the benign reach of state agencies. The footloose proletarians are subjected to repression and exploitation in a capitalist framework remarkable for its nakedness and rawness. We have here a reserve army of labour moving around in an economic jungle—a predominantly male workforce of aliens, with no or meagre skills, which is casualized and forever kept on the run. The official in charge of Gujarat's labour inspectorate in the city told me that politicians who kept coming to collect with impunity their illegal dues from Surat's booming but thoroughly informalized economy—constantly bothering him with requests for licences, exemptions from regulations, and remission from taxation—had never questioned him on the non-implementation of minimum wages or other labour laws that exist on paper for migrant workers. Informality has spread to the realms of governance and politics or may even have started there. In accordance with management practices characteristic of flexibilized employment, the migrants are alienated from their identity on arrival, and throughout their stay in the city, continue to remain deprived of entitlements that make a social system worthwhile to belong to. The transients are reduced to a passing labour commodity in a cycle of attraction and expulsion, condemned to a life which is inhuman by any definition. For the flourishing condition of the informal economy, the people who have come to join the urban workforce pay a very high price. The footloose labour that constitute a vast reserve army do not easily team up in collective action but are divided along lines of caste, ethnicity, religion, and other primary loyalties. Their interaction is based more on rivalry, often instigated by those who hire them, rather than on a kind of natural solidarity.

## THE JOBBER

The magnitude of seasonal migration in south Gujarat warrants special attention for the modus operandi of the jobber who also acts as boss of the gang he has recruited. Ambiguity is inherent to his role as mediator.

He has the same origins as the workers but acts under orders of the employers. During the rainy season, the cooperative sugar mills use labour contractors to recruit many tens of thousands of harvest workers for the duration of the campaign which starts towards the end of October. In the villages of the hinterland where the cane cutters live, the jobbers hand out a cash advance to *koyta*s, teams consisting of a man and a woman and often also a child worker. A number of these teams together—some 10, 20, or more—constitute the gang contracted by the jobber and accompany him to the plains when the rains are over. As gang boss, he continues to be the link between the management of the mill and the migrants who belong to his gang. Work is allocated through his agency, he keeps a check on the daily state of affairs, and distributes the fortnightly grain and cash allowance. When the campaign ends, the final account is settled through him. The labour contractor also holds absolute sway in the bivouac that the cane cutters set up for their night halt and which has to be moved after some time for harvesting new fields. Thus, the workforce remains mobile and rotates around the mill area in the course of the campaign.

In the vicinity of the villages of my research, labour from far away is mobilized for a variety of activities such as harvesting sugarcane, digging sand, working in stone quarries, and road building. But large groups of labourers from south Gujarat go off in search of work elsewhere, mostly in brick kilns, salt pans, or picking cotton. They are recruited by a jobber who mediates between employers located elsewhere and the seasonal migrants. In all these instances, recruitment starts during the monsoon when there is little work in agriculture. The lack of income means that most landless labourers and marginal peasants have no other choice than to accept the advance held out as bait by the jobber. They need money not only for food, other daily necessities, and cost of illness, but also for such expenses which they can meet only once a year: a wedding in the family or repairs to the house. In the past, the bigger class of farmers were prepared to meet such needs by providing a loan that was repaid later in labour power, but they are no longer interested in attaching labour in advance in this way.

The jobber is one of the few whom the poorest households in the village can approach for obtaining credit, which they so desperately need in their struggle for survival and reproduction. The price they have to pay is the loss of all control over the hiring out of their own labour power, and often also over that of other members in their household, for the duration of the season or even a few seasons in succession. In their attempt to get their hands on the highest amount of credit possible, labourers do not hesitate to accept cash advances from different and even conflicting sides. It sometimes happens that they collect earnest money without even intending to go away. This risk in itself shows how important it is that the jobbers are rooted in the same milieu as their catch. Only then they are able to assess the quality of the labour on offer, to judge who is suitable for heavy work and who will submit to management's rules without creating problems. It is also essential to be in close vicinity of their catch to ensure compliance with the labour contract. These considerations explain why jobbers recruit mainly in their own village and its environs. The jobbers have been employed in the brickfields or stone quarries themselves from young age onwards. Why have they been singled out to become jobbers? Intimate familiarity with the work at hand on the basis of own experience helps the labour broker to keep control over production in his role as boss of his work gang. The set of people he takes with him are contracted for specific tasks: the male brick maker is assisted by 9–10 men, women, and children who are part of his team. In addition, there are the men who accompany the truck or tractor as loaders–unloaders if the earth has to be fetched from outside as well as women who carry the ready-made bricks to and out of the kiln. The owner of a large brickworks will engage more than one jobber, because only then is he assured of the right combination of men and women, adults and minors, old hands and newcomers.

The jobber should have the ability to handle the workers recruited by him. That is to say, he has to know how to get the work done in a way that will satisfy the employer but without arousing bad feelings, let alone antagonism, from among his work gang. He has to find the right mix of cursing and yelling, persuasion and encouragement. Harshness and forbearance alternate in a relationship that produces the highest possible output. On the other hand, he is supposed to show utter deference to the brickworks owner. Did he really arrive with the specified number of workers at the agreed time, have the migrants not run away during the season, and did they work to full satisfaction? Good performance on all these scores may be rewarded by the employer next time with the order for a larger number of gangs and with more generous credit. At the same time, the workers should not get the impression that the gang boss is negligent in his care for their interests. The employer himself usually avoids any contact with his workforce, neither can he be directly approached by them. The jobber conveys instructions from above to the workers, and passes on any request for favours from below, for example, for a short leave, an extra allowance, and permission to see a doctor. He must be able to maintain a simple handwritten notebook in which, at the time of recruitment, he writes down how much is paid to whom and when. Also, after reaching the brickworks, he records the size of the daily production, the petty cash allowances and food rations handed out every fortnight, and any other information regarding his work gang. Migrants who are not able to read and write cannot be promoted to the rank of jobber. An equally important precondition is having some property— land, house, cattle, agricultural implements—that can be forfeited in case of default. The payment of cash advances at the time of recruitment involves a considerable amount of money which the employer does not hand over without covering his own risk by making the jobber liable on paper and by demanding collateral. In the event of mala fide practices, the jobber runs the risk of losing whatever property he has, or can at least be put under pressure by the threat of such a consequence. Loyalty and integrity are the jobber's capital. For the sake of his advancement, he is more dependent on good contact with his employer than the other way around. This is an ambiguous relationship. Labour brokers used to tell me that, without them, the *sheth* would never have achieved his prosperity. But in the same breath, they praised their 'benefactor' humbly and profusely for the progress they themselves had made.

## LINKING LABOUR TO CAPITAL

To be a jobber is extremely lucrative. He is paid a commission that not only varies with the size of his gang but also with his track record. This is how employers reward the loyalty and increased creditability of their agents. In addition, the jobber gets a premium for supervising the work during the season, expressed in a percentage of the total labour cost paid in wages. A gang boss earns many times more than the migrants whom he brings along. At the start of his career, the jobber is still on trial. He needs means of his own to invest in brokerage. To prevent default, the employer tries to defer providing credit to the latest possible date, until late in the rainy season, and also keeps the amount as low as possible. The workers' dire need for an advance forces the jobber to bind the migrants he wants for his gang by paying earnest money out of his own pocket. Experienced workers demand a larger sum that he is obliged to pay to avoid the risk of losing them to a competitor. If he lacks sufficient cash in hand he has no other option than to borrow from a local moneylender, who naturally demands the customary exorbitant interest. Besides, you can only become a jobber with the support of others who already hold that position. Some have been introduced to the business by father, brother, or uncle, but such recommendation need not necessarily be along lines of kinship. The somewhat bigger contractors of seasonal labour build up a network of helpers who act as their eyes and ears in the neighbouring villages. The services rendered by such henchmen are not restricted to scouting around for recruits but include reporting on their good conduct as workers, the sort of households to which they belong, and on their credibility. These touts are given a premium and a jobber with a large workforce will choose some of them as his assistants for supervising the labourers in the brickworks. They are paid out of his own commission. Thus, by building up experience, a tout may win the trust of the patron and permission to establish himself as a labour broker in his own right.

In the landscape of labour, the jobbers stand out noticeably from the mass of migrant workers that they lead, but too great a detachment from their catchment milieu can also be counterproductive. They need to be sufficiently close to the clientele's world and they cannot operate successfully beyond the space with which they are familiar. Their room of manoeuvre is thus limited to the terrain to which they themselves belong. Jobbers do not have a permanent gang of workers but recruit a new gang each and every year. The personal merits or demerits of the gang boss do play a role in this rotation, but other motives have priority in the choice that the migrants have to make anew each year. Their first priority is for a cash advance as large and as early as possible at the time of recruitment. Migrants from Ahmedabad whom I came across in a brickworks near Surat told me that the piece rate per 1,000 bricks in south Gujarat was lower than in their own region, but that the attraction of working closer to home for this reason was nullified by the much lower amount of credit in their area of origin which, moreover, was only paid just before the start of the season. They simply had no other option than to attach themselves much earlier. One jobber confirmed this information with the complaint that his own boss was always so late in paying the advance that he hopelessly got behind-hand at the peak of the recruitment and had to incur extra trouble and expense, by taking high-interest loans from a moneylender, to avoid being lumbered with the poorest quality of workers.

I have described the jobber as a broker of seasonal labour who has his basis of operation in the countryside of south Gujarat. Without fundamentally qualifying that notion, I have to point out that the labour contractor is not an unknown figure in the urban informal economy as well. He is, for instance, markedly present in the early morning labour market held in small towns and big cities. In that scene, the jobber acts as an agent on behalf of an employer whose confidence he has gained. Usually, this is a building or road construction operator, the owner of a transport firm, etc. The jobber supervises the work of a gang (*toli*) which he himself has brought together and which he dismisses once the work is done. It may happen that male and female job seekers are quite familiar with a particular contractor and try to cultivate a more regular relationship with him. They are the first ones to be selected and his favourites may also advise him whom to choose among the waiting crowd. Those who enjoy preferential treatment are favoured with other benefits, such as advance payment. It is a form of credit which they repay by making themselves available at a later date with or without receiving prior intimation. The jobber receives a commission from his patron for his mediation and in addition to that reward, takes his cut from the wages paid by the employer and passed on via him to the gang. Thus, the jobber operates in both the rural and the urban informal economy. He keeps a high profile in circuits of seasonally employed labour, inside and outside agriculture, and is by and large active in modes of employment that are low skilled and casual in nature.

Finally, recruitment is not organized along territorial lines. Most jobbers operate within a radius of 15 km from their place of residence, and they are not the only ones doing business within this area. Does this give rise to fierce competition among them? Definitely so. It occurs quite frequently that a seasonal migrant gets offers from more than one jobber. If he accepts advance payments from different sides, he is the one who gets blamed for the problem created. Actually, it is the gang bosses themselves, anxious to make up the required strength of their gangs, who use money unscrupulously to entice away workers already under contract to another agent. There is a standard solution to the tussle that follows. The jobber who in the end goes off with 'the swindler' repays his competitor the amount that the latter had already paid and claims the entire advance against the workers' earnings. Knowing all too well that they are the losers when the competition is heavy, the jobbers consult each other if they doubt the bona fides of a candidate and if necessary, swap gang members if one of them has too many for the work at hand that another lacks.

## NEO-BONDAGE

The shortage of income required for the cost of survival and reproduction forces members of landless and land-poor households to accept advance payment for their labour power in a contract constituting unfree labour that I have defined as neo-bondage. The starting point is an absence of choice which confronts these workers. Earnings are low and uncertain, a situation which leads to loss of autonomy. Their labour power is the only collateral they possess. Work indicating economic dependency, expressed in a debt relationship, is a very common phenomenon in the informal economy. Employers present such arrangements as 'advances' on wages that will be repaid by utilizing the labour power of the borrower. However, such 'advances' are solely intended to immobilize labour, whether immediately or at a later date. Neither party views the transaction as a loan that is going to be terminated on repayment. Debt bondage is by no means a new phenomenon. In the past, it was the customary manner by which landless low-caste workers were attached to landowning households of higher castes. This master–serf relationship was common throughout the South Asian subcontinent. The outcome of my first round of fieldwork in south Gujarat during the early 1960s led me to characterize such bondage as a pre-capitalist system of unfree labour (Breman 1974). The bondage was lifelong, could even stretch from generation to generation, and also included the wife and children of the landless household. The landowner claimed a broad range of services, both economic and non-economic, that demonstrated the subjugation of the farm servant. The social context in which this master–serf relationship operated was a localized and non-monetary rural order with an economy based on subsistence production.

In the course of my fieldwork, then and later on, I found that although the former system of bondage no longer existed, the members of the landless underclass had not become free labourers. Indebtedness continues to be a crucial feature of the capitalist work regime that I have called new or neo-bondage. It is a mode of employment that is not restricted to the shrinking category of farm servants. Similar arrangements also characterize a diversity of labour in the rural as well as urban sectors of the informal economy. Men, women, and children recruited for cane cutting or brick making receive, through the jobber, a sum of money that binds this army of migrants for the whole season, a period for up to six or seven months. Payment of an advance obliges them to leave home, and also prevents them from withdrawing prematurely from their contracts. To ensure immobilization of the floating workforce for the full length of the production process, settlement of the wage is deferred until the season ends. The new regime of bondage differs from the traditional one in terms of the short duration of the contract (often no longer than for one season), its more restricted character (labour instead of a more encompassing beck-and-call relationship), and finally, its easier termination or evasion (even without repayment of the debt). The far greater risk nowadays of breach of contract discourages employers from being imprudent and generous in granting an advance on wages. It is difficult to recoup losses made in this way and it has become useless for employers to appeal to authorities for help in taking absconders to task. Finally, today's bosses lack the natural superiority that, in the past, made it highly unlikely that a contract would be broken. The gap that existed in the past between high-caste master and low-caste servant has gone. Often, the social identity of the jobbers is the same as that of the labourer recruited by them and consequently, their relationship is not any longer one of superiority versus inferiority. Unfree labour is, of course, unlawful and also immoral since it thrives on the vulnerability of people who are driven by economic need to sell their labour power in advance and by doing so, see their vulnerability perpetuated. It is a huge problem that is much underplayed in official statistics, as the National Commission has reported (NCEUS 2009: 147–8). As part of the strategy for a low route to capitalist growth that is based on cheap labour, the government so far has turned a blind eye to what is a socially objectionable work contract.

In a recent report, *The Cost of Coercion*, the ILO (2009) draws attention to millions of people worldwide who are entrapped in regimes of coercion—ranging from slavery, forced, or bonded labour to human trafficking.[2] In the South Asian subcontinent in particular, debt bondage is widely practised. The relationship between an employer and an employee can only be referred to as one of bondage if the loan is provided at the outset with the clear intent of disposing over the labour power of the borrower, and if the amount is disproportionate to the terms imposed in scale and duration. Debt bondage is a form of servitude which does not have to be enforced with non-economic sanctions. Workers turn to this mode of employment out of economic compulsion because they have no choice but to sell their labour power in advance. The paucity of estimates on the magnitude of debt bondage in India has its roots not only in the reluctance of official agencies to gather statistical information on the phenomenon, but is also related to the problem of establishing a clear dividing line between free and unfree labour. The lives of the working masses down at the bottom of the labour hierarchy are conditioned by far-reaching deprivation, denigration, and discrimination, making the distinction between working voluntarily or involuntarily a very elastic concept. Modalities of free and unfree labour cannot be described in a clear-cut dichotomy but have to be seen on a sliding scale, a continuum on which only the extremes on both sides are in sharp contrast to each other (see also Lerche 2012). In other words, debt bondage needs to be classified as belonging to a whole gamut of decent-deficit labour practices (understood as brutal, harsh, unfair) in the informal economy.

The disappearance of agrestic servitude in large parts of South Asia, at least in the way in which it was practised in the pre-capitalist past, does not mean that the working population at large is now in a position to determine for themselves where, when, and for whom to work. That conclusion contradicts the classical assumption that the transition to capitalism is marked by a mode of production based on free labour, that is, free from means of production and free to decide how to use their labour power. The debt bondage of today may even be practised on a scale larger than traditional agrarian bondage ever was. It is a form of unfree labour that has received a strong boost as the capitalist economy has risen to dominance. No doubt, there are similarities between past and present forms of dependency. Bondage then and now is deeply embedded in a milieu that is exposed to economic deprivation and social discrimination. There is a demonstrable link between debt bondage and origins in low castes and tribal communities. Both stark poverty and an ingrained ideology of inequality gave shape to a partnership of bondage and still do.

However, the similarities should not blind us to major differences that have come about with the passage of time, as I have argued in the sixth of the *Selected Readings*, 'Neo-bondage: A Fieldwork-based Account'. The debt bondage typical of current capitalism strongly displays the characteristics of an employment relationship in which other than economic dimensions are largely or completely absent. The boss is not interested to use the relationship for gaining power or enhancing his social status, nor is he obliged to guarantee that his employees can meet their basic needs, irrespective how long the employment contract lasts. He lays claim to their labour power and that, not the need to act as a patron, is why he is willing to provide a 'loan' which results in indebtedness of the worker. The contract has none of the social and cultural features that gave the relationship between bonded farm servants and their masters a much more encompassing quality. The reduction to a labour commodity, pure and simple, is also apparent from the exact specification of who falls under the contract. In addition to those to whom the agreement first applies, usually a man, the amount of the cash advanced increases if his wife and children are also ready and able to work. This means, in effect, that the man can demand a higher wage by expanding his own bondage to include the members of his household. Especially in the case of seasonal migrants, the lifelong or even intergenerational attachment that was characteristic of traditional agrarian bondage is lacking. I am inclined to attribute the shorter duration in the practices of neo-bondage to the unwillingness of employers to hire labour any longer than is strictly necessary. The regular replenishment of the workforce is, in any case, not motivated by any voluntary limitation of the employer's span of control. Workers are always hired and fired, when, and to the extent that the material benefits exceed the cost.

## THE DECENT DEFICIT

Debt bondage is the way in which seasonal migrants are pried loose from their rural habitat and pushed into a state of mobility. Millions of workers throughout South Asia have to sell their labour power in advance because of lack of employment in the rural economy in combination with the low price they receive for their toil. But neo-bondage is a frequent practice also in the urban informal economy: in diamond cutting and polishing; processing gems; making bangles; glass blowing; fabrication of cloth; garment manufacture; embroidery; carpet weaving; manufacture of, for example, bidis, incense, and matches; production of toys and packaging materials; and the construction industry. A host of service providers also fall in the bondage category, such as street vendors who are indebted to their suppliers and a wide range of cleaners and domestic servants who are, for the same reason, not free to change their employ. The distribution of gender and age groups varies sector- and branch-wise. Sometimes, an employment contract will apply to all members of the household able to work; in other cases, it applies specifically to a man, woman, or child. My estimate is that roughly 10 per cent of South Asia's working population in the informal sector of the urban and rural economy is engaged on terms that amount to debt bondage. The NCEUS is equally critical of the blissful ignorance shown by state agencies.

No credible estimate of the magnitude of bonded labour is yet available. In any case, the Commission views the problem as a huge one in view of the overwhelming empirical evidence arising from a number of studies and surveys. Officials have tended to underplay the incidence of bonded labour. In fact, it is almost a non-existent problem if one takes the reported figures of bonded labour seriously. (NCEUS 2008: 108)

Important to emphasize also is that labour bondage comes in various shades and gradations. Of relevance here is the distinction made between relatively 'mild' forms to practices which are more brutal. It is a continuum that reminds us, once again that the opposition between free and unfree is a sliding scale rather than a dichotomy (Breman *et al.* 2009: 285).

The employment of unfree labour is not permitted but the Bonded Labour System (Abolition) Act, passed in 1976, incorrectly assumed that debt bondage was a problem restricted to agriculture, a leftover kind of servitude that attached landless farmhands to their landlords. This was a fallacy and completely ignored practices of neo-bondage also beyond the agricultural sector and in both town and countryside. My assessment of the lack of public action is that authorities at the central and state level are reluctant or outright unwilling to track down, identify, and prosecute employers in the lower circuits of the informal economy who use bondage to minimize labour cost and to exercise an unrestrained control over their workforce in order to raise production and maximize profits. The regional office of the ILO in India has argued for an approach based on tripartite consultations between employees, employers, and official agencies. Reports on pilot projects at district level in south India describe them as reasonably successful. My hunch is that more objective evaluation by non-stakeholders might not confirm the claim that, if the current course is pursued, the end of bondage is in sight. My reservations are based, to begin with, on the lack of genuine representation from the bonded labourers themselves. Agreeing to an employment relationship in which the freedom of the worker takes priority would inevitably lead to a rise in the price of labour. Achieving a shift in the balance between the greatest possible profit for the employer and the costs of a decent standard of living for his workforce will not come easily. Any strategy aimed at redemption from bondage which relies on the consent of those who minimize their cost of production by tying down the workers they contract is doomed to end up in a fiasco. If I do not doubt the ultimate emancipation of labour, it is because I discern a growing assertion at the foot of the economy. When I take as my point of departure the land-poor and landless milieu in south Gujarat that has been my field of empirical study for half a century, I see no attitudes of lethargy and, even less so, any internalized dependency and subordination with respect to employers or the better-off social classes in general. Nor do the workers caught up in debt bondage give the impression of quietly accepting their fate. Docility is certainly not a distinct feature of their behaviour. The state of deficiency in which they live is the reason why they are unable to escape their servitude. But they will respond alertly to any initiative from outside to expand their narrow room for manoeuvre. Living unfree erodes their self-respect and the desire to dignify their lives does not need to be imbued from outside. A telling indication of that growing assertion is to be given a piece of land to call home in their rural habitat. As elsewhere, the landless in the villages of my fieldwork in south Gujarat also have built their huts/houses on plots they do not own. In the fall of 2012, from many parts of the country the landless poor went on a march which was scheduled to end in a massive demonstration in Delhi to confront the top-ranking politicians with their demand. It is a movement asking for land reform, for the time being, limited to get the title deed for the site on which they are sheltered. In an interview, a woman explained why she has joined the march: 'We have already tried to fight for our rights in Tamil Nadu. But if we tell the Collector we want our rights, he claims that there is no land, even though there is plenty of land for SEZs and industries. He says, you get an order from above. So we are going to Delhi to get an order from above'.[3]

## REQUIRED AS WORKERS, NOT CITIZENS

The cost of migration, in both economic and non-economic terms, is highly understated in much of the literature on the subject. The World Bank has been in the forefront of policies claiming that because of the pressure on agrarian resources, migration to wherever work and income outside the primary sector of the economy can be found is a must. In its *World Development Report* in 2009, the Bank suggests that large-scale labour mobility is a win-win game for all stakeholders (World Bank 2009). It carefully refrains from referring to evidence that shows what migrants loose rather than win. In the first place, the departure of many landless and land-poor peasants is often a form of distress migration, away from misery or even destitution due to scarcity of employment and low wages, without necessarily resulting in better work and higher pay. It is an escape for the duration of a season, a short-term remedy in response to the structural lack of wherewithal to survive by staying put. The compulsion to go elsewhere may also last for the duration of the working life. For many of the footloose, migration is bound to remain circular in nature because of the absence of physical and social capital to settle down elsewhere. The decision to leave is also not based on the exercise of free but forced choice imposed by the need to sell one's labour power in advance and thus, become entrapped in a relationship of debt bondage. Heralding departure from home as the way out of poverty, the Bank strongly condemns what it calls the setting up of barriers against labour mobility (World Bank 2009). Efforts to increase rural employment opportunities, such as the recently introduced scheme in India to generate rural public works, are rejected out of hand as a waste of time and money, ill-advised because such interventions tend to undercut the free flow of labour praised as being in the best interests of all parties concerned. The Mahatma Gandhi National Rural Employment Guarantee Scheme (MGNREGS) was enacted in 2005 with the objective to provide work for one hundred days a year at statutory wages (see Khera 2011). The scheme has been helpful in the sense that it has increased incomes for land-poor and landless households in some regions of the country. However, it does not seem to have stemmed the swelling tide of seasonal migration. In a forthcoming publication (Kannan and Breman 2013) I shall report that in the villages of my fieldwork in south Gujarat *narega*, as it is commonly called, has failed to generate employment for the labouring poor. The MGNREGS seems to have lost the bite it initially had. While safe drinking water and sanitation are badly required in the rural colonies where the labouring poor dwell, more than half of the total population has still to go for defecation in the open fields. Instead of expanding the job scheme to improve the physical and institutional infrastructure of their colonies, the budget allotted for this purpose might be reduced because of the slowing down of the economic boom.

Together with other policymakers, the World Bank is fully aware that migrants need at least a foothold to enable them to settle down more permanently in the urban milieu. By not taking care of their basic needs, the newly arrived may find the terrain to which they have come not congenial for staying on. Without access to minimal welfare facilities, such as cheap shelter and food subsidies made available to the urban poor, the cost of life in the city becomes prohibitive. Also, granting property rights and tenure security to the plots on which the squatters have built their shelter is pre-conditional to the acceptance of migrants as urban residents with a legal status. The question is whether this minimum packet, presented in the World Bank's document as selective interventions, has been put into practice. Hardly or not at all, it seems.

Urbanization in the main growth poles of India has accelerated in the past decades but to a lesser extent than one would have expected given the sharp fall in the man–land ratio as a steady trend in the rural hinterland (Kundu 2011). Lack of livelihood drives the landless and land-poor out of the rural habitat but their inability to establish a foothold in the urban economy drives them back again to the village. In a follow-up article the same author discusses the impasse in which the labouring poor get stuck on both ends of their trajectory. Barriers for mobility of the poor are being raised.

> With present rigidities in the agrarian system, growing regionalism, higher skill requirements in the labour market, etc., the emerging production system and governance structure in the cities have become hostile to newcomers. These factors have made the migration process selective such that poor and unskilled labourers are finding it difficult to access opportunities coming up in developed regions and large cities. (Kundu 2012: 225; see also Sainath 2012)

In the restructuring of the balance between town and countryside, the main stakeholders in the urban habitat have turned increasingly hostile to outsiders who do not only come to work but also to occupy space for their livelihood. Slum dwellers have to face many difficulties in their efforts to get official permits required for urban citizenship. They encroach on wastelands, in either public or private hands, but have to move on again when the plots on which they have squatted down are required for expansion of the urban infrastructure or are converted into housing colonies for people with higher and regular incomes. The footloose settlers try to hang on at the outskirts of the city, but they have to keep a low profile because they cannot afford to buy the plot on which they erect their makeshift shelter since land prices are far above their budget. Without assets and assiduously kept beyond the visibility and reach of municipal authorities, the nomads are what I have called 'nowhere people', made to drift around in a nowhere landscape. Those who manage to gain a foothold in one of the more regularized slums belong to the category of somewhat better-off migrants. It does not mean, however, that they have found a more permanent niche in which they are safe from eviction. Even whey they manage to get registered in the municipal administration, their houses are demolished because the cheap land they occupy becomes a target for real estate dealers or building contractors who terrorize the slum dwellers to vacate.

The growing prosperity of the more well-to-do, living far above the poverty line, has encouraged local governments to design projects for the beautification of city space. The hostile reception awaiting the resourceless army of migrants in the urban arena is inspired by new civic movements launched by bourgeois and politically well-connected sections of the population in India's metropoles. The strongly neoliberal bias underlying the Jawaharlal Nehru National Urban Renewal Mission (JNNURM) results in excluding rather than including the labouring poor in the urban space (see Banerjee–Guha 2010). The campaign for the disenfranchisement of slum dwellers is backed up with the argument that their illegal status and inclination to criminal behaviour pose a threat to the maintenance of law and order. In Ahmedabad, many of them are thrown out from the city centre to the urban–rural periphery and resettled for the time being in what are called 'temporary relocation sites'—waiting there, until the next round in their ongoing rotation will take place (see Mahadevia 2011 and Desai 2012). The labour power of these outsiders is required, off and on, but not their cumbersome and defiling presence as regular urban residents.

## NOTES

1. For a visual portrait of their life and work in Surat and south Gujarat, see Breman and Das (photographs by Ravi Agarwal) (2000).

2. Global report on the follow-up to ILO Declaration on Fundamental Principles and Rights at Work, International Labour Office, Geneva, 2009, Report I (B). The ILO addresses unfree labour practices in its annual reports and publishes regular reports on the theme. The most recent ILO report on forced labour was published in 2005 (see 'A Global Alliance against Forced Labour' 2005). The type of agrarian bondage that used to exist in south Gujarat still lingers on in other parts of the country. For a portrait of the hali system as it operates until today in Baran district of Rajasthan, see Bhatia (2012).

3. 'Landless Poor on Long March to Delhi', *The Hindu*, 1 October 2012.

# 5

# Social Profile and Locale

While class and caste identities are crucial for drawing the social profile of the workforce, the regime of informality is also marked by the locale in which it is set, the slum habitat. These three structuring features and their congruence are discussed in this chapter. In my first publication on the regime of informality in the mid-1970s, 1 drew attention to the limited knowledge and also preconceived ideas that existed on the relationship between the informal economy and social hierarchy. I challenged the then prevailing notion of the informal sector as an urban phenomenon and in that context, also rejected the assumption that the workforce could be split up into two segments, a formal one recruited from the higher social strata and an informal one consisting of lower-class workers. I followed up my critique by presenting a more complex analysis of the social structure on both sides of the suggested divide. This chapter starts with what I wrote then, since my earlier views relate to the portrait of the informal economy in the way it was initially crafted as an urban sector.

## LABOUR ARISTOCRACY AND LUMPENPROLETARIAT

Those who accept the suggestion that the urban system is divided into two sectors have little difficulty in extending this duality to the social structure. In distinguishing the working population into two separate circuits, the members of which are absorbed into the production process in entirely different ways, the contrast made between the formal and the informal sectors parallels that between a labour elite and a lumpenproletariat. It is not difficult to consider the minority, engaged on the basis of regular employment and standardized working conditions and thus privileged to lead a relatively secure existence, as a labour elite. This includes the employees of private enterprises and government institutions, workers in large factories, and other groups who, in view of their social standing, comply more with the image of a salariat than of a proletariat. The principal characteristics of such employment, linked to major enterprises and government offices, have already been discussed. But it is important to note that this favoured part of the labour force can also be recognized by its lifestyle, such as in the type of housing, its furnishings, intake of food (quality and quantity), clothing and dress code, and other symbols of material affluence. Housekeeping shows regularity, the rhythm being attuned to fixed working hours, holidays, etc. Considerable value is attached to formal education. Even when women work outside the home, a major concern is to pay attention to the care and socialization of their children. People are well informed as to what goes on outside their locality, show great interest in non-routine events, and evince signs of a long-term perspective with regard to the future. But can the multitude of small self-employed and casual labourers be classified as a marginalized mass and absorbed under the concept 'lumpenproletariat', which has the reverse characteristics? When writing in the mid-twentieth century, Fanon (1961) thought this was possible with relation to the populations of Third World countries who migrate to the cities, live a precarious existence for lack of permanent work and income, and remain uprooted. In his view, they represented a mixture of people who were no longer peasants but who had not yet crystallized into a proletariat. Fanon saw them as bearers of the revolutionary spirit so lacking among the established working class who fear everything that is likely to affect their elitist position.

The realization came that the poor settled in the slums were closely intertwined with, and not dissociated from, the overall socio-economic order. This apparently nullifies the wider significance that Fanon gave to the concept, and makes it just as inappropriate as that of the informal sector. Lumpenproletariat is taken to include widely varied classes whose only common characteristic is that none of them belongs to the labour aristocracy. This is quite inadequate to take as a point of departure in a definition of social classes. In agreement with the meaning originally given to it by Marx, therefore, it seems wiser to reserve the term 'lumpenproletariat' for the urban residual lot with criminal tendencies whose presence is appreciated by no one. These are the declassed, who have broken all ties with their milieu of origin, who have nowhere to live, and who have no proper or regular contact with others in their immediate surroundings. Having fallen into a state of pauperization, they form a beaten and apathetic muster of lone men, women with children, children without parents, the maimed, and the aged. Prepared to do anything that will earn them a penny, the majority roam the streets begging, collecting old paper, plastics, and bottles, and scavenging through the city's garbage for anything edible or usable. These are the genuinely uprooted, and it is quite inconceivable that they could ever act as a revolutionary force.

The working elite and the lumpenproletariat—the latter concept taken in its original meaning of a residue of pauperized elements—can be regarded as the extremes of the social hierarchy of the labour force. The dynamics of the two social classes are very different. While employment in the formal, large-scale segment shows little sign of expansion, and even appears to be at a standstill, the dregs of society gradually increase because the production process is unable to absorb the inflow of rural migrants. However, these two categories are not the only, or even the most important, social classes. Is it conceivable that the majority of the working population, situated between the labouring aristocracy and paupers, form one social class whose members are absorbed in similar manner in the production process and who have identical living standards? This view would seem to be confirmed by the idea of the terrain of informality as lacking sectoral differentiation, a homogeneous contingent formed principally by a multitude of self-employed who earn their living independently or with the aid of family labour. As I have mentioned earlier, however, this conception disregards the quite substantial heterogeneity that exists at this level of activity. To suggest, as Sanyal does, that small-scale entrepreneurs and the workers they sweat are from the same social stock is a misrepresentation of the class differentiation that exists and amounts to a denial of the capitalist features structuring social relations in petty commodity production (2007: 239). Any classification is quite unacceptable when it starts from the assumption, as Sanyal does, that both the owners of workshops and of other small establishments and the labourers whom they exploit share the same social plane. Instead of maintaining this fiction of homogeneity in employment and lifestyle, I wish to introduce another differentiation in social classes, namely, a distinction between a petty bourgeoisie and a sub-proletariat.

## PETTY BOURGEOISIE AND SUB-PROLETARIAT

The petty bourgeoisie includes the owners of small-scale workshops, a wide assortment of self-employed craftsmen, petty traders and shopkeepers, and those who earn their daily bread by economic brokerage, such as moneylenders, labour recruiters, contractors or subcontractors of piecework, suppliers of home-based manufacturers, rent collectors, drug dealers, booze distillers and sellers, black marketeers, and slumlords. Their incomes are often quite high even when compared to those in protected employment, and they are given pride of place in those reports which praise the informal sector as a nursery and training ground for entrepreneurs. All such groups have some capital of their own, know how to get access to credit for doing business, and cling strongly to their relative autonomy—guarding against subordination to others—while as individuals, they show signs of wanting to improve their position within the existing social hierarchy by such bourgeois characteristics as hard work, thrift, and deferred gratification. In other words, as petty capitalists, they have a great urge towards self-achievement, confidence in the openness of the system, appreciation of the value of education, and realization that to climb the social ladder, they have to depend on favourable contacts with those of higher status. Without going to the extreme of an antithetical stereotype of a culture of poverty—which half a century ago became a fashionable construct, particularly in anthropological studies (see, for example, Lewis 1968)—I cannot agree with a concept that attributes bourgeois habits to all layers of the urban poor. The differences in style of living are, in my opinion, far too great.

The urban labour force is primarily made up of the sub-proletariat. This social class forms the largest section of the working population.[1] In my view, it includes not only the casual and unskilled labourers but also those employed by small-scale workshops and labour reserve of large enterprises; they are split up in small groups, gangs of labour, which are continuously changing in composition and which are rarely tied to a permanent place of work. It further includes those who are condemned to self-employment such as the ambulant craftsmen who each morning tender their labour and paltry set of tools in the urban marketplace, the home-based workers, street vendors, and a long list of others, including the inevitable shoeshine. The wages of this sub-proletariat are half, or even less than half, of the earnings of the labour elite; and the low return to their labour power is also subject to great fluctuation. The expenditures of households in this category regularly exceed their incomes, a fact that can only be explained if debt mechanisms are included as an important feature in determining the price of labour. Such workers are pitiably housed and although a family may manage to pull on, their housekeeping is very makeshift. Members of the sub-proletariat are often better educated than might be assumed and their attitude towards education is not necessarily negative. They put forward many excuses for not sending their children to school regularly: no money for clothing and books; the distance to the school is too great; the care for younger siblings; or the contribution children have to make to the household budget. They also question the usefulness of education that does not lead to any obvious economic improvement. Nevertheless, the opinion prevails that those who cannot read or write are deficient and shiftless members of society. It is all too usual for them to seek to escape their daily misery with the aid of alcohol. Their day-to-day existence precludes any long-term orientation. Major and minor crises such as lack of employment and the inability to work due to illness are chronic and consequently, their coping power is very limited. The consciousness that they lack dignity, that they are stigmatized in the eyes of others, makes them feel inadequate. However, their class consciousness should not be underestimated. Their perception of their situation, and the social determinants which cause it, are frequently quite accurate; but equally accurate is their awareness that they are unlikely to find a way out.

Although their misery is great, these labouring households at the bottom of the sub-proletariat are still distinct from the category of the last resort, the *Lumpen* torn loose from the social fabric. Equally improvident but not in the forefront of public notice is the segment that has no property to fall back on but is also deplete of the labour power and stamina needed to secure their livelihood. Alienated from adequate means of consumption that are required for survival, they consist of a ragbag of crushed, broken-spirited rejects: single living men, widows or divorced women with children, children without parents, the mentally or physically handicapped, and the superfluous elderly. My latest round of fieldwork in south Gujarat is targeted on these destitutes and their pauperized lives. The findings will be published in a forthcoming publication (Kannan and Breman 2013).

The attempt made to split up the workforce in the informal economy in a three-class profile—petty bourgeoisie, sub-proletariat, and the non-labouring poor—is not a very sophisticated one. The exercise lacks nuance because it clubs together categories quite disparate in their social identity. As I suggested earlier, the same multidimensional heterogeneity that fragments the informal economy is also a characteristic feature of its social landscape. While I have tried to demarcate the lines between the distinct segments on the basis of their internal congruency, a hierarchical model neatly divided into three discrete social strata is difficult to substantiate with factual evidence. A household can include members who have been absorbed in the labour process in various ways; not always all of them are involved either in the informal or formal sector. Still, a consequent absence of consistency in terms of class position and associated lifestyle can be overcome by part of the household breaking away or pushed off to form a new unit of cohabitation. The fluidity in the transition between the different social classes, as well as shifts in the proportional distribution among them that occur over time under influence of contraction or expansion of the economy and its sector-wise distribution, mitigate against a structural division which is either unduly rigid or too static. Hence, it is empirically not easy to delineate the largest segment of the workforce in the informal economy, the sub-proletariat, from the other collectivities. Hypothetically, upward and downward mobility are both possible and occur at all levels to some degree, but very rarely all the way, that is, from the bottom to the top or vice versa. In most cases, mobility is limited to much shorter movements up or down.

## HETEROGENEITY ABOVE ALL

The given analysis dates back to the mid-1970s and cannot any longer be held up as a frame for constructing the social outlines of the informal economy. It does not fit the contours of this landscape, mainly for two reasons. In the first place, the argument that informality is not a major feature of the urban setting only has found general acceptance recently. The extension of the concept to all branches of the economy, including agriculture, has resulted in a huge scaling up of the magnitude of the workforce employed on these conditions. While prior estimates were that about half or maybe a little more of the labouring classes in the cities were not engaged on formal sector terms, the latest figures show that in India, nine out of every 10 workers—either urban, rural, or in between—depend for their livelihood on the informal economy. The increase is not merely caused by a redefinition of the concept of informality, applying it to all forms of gainful work without public regulation and protection, but is also the outcome of the neoliberal politics of informalization that have been relentlessly pushed since the last decade of the twentieth century. The earlier trend to regulate and protect conditions of employment, backed up by public agency, was abandoned to be replaced by a labour regime that denies both employment and social security to the working classes and leaves them unprotected and vulnerable in the free interplay of market forces. The size and shape of the informal economy differ in important ways from earlier appraisals. Which are the consequences of these reconsiderations for the social profile of its workforce?

The very broad range of activities clubbed together under the label of informality are performed by just as heterogeneously composed categories of working people. Despite the wide diversity, there are still a number of common features in the identity of these masses. For the large majority, their economic status is one of stark and lasting poverty due to the low price their labour fetches. There are various dimensions to this condition of acute deprivation. In the first place, they belong to households that have no, or not enough, means of production from which income can be derived. Their labour power, which is the main or only source of income, remains unskilled, and bringing them up to the educational level required for upgrading their trade or craft to a higher level of competence is out of question. A toolkit or other equipment with which to increase their labour earnings is an expenditure they cannot afford or for which they have to take out a loan at a high rate of interest. When informal sector workers lack creditworthiness, it is because of the low wages they receive, which do not allow them to save up for making investments in whatever is the mainstay of their livelihood. It is precisely the paltry returns that force these workers to make use of all hands, nimble fingers as well as over-aged ones, available in their households. Or in the case of migrants, to leave behind 'dependent' family members who no longer or not yet have the ability to work to an extent that would at least compensate for the cost of their maintenance. Still, the informal economy is not the exclusive domain of migrants. Many workers in the informal economy are born and bred in the city, and the work they do has frequently been handed down to them by the older generation.

By now, there are a number of case studies available that inform us about the economics of labour migration (for example, Breman 1996 and 2010a; Deshingkar and Farrington 2009; and Srivastava 2011)—the work they do, the wages they get for it, their abysmal accommodation, etc.—but we know much less about what it means to break up the household between those who go off and those who stay behind. The social cost is enormous but we are short of data on the coping behaviour of wives and children in the absence of the main income providers and on the loneliness of the migrants in the months or years they have to spend away from home and family as well as the lack of care and support in case of illness or other adversities they are bound to experience. Last but not the least is the degraded status associated with most informal jobs. This is partly the sum total of the features mentioned earlier in combination with the irregularity and substitutability of the work that, in addition to all this, is often also demeaning and defiling in a physical sense. The strenuous effort demanded goes together with stench, noise, sweat, filth, and other such bodily symptoms which bear the odium of inferiority and subordination. Tainted with the stigma of pollution, these characteristics also undermine the health of the workers in a way which incapacitates them from working on. Many are already worn out long before old age sets in. In further aggravation of all these hazards, women and children are also exposed to sexual abuse. Female and child domestic servants, for instance, are at risk from their employers, or mates in the same work gangs, or from the foremen and other bosses. Lack of dignity results from their inability to cope with misfortune, such as illness, or to save for the considerable expense which cannot be avoided for important life cycle rituals which have to be observed at the time of birth, death, and in particular, marriage. By taking an advance on these occasions, they try to meet their social obligations even if it leads to a form of debt bondage, to their employer or a jobber, which restricts even further their already limited room for manoeuvre. The resulting dependency means living in a state of subordination. Labour is treated as a commodity, has already been stripped from its human quality on entering the workforce, and becomes more dehumanized in the labour process. In that sense, the word coolie, widely used in the colonial setting, is still an apt phrase for the men, women, and children milling around but stuck at the bottom of the informal economy.

In comparison with the labour aristocracy firmly embedded in the formal economy—in regular employ, well educated, with a daily rhythm in which work and free time are sharply marked, reasonably well paid, able to save and invest in the future of the next generation, living in reasonable comfort, and consequently aware of their social dignity and respect—the huge workforce without all these prerogatives and labour rights seem to form a homogeneous mass. A closer examination, however, reveals that the working population is not divided into just two social classes. In the lower circuits of the informal economy, there are striking differences in lifestyle between, for example, migrants forced to wander around sites of employment in the open air and labourers who operate power looms in small workshops. The latter have more steady jobs, although they cannot derive from their ongoing employment by the same boss any claim for decent treatment or even the right to a minimum form of security.

## THE COMMON PEOPLE

An approach from a different angle on the social classification of the informal workforce has been presented by K.P. Kannan (2009). As one of the members of the NCEUS, set up by the government to report on the informal economy and its workforce, he had a major role in the investigations leading to the disconcerting finding that in 2004–5, not less than three-quarters of the population were unable to spend more for their living cost than 20 rupees per day per capita, an amount that led the commission to classify this multitude as poor and vulnerable. They are the people who form the backbone of the workforce in the informal economy and who are, in the Commission's documentation, classified as hovering around the poverty line, the slightly better-off somewhat above the statistical demarcation of income deficit but at constant risk to fall back to a worse condition and the worst-off segment far below this line of minimal well-being. Having established the interrelationship between poverty and informality, the social segments to which they belong were clubbed together as *aam admi*, a generic name for the common people. A further deconstruction of this all too general label was required. Following up on his work as a panellist of the NCEUS, Kannan co-authored an article on the social profile of the various categories brought together on a platform of commonality that suggests uniformity where diversity prevails (Sengupta *et al.* 2008). That diversity, the authors argued, stems from 'systematic and hierarchical segmentation' (ibid.). In his Presidential Address in 2008 to the Indian Society for Labour Economics, Kannan held forth on the close nexus that exists between social identity, economic vulnerability, and informality (Kannan 2009). The common denominator underlying this triangular setting of inequality is, in his opinion, the entrenched inequitable distribution arising out of the hierarchical nature of India's social order. He makes a threefold classification—with the SCs/STs at the bottom of the heap, a cluster called 'Others' consisting of upper-caste Hindus and similar elite formations at the top, and Other Backward Castes (OBCs) together with Muslims ranked in the middle—and concludes that 'those who are clustered at the lower layers of social inequality are also the ones, as a group, who are disproportionately represented in the informal economy and are poor and vulnerable' (Kannan 2009: 12).

Based on data presented in one of the NCEUS reports (2008), Tables 5.1 and 5.2 specify the state of poverty of the classified social groups among the informal workforce in a macro-level analysis of socio-economic correlates. The social groups distinguished show a clear and differential pattern in their level of poverty and that same gradation comes back when all poor and vulnerable are clustered in one group with the better-off (middle and high income) in another cluster. The association between poverty, social identity, and working in the informal economy is equally close.

The NCEUS has focused its analysis on the decade of high growth rate between 1993–4 and 2004–5. Have the labouring poor not benefited at all from this impressive outcome of the neoliberal policy? In his foreword to the final report, the Commission's chairman agreed that there has been some increase in employment during these years, but he adds immediately,

TABLE 5.1    Percentage Distribution of Population and Informal Workers
             by Poverty Status and Social Groups, 2004–5

| Poverty Status | Population | | | | | Informal |
| --- | --- | --- | --- | --- | --- | --- |
| | Total | SC/ST | Muslim | OBC | Others | Workers |
| 1. Extreme poor | 6.4 | 10.9 | 8.2 | 5.2 | 2.1 | 5.8 |
| 2. Poor | 15.4 | 21.5 | 19.2 | 15.1 | 6.4 | 15.0 |
| 3. Marginal | 19.0 | 22.4 | 22.3 | 20.4 | 11.1 | 19.6 |
| 4. Vulnerable | 36.0 | 33.0 | 34.8 | 39.2 | 35.3 | 38.4 |
| 5. Middle income | 19.3 | 11.2 | 13.3 | 17.8 | 34.2 | 18.7 |
| 6. Higher income | 4.0 | 1.0 | 2.2 | 2.4 | 11.0 | 2.7 |
| 9. Poor and vulnerable (7 + 8) | 76.7 | 87.8 | 84.5 | 79.9 | 54.8 | 78.7 |
| 10. Middle and high income (5 + 6) | 23.3 | 12.2 | 15.5 | 20.2 | 45.2 | 21.3 |
| 11. All | 100.0 | 100.0 | 100.0 | 100.0 | 100.0 | 100.0 |

*Source*: Kannan (2009: 12).
*Note*: The official poverty line (PL) is the benchmark used for determining the
different categories of the poverty status. Extreme poverty means those below
0.75 PL; poor means 1 PL; marginal means between 1 and 1.25 PL; vulnerable
means between 1.25 and 2 PL; middle income means between 2 and 4 PL; and
high income means above 4 PL. For details, see the Appendix in Sengupta *et al.*
(2008). The data on consumer expenditure computed for determining poverty
status are from the consumer expenditure schedule attached to the Employment
and Unemployment Survey of the National Sample Survey 61st Round. This is a
slightly abridged version of the detailed consumer expenditure survey conducted
separately. The incidence of poor and vulnerable by using the detailed survey works
out to 75.3 as against 76.7 arrived at by using the abridged schedule.

almost entirely of informal employment of a casualized and contractual
nature and informal regular low-wage workers (Sengupta 2009). His
succinct observation was that both in terms of quantity and quality of
employment, the poor and vulnerable groups have been lagging far behind
during the period of rapid economic growth (ibid.). The social dynamics
have been those of progressive polarization, a further widening of the
already yawning gap separating the *haves* from the *have-nots*. It is not for
the first time that the trend towards more rather than less inequity has been
highlighted in a report commissioned by the government. The report of the
NCRL, submitted shortly before the economic policy became relentlessly
market driven, held the slow increase in per capita income, as well as the
labour-unfriendly policy framework, responsible for the deprivation in

TABLE 5.2  Percentage Distribution of Informal Workers by Socio-Religious Groups Within Different Categories of the Poverty Status, 2004–5

| Poverty Status | Socio-religious Category | | | | |
| --- | --- | --- | --- | --- | --- |
| | SC/ST | Muslim | OBC | Others | Total |
| Shares of workers in each social group | | | | | |
| Poor and vulnerable | 88.5 | 84.7 | 80.1 | 58.8 | 78.7 |
| Middle and high income | 11.5 | 15.3 | 19.9 | 41.2 | 21.3 |
| Total | 100.0 | 100.0 | 100.0 | 100.0 | 100.0 |
| Shares of social groups in total informal workers | | | | | |
| Poor and vulnerable | 34.3 | 11.3 | 38.7 | 15.6 | 100.0 |
| Middle and high income | 16.5 | 7.6 | 35.6 | 40.4 | 100.0 |
| Total | 30.5 | 10.5 | 38.1 | 20.9 | 100.0 |

*Source*: Kannan (2009: 12).

which the lower classes in the countryside remained stuck and concluded that the trickle-down effects of growth had been negligible for India's rural poor (GoI 1991). This assessment came after more than four decades of public development praxis as specified in the five-year planning documents that formed the directory for the policies to be followed. Turning the compass around in the opposite direction and leaving the field open for the free interplay of market forces suggested that flexibilization of employment would not only raise production and productivity but also alleviate poverty in the lower echelons of the informalized economy. It is a sobering thought that both policy regimes, though in stark contrast to each other, have not resulted in a levelling down of the social discrepancies.

## PROGRESSIVE POLARIZATION

Have the prospects for socio-economic progress across the board become brighter in more recent years? An unequivocal turn for the better is not what Kannan has found in his ongoing documentation of the ordeal India's common people are forced to face in their fight for a better deal (Kannan 2011b; Kannan and Raveendran 2011). Certainly, his updated analysis confirms that the incidence of extremely poor and poor has declined in all states and thus, also nationwide. In other words, the segment of the population below the official poverty line is lower in 2011 than it was five years ago. But that happy tale needs to be toned down on several counts: first, in the light of the criticism raised against the way in which the policymakers have drawn the divide between the poor and non-poor. The Government of India, in mid-2010, has accepted an expenditure threshold set at 22 per cent above the old poverty line. According to many commentators, this reappraisal is not good enough by far. In terms of purchasing power parity (PPP), it is fixed still lower than the international extreme poverty line of 1 dollar per capita per day. Acceptance of the standard of 2 dollars a day would include in the ranks of the poor, the categories that are now classified as vulnerable and marginal. Second reason is because the poverty reduction is not proportionally spread over the various social groups affected by an income deficit. As Kannan (2011b) demonstrates with statistical evidence, the segments classified as the least deprived among the poor and vulnerable have done better than the cluster of STs and SCs at the tail end of the list with respective 81 per cent and 66 per cent of their constituency stuck in insecurity. Without doubt, access to work has remained firmly caste based. Workers try to fence off the niche in which they have found employment from outside intrusion by articulating their caste identity. This also applies to the somewhat better-skilled and better-paid jobs in the informal economy. In the recruitment to such work, intermediate and OBCs are strongly represented. In contrast, workers performing the most strenuous and menial forms of work are mostly recruited from the lowest social rank and are often from tribal and Dalit communities. The consequence is that the distance between them, stagnating at the bottom, and the groups somewhat higher up has increased.

Summing up his findings, this economist of the aam admi or the common people (Kannan 2011a) concludes that in most states of India, escaping from poverty has meant an extremely tenuous process with some segments of the poor finding themselves upgraded to the category of the marginally poor; for those in the latter category, the movement has meant a similar escape from the milieu of absolute poverty, but not out of vulnerability. At best, the transition has been one from 'more poor' to 'less poor' but remaining poor nevertheless. While acknowledging some improvement in the poverty profile since 2004–5, Kannan's conclusion does not come as a surprise that the social dynamics have been of exclusive rather than inclusive growth. There still exists a vast mass of labouring poor in the country constrained by hunger, poverty, and low capabilities, all of which work as formidable barriers towards the move to a life of dignity. 'Such a grim picture of low human development in India is very much related to the issue of embedded inequality as well as a process of inequalising growth along with slow progress in raising human development' (Kannan 2011b: 15). More fundamental is the critique that by focusing on the distribution of expenditure, the existence of inequality is shown to be less sharp than when income would have been chosen as the main yardstick of class disparity (Weisskopf 2011). Indeed, the degree of inequality is even more pronounced than can be distilled from official statistics since the capital circulating in the informal economy remains beyond the records of the state. The magnitude and power of informalized capital spill over in circuits of politics and governance, adding to the maldistribution in the representation of class interests.

Indicative of the polarization trend is that the incidence of deprivation has not progressively gone down in states characterized by high industrialization and urbanization. As a matter of fact, together with Tamil Nadu, the state of Gujarat with the highest growth rate has also the dubious virtue of having the sharpest inequality between the top and bottom slots of poverty. The final conclusion, which should come as no surprise, is that India's unresolved poverty question is closely related to the political unwillingness to tackle the social question. The neoliberal faith that growth trickles down, if not instantly than soon enough, has been belied so often and so strongly that it cannot be accepted any longer as a trustful and truthful announcement on what will happen next. In an affidavit submitted to the Supreme Court in September 2011, the Planning Commission has brazenly testified that a daily per capita income of just 26 rupees in rural areas and of 32 rupees in urban areas constitutes adequate private expenditure on food, education, and health. This cash amount is in accordance with the recommendations made by the Tendulkar Committee that pegged the poverty line at roughly 15 rupees per day at 2004–5 prices for rural consumers and 25 rupees per day for urban consumers.

The exercise led to a modest upward revision of poverty, now calculated to be 27.8 per cent. Of the amount stipulated about 80 per cent is generally considered to be meant for food requirements, while a stingy 20 per cent is all that remains for housing, health, education and transport. In the uproar that followed a number of leading economists publicly spoke out against the measurement of poverty as fixed by the Planning Commission (Breman 2010c).

The estimates are fixed at this low level for no other purpose than to drive down the below the poverty line (BPL) figure, and thus reduce government expenditure on the poor in the years to come.[2] The current BPL list has now become invalid and will be revised on the basis of an ongoing survey with the clear intent to remove a large number of households which appear on the current list.[3] What will remain is the nexus between informality, economic insecurity, and a social status regarded as 'inferior'. If indeed India's poverty question is as unresolved as its social question, it is because of the policies of exclusion that dominate over the faint promises of inclusion. What is the upshot of all this? Including the aam admi in the ranks of the labouring poor, Kannan (2011b: 21) contrasts 'Shining India' to 'Suffering India', a two-class model in which the well-to-do top consists of 368 million people (31 per cent) and the broad bottom of the more or less deprived is enumerated at 820 million (69 per cent).

## FROM HIERARCHY TO INEQUALITY

Is there no countervailing power, the opening of a prospect for better days to come? What I find a very hopeful sign in the milieu of the down and out is the absence of people sunk in a culture of poverty, the acceptance of life and work at the bottom as it is. That kind of submissiveness, if it has ever existed, has gone. The seventh of the *Selected Readings*, 'Proletarian Life and Social Consciousness', describes and analyses the self-perception of the workforce at the bottom of the informal economy in my fieldwork arena. Caste as a system of social structure and culture has not withered away in modern India. In some respects, certainly in the labour market, it has even gained in strength as a marker of identification. However, the hierarchical features that were the organizing principles of the caste-cum-tribe order, modelled on a domination–submission complex, have increasingly become inoperative. This shift that has come about in a long drawn-out process can be summed up as an institutional change from stratification along lines of verticality to one of horizontality. That is, the caste system seems to have lost its high versus low imprint. Superiority is still claimed at the top but not granted from below; and the label of inferiority, instead of having been internalized, is nowadays openly contested. It means that the social system has graduated from one based on hierarchy to one structured along lines of stratified differentiation. Of course, the class angle was also crucial to the caste ranking of the past. But in the transition to a capitalist mode of production, economic status, in terms of power and property, has gained in prominence, while ritual status has receded in the attribution of positions within the system of social organization. An extension in scale of interaction and a lengthening as well as widening of the chain of differentiation has increased social distancing. Therefore, I wholeheartedly disagree with Sanyal (2007: 259) that the landscape of informality can be summed up as one of classlessness. Growing inequality rather than a levelling down of disparities and inequities is the driving force in what has emerged as an unregulated regime of capitalism flourishing under a free market doctrine. The masses at the bottom are dependent on the informal economy for their survival. Worst off is the substantial segment depleted from income sources of their own and who, because of old age or a variety of handicaps, are not able to work. Widening class divides bordering over into acute pauperism are the outcome of this social meltdown of decency. The fear of the dangerous hordes that in the Western world became a major motive towards inclusion of the working and non-working poor towards the end of the nineteenth century does not bother India's dominating elite which enjoys increasing prosperity. There seems to be no lurking suspicion that the excluded masses might challenge the established order and rise in revolt. That disregard may have to do with the assumed natural inferiority per se of the down and out. It is also caused, however, by the informalism of the political economy that puts a premium not merely on cheap labour but also sees to it that the fragmented and segmented workforce is kept footloose. Oppressed and exploited as they are, it does not mean that the down and out have been cowed down and bridled in defeatism. Underlying their spirit of resistance is the claim on life and work in decency and dignity, an insistence on inclusion.

## UNDERCITIZENSHIP[4]

Slums are the habitat *par excellence* for a very substantial part of the workforce in the informal economy. These settlements can be either urban or rural but their defining feature at first sight is the poor quality of the housing and the paltry provisioning of basic utilities. There is no dearth of slum profiles but it is clear that Katherine Boo's recently published chronicle of Annawadi in Mumbai stands out as a magnificent account of work and life at the margins of the urban economy (Boo 2012). The undercity that has come under her lense consists of 335 huts in which more than 3,000 people are packed. Slums have a complex class configuration and Annawadi is no exception. A few of the households have, or aim at, the lifestyle of petty bourgeois. They are the ones connecting the residents to the power mongers in the overcity—politicians, bureaucrats, and non-government associations in particular—whose help is sought to get out of trouble, gain a free benefit or ward off some threat. Sub-proletarian is the class identity of the large majority of slum dwellers. A freak residue of the good-for-nothing constitute the Lumpen element—eaters of rats, frogs, and scrub grass— whose presence is required as a reminder that life can still be worse than it has been so far. The author has selected her terrain for a number of reasons. Mainly for the stark contrast with the wealth all around. In the shadow of Mumbai's airport Annawadi actually came up as a slum when a gang of construction workers, brought in from Tamilnad to repair a runway at the airport, decided to stay on when their job was finished and fabricate a settlement out of a swamp. Today's inhabitants live on the leftovers of the nearby opulence, the garbage and waste spilled out from the luxury hotels, airconditioned offices and airport buildings. If not salvaging trash, they resort to pilfering material and goods from the construction sites or warehouses scattered around the airport. A second ground for choosing this enclave as her research site was its contained and small-scale size that allowed for a door-to-door survey and for what Boo calls the vagrant-sociology approach. What adds to the impressive quality of her findings is that she did not limit herself to a single round of investigations. Boo came to stay on for over three years, from late 2007 to early 2011. The monitoring of the day-to-day life experiences of the slum dwellers over such an extended stretch of time has enabled her to change her initial perception as outsider to one of an insider. While to a certain extent overlooking the wider context, she has managed to come close to the ups and downs of a small number of households and these tales are extensively documented from beginning to end.

The opening sentence of Boo's narrative is the arrival of the police at midnight to arrest Abdul and his father, victims of a faked crime for which they will nevertheless be sent to prison. The author's technique is that of an investigative journalist who weaves into the non-fictitious story told meaningful facts that demonstrate how the progress hoped for remains frustrated and setbacks are in the order of the day. That bitter lesson has much to do with the lack of decent work and adequate income for almost all slum dwellers. Among the more than three thousand inhabitants of Annawadi only six had found access to a permanent job. What is the sort of daily work schedule men, women, and children are engaged in?

One by one, construction workers departed for an intersection where site supervisors chose day labourers. Young girls began threading marigolds into garlands that they would hawk in the evening's rush-hour traffic. Older women sewed patches onto pink-and-blue cotton quilts for a company that paid by the piece. In a small, sweltering plastic-moulding factory, bare-chested men cranked gears that would turn colored beads into ornaments to be hung from rearview mirrors- smiling ducks and pink cats with jewels around their necks that they couldn't imagine anyone, anywhere buying. And Abdul crouched on the maidan, beginning to sort two weeks' worth of purchased trash, a stained shirt hitching up his knobby spine. (Boo 2012: 4)

Adding to the merits of staying on and observing from close-by is that the scene of action is looked at through the eyes of kids and youngsters. As Boo pointed out in her author's endnote, children are indeed more dependable witnesses, more open minded in talking about the doings, misdoings and undoings of adults. But also among the up and coming generation hopes for a better future are inevitably dampened by a realism that windows of opportunity are a rare occurrence. Trajectories leading out of abject poverty can be dreamt off but all too often turn out to be chimeras leading into dead-end alleys. Those notions seem to go together with a matter of fact acceptance that the heartfelt desire for upliftment from undercitizenship to citizenship implies a claim to respectability that is more often denied than granted. No doubt, there are the once-in-a-while windfalls, an unexpected gain which brings temporary relief but which is soon reversed in a new setback. The mood of being deprived is starker because at short distance glamour and glitter abound. 'Everything around us is roses', is how Abdul's younger brother Mirichi, put it. 'And we are the shit in between' (ibid.: xii). And his elder brother knew that the commodity in which he traded was also the label attached to his own identity: garbage. 'But in the hierarchy of the undercity's waste business, this teenager was a notch above the scavengers: a trader who appraised and bought what they found. His profit came from selling the refuse in bulk to small recycling plants a few miles away' (ibid.: xiii).

Let alone the inadequate food intake, pollution at the work sites in the open air is as hazardous to health risks as the abysmal terms of employment inside the workshops. Conditions in an industry-heavy slum nearby provide a good example.

Among Saki Naka's acres of sheds were metal-melting and plastic-shredding machines owned by men in starched kurtas—white kurtas—to announce the owners' distance from the filth of their trade. Some of the workers at the plants were black-faced from carbon dust, and surely black-lunged from breathing iron shavings. A few weeks ago, Abdul had seen a boy's hand cut clean off when he was putting plastic into one of the shredders. The boy's eyes were filled with tears but he hadn't screamed. Instead he'd stood there with his blood-spurting stump, his ability to earn a living ended, and started apologizing to the owner of the plant. 'Sa'ab, I'm sorry', he'd said to the man in white. 'I won't cause you any problems by reporting this. You will have no trouble from me'. (Ibid.: 15)

Heavy drinking and drug addiction, which for youngsters takes the shape of sniffing correction fluid, are vices that weaken the ability to work and result in a downward spiral marked by lumpenization. Boo's narrative is replete with illness, injuries, either temporary or chronic invalidity and a protracted debilitation of body or mind ending in premature loss of life. But also self-inflicted death in order to be released from pain, expressing inability to endure further physical or mental agony. This leads me to comment on the shallow demographic range of Annawadi's population, which is the remarkable absence of elderly people. The generational interaction reported is between adults and children while the old age cohort is simply not around. High morbidity leading to progressive disability and demise already at or shortly beyond middle age cannot be the only or even the main explanation for the lack of grandparents in the slum. A more likely cause seems to be that when the labour power required to make a living is gone, people faced with that ordeal cannot afford to stay on. Only those strong and hardy enough to earn at least their own keep, be they adults or youngsters, can claim the right of survival in the slum locality. Those who do not qualify, who have lost their strength to cope and do not chip in anymore to what is required for mere survival, cannot depend on other members of the household to take care of them. They have to disappear from the scene. Where do people go who, on a life-long diet of severe malnourishment and in a state of growing incapacitation, have no option but to join the ranks of the non-labouring poor?

A striking feature of the slum settlement is the continual passing through of people from all over India. Moving on or going back, Boo explains, is conditioned by the paucity of regular work and without earning an income it is well-nigh impossible to hold on to the foothold established in Annawadi. Households may every now and then tolerate members not able to contribute fully to the budget because bouts of unemployment do occur frequently. But growing old and losing one's labour power is too a heavy burden for the next generation to carry and forces people facing that predicament to go off. Ill equipped for survival most of them return to their place of origin to silently fade away in starvation. Although the author has ventured on trips to the rural hinterland, it is clear that she is more familiar with, and also has a much better grip on, her slum niche in Mumbai. The village is a site from which people come or move back to but Boo has little to tell on those points of departure. Consequently, she touches in haste on issues—such as the maoist movement, farmers' suicide, public works for the rural poor, vain attempts to find work in the city—that, in order to become meaningful, would require more space and context. The very diversity of the slum population makes it all the more necessary to sharpen separate identities. Cementing bonds along lines of ethnicity, religion, caste and language becomes instrumental in the search for work or finding access to political patronage. To that extent collective action does exist though fractured on the basis of primordial attachments. Bereft from such links of mediation and just walking into the urban labour market will not do, as Anil found out. Seeing no future as an agricultural labourer in his village, he had become one of the half a million rural Indians who annually try their luck in Mumbai. 'Each dawn, he stood with other work-seekers at Marol Naka, an intersection near the airport where construction supervisors come in trucks to pick up day labourers. A thousand unemployed men and women came to this crossroads every morning; a few hundred got picked.... After a month of rejection, he'd gone home' (Boo 2012: 140).

Economic misfortune was not the only reason why migrants left, as many Tamils had done. To become footloose again might also result from the kind of political turmoil instigated by Shiv Sena. This party wanted to purge Mumbai of outsiders, the Muslims among them in particular, and attempted to replace them by Maharashtrians. When Boo started her investigations, the locality was only eleven years old but already three waves of migrants had passed through.

... shortly after the turn of the century, the Maharashtrians had disempowered the Tamil laborers who had first cleared the land. But a majority is a hard thing to maintain in a slum where almost no one has permanent work. Annawadians came and went, selling or renting their huts in a thriving underground trade, and by early 2008, the North Indian migrants against whom Shiv Sena campaigned had become a plurality. (Ibid.: 18)

Annawadi's short life cycle would soon come to an end in a clearance operation that loomed large over the immediate future of the last spate of settlers. They had already started to position themselves for relocation. Two-thirds of the inhabitants, however, had not lived in their huts long enough to qualify for rehousing. They have no option but to move on to other slums or become squatters on waste land elsewhere. Mobility is continual but upward only in rare cases. The label of undercity is not only a comment on the inadequate habitat, the improvident shelter and the lack of basic amenities with which slum dwellers have to make do. Simply living in Annawadi is illegal, a stigma of subversion and criminality from which people belonging to overcity are spared by definition. It means that from beginning to end undercitizens are on the receiving end of the stick and do not qualify for a modicum of respectability and honour. Why then participate in elections? As is common knowledge, the poor do so with more fervour than the better-off segments of the electorate. Boo suggests that their eagerness to turn up demonstrates their claim to inclusion. 'The crucial thing was the act of casting a ballot. Slumdwellers, who were criminalized by where they lived, and the work they did, living there, were in this one instance equal to every other citizen of India. They were a legitimate part of the state, if they could get on the rolls' (Boo 2012: 231).

Voting is stepping over the threshold that the authorities have thrown up to keep the masses floating and firmly beyond the purview of the state. To get registered is to be acknowledged as local residents and gives the *sans papiers* a claim on legality. This is why Annawadians are so eager to get a voting card, more as an official document of their presence than as an act of suffrage. The other way around, the political bosses in overcity need the vote banks in the undercity to hold on to their power. Slumlords are indispensable to do the canvassing and distribute the cash and booze that have to be doled out to gain or consolidate a seat in the municipality or state assembly. Besides, where and when the poor cast their votes, it does not mean that the political outcome is pro-poor.

The praise I have for Boo's findings does not mean that I accept her assessment of them as valid and fair. Exasperated by Annawadi's layers of deep misery she has brought to the surface in minute detail, Boo wonders at the finale of her narrative: 'Why don't more of our unequal societies implode?' (ibid.: 246). The facile answer given to this crucial query is that, regrettably, she has found no base for the idea of a mutually supportive poor community. Earlier on she conveys how the poor get screwed and squeezed by the somewhat less poor who happen to be their own neighbours. That shocking fact comes back elsewhere in the script, for example, when mentioning that scavengers have to sleep on top of the garbage heap they have collected to prevent other scavengers from stealing them. The nastiness of life and work in the city's underbelly is compounded by fights in which people who are the foot soldiers of a brutal economic regime turn against each other and go hunting for victims even more vulnerable than they themselves are. Although many instances of breach in tolerance escalating into orgies of violence are there for all to see, they do not seem to undermine the myth of communal harmony. While having sympathy for Boo's disillusionment and agony about the lack of solidarity in the milieu of the downtrodden, their envy and suspicion of each other, I thoroughly disagree with her that their exploitation and oppression are caused by an inability and unwillingness to unite in concerted action. It is not so much that the factual evidence is flawed or twisted but it is incomplete. To acknowledge and be involved in collective action along vertical lines of dependency suits some of her informants better than investing in horizontalized bonds of reciprocity and commonality. As, for instance, Asha, who does not mind having sex with a policeman or a politician, to play up to the high and mighty if that is required to be nominated as slumlord and in the end to reach out to overcitizenship. The children of these women are the uncomfortable witnesses to such instances of extra-marital intercourse. I do not dispute Boo's statement that the slum is a vicious battleground with people apt to articulate their self-interest rather than to try and transcend what keeps them divided. As one woman lamented, 'we are so alone in this city' (Boo 2012: 109). However, to seek the origin of poverty in their midst and accuse them of failing to find the remedy for their redemption from deprivation in collective action comes in my reading close to blaming the victim. What may have led her to express that opinion is that the locale of her investigations has also remained the frame of her analysis.

In a way Boo is caught up by having stayed in her search for a rationale too close to the people portrayed. It may be a debatable point of view since she has made the effort to go through three thousand public records accessed after petitioning various government agencies under the Right of Information Act. Procuring these documents enabled her to find out about the interaction between the Mumbai police, the public health department, education bureaucracies, electoral offices, city ward offices, public hospitals, morgues and the courts on the one hand and Annawadi's population on the other hand. It meant that the research did reach out to comprehend and contextualize local affairs in a wider setting. This commendable extension in scale of operation enabled Boo to reveal the means by which a mixture of corruption and indifference erases from the public record the experiences of poor citizens. It is not that do-gooders from civil society have a much better reputation in caring for the poor. Non-government agencies are strikingly absent in Annawadi but in the few instances these voluntary suppliers of benefaction happen to come on stage, they are not less corrupt than most state officials.

While Sonu's father was a good for nothing, his mother was running the household. At night, she and her four children pulled the stringy manufacturing remnants from pink clothespins—piecework for a nearby factory. During the day she sold packets of ketchup and tiny jars of jam, past their expiration date, on a sidewalk near the Hotel Leela. Airline catering companies had donated the jam, along with plastic-wrapped packets of cake crumbs, to Sister Paulette, for the needy young wards. Instead she sold the expired goods to poor women and children, who in turn tried to resell them. Sonu resented Sister Paulette even more than Sunil did. (Boo 2012: 157)

Sister Paulette is the nun who runs the Handmaids of the Blessed Trinity Children orphanage. The children in her custody saw through the racket on which her charity work was based and at the age of 11, Sunil was thrown out of her institutional care to go and fend for himself.

Boo has given us an incisive portrait of slum life and I do not share the criticism that the way in which she takes the politicians and bureaucrats to task shows her subtle alignment with the neoliberal credo out to scale back the state and promote free enterprise (Sengupta 2012). This seems to me to be an unfair distortion of both her findings and write-up. The rampant practice of extortion to which the slum dwellers fall prey are committed by officials and politicians who privatise their public authority and exemplify what I have called the informalization of politics and governance. Indeed, the state does not figure in a benign role and could not care less about the promotion of well-being for its undercitizens. The government does not even acknowledge the intense misery to which the slum dwellers are exposed. Sarcastically Boo sums up the received wisdom of the state.

... almost no one in this slum was considered poor by official Indian benchmarks. Rather, Annawadians were among roughly one hundred million Indians freed from poverty since 1991, when, around the same moment as the small slum's founding, the central government embraced economic liberalization. The Annawadians were thus part of one of the most stirring success narratives in the modern history of global market capitalism, a narrative still unfolding. (Boo 2012: 6)

There is nothing amiss with critical review of the impact of globalization on the lives of the poor. Apart from mentioning the fact that more than half of Mumbai's population are slum dwellers, Annawadi is not set in the wider fabric of the city's economy. Fair enough, since Boo is not interested to discuss her findings as social scientists are habituated to do, that is, by framing them in a larger and more encompassing canvass of studies. For sure, she could have strengthened her story by taking on board the gist of other reports on life and work at the bottom of the urban growth poles. The absence of comparison and of contextualization, however, does not mean that her slum profile is an atypical one. Also reviewers critical of her work praise the quality of Boo's vignettes. Still, there is a kind of myopic gaze in the narrative, the I-am-a-camera syndrome with which Isherwood zoomed in on the company he kept in Berlin in the early 1930s. To clarify what I have in mind, Boo could have benefited, for instance, from the study of scrap trading that links up the localities in which scavengers move around to the waste recovery market (Gill 2010). Just pointing out that Mukesh Ambani is looking down on the undercities of Mumbai from his 27-storey-high skyscraper, in which his family of 5 is serviced by 600 servants, does not compensate for the lack of a wider perspective: a society bent on inequality and inequity together with an economy of predatory capitalism unwilling to incorporate the labouring poor in decent conditions of employment.

The regime of informality does not come up for discussion in Boo's account although that is the backdrop to all that transpires in Annawadi. It is more than just the absence of a spirit of togetherness among the slum dwellers, their steadfast refusal to share the scarce work and livelihood available, that Boo feels rightly upset about. Why can these households not team up and replace their mutual antagonism by helping each other? Because investment in kinship can be risky and costly business and the tendency is not to give in easily to calls for help even from close relatives. Of course, the real question here is how to overcome the commodification of relationships as the organizing principle structuring not only interaction between neighbours but also among members within one and the same household. Children's voices have told Boo how the ties binding them to their parents are instrumental and contractual, often void of love and care, why the labour power they command rather than filial dependency and need of protection become the true measure of their standing in the pecking order at home. In their upbringing, Annawadi's children gradually lose the feelings of empathy that they are not shy to express freely and generously at a tender age. But it is a morality that they cannot afford to nurture in the desperate quest for survival. Is it a deficit of goodwill for which the labouring poor can be held complicit? Boo's answer is not in the affirmative.

In my reporting, I am continually struck by the ethical imaginations of young people, even those in circumstances so desperate that selfishness would be an asset. Children have little power to act on those imaginations, and by the time they grow up, they may have become the adults who keep walking as a bleeding waste-picker slowly dies on the roadside, who turn away when a burned woman writhes, whose first reaction when a vibrant teenager drinks rat poison is a shrug. (Boo 2012: 252)

The multiple forces that account for the change in morale when becoming of age, that is, before reaching puberty, are not spelt out. But shedding light on the process of commodification, which is so intimately and powerfully narrated, and an exposé of what the informal economy is all about, or at least showing an awareness that this is the heart of the matter, might have been a good beginning. It would also require an analysis that goes beyond the locale of investigations. So much is certain, remaining mired in poverty in the undercity is not the failure or shortcoming of the down and out but stems from outside culpability, the politics and policies as directed and imposed from overcity. That verdict, if Boo is willing to owe up to it, could have been substantiated in more articulate and explicit wording.

## NOTES
1. Following Fanon, Worsley also gives a very broad meaning to the concept of sub-proletariat which he places between the peasant mass on the one hand, and the urban labour aristocracy on the other (Worsley 1972: 210–11). He ascribes a lifestyle to this class—in his terminology, the victims of urbanization without industrialization—that differs from that of the bourgeoisie and also from that of the labour aristocracy. T.G. McGee (1971) uses the term proto-proletariat in his writings. Even in the more restricted significance that I give to the concept—omitting paupers and petty bourgeoisie—it still represents the largest social class of the urban working population.
2. In an immediate reaction, the Deputy Chairman of the Planning Commission remained adamant on the correctness of the poverty estimate provided but granted that there would not be an automatic connection between the fixed poverty line and the eligibility for subsidized food (or any other social support benefits).
3. The new BPL census, restricted to rural areas, has already started in late 2011. The questionnaire includes an automatic exclusion category as well as an automatic inclusion category. It retains, however, a ranking system for the rest, who will make up the large majority of the rural population. Destitute people have been defined as those living on alms. But if, for example, a household consists of two senior citizens are forced to work for about a week each month just to survive, then they will not be included as destitutes as they do not beg. Others in this category include 'households

without shelter, manual scavengers, primitive tribal groups, legally released bonded labourers'. But if the worker has run away from bondage, he or she is not legally released, and therefore is not eligible for automatic inclusion. Even social categories such as SCs and STs, the disabled, the widows, and casual manual workers are not automatically included.

4. This section is also being published as a review essay titled 'Stuck in Mumbai's Undercity', *New Left Review*, vol. 78, November–December 2012.

# 6

# Resistance to Exclusion and Coping with Insecurity

## FORMALIZING INFORMALITY?

Lack of public regulation in the hire of labour power is what distinguishes the informal from the formal economy. However, the divide is not watertight because in the first few decades after independence, the Indian government made efforts to reduce the vulnerability of the working classes unprotected by the labour legislation promulgated for the organized segments of the urban proletariat. I shall comment on these efforts for the state of Gujarat in which I have located most of my fieldwork. In the wake of the green revolution that led to a breakthrough in the stagnating agricultural production and productivity, policymakers became sensitive to the idea that the increasing inequity in the countryside might affect social stability. In 1964, the Government of Gujarat set up a committee to recommend a minimum wage for agrarian labour. The growing fear of radicalization at the rural bottom played an important role, but equally important was the need to cater to the interests of an underprivileged class that was a major vote bank for the ruling Congress party. After all, the votes of the landless carried no less weight than the votes of the landowners. Universal suffrage in the frame of democratic politics required to open up the prospect of a better life for a major segment of the nation and the slogan *garibi hatao* (remove poverty) underscored that pledge. One of the committee's findings was that 80 per cent of the daily budget of agricultural labourers had to be spent on food and even then this was not enough to fill their belly. Striking in the report that the committee submitted was the condescending style, in a way blaming the proletariat for their hapless existence.

Visits to Halpati colonies presented a picture of unhealthy and unhygienic conditions of accommodation with meagre household effects or less than a bare living. The surroundings were filthy and neglected. Vices, particularly of illicit drinking were the rule. The *halis* [serfs] and their families were undernourished and in poor health. Large families with many children doing nothing or little and living in a purposeless or directionless life were other tragic features. (Government of Gujarat 1966: 39)

Later on, I shall argue that this derogatory tone is a recurrent feature in views from above on the people down and out in the informal economy and purports to justify their ongoing discrimination. The committee rejected the idea of fixing the wage in relation to the minimum cost of living for an agricultural labourer's household. It was impossible to give an unambiguous answer to the question of quality and quantity of the most essential needs, restricted to food, clothing, and shelter. Moreover, it would be incorrect to stipulate a specific amount without considering the state of agriculture and the capability of the farmers to pay it. Thus, the proposal was that the government should raise the going wage only slightly and also maintain the lower rate for women than for men. While conceding to the compelling urge for social reform, the members of the committee argued that a drastic rise in the price of labour would antagonize agrarian employers. Another argument in favour of taking a conservative stance was that the wages of agrarian workers must, in any case, remain below the minimum rate paid in other economic sectors. Otherwise, there would be no incentive to leave agriculture which was replete with redundant labour.

It was not until 1972 that the Government of Gujarat introduced the first Minimum Wage Act for Agricultural Labour. It was fixed only slightly above the level proposed by the committee six years earlier. Rising cost of living made periodic revisions necessary and that usually occurred shortly before elections for the state's assembly. As I have amply documented in my fieldwork findings, the legal instruction was not effective. In one of my reports, I quoted a minister who, confronted by hostile farmers, pacified them by saying that some laws were not meant to be implemented (Breman 1994: 311). The landowners' obstruction was caused not by their economic inability to pay but by their political unwillingness to do so. Their anger was driven by an inherited ideology of social inequality that did not tolerate any progress of the landless whom they considered inferior and as the undeserving poor. But the attention of policymakers now also extended to the non-agrarian workforce at the bottom of the economy with the shared characteristic that they had remained unorganized. Following up on the *Report of the National Commission on Labour* (GoI 1969), the Government of Gujarat instituted a commission in 1971 with the task to investigate employment and working conditions in branches of industry that made use of unprotected and unorganized manual workers. The instruction was that the investigation should lead to recommendations of legal regulations to improve the conditions of such labour. Ultimately, the whole exercise had little result. The complexity of the task was a major obstacle in reaching a satisfactory outcome. Apart from terminological vagueness, efforts made to estimate the volume of labour involved had to be abandoned in the absence of statistical and other data. In its report, the committee complained that information on the subject was almost non-existent and the attempt to collect data that could be fitted in an operational policy frame failed miserably (Government of Gujarat 1972: 11).

The Government of Gujarat tried to follow the example set by the state of Maharashtra which had introduced legislation in response to a series of strikes by head loaders (*hamalis*) in Bombay in the early 1960s. They exerted pressure on the municipal authorities to regulate their employment. The result of that arbitration amounted to a formalization of the working conditions for this loosely structured occupation under a law that was enacted in 1968. It is a milestone in the jurisprudence on work and welfare in the informal economy and became incorporated in the *Report of the National Commission on Labour* (GoI 1969: 436–7). However, the regulation of head loaders' labour was fated to be short in the absence of a strong trade union movement. It is, of course, not so easy to organize the casual and footloose workforce that can be found in the early morning labour markets. Bombay had 80 such nakas in different parts of the city that attracted, on an average, 200,000 labourers in the post-monsoon months. The Labour Office conveniently classified them as 'self-employed', implying that these people did not need the help of government in their search for work and managed to get by on their own. As has been demonstrated in Kerala, concerted action was not, in principle, out of the question for such categories in the past. Toddy tappers, bidi workers, and a number of other occupations were able to protect and harmonize their interests collectively (Kannan 1988). The formalization of labour relations is shown not only by the ratification of work conditions by government. Modelled on industrial legislation in Kerala, officials of state agencies became involved in the regular consultations between employers and employees. It was the start of the Scheduled Employment Act that regulated employment conditions in far more branches of industry in Maharashtra than had formerly been the case.

Similar measures were enacted in Gujarat. The Committee on Unprotected and Unorganized Labour set up in 1972 was able to refer to a Minimum Wage Act that had been promulgated many years previously for 19 scheduled employments. One criterion for government action was that the branch of industry in question should employ minimally 1,000 workers within the state's borders. That was no problem, for instance, for road construction and brick making. Their combined labour force was estimated to be more than 100,000 by the Committee. The procedure prior to the introduction of a Minimum Wage Act was always the same. The government appointed a small committee chaired by an independent outsider and with a membership of representatives of employers and workers in the branch of industry concerned. In the absence of the latter, a social activist would be appointed to speak up for them. The position of secretary was entrusted to an assistant labour commissioner who served in that capacity many such task groups. If it was a new initiative, the Office of the Labour Commissioner would conduct a brief preliminary survey of the number and size of such enterprises, their distribution throughout the state, their management, the composition of the workforce, and so on. The committee always attempted to gain additional information. The questionnaire specially designed for the purpose was sent to employers, their association, social workers, and other persons, knowledgeable and able to speak on behalf of the workers. The final report invariably included the comment that the response to the questionnaire had been lamentably low and that it was therefore impossible to draw any general conclusion. Equipped with little prior knowledge, the committee members toured around the sites of the investigated industries in order to acquaint themselves with the prevailing practices, in particular with regard to wages and modes of payment. Their visits were announced in advance in the local press, with an open invitation to all stakeholders to appear before the committee. Often, no one turned up for these hearings. In drafting the final report, the committees mainly deliberated on the mandatory wage rate but it also happened that the working group made other suggestions. For example, the Committee on Brickworks recommended that child labour should be prohibited in the industry and that government take responsibility for educational facilities at the sites of employment.

One question discussed by almost all committees was the yardstick for establishing the minimum wage. Their point of departure was the views expressed by the Committee on Fair Wages set up by the central government in 1948. In that panel's opinion, a minimum wage should encompass not only what the industrial worker needed for mere survival but also allow for expenditure on education and health, for example, in order to ensure an adequate labour performance. If payment should remain below the level at which labourer's physical health was threatened, then the industry in question should lose its right to exist. On the other hand, to fix the minimum wage at too high a level would defeat its purpose, if it should result in less employment. In 1957, the Indian Labour Conference specified the subsistence minimum to which workers had a right. The packet of commodities that should be made available to a working family of husband, wife, and two children consisted of: (*a*) a quantity of daily food based on 2,700 calories per adult person; (*b*) a total of 72 yards of clothing per year; (*c*) for shelter, the amount the government charged its own employees in the lowest-income brackets for rent; and (*d*) a 20 per cent latitude in the budget for expenditure on fuel, lighting, and other items.

Although no serious attempt was made to subject the paying capacity of employers to any thorough scrutiny, all committees agreed that it was necessary to adjust the wage level to increases in the cost of living. The viewpoint of employers was expressed more emphatically than that of the workers. The latter were unorganized, but not the industrialists, and the arguments put forward both in writing and verbally by their representatives never failed to impress the committees. In one of the stone quarries in south Gujarat, which I also happened to visit myself in the course of my fieldwork, the owners acknowledged that the wages paid were less than the rate needed for the reproduction of labour, but claimed that it was 'impractible' to pay more (Government of Gujarat 1974: 16). The committee on wage fixation in brick manufacture was one of the few to calculate the profit made by the employers. Their estimate was a figure of 20–40 per cent, while my own data showed a profit margin between 40–60 per cent of the cost of production. Even on the basis of the figures supplied by the industrialists, the committee members would have had good reason to advise a higher rate than they actually did. The information accepted was that no less than 84 per cent of the wages paid to a brick-making family had to be spent on food, and even at that level it was not enough to avoid malnutrition.

## A FAINT ATTEMPT

Due to a lack of empathy with the workforce, the regulation of wages in the informal economy did not result in any real improvement. The instructions given to the committees and the outcome of their assignments implied a sanctioning of existing industrial practices. In a few instances, abuses were duly noted—for example, that brick makers had to work 14–15 hours each day for their wage—but such findings were not addressed in the conclusions and recommendations. Rather than insisting on an individual-based labour contract—as prescribed by the code established for formal sector workers—the committee accepted the employer's explanation that in this branch, it was customary to hire labour on a family basis. Perhaps the most important decision taken by all these committees was not to give in to the demand repeatedly expressed by workers' representatives for the introduction of a time-based wage. The going practices of piece-rate payment and subcontracting were not disputed, and the committee that had to advise on more general lines of policy regarding unprotected workers even wondered if they should be qualified as wage workers. In line with the stereotyped image of the informal workforce as a reservoir of self-employed, the dominant opinion among policymakers was that this heterogeneous multitude was better off without state regulation. What at first sight seems to have been a half-hearted attempt to formalize industrial relations in the informal economy, did not add up to much more than somewhat streamlining current and informal practices. There are some immediate explanations for this disappointing outcome: the weak bargaining power of discriminated labour; the rigid opposition by employers against all regulative measures; and the high-caste identity of policymakers within the government bureaucracy.

The voice of the workers themselves was hardly heard. The employers' interests were put across more powerfully and clearly, expressed by themselves and by the spokesmen of their orchestrated lobby. On the opposite side, the designation 'unorganized workers' in itself indicates that there was little if any evidence of collective action. Trade unions did not exist at all in most branches of industry. Spokesmen on behalf of these unprotected workers were caretakers who acted with sympathy but from a distance. A serious handicap was also the considerable social gap that separated the regulators from a clientele that for so long had remained invisible to policymakers, people who led an incomprehensible existence at the bottom of society. The condescension with which industrialists discussed their workers, often in front of the committee, was, in fact, not very different from the denigration that imbued the attitude of many committee members towards this workforce. In no instance did the role of the jobber, a pivotal figure in the landscape of the informal economy, come up for discussion or regulation. This omission was rectified by the central government after being exhorted in 1969 by the National

Commission of Labour to put an end to the exploitation of workers by these contractors who acted as agents of employers (GoI 1969). The Contract Labour (Regulation and Abolition) Act 1972 was meant to cover the country as a whole and made it mandatory for state governments to take appropriate measures. This Act intended to check the authority of jobbers and subcontractors over the gangs they recruited and supervised. Employers had to register when they used contract labour, while jobbers who supplied and led such gangs had to be licenced. The effect of this regulation was considerably restricted by the clause that it did not apply in situations where employment was incidental or intermittent. In my research for decades in south Gujarat on seasonal migration—huge armies of many thousands of gangs of men, women, and children—I have never come across brick makers, cane cutters, road workers, salt pan workers, and quarrymen who were able to benefit from the provisions under the Act that regulated conditions of employment in their branch of industry. The flexibility of the labour market in which these super-vulnerable people have to operate was praised rather than harnessed.

Non-application also became the fate of the Inter-State Migrant Workers (Regulation of Employment and Conditions of Service) Act introduced in 1979. In this ordinance, the jobber–gang boss again plays a major role. As middleman, he is supposed to supply the members of his gang with a workbook that includes details of the nature of the work, wage rate, mode of payment, deductions, and compensation for travel cost. More costly still than this compulsory registration is the relocation allowance amounting to 50 per cent of the monthly wage to which gangs of migrant workers are entitled. Most state governments have not made the least effort to enforce compliance with these rights. When I broached the non-implementation of this Act at a high political and bureaucratic level in Gujarat, I was told that the country's constitution stipulates freedom of movement and this principle could in no way be circumscribed. I was also told that labour migration was not only inevitable given regional imbalances between supply and demand, but that it was also a sign of progress on the path to economic development. However, to suggest that the cane cutters from Maharashtra deployed for the duration of the harvest campaign in the fields of south Gujarat, the Oriya power-loom operators in Surat, or the landless labourers who trek each year from the villages of my fieldwork to brickworks in other states are migrants who leave home out of their own free choice, who resort to this option due to well-considered self-interest, and thus become a vanguard in paving the route towards modern industry, in my opinion testifies to a grotesque distortion of social reality. In similar words, I could criticize three other laws that have been promulgated: the Bonded Labour (Abolition) Act (1976); the Equal Remuneration Act (1976); and the Child Labour (Prohibition and Regulation) Act (1986). In all these cases, the legislation seems at best to have arisen from good intentions, but these have been formulated too hastily and carelessly and therefore lack efficacy. According to another, that is, my own and less benign assessment, the regulations were merely a façade of formalism with which, for political convenience of national and international legitimacy, government pretended that it cared for the well-being of unprotected workers.

The lacklustre performance of the machinery established to accomplish the formalization of employment in the informal economy strengthened my scepticism on the commitment of the government to improve the plight of the massive workforce in the informal economy. In 1982, as one of the first states in India, Gujarat set up an Inspectorate for Rural Labour with the mandate 'to improve the conditions of unorganized rural labour and to protect them against exploitation and malpractices of their employers'. The initiative was taken in the wake of an open clash between agrarian labourers and farmers in a south Gujarat village close to the site of my fieldwork. District and sub-district branches of this agency had to check on the implementation of the minimum wage legislation. In an essay first published in 1985 on the daily routine of this agency, I concluded that the inspecting officials totally failed to achieve what they set out to do (Breman 1994). My critical appraisal, which highlighted official misdemeanour and corruption, was vindicated in the report of the NCRL published a few years later:

The organization has not been effective. The officials are not adequately informed on their subject. They are not sufficiently motivated. The quality of the inspections is poor. In its totality also, the organization has not done well. There does not seem to be adequate understanding of and identification with the objectives of the organization. In the four years ending in 1988, the performance has been particularly poor in some respects. The number of inspections and consequent detection of violations and defaults are expected to go up following the revision of the minimum wage. In Gujarat the experience following the 1986 revisions is in reverse. The morale of the inspecting officers is low. (GoI, vol. 1, 1991: 208)

I have quoted this official source at length because it shows that already before the shift to neoliberal policies, the way in which the labour legislation for the workforce in the informal economy was practised, defeated the very purpose for which it had been introduced: to make their employment more decent and dignified.

It is as if the defilement arising from the unenviable task of inspecting work conditions at the bottom of the informal economy also diminishes the status of the government official charged to do so. His reluctant excursions into this demeaning landscape have another purpose than for which he is sent. Breaches of the law are not identified in order to declare the employer in default and impose a penalty. Far more frequently, the inspector will use his knowledge of the rules and regulations to demand hush money for covering up the transgression. This is easily done since not a single employer, for instance, pays the special allowances granted to wage labourers in scheduled employments by way of price compensation. Capitalizing on the discrepancy between practice and law provides the inspector with an income that is many times higher than his salary. It also explains why candidates for a vacant post are only considered if they are prepared to 'buy' it. This is done by paying cash to their superior or a local politician in compensation for the income that will flow so readily and substantially. The workers themselves remain invisible, also to the handful of government agents charged with their protection, and know quite well that the statements they are invited to make tend to be used for the extortion of a bribe rather than to see to it that justice is done.

On the side of the employers, more than distrust of these officials is at stake. Naturally, no workshop owner is prepared to voluntarily increase the market price for labour to the legal minimum or improve the wretched work conditions. But many are even unfamiliar with the regulations that they have to comply with, and also lack the knowledge necessary for keeping the registers demanded by the government. This applies, for example, to the owners of small brickyards, self-made men who have worked their way up to become petty entrepreneurs from an artisanal background and without much education. Government officials who visit their worksites equipped with their book of rules and forms are given bribes simply to avoid the fuss and bother. They very well know what their workers want: a fair wage, permanent employment, and its prerequisites. Granting these privileges would raise the cost of production. Even that they do not mind since profit margins are extremely high. The problem, however, is that this route to formalization of industrial relations would give the authorities a handle to find out the real size of their turnover and, on that basis, impose higher taxes as well as other levies. Such a drastic appropriation of their surplus value cannot be tolerated because it would impinge on their cash flow. Not only their incomes but also their expenses are largely illicit, that is, received as well as paid in black money.

## THE INFORMALIZED STATE

This is what I meant when I commented earlier that informality is a concept that does not only concern labour but also intrudes into the domains of politics and governance: employment as well as capital are outsourced from the formal economy. The informalization of the latter factor of production is highly understated in the literature and needs to be explored and documented in much greater detail than has been done so far. Both in the rural and urban economy of Gujarat, a class of businessmen operate who have become the backbone of the political wheeling and dealing that is going on. They are accustomed to buying what they need, including state support or the reverse, abstinence. Their attitude towards government is marked by rancour, a frustration that they are curtailed in their economic freedom of action, and moreover, that their social value is not sufficiently respected. They feel that the busybodies in the service of the state interfere in their industries and do not heed the informal rules that also operate in the formal economy. The real administrative records, the ledgers these entrepreneurs keep for their transactions called *number be* (no. 2) or *kalum* (black), are for their eyes only. The whitewashed bookkeeping shown to officials is fake, written down with no other intention than to pretend a semblance of legality. Workers do not receive a wage slip, only permanent employees are issued an identity card, and the majority do not appear at all, or under a false name in the company's register that has to be submitted on inspection. In such a policy climate, it cannot be expected that workers will submit complaints to the labour inspectors about the abuses from which they suffer. They know about the rules and regulations from which they hypothetically stand to benefit. They may not be familiar with the precise details, but are well aware of minimum wage rates, for example. The official does not interact with them because he is separated from his real clientele by a wide social rift. He has little if any understanding of their way of life and nor does not feel obliged to improve it. The workers are helpless witnesses in transactions that occur outside their sight and over which they have no control. Any recalcitrance, let alone militancy, even if shown in body language, is running a risk that most of them cannot and will not afford. When publicly challenged on their pitiable record, the government officials tend to fall back on a standard mantra, a ritualized summing up of the action taken: the prescribed number of monthly inspections and their spurious findings, ending with the complacent statement that everything has been done to ensure a successful outcome.

By way of excuse for the inefficacy of the labour laws meant for improving conditions in the informal economy, the bureaucrats in charge frequently complain about the passivity of the workforce. This line of thinking suggests that the target group, uneducated and ignorant as it is, lacks the assertion to make use of the protection offered. More generally, fatalism as a prime feature of their behaviour is said to frustrate all efforts made to raise their standards of work and life. It comes close to a definition of the problem of backwardness in terms of a culture of poverty. The ascribed inertia caused the Government of Gujarat to launch a campaign for stimulating the social consciousness of the rural proletariat. In a few villages of districts with a high density of landless, Rural Workers' Welfare Centres (Gram Majur Kalyan Kendra) were opened in 1982 with a rural organizer supposed to coach the workers on what the government was doing for them. Nominated as social activists, these unemployed, educated youngsters from low castes had to increase feelings of solidarity among the agricultural labourers. A couple of years later, I have described the futility of this scheme and criticized the preconceived ideas underlying it (Breman 1994: 314–7).

How genuine is an appeal to this footloose class at the bottom of the informal economy to show greater defiance and engage in collective action if, whenever this is made manifest, the authorities take immediate and hard-handed action to de-escalate the conflict on the pretext of maintaining law and order? Labour agitation is a frequent occurrence in the informal economy, although such outbursts are often spontaneous rather than organized, short in duration, and restricted to a few locations. It has been said that compliance with the Minimum Wage Act is weakened by the small size and fragmented nature of much informal activity. How would it be possible, for instance, to check on each and every farmer who off and on or even on a regular basis employs one or more labourers? This argument, however, does not apply to employment in large-scale enterprises. The administrative capability at the disposal of the cooperatively run sugar mills in south Gujarat is quite adequate to handle official instructions on payment of minimum wages. The reason for not doing so stems from political unwillingness rather than from logistical problems. That conclusion was confirmed when I found in the

Surat office of the Rural Labour Inspectorate, a secret memorandum that instructed the inspectors 'until further order', not to take any action against the management of this powerful agro-industrial lobby for non-payment of the prescribed wage rate to this huge harvesting army of seasonal labourers brought in from outside. The cane-cutters' earnings, till today, remain below the basic rate to which the local landless are entitled. A leading politician in Gujarat told me why the multitude of migrant workers are deprived from the provisions granted to them by law. These labouring nomads, he said, are unable to cast their votes neither where they live nor where they work. His comment was not meant to be cynical or indifferent but a matter-of-fact explanation why the voices of the people drifting around are not heard and do not count.

Writing the concluding part of a survey-based report on workers employed in the thoroughly informalized textile industry in Surat, U. Baxi, in his capacity as Vice-Chancellor of the South Gujarat University, referred to a distinction made by the Second Law Review Committee (Government of Gujarat 1983–4) between transgression and subversion of the law, the latter being a more serious misdemeanour with consequences much graver in nature. The Committee stated:

Subversion means planned systematic disregard of labour legislation involving an organized anticipation of immunity from any kind of credible law enforcement process. In other words, subversion of labour law is a public conduct which denies the relevance and reality of law as providing norms for social action. It, therefore, implies a trend towards collective lawlessness which involves on the side of organized capital and organized labour an assertion of superior political power over the state and the law and on the side of the state a public admission of its inability to impose social justice. For the workers who are the victims of subversion of labour law, subversion prevents the growth of social consciousness and organization which alone could provide sources and stimuli for a more vigorous and just administration of the law, and constant redefinition. (South Gujarat University 1984: 105)

This passage adequately sums up the state of exclusion in which people at the bottom of the informal economy are entrapped. While on the one hand, propaganda of the state apparatus upheld its commitment to improving the lot of unprotected workers, on the other hand, it already then, before the switch to the neoliberal doctrine, made great effort to portray Gujarat as a capitalist's paradise with the message that its people are of a peaceable nature and that industrial relations were harmonious with hardly any days lost to labour strikes. The least that can be concluded is that government showed little interest in taking up the cudgel for 'the untouchables' under the capitalist mode of production. I am inclined to go one step further and suggest that informalized employment modalities came to dominate the economy not despite but thanks to state intervention. It was in these years that the textile mills that had, for more than a century, been in the forefront of the formal economy of Mumbai and Ahmedabad were being dismantled. Their looms that had become redundant were now sold and installed in the power-loom workshops of Surat. Being unable to insist on the formalization of employment, large segments of the workforce have even lost the feudal-type protection that formerly accompanied their agrarian life and work. Against this background, it is easy to understand the litany with which the NCRL in 1991 commented on the dualism in the labour market.

The conspicuous co-existence of mushrooming high-wage islands in the organized sector on the one hand and miserable conditions of labour in informal urban and rural sector (both farm and non-farm) on the other, and the corresponding dualism in capital/labour intensities and associated levels of productivity are the result of our inability or even unwillingness to implement a sound and firm wage policy. (GoI, vol. 1, 1991: 23)

Unable or even unwilling, thus is my verdict on the government's endeavour in the preceding decades to regulate and protect labour in the informal economy. The attempt to extend labour legislation, the right to a minimum wage first and for all, to this majority of the workforce broke down on lacklustre and faulty implementation. In the end, also the pretension was not kept up any longer. Even the contrast with employment conditions in the formal economy are not as sharp as they are pretended to be.[1] While the campaign of corporate business against what are called 'stifling labour laws' goes on unabated, it is for the sake of the argument more than anything else, as Kannan has rightly concluded.

The fact that the majority of workers in the formal economy currently consists of informal workers is a testimony to the ability of capital to circumvent the labour legislation which in law was intended to offer a degree of protection. This shows that capital in India seems to have achieved its goal of a flexible labour market without any change in the existing labour laws. (Kannan 2011b: 26)

With the resolute switch to neoliberal politics, informalization of employment across the board became the clarion call. Opinions differ on how to interpret the near-monopoly of informality. The following one is in line with the neoliberal credo and implies that not steady but casual employment is in the best interest of the labouring poor. 'The primary reason for the dominance of the unorganised sector is the rigid and cumbersome labour laws, which employers circumvent by setting up much smaller units which fall outside the preview of the law.' Thus said Kaushik Basu, who was recently appointed as Chief Economist to the World Bank.[2] His explanation of how and why the informal sector came about blatantly twists around the causal logic of the informalization process. The eighth *Selected Reading*, 'Informality as a Regime of Exploitation and Marginalization', is concerned with the consequences of the turn around, which benefits capital and victimizes labour.

## THE PROMISE OF INCLUSION

Revisiting these issues two decades later, one wonders whether the government, in its policy to increase economic growth at the highest rate possible but also to generate more employment, has tried to see to the interests of labour while giving priority to the demands of capital? Have the market-driven benefits trickled down to the working classes in the informal economy? The urge for flexibilization led to getting rid of 'inspection raj', as the Prime Minister of India called it. Employers need not worry any longer that an inspector would turn up and find fault with the labour regime practised. Giving a free hand to the barons of the economy, the politicians insisted, would not at all be in contravention to the promise of inclusive growth. My ongoing fieldwork all these years in Gujarat shows that this pledge with which the formation of the United Progressive Alliance (UPA) was sealed, and repeated ad nauseam since then, has not been honoured. My negative assessment on the government's record is backed up in a recent essay analysing various features of the neoliberal growth scenario (Hirway and Shah 2011: 57–65). While capital intensity in industrial production rose rapidly and profits were very high, the authors found that wage increase remained very low and that the major gains made in productivity were not passed on to workers. Although the state prides itself on leading the country in the economic boom, the wage rate of casual male workers is lower than in India as a whole. Since 2003, enterprises still covered by formal labour laws are permitted self-certification, which essentially means that compliance on the part of management with statutory regulations is taken for granted. The main objective of this hands-off instruction is to avoid 'unnecessary litigation' and to promote a friendly relationship between government and business. In the light of this 'liberalization', it comes as no surprise that the share of wages in the state's domestic product has gone down.

As part of its vigorous pro-growth strategy, Gujarat has plans to set up more SEZs than any other state in the country. An amendment to the Industrial Dispute Act 1947 exempts the workforce in these SEZ's from the right to file a complaint when they lose their jobs. Employers are allowed to dismiss workers when it suits them and the power of employees to fight against illegal retrenchment is much weakened. Already, earlier on, the government machinery in charge of enforcement of the labour legislation left much to be desired, but it has further shrunk in the past two decades. There is a severe shortage of staff, a consequence of the decision not to fill up vacancies in all ranks of the agencies concerned. Nowadays, the deputy labour commissioner's office in Surat has only three officers, as compared to nine in 1993, and the official in charge is quoted saying that closing the labour department will not make any difference to labour in the city. In the towns of Navsari, Vapi, and Valsad, major industrial centres in south Gujarat along the north–south railway line, it was not any better. The conclusion reached puts the overall failure on record.

The department of labour is therefore not in a position to conduct inspections. It is not even in a position to attend to complaints, let alone enforce labour laws. Its officers and staff are unmotivated and frustrated; and have little enthusiasm to enforce labour laws. In addition, there are political pressures frequently working on them. Many of them have become corrupt in this environment. (Hirway and Shah 2011: 62)

All the failings listed above are corroborated in the autobiography of a high-ranking official who was in charge of the labour inspectorate of Gujarat (Luke 2015). On his appointment in 1990 he found how this state apparatus had become one big extortion racket. These were payments received from industrialists and businessmen for not doing what the inspectors, right from the central to the district level, were mandated with, that is, to see to the proper implementation of the labour legislation which was still intact. When the Labour Commissioner refused to be co-opted in the scam going on, he was first warned and then demoted to another agency. It took him not long to find out that similar embezzlement and fraud went on in his new job. Instead of distributing equipment to weavers in order to raise their productivity and income, officials, politicians and other stakeholders teamed up to pocket the money allocated for this purpose. The public campaign going on against corruption has remained targeted on cases in which ministers and other politicians are implicated. While the uproar this has caused is quite understandable, Hazare and his well-wishers have insufficiently articulated that corruption is a relationship in which a substantial part of their middle-class clientele is embroiled, now eager to join the bandwagon for cleaning up India. Also understated in the frenzy that has become popular against dirty politics is that the poor, much more than the better-off, are made to pay the price for corruption, either directly or indirectly, which they can least afford.

All said and done, workers with no security of employment have forfeited their right to lodge complaints about non-payment of minimum wages or violation of other labour acts supposed to cover them. For

TABLE 6.1    Inspections in Gujarat under Labour Laws Applying
to the Informal Economy, 2008

| Labour Law | Number of Inspections | Number of Prosecutions | Number of Total Beneficiaries |
|---|---|---|---|
| Minimum Wages Act | 12,398 | 2,633 | 9,227 |
| Contract Labour Act | 5,629 | 351 | 11,201 |
| Child Labour Act | 10,242 | 235 | 11 |
| Inter-State Migrant Workers Act | 428 | 21 | 42 |
| Equal Remuneration Act | 2,093 | 45 | 7 |

*Source*: Website of the Labour Commissioner's office, Government of Gujarat (2010), cited in Hirway and Shah (2011: 63).

the total workforce in Gujarat of approximately 14 million—of which 8.5–9 million are employed in the rural economy—one labour officer is needed for every 10,000 workers, and he is expected to carry out 100 inspections a month to enforce one of the statutory labour laws. The actual number of inspections carried out by the Labour Inspectorate in Gujarat (at least the ones reported) is woefully inadequate, as Table 6.1 clarifies.

The Rural Workers Welfare Board, set up in the 1982, is no longer entrusted with the mandate to boost the organization of rural labour and is hardly active in the only job left now, which is to help workers to get access to social security schemes. Gujarat's performance in poverty reduction and human development is lagging behind the progress made in some other states, even when they are growing at a lower rate. The relatively high percentage of working poor is also reflected in the hunger index. On this score, India ranks 66 among 88 countries figuring on the Global Hunger Index. Together with Bihar, Madhya Pradesh, Chhattisgarh, and Jharkand, Gujarat belongs to the five worst-performing states in the country. In striking contrast to this dismal performance is the rapidly rising share of profits in the economy that gets appropriated by the owners and providers of capital. Under the market-friendly regime in place, they qualify in addition for a wide range of subsidies, tax breaks, grants, as well as reduced rates for land, water, and electricity supply. Pointing out that the success of private business is determined not by a free market but by favouritism extended to corporate business, Hirway and Shah (2011) end their essay with the conclusion that the Gujarat model of growth is a case of crony capitalism that is unsustainable in a social, economic, as well as political sense: socially, because of the stigma of inferiority attached to a poor, undernourished, and illiterate underclass deprived from their human rights; economically, because these people are denied the purchasing power for consuming the goods and services the market produces; and politically, because the suppression of political agency will escalate in large-scale class antagonism and revolt. Gujarat, they argue, is certainly not atypical but the distortions found here between the people at the top and the bottom of the economy are more extreme than elsewhere in India.[3]

## COLLECTIVE ACTION

In line with the multiple barriers thrown up against collective action, the combined effect of labour fragmentation and segmentation, trade unions are a rare phenomenon in the informal economy. In a monograph on the closure of the corporate textile mills in Ahmedabad, once known as the Manchester of India, I described how with the loss of their secure and protected mill job, the workforce of more than 125,000 was also thrown out of the formal economy (Breman 2004). The purport of my study was to shed light on what happened next to the dismissed mill hands. The textile workers were not a homogeneous lot and the low skilled and lowest paid among them were often members of SCs or belonged to religious minorities. Did they constitute, despite their subordinate position at the base of the hierarchy in the textile mills, a labour aristocracy among the working population of Ahmedabad? This label can easily lead to an exaggerated image of the comfort the industrial vanguard used to enjoy in terms of welfare, security, and protection. This view needs to be modified given the industrial accidents and diseases that impaired the health of many workers sooner or later. While accepting that the conditions in the mills left much to be desired, the workers themselves considered their dismissal from the mill as a fall from paradise. That sentiment says more about the misery they suffer now than how auspicious and enviable life used to be.

Was there no resistance to the restructuring of the labour market? The dismantling of the corporate textile industry in Ahmedabad was a process that unfolded over many years, but at no point were the victims able to mount a sustained or concerted protest. Certainly, when looking back, there was much bitterness and agitation. The trade union, which could have channelled these frustrations into forceful action, was prevented from doing so because of an imbibed doctrine that preached industrial peace, an eagerness to make concessions and seek compromises at all times. This ideology explains why the TLA failed to take decisive action at the crucial conjuncture. The Gandhian strategy to which the union leaders firmly adhered in the decades preceding the closures had undeniably produced many benefits for the members, not least because of the strong political clout of the union in both Gujarat and nationwide. In addition to higher wages and a range of secondary benefits, this well-organized political lobby resulted in a body of advanced legislation of industrial relations together with a tripartite framework for implementing it. However, at the critical moment when they should have insisted that the agreements be honoured, the leaders made a conscious decision not to mount any organized protest against the mass redundancies, thereby surrendering the rights that the workers had fought for throughout the twentieth century. In retrospect, it has to be pointed out that the solidarity the Gandhian activists envisaged was based on recognizing the segmented group identities of caste and religion to which the union members belonged. The main objective was not to form a united front of labour against capital, but a civilizing mission designed to discipline and raise the industrial proletariat to a higher moral plane. On the other hand, it should be noted that other trade unions with a more radical agenda met with little success in the working-class neighbourhoods of Ahmedabad. It would be difficult to deny that the caste and religious sentiments that were articulated, not only by the division of labour in the mills but also by a policy of residential segregation, became the primary source of care and protection when the mills were shut. Receiving no support from employers and government, but also let down by their own association, the workers had no other alternative than to fall back on their primordial loyalties.

Loss of job implied that the sacked workforce also forfeited membership of the trade union because their contribution was deducted from their weekly wage. 'How can we keep them on our register when they do not pay their dues any longer', was the answer from the secretary of the TLA to my question regarding the membership of the sacked workforce. 'When there is no mill to work in, there can be no trade union', he added despondently. Is that really so? No doubt, labour unions are a rare phenomenon in the landscape of the informal economy but they do exist. A major one which immediately comes to mind is the Self Employed Women's Association (SEWA) founded by Ela R. Bhatt. As a TLA staff member, she was in charge of the Women's Wing set up in 1954 to look after the needs of women in the households of male mill workers. Ela Bhatt soon came to know that the women, in addition to being housewives, contributed to the household income by working in the informal economy. She took up the plight of these women workers, an activity not much appreciated by the union's patriarchal leadership. The obstruction she encountered made her decide to launch an independent movement for poor women living on their own labour or doing small business; in short, all those who were not in regular employ and did not receive social benefits. In 1972, SEWA was registered as a trade union organizing home-based workers engaged in manufacturing bidis, incense sticks, ready-made garments, toys, and other commodities subcontracted to them for processing, and as domestic servants and street-based workers, among whom were vegetable vendors and hawkers, cart pullers, head loaders, scavengers, etc. Since the early years when the activity was mainly concentrated on Ahmedabad, SEWA has branched out not only to the rural economy of Gujarat, bringing female artisans and rural workers, agrarian as well as non-agrarian, into its fold, but also spread to other states in the country. The founding mother of the association has provided a powerful account on the role of women in the informal economy and the urgent need to promote their collective action.[4] While at birth a mere 700 females were enrolled—head-loaders, street vendors, and homebased stitchers—by end of 2012 membership has increased to 1.7 million spread over 10 states in the country. It means that this trade union is much bigger than the TLA has ever been. Throughout India, a large a number of trade unions have sprung up, organizing the proletariat in different sectors of the informal economy. The long-established trade unions in the formal economy used to neglect workers in informal employment in the past and have only recently shown signs of becoming interested in this huge workforce.

Underlying that hostile attitude was the suspicion that in the event of strikes, this was the milieu from which blacklegs would be recruited. Consequently, the union leadership tended to ignore what went on in the unorganized economy. The onerous task to mobilize this amorphous and footloose proletariat on the basis of a presumed solidarity is further complicated by the necessity to promote their widely diverse interests in a bargaining dialogue with a very great number of small-scale employers. This effort requires large overhead costs that would be impossible to finance for members who belong to the lowest-paid and most-vulnerable economic categories. Furthermore, experience shows that the needs and problems of unregulated workers are quite distinct from labourers in the formal economy, of whom, at best, half are members of trade unions (Bhowmik 1998). These differences demand a type of organization and a promotion of interests with which the since long established trade unions have little empathy, many of them none at all. Even more important, the conventional union leadership is ill prepared to reformulate its mission and to frame the new and revitalized agenda into a concrete plan of action. In the final analysis, the trade unions accustomed to operate in the landscape of the formal economy tend to close ranks to restrict access. The miserable lot of the down and out is often not seen as a challenge but as a possible threat to the much better deal—the result of a long-lasting struggle for a reasonable degree of security and protection—enjoyed by the remaining vestiges of formal sector labour. The strategy of fending off the mass of excluded workers explains why, conversely, the latter feel little affinity with the trade union movements that have been in existence since long. Both the leadership and the members do not appear to unduly worry themselves over the question of how they could help to improve the condition of the unregulated and unprotected segments. Rather they seem to share the class-biased prejudices about the inferior, backward quality of the people milling around at the bottom of the economy. But this has changed now.

How could indifference be maintained if, according to the 2011 census, of the total workforce in the country—a multitude somewhat below half a billion—nine out of every 10 have to depend on labour arrangements that clearly identify them as being part and parcel of the informal economy? It has become clear to insiders as well as outsiders that the classical trade union movement was threatened with marginalization by its exclusive concentration on a small and shrinking labour segment hired under regulated and protected terms of employment. The stupendous task at hand is to regulate the unregulated and to claim protection for the unprotected. Still, in practice, the representatives of formal sector employees do not pay much more than lip service to the mobilization of what they consider to be an elusive reserve army that is far beyond their horizon and defeats all efforts to bring them together on a common platform. A major exception to this widespread attitude of negligence is the New Trade Union Initiative (NTUI), a federation of associations in the formal and informal economy which started in 2001 and by the end of 2009, had more than one million members, mainly employed in the industrial sector, and spread over 300 affiliated unions. Other than the standard trade union movements in the formal economy, the NTUI has refused to become identified with parties in the political mainstream.[5]

## A MOOD OF RESILIENCE AND RESISTANCE

In the absence of much organized collective action, the workforce in the informal economy has to rely on other forms of agency in the search for work or mediation required to move around in the labour market and to bargain for a better deal. Their social identity is a major determinant for the line of job they might be able to access. Neighbourhood ties are a good beginning because back at home, in their own habitat, are the people who share the same socio-economic profile. Primordial loyalties of family, caste, clan, tribe, religion, and ethnicity are the social capital that enable job seekers to trace their route in unknown terrain. It helps them to arrive wherever they go, not only in applying for work but also in finding shelter, survival loans to hold on, to cope with bouts of unemployment, and last but not least, calling on testimonies of goodwill if they need to establish their bona fides to employers. In the labour market hierarchy of the informal economy, social clusters that reflect the inegalitarian structure of society as a whole are of preponderant significance. Clearly, in the search for employment, one should take account of such separated niches and rely on the social capital that goes together with it. They act as networks of solidarity for insiders, those who share the same identity, while at the same time, throwing up fences to prevent the intrusion of outsiders into these enclaves.

Still, this does not mean that the whole amalgam of occupations is structured solely by primordial ties. Individual characteristics and choices, to a large extent dependent on good luck and bad luck, can also be decisive in practice. What in the terrain of the informal economy is often lacking, however, is the capability to realize a better deal through collective bargaining. Joint action does happen and in the course of my fieldwork, I have often come across instances of strikes in which labour teamed up to confront the power of employers. Even then, the contestation was not organized but broke out spontaneously, remained localized, rarely spread to other sites of the same industry, and did not last long because the workers could not afford to continue their agitation for more than a few days. Driving the cost of labour down to the lowest possible level, I have argued, is the main rationale for the informalization of employment. But there are additional reasons and one of them is to pre-empt the building up of collective action that would change the skewed balance of power away from privileging capital and tilt it more in favour of labour. The infinite fragmentation of the informal workforce is compounded by the compelling need to remain footloose, to trek around between sites and sectors of trade and industry.[6]

The lack of support from the established trade union movements does not mean that the informal proletariat passively accepts the labour regime imposed on them. Many make efforts, often repeatedly so, to combat the insecurity and miserable conditions of employment by trying to negotiate, on an individual footing, a somewhat better deal with their employer. They do this by emphasizing their subordination and loyalty to their patron for which, in exchange, they appeal to his discretionary power to grant favours. In turn, employers are bent on narrowing even further the small space in which the massive army in search of work must operate, given the abundant supply of and limited demand for labour. The employers make use of all sorts of arrangements, such as advance payment or postponed wage settlement, to cut short their employees' room for manoeuvre. Mechanisms to tie the worker down, as, for example, loans for meeting urgent cash needs in case of illness in the family, house repair, or cost of marriage, show similarities with forms of bondage that existed in the past but differ from them by a more articulated contractual and capitalist slant. The need to accept an advance on wages subjects the worker to the employer's claim on his or her labour power for the direct future. The loss of independence that adheres to such a labour contract explains why it is only entreated because of lack of a better alternative. The fact that so many, nevertheless, have to seek recourse to this unfree employment of the last resort indicates the enormous pressure on livelihood resources at the bottom of the economy. The work agreement is often for the duration of the season only and is seldom entered into for an indefinite period of time. The neo-bondage is not only time bound but also specifically restricted to the labour power of the worker and does not include his or her social or political submission to the employer. For the wage hunters and gatherers, it is a way to cope with insecurity but not to the extent that they are willing to seek security in bondage. Theirs is a type of resilience and resistance that might be expected from a proletarian class.

The footloose proletariat adopts various ways by which to resist employers' endeavours to appropriate their labour power through indebtedness. Workers do not hesitate to leave without notice if the employer, the jobber, or the work itself is found to be too oppressive, and certainly do so for an eventual offer of a somewhat higher wage. Creditors today lack the social and political power to prolong the contract until the debt has been worked off. They are no longer able to call on the authority of government officials for help, and attempts to exclude 'defaulters' from future employment usually fail due to competition and rivalry between employers. In short, labour bondage has lost social legitimacy and this means that employers who pay an advance wage are no longer assured that the labour power they have attached will indeed be provided. The chance that compliance with the contract can be enforced does not necessarily increase as the social gap between employer and employee widens. As a matter of fact, the labour contractor who comes from the same milieu as the worker is more effective in seeing his discipline respected. And even more effective than the jobber–gang boss is the male head of the household who does not shy away from using physical force to obtain control over the dependent members, that is, wife and children, of his household.

Modes and degrees of resistance show great diversity. Despite severe sanctions, which are particularly brought to bear on attempts to form a common front and thus openly express latent feelings of solidarity, concerted signals of resistance are frequent occasions in the informal economy. But as observed earlier, strikes 'suddenly' break out, hardly spread beyond the site of the agitation, and also die out relatively quickly. Given the vulnerability and dependency of the workforce in the informal economy, it is not surprising that resistance is mostly on an individual basis. Earlier, I have attributed occupational multiplicity to the lack of permanent employment in any particular branch of industry or trade. Recurrent rotation of job and workplace, however, can also indicate a strategy by which workers avoid reliance on a single source of livelihood and thus increase their bargaining power. Also, when a man migrates alone, it may be due to his attempt to protect the other members of his household from becoming subjected to the dependency and degradation inherent to life and labour away from home.

Similarly, I do not see labour circulation as exclusively indicating fluctuations in the supply of work. Refusal to continue a contract indefinitely may embody a protest against a merciless work regime. Covert resistance includes inertia, feigned lack of understanding, foot dragging, avoidance, withdrawal, sabotage, loitering and shirking, obstruction, and other weapons of the weak before it flares up in overt confrontation. These types of behaviour give footloose labour the reputation of being unpredictable, impulsive, and liable to abandon work for no good reason and on the spur of the moment. Employers make such complaints, censuring the 'lack of commitment' of wage hunters and gatherers. But seen from another angle, such evasive action is an attempt to obtain or maintain a fragile dignity. There is a degree of solidarity, although it is not based on any realization that all workers belong to an undivided working class. Having said that, I would like to add that there is a dearth of documentation on forms of collective resistance that occur much less, or even not at all, in employment modalities characteristic for the formal economy. The reporting on labour resistance has been unduly focused on the nature, course, and outcome of the social struggle at the bright side of the spectre, neglecting what goes on in the fragmented and segmented landscape of the informal economy that is much more difficult to access and document. Employers are accustomed to making use of primordial ties in order to exercise control over labour, either for the season or more indefinitely. Conversely, however, such parochial attachments are equally important for the workforce in the informal economy to heighten its resistance and manoeuvrability, to distance themselves from a world in which they are exploited and oppressed. This countervailing power may not be expressed in a generalized horizontal strategy, that is, made manifest in regular class organization and action. Gujarat's thoroughly informalized workforce does not accept the treatment meted out willingly and docilely. *The Economic Survey of 2011*, an indisputable source reference, reports that in the country at large Gujarat stands out as being the 'worst' state for labour unrest. 'Gujarat witnessed the highest number of strikes and other forms of labour unrest in recent times on account of various financial and disciplinary issues.'[7] The vibrance of Gujarat is different from the one Chief Minister Modi has in mind. I conclude that the state's huge army of labour, at drift, fragmented and casualized as it is, has a social consciousness which is essentially proletarian in nature.

## NOTES

1. Labour unrest which broke out in the Maruti car plant exposed the simmering discontent among the workforce in India's automotive industry in the Gurgaon–Manesar–Dharuhera–Ravri belt. The agitation that began in mid-2011 cascaded into a strike a year later, which was joined by both temps—consisting of contract workers, casuals, and apprentices, which constitute the large majority of the employees—and permanents. The latter segment constituted the core workers but added up to no more than 15 per cent of all factory hands. They closed ranks

with their casualized mates in a united front organized by a new trade union which insisted on equal pay for equal work, rejecting the management offer of a wage rise which would only benefit the privileged segment of the workforce (Sehgal 2012; for a report on the grim working conditions in the plant, see Annavajhula and Pratap 2012). In the riots that took place in mid-2012, one plant executive was killed and 40 others were injured. At the behest of the management, the police arrested 147 workers and slapped murder charges on all of them. A total of 2,300 workers were instantly dismissed and in the wake of the agitation a new system of company temps was introduced, which stipulated that those recruited would work for not more than six months after which they were laid off for five months to be rehired again, or not, for another round of six months. The hire-and-fire policy was a move that the management had designed to defuse the threat of a joint platform of temporary and permanent workers by rotating the former category and thus pre-empting labour unrest. In a scathing comment G. Sampath pointed out how and why corporate India, with state collusion, crushed in one stroke both the strike and the trade union which had brought it about. The demand of corporate India, he wrote, is for a labour regime that allows companies to freely hire temporary workers even for core operations. The labour reforms on the anvil essentially boil down to two things: make it impossible to form a truly independent trade union; and make it legal to keep temporary workers permanently temporary, while paying them subsistence wages ('Labour's love lost', *The Hindu*, 1 January 2016).

2. See Editorial, *The Times of India*, Ahmedabad edition, 14 November 2012.

3. For an overview of Gujarat's agenda towards capitalist development, see Sud (2012).

4. In a reflexive account of the struggle started by her, Ela Bhatt elaborated on the Gandhian principles which inspired her life's journey (Bhatt 2005).

5. For more information on the federated structure and activity of the newcomer, see the website, www.ntui.org.in.

6. A portrait of the hired-and-fired workforce in Surat shows the deprived state in which they wander around in the urban economy and which prevents them from mutually supporting each other. 'Workers in the fringe sector are never able to pool their resources adequately in order to support the very needy among them during sickness, accidents, loss of one's work, and different types of social crises. At best, this social network us a very precarious coping mechanism to see them through the next phase of economic and social crises' (Desai 2002: 171).

7. *The Economic Times*, 25 February 2011.

# Conclusion

## THE CONCEPT OF INFORMALITY IN RETROSPECT

The early writings on the informal sector were purely descriptive and empirical. The concept was explored and dealt with in a series of local-level case studies on the changing fabric of the urban economy and was considered to be peculiar to the Third World. It did not find ready acceptance in the literature on developmentalism because of its lack of theoretical and analytical rigour. When the realization came that the spread of informality was huge and also expanding rapidly, a more systematic inventory had to be made to comprehend it as 'an object of statistical enquiry, enumerable and classifiable' (Sanyal 2007: 205). I am quite sceptical of what Sanyal (2007) perceives as the next stage, a variety of policy interventions aimed at improving the lot of the workforce unable to find access to the formal economy or, and increasingly so, being driven out from this higher circuit to the margins of the economy. While Sanyal wants to distance himself from the empiricist overload of the informality concept, I in turn tend to be critical of his refusal to frame and validate the dualism he perceives in a body of quantified and qualified data sets. In my opinion, his paradigm does not stand the test of thick description à la Geertz (2003). My second remark concerns the situation of informality in the post-colonial Third World. While the origin of the concept has, for good reasons, been located in this terrain inhabited by the majority of mankind (Peattie 1985), it has broached out from there to reach the economies in the developed zones of the world (see, for example, Tabak 2000). This trend has reversed the direction of the earlier development paradigm: the 'Rest' not following the West but rather the other way round. But now back to where we started.

## RESHAPING THE SOCIAL CONTRACT?

Does the promise of inclusion not find confirmation in the democratic frame that provides agency and representation to the subaltern classes that have for so long been invisible and without a voice of their own?

The growing assertion noticeable in the milieu of the labouring poor is fuelled by a revolution of rising expectations difficult to ignore. Also, the people at the bottom end want their share in the spoils of an economy bent on consumerism. Where there is universal suffrage, which is actually exercised in reasonable freedom in India, the political system cannot afford to completely frustrate the demands of the reserve army for everyday and durable commodities. The working masses make up the majority of its mandate. This consideration is of relevance for explaining why minimum wages were fixed for landless labourers, why the practices of labour contractors are restricted, why child labour has been prohibited, or why violations of the prohibition of bonded labour are punishable by law, to mention just a few examples. In many states, there are detailed rules regulating employment for a great many occupations, including for casual workers hired for the season only. What is lacking, as discussed in the preceding chapter, is an effective public administration to implement these regulations as well as the appointment of an adequate number of officials responsible for their affirmative enforcement. This is because the government machinery, as it operates, is not held accountable to the people for whom it is supposed to act. Limiting their agency and representation only to the moment of election but denying their rights to be actively engaged in deliberations and control over wage levels as well as other terms of employment is a major reason why civil servants use their authority not to protect and regulate conditions of the workforce in the informal economy. Instead, and in collusion with employers, they deprive these masses from decent work and a somewhat dignified life. In a recent article, Agarwala (2008) is much more hopeful about the prospect of social progress for the Indian proletariat. She suggests that informal workers have changed their strategy and, rather than demanding workers' benefits from employers, address the state to provide welfare entitlements in their quality as citizens. Her argument on the reshaped social contract is as follows: 'To attain state attention, informal workers are using the rhetoric of citizenship rights to offer their unregulated labor and political support in return for state recognition of their work. Such recognition bestows informal workers with a degree of social legitimacy, thereby dignifying their discontent and bolstering their status as claim makers in society' (ibid.: 375).

The empirical evidence with which the author backs up her optimistic assessment is, in my opinion, not very persuasive. It is based on a survey of conditions in two urban industries, construction and bidi manufacture, and interviews held with members and leaders of seven informal workers' organizations in the cities of Mumbai, Chennai, and Kolkata. My first note of dissent is that I consider this data set neither adequate nor representative for the workforce at large but skewed in various ways: location (all urban, not one rural); type of work (two, both industries); and agency (all interviewed stakeholders involved in collective action). My more substantial criticism is that the reformulated model of state–labour relations as presented by Agarwala implicates a measure of success that is difficult to concur with. In contrast to her claim that the state is willing to ensure, instead of work benefits, welfare benefits such as health and education, I tend to be more sceptical that these promises are indeed delivered. Neither do I agree that the few and industry-specific workers' welfare boards that have been established in several states can be held up as demonstrating that the new formula (of state–labour collaboration) will succeed where the discarded one (getting a better deal from employers) has failed. As a matter of fact, in her conclusion, Agarwala (2008) concedes that the informal workers do have a long way to go before receiving all the welfare benefits that they have been promised by the state. Finally, I would qualify her statement as unfounded and misconceived that the informal workers, in return for acknowledgement of their citizenship rights, accept as part of the bargain the unregulated and unprotected nature of informality and, either implicitly or explicitly, are willing to forego their rights to work in decency and dignity.

No doubt, there is a growing divide between the economics of market and the language of citizenship. Under pressure of democratic politics, several states, and to some extent also the central government of India, try to compensate for the low and irregular income of informal workers' households by provisioning some public services (education and health) and basic goods (foodgrains in particular) at below market prices. However, I am inclined to read such schemes more as goodwill signals of populist-style politics, inspired by the need to safeguard vote benches for the next round of elections, than as an expression of a political commitment in respect of claims made from below for decommodification. A commitment to inclusive growth entails much more than just fixing a floor for the reduction of deprivation. While operationalized as eradication of poverty, the policy attempt would have to focus on levelling down the gap separating the poor from the better-off and the rich. Bringing down inequality rather than the alleviation of poverty should be accepted as the issue at stake. Acknowledging the aspirations for social assertion and emancipation would require a redistribution of power, a major redress of the balance that remains so heavily tilted in favour of capital and against labour.

Social theories in an earlier round of globalization, when more than a century ago the process of industrialization and urbanization in the Western economies was in full swing, maintained that progress for the labouring poor was improbable because they themselves were responsible for their improvidence. Proponents of social Darwinism scorned any claim by or on behalf of this underprivileged crowd at the tail end of the economy for a better deal as improper and subversive. A century later, awareness seems to have slowly grown that steadfast pursuit of market-driven economic and social policies is not going to solve the problem of mass poverty. The circumstances which eventually allowed the land-poor and landless, thrown out of agriculture and their rural habitat, in the first industrialized nations of the Northern hemisphere to gain access to mainstream society do not apply to these far larger contingents in countries where the triumph of capitalism is a more recent phenomenon. The once 'empty' regions in the world do not need these surplus people any longer. Moreover, technological development has made production much less labour intensive than it used to be and explains why labour redundant in the primary sector can only be partially absorbed in industry. In this late phase of capitalism, informalization is dominating the economy, above all in the Southern hemisphere, but not only there. This neoliberal policy, capital friendly and labour hostile, replaces regulated and protected employment with casual, irregular, and spasmodic arrangements that suggest own-account work but are disguised forms of wage labour. It is a regime that discourages militancy and obstructs the mobilization of the footloose proletariat into unions and other mass-based organizations.

The agendas of the transnational institutions in charge of the globalized policies pay lip service to combating poverty, as I have argued in the ninth of the *Selected Readings*, 'Myths of the Global Safety Net'. However, the neoclassical doctrine underlying these politics seems to convey that the poor masses themselves are to blame for their survival in distress. Deprivation and subordination has not yet been transformed into systemic exclusion, but that moment may not be far off in the subcontinent of South Asia. The social question in India remains unresolved. It is very clear, however, that whatever claims are made on the state, they cannot absolve capital from its beholden duty to share proportionately and fairly in the cost of making work and life decent

and dignified for the labouring poor. Where informalization of work
and employment is the outcome of a policy dictated by capital and the
state, a better deal for the deregulated and unprotected workforce can
only be realized by a formalization of their rights. Levelling up, is how
the NCEUS has labelled the urgent need to halt the race to the bottom,
and the substantial expenditure this reverse trend requires can not only,
or even mainly, be paid out of the public budget.

## THE CRISIS OF GLOBAL CAPITALISM
How to qualify the footloose victimhood of a political economy that
refuses the formalization of the down and out, that is, to regulate and
protect their work and life conditions? In the first place, I do not want
to subscribe to the opinion that informal workers are wandering around
in a kind of in-between landscape: on the one hand, outside the domains
of capital; and on the other hand, not any longer firmly entrenched in
traditional subsistence.[1] When I reject the notion of an intermediate
zone, it is because I am in endorsement with the label of reserve army
that Karl Marx attached to the workforce, contracted when their labour
power is required and sent off again as soon as they are redundant to
demand. Marx left no room for discussion on the essential capitalist
character of these labour nomads.

But if a surplus labouring population is a necessary product of accumulation
or of the development of wealth on a capitalist basis, this surplus population
becomes, conversely, the lever of capitalistic accumulation, nay, a condition of
existence of the capitalist mode of production. It forms a disposable industrial
reserve army, that belongs to capital quite as absolutely as if the latter had bred it
at its own cost. Independently of the limits of the actual increase of population,
it creates, for the changing needs of the self-expansion of capital, a mass of
human material always ready for exploitation.[2]

Thus, the global economy is faced with a reserve army that is firmly
part of the capitalist mode of production, hired and fired off and on.
The other point I would like to make concerns what will happen next.
In an earlier publication (Breman 2003: 9), I thoroughly disagreed
with I. Wallerstein, according to whom world capitalism is in an acute
and terminal state of crisis, as he argued in an essay published at the
beginning of the twenty-first century (Wallerstein 2000). My conclusion
was that the squeeze of capital in the globalized economy, as evinced by
sharply falling profit rates, has not taken place. Nor did I find empirical
support for his assumption of stagnation in the accumulation of capital.

I suggested that it would be easier to argue in favour of the opposite, that is, of an acceleration in capital formation outside the purview of national or transnational governance. Capital has actually become more footloose between countries and continents, but its volatility has not been accompanied by increasing transparency, let alone control. Freeing capital from official regulation has been paralleled by a concentration of the surplus, resulting in a progressive tilting of the balance between the haves and the have-nots.

I would offhand reject the suggestion that my findings have no other validity than for the sites of my fieldwork in south Gujarat. South Asia is one out of many regions in the world where the social unrest index has prominently gone up in 2010, as reported by the ILO (2011). Characteristic of the globalized regime of capitalism today is the stubborn and pernicious unwillingness to enable a very substantial part of mankind to qualify both as producers and consumers for full and fair participation (Breman 2003: 13). Here I would like to differentiate between people made to live at the fringe of the global economy. The promise of inclusion is still held out to people whose labour power is required off and on as a badli class of coolies. They fulfil the classical role of a reserve army in the political regime of capitalism worldwide. Down and out are the truly excluded, the surplus people who have outlived their usefulness and are increasingly considered to be an intolerable burden to the well-being of the better-off classes of mankind.[3] Are well-being and democracy for a minority of the world population really compatible in the long term with the exclusion from these welfares of a larger part of humanity condemned to live in dire poverty and subordination? A point of no return is reached when a huge reserve army waiting to be incorporated in the labour process becomes stigmatized as a redundant mass, an excessive burden that cannot be included, now or in future, in economy and society (see the tenth of the *Selected Readings*, 'The Eventual Return of Social Darwinism'). The phenomenon of jobless growth is going to haunt us in the years to come. In my opinion, that metamorphosis is the real crisis of world capitalism.

## NOTES

1. In an interesting article on welfare provisions and state benefits for informal labour, Vijayabaskar (2011) contrasts the early history of capitalist accumulation in the Western economies with those of post-colonial societies in the present era. According to him, in the latter case, as, for example, in India, the transfer is from the capitalist to the non-capitalist sector to counter the negative effects of primitive accumulation. He articulates his position, and I quote him: 'The pressure

of democratic politics force the state to implement asset of schemes targeted at improving the welfare of those trapped outside the domains of capital and traditional subsistence' (ibid.: 40).

2. Available at http://www.marxists.org/archive/marx/works/cw/volume35/index. htm (p. 623).

3. There is a growing literature on these rejects, all those who are permanently, and not off and on, superfluous to demand. See, for example, the essay in which Li (2010) contrasts the regimes of informality in Indonesia and India. While in the last country there is still hope for the underprivileged to become included in mainstream society, she is more worried about their plight in Indonesia where the massacre of the organized left in 1965 has left the dispossessed people brutally exposed to exclusion.

# Bibliography

Agarwala, R. (2008), 'Reshaping the Social Contract: Emerging Relations between the State and Informal Labor in India', *Theory and Society*, vol. 37, no. 4, pp. 375–406.

Annavajhula, J.C.B. and S. Pratap (2012), 'Worker Voices in an Auto Production Chain', *Economic and Political Weekly*, vol. 47, no. 33, 18 August, pp. 46–59.

Arunachalam, R.S. (2011), *The Journey of Indian Micro-finance: Leassons for the Future*. Chennai: Aapti Publications.

Banerjee–Guha, S. (ed.) (2010), *Accumulation by Dispossession: Transformative Cities in the New Global Order*. New Delhi: Sage Publications.

Bangasser, P.E. (2000), 'The ILO and the Informal Sector: An Institutional History', ILO Employment Paper No. 2000/9, Geneva. Available online at www.ilo.org.

Barta, Patrick (2009), 'Global Economics: The Rise of the Underground', *Wall Street Journal*, 14 March.

Bernstein, H. (1988), 'Capitalism and Petty Bourgeois Production: Class Relations and Divisions of Labour', *Journal of Peasant Studies*, vol. 15, no. 2, pp. 258–71.

Bhatia, B. (2012), 'Of Human Bondage in Baran, Rajasthan', *Economic and Political Weekly*, Review of Rural Affairs, vol. 47, nos 26 and 27, 30 June–7 July, pp. 159–69.

Bhatt, E.R. (2005), *We Are Poor but So Many: The Story of Self-Employed Women in India*. New York: Oxford University Press.

Bhowmik, S. (1998), 'The Labour Movement in India: Present Problems and Future Perspective', *The Indian Journal of Social Work*, vol. 59, no. 1, pp. 147–66.

Boeke, J.H. (1910), 'Tropisch–Koloniale Staathuishoudkunde: Het Probleem' (Tropical–Colonial Economics: The Problem), PhD thesis, University of Amsterdam, Amsterdam.

Boeke, J.H. (1953), *Economics and Economic Policy of Dual Societies as Exemplified by Indonesia*. Haarlem: H.D. Tjeenk Willink.

Boo, Katherine (2012), *Behind the Beautiful Forevers; Life, Death and Hope in a Mumbai Undercity*. New Delhi: Penguin Books.

Breman, Jan (1974), *Patronage and Exploitation: Changing Agrarian Relationships in South Gujarat, India*. Berkeley, CA: University of California Press.

——— (1976a), *Een dualistisch arbeidsbestel? Een kritische beschouwing van het begrip "de informele sector"* (A Dualistic Labour Order? A Critical Appraisal of the Informal Sector Concept). Rotterdam: Van Gennep.

——— (1976b), 'A Dualistic Labour System? Critique of the "Informal Sector" Concept', *Economic and Political Weekly*, vol. 11, no. 50, part 1, November, pp. 1870–6; and parts 2 and 3, December, pp. 1905–8 and 1939–43.

——— (1989), *Taming the Coolie Beast: Plantation Society and the Colonial Order in Southeast Asia*. New Delhi: Oxford University Press.

——— (1990), *Labour Migration and Rural Transformation in Colonial Asia*. Amsterdam: Free University Press for Centre for Asian Studies Amsterdam.

——— (1994), 'State Protection for the Rural Proletariat', in Jan Breman, *Wage Hunters and Gatherers: Search for Work in the Urban and Rural Economy of South Gujarat*, pp. 291–332. New Delhi: Oxford University Press.

——— (1996), *Footloose Labour: Working in India's Informal Economy*. Cambridge: Cambridge University Press.

——— (2001a), *Op weg naar een slechter bestaan* (A Turn for the Worse). Amsterdam: Vossius Pers, Universiteit van Amsterdam.

——— (2001b), *A Turn for the Worse: The Closure of the Ahmedabad Textile Mills and the Retrenchment of the Workforce*, The Wertheim Lecture. Amsterdam: Amsterdam University Press.

——— (2003), *The Labouring Poor in India: Patterns of Exploitation, Subordination and Exclusion*. New Delhi: Oxford University Press.

——— (2004), *The Making and Unmaking of an Industrial Working Class: Sliding Down the Labour Hierarchy in Ahmedabad, India*. New Delhi: Oxford University Press.

——— (2008), 'A Methodological Note on Investigating Poverty', Special Guest of Honor Lecture, The Indian Econometric Society, 44th Annual Conference, University of Hyderabad, 5 January.

Breman, Jan (2009), 'Myths of the Global Safety Net', *New Left Review*, no. 59, September–October, pp. 1–8.

——— (2010a), *Outcast Labour in Asia: Circulation and Informalization of the Workforce at the Bottom of the Economy*. New Delhi: Oxford University Press. (Paperback edition 2012.)

——— (2010b), 'The Social Question in a State of Denial', *Economic and Political Weekly*, vol. 45, no. 23, pp. 42–6.

——— (2010c), '"A Poor Deal", Symposium Estimation of Poverty and Identifying the Poor', *Indian Journal of Human Development*, vol. 4, no. 1, January–June, pp. 133–42.

——— (2010d), *Koloniaal Profijt van Onvrije Arbeid; Het Preanger Stelsel van Gedwongen Koffieteelt op Java, 1720–1870* (Colonial Profit from Unfree Labour; The Priangan System of Forced Coffee Cultivation on Java, 1720–1870). Amsterdam: Amsterdam University Press.

——— (2012), 'Undercities of Karachi', *New Left Review*, no. 76, July–August, pp. 48–63.

Breman, Jan and Arvind Das (photographs by Ravi Agarwal) (2000), *Down and Out: Labouring under Global Capitalism*. New Delhi: Oxford University Press.

Breman, Jan, Isabelle Guerin, and Aseem Prakash (eds) (2009), *India's Unfree Workforce: Of Bondage Old and New*. New Delhi: Oxford University Press.

Breman, Jan and Gunawan Wiradi (2002), *Good Times and Bad Times in Rural Java: Case Study of Socio-economic Dynamics in Two Villages towards the End of the Twentieth Century*. Singapore: Institute of Southeast Asian Studies.

Chowdhury, S. (2011), 'Employment in India: What Does the Latest Data Show?', *Economic and Political Weekly*, vol. 46, no. 32, August, pp. 23–6.

Cohn, B.S. (1980), 'History and Anthropology: The State of Play', *Comparative Studies in Society and History*, vol. 22, no. 2, pp. 198–221.

Davis, M. (2006), *Planet of Slums*. London and New York: Verso.

Desai, K. (2002), 'Searching for Space: Workers in the Fringe Sector of Surat', in G. Shah, M. Rutten, and H. Streefkerk (eds), *Development and Deprivation in Surat*. New Delhi: Sage Publications, pp. 150–72.

Desai, R. (2012), 'Governing the Urban Poor: River front Development, Slum Settlement and the Politics of Inclusion in Ahmedabad', *Economic and Political Weekly*, vol. 47, no.2, 14 January, pp. 49–56.

Deshingkar, P. and J. Farrington (eds) (2009), *Circular Migration and Multilocational Livelihood Strategies in Rural India*. New Delhi: Oxford University Press.

Fanon, F. (1961), *Les damnés de la terre* (The Wretched of the Earth), translated by C. Farrington in 1963. Paris: François Maspéro.

Geertz, C. (2003), 'Thick Description: Towards an Interpretive Theory of Culture', in C. Jenks (ed.), *Culture: Critical Concepts in Sociology*, pp. 173–96. London: Routledge.

Ghose, A.K. (1999), 'Current Issues of Employment Policy in India', *Economic and Political Weekly*, vol. 34, no. 36, pp. 2592–608.

Gill, K. (2010), *Of Poverty and Plastic; Scavenging and Scrap Trading Entrepreneurs in India's Informal Economy*. New Delhi: Oxford University Press.

'A Global Alliance against Forced Labour' (2005), International Labour Office, Geneva.

Government of Gujarat (1966), *Report of the Minimum Wages Advisory Committee for Employment in Agriculture*. Ahmedabad: Government of Gujarat.

——— (1972), *Report of the Committee on Unprotected and Unorganized Labour*. Gandhinagar: Education and Labour Department, Government of Gujarat.

——— (1974), *Report Minimum Wages Stone Breaking and Stone Crushing*. Ahmedabad: Government of Gujarat.

GoI (Government of India) (1969), *Report of the National Commission on Labour*. New Delhi: Ministry of Labour, Employment and Rehabilitation, GoI.

——— (1991), *Report of the National Commission on Rural Labour* (2 vols) (Reports of Study Groups). New Delhi: Ministry of Labour, GoI.

Gupta, S.P. (2002), *On Targeting Ten Million Employment Opportunities per Year over the Tenth Plan Period*. New Delhi: Planning Commission, GoI.

Haan, de A. (2011), 'Inclusive Growth? Labour Migration and Poverty in India', *The Indian Journal of Labour Economics*, vol. 54, no. 3, July–September, pp. 387–409.

Harriss–White, B. (2003), *India Working: Essays on Society and Economy*. Cambridge: Cambridge University Press.

Harriss–White, Barbara and Nandini Gooptu (2001), 'Mapping India's World of Unorganized Labour', in L. Panitch and C. Leys (eds), *The*

*Socialist Register 2001: Working Classes, Global Realities*. London: Merlin Press, pp. 89–119.

Hart, K. (1973), 'Informal Income Opportunities and Urban Employment in Ghana', in R. Jolly, E. de Kadt, H. Singer, and F. Wilson (eds), *Third World Employment: Problems and Strategy*. Harmondsworth: Penguin, pp. 66–70.

Haynes, D. E. (2012), *Small Town Capitalism in Western India: Artisans, Merchants and the Making of the Informal Economy, 1870–1960*. Cambridge Studies in Indian History and Society. Cambridge: Cambridge University Press.

Hirway, I. and N. Shah (2011), 'Labour and Employment under Globalisation: The Case of Gujarat', *Economic and Political Weekly*, vol. XLVI, no. 22, pp. 57–65.

ILO (International Labour Organization) (1972), *Employment, Incomes and Equality: A Strategy for Increasing Productive Employment in Kenya*. Geneva: ILO.

——— (1974), *Sharing in Development: A Programme for Employment, Equity and Growth for The Philippines*. Geneva: ILO.

——— (1991), *The Dilemma of the Informal Sector*. Report of the Director-General, International Labour Conference, 78th Session, International Labour Office, Geneva.

——— (1996), *India: Economic Reforms and Labour Politics*. New Delhi: South Asia Multidisciplinary Advisory Team, ILO.

——— (2002), *Decent Work and the Informal Economy*. Report VI, International Labour Conference, 90th Session, International Labour Office, Geneva.

——— (2009), *The Cost of Coercion*. Geneva: ILO.

——— (2010), *Extending the Scope of Application of Labour Laws to the Informal Economy*. Geneva: ILO.

——— (2011). *World of Work Report*. Geneva: International Institute for Labour Studies, ILO.

Jenks, C. (ed.) (2003), *Culture: Critical Concepts in Sociology*. New York: Routledge.

Kahn, J.S. (1982), 'From Peasants to Petty Commodity Production in Southeast Asia', *Critical Asian Studies*, vol. 14, no. 1, January–March.

Kanappan, A. (1970), 'Labour Force Commitment in Early Stages of Industrialisation', *Indian Journal of Industrial Relations*, vol. 5, no. 3, pp. 290–349.

——— (ed.) (1980), *Studies of Labour Market Behaviour in Developing Areas*. Geneva: International Institute of Labour Studies, ILO.

Kannan, K.P. (1988), *Of Rural Proletarian Struggles: Mobilization and Organization of Rural Workers in Southwest India*. New Delhi: Oxford University Press.

———— (2009), 'Dualism, Informality and Social Inequality: An Informal Economy Perspective of the Challenge of Inclusive Development in India', *The Indian Journal of Labour Economics*, vol. 51, no. 1, pp. 1–32.

———— (2011a), 'India's Common People: The Regional Profile', *Economic and Political Weekly*, vol. 46, no. 38, September, pp. 60–73.

———— (2011b), 'How Inclusive is Growth in India?' Paper presented at the International Expert Workshop on Inclusive Growth, 'From Policy to Reality', Indian Institute of Dalit Studies, New Delhi, 12–13 December.

———— (2012), 'How Inclusive Is Inclusive Growth in India?' Working Paper WP03/2012, Institute for Human Development, New Delhi.

Kannan, K.P. and G. Raveendran (2011), 'India's Common People: The Regional Profile', *Economic and Political Weekly*, vol. 46, no. 38, September, pp. 60–73.

Kannan, K.P. and J. Breman (eds) (2013), *The Long Road to Social Security: Assessing the Implementation of National Security Initiatives for the Working Poor in India*. New Delhi: Oxford University Press.

Karnik, V.B. (1967), *Strikes in India*. Bombay: Manaktalas.

Khera, R. (ed.) (2011), *The Battle for Employment Guarantee*. New Delhi: Oxford University Press.

Kundu, A. (2011), 'Politics and Economics of Urban Growth', *Economic and Political Weekly*, vol. 46, no. 20, May, pp. 10–12.

Kundu, A. and L.R. Saraswati (2012), 'Migration and Exclusionary Urbanization in India', *Economic and Political Weekly*, vol. 47, nos 26 and 27, 30 June–7 July, pp. 219–27.

Lerche, J. (2012), 'The Unfree Labour Category and Unfree Labour Estimates: A Continuum within Low-end Labour Relations?' Forthcoming.

Lewis, O. (1968), *La Vida: A Puerto Rican Family in the Culture of Poverty—San Juan and New York*. New York: Random House.

Lewis, W.A. (1954), 'Economic Development with Unlimited Supplies of Labour', *Manchester School of Economic and Social Studies*, vol. 22, pp. 139–91.

Li, T.M. (2010), 'To Make Live or Let Die? Rural Dispossession and the Protection of Surplus Populations', *Antipode, A Radical Journal of Anthropology*, vol. 41, January, pp. 66–93.

Lubell, H. (1991), *The Informal Sector in the 1980s and 1990s*. Paris: OECD, Development Centre Studies.

Luke, A.K. (2015), *Passport of Gujarat: Hazardous Journeys*. New Delhi: Manas Publications.

Mahadevia, D. (2011a), 'An Integrated Approach to Decent Work in Asia's Cities: Ahmedabad', Paper presented at the Workshop on Decent Work and Social Security, Centre for Urban Equity, CEPT University, Ahmedabad, December.

———— (2011b), 'Branded and Renewed? Policies, Politics and Processes of Urban Development in the Reform Area', *Economic and Political Weekly*, vol. 46, no. 31, pp. 56–64.

McGee, T.G. (1971), *The Urbanization Process in the Third World*. London: Bell.

NCEUS (National Commission on Enterprises in the Unorganized Sector) (2008), *Report on Conditions of Work and Promotion of Livelihoods in the Unorganised Sector*. New Delhi: GoI.

———— (2009), *The Challenge of Employment in India: An Informal Economy Perspective, Vol. 1*, Main Report. New Delhi: Government of India.

Papola, T.S. (1981), *Urban Informal Sector in a Developing Economy*. New Delhi: Vikas.

Parry, J.P., J. Breman and K. Kapadia (eds) (1999), *The Worlds of Indian Industrial Labour*. New Delhi: ILO–ARTEP.

Peattie, L. (1985), 'An Idea in Good Currency and How it Grew: The Informal Sector', *World Development*, vol. 15, no. 7, pp. 851–60.

Polanyi, K. (1944), *The Great Transformation: The Political and Economic Origins of Our Times*. Boston: Beacon Press.

Sainath, P. (2012), 'Census Findings Put to Decade of Rural Distress', *The Hindu*, 25 September.

Sanyal, K. (2007), *Rethinking Capitalist Development: Primitive Accumulation, Governmentality and Post-colonial Capitalism*. New Delhi: Routledge.

Sehgal, R. (2012), 'Maruti Workers Are the Villiam: Truth or Prejudice?' *Economic and Political Weekely*, vol. 47, no. 31, 4 August, pp. 12–15.

Sengupta, Arjun (2009), 'Preface', in NCEUS, *The Challenge of Employment in India: An Informal Sector Perspective, Vol. 1*, Main Report, p. iv. New Delhi: Government of India.

Sengupta, M. (2012), 'The Organized Poor and *Behind the Beautiful Forevers*', *Dissent Magazine*, Summer. Available online at http://dissentmagazine.org/online.php?id=603 (accessed on 14 July 2012).

Sengupta, A., K.P. Kannan, and G. Raveendran (2008), 'India's Common People: Who Are They, How Many Are They and How Do

They Live?', *Economic and Political Weekly*, vol. 43, no. 11, March, pp. 49–63.

Sethuraman, S.V. (1976), *The Urban Informal Sector: Concept, Measurement and Policy*. Working Papers, World Employment Programme Research, ILO, Geneva.

Sinha, A., N. Sangeeta, and K.A. Siddiqui (1999), *The Impact of Alternative Policies on the Economy with Special Reference to the Informal Sector*. New Delhi: National Council for Applied Economic Research.

Sood, A. (ed.) (2012),*Poverty amidst Prosperity: Essays on the Trajectory of Development in Gujarat*. Delhi: Aakar Books.

Soto, H. de (1989), *The Other Path: The Invisible Revolution in the Third World*. New York: Harper and Row.

——— (2000), *The Mystery of Capital: Why Capitalism Triumphs in the West and Fails Everywhere Else*. London: Bantam Press.

South Gujarat University (1984), *Working and Living Conditions of the Surat Textile Workers: A Survey*. Submitted to the Honourable Chief Justice of the Gujarat High Court (17 December). Surat: Department of Sociology, South Gujarat University.

Srivastava, R. (2011), 'Labour Migration, Inequality and Development Dynamics in India: An Introduction', *Indian Journal of Labour Economics*, Special Issue on Labour Migration and Development Dynamics in India, vol. 54, no. 3, July–September, pp. 373–85.

Sud, N. (2012), *Liberalization, Hindu Nationalism and The State: A Biography of Gujarat*. New Delhi: Oxford University Press.

Swaan, A. de (1988), *In Care of the State: Health Care, Education and Welfare in Europe and the USA in the Modern Era*. Cambridge: Polity Press.

Tabak, F. (2000), 'Introduction: Informalization and the Long Term', in F. Tabak and M.A. Crichlow (eds), *Informalization: Process and Structure*. Baltimore: Johns Hopkins University Press, pp. 1–19.

Thompson, E.P. (1991), *Customs in Common: Studies in Traditional Popular Culture*. London: Merlin Press.

——— (1993 [1967]), 'Time, Work-Discipline, and Industrial Capitalism', *Past and Present*, vol. 38, December, pp. 56–97.

Vijayabaskar (2011), 'Global Crises, Welfare Provision and Coping Strategies of Labour in Tiruppur', *Economic and Political Weekly*, vol. 46, no. 22, May, pp. 38–45.

Wallerstein, I. (2000), 'Globalization or the Age of Transition: A Long-term View of the Trajectory of the World System', *International Sociology*, vol. 15, no. 2, pp. 251–67.

Weber, M. (1949), 'Objectivity in Social Science and Social Policy',
in E.A. Shils and H.A. Finch (eds), *The Methodology of the Social
Sciences*. New York: Free Press.

Weisskopf, T.E. (2011), 'Why Worry about Inequality in the Booming
Indian Economy?', *Economic and Political Weekly*, vol. 46, no. 47,
November, pp. 41–51.

Wertheim, W.F. (ed.) (1961), *Indonesian Economics: The Concept of
Dualism in Theory and Policy*. The Hague: Van Hoeve.

World Bank (1995), *World Development Report—Workers in an Integrating World*. Washington, DC: The World Bank.

——— (2009), *World Development Report—Reshaping Economic Geography*. Washington, DC: The World Bank.

Worsley, P. (1972), 'Frantz Fanon and the "Lumpenproletariat"', in
R. Miliband and J. Savile (eds), *Socialist Register*. London: Merlin
Press, pp. 210–11.

# Index

abuse of workers 71–2
accumulation 20, 22, 63, 141, 142n
Agarwala, R. 138–9
agrarian economy 1, 34
agrarian resources, impact of
   increasing pressure on 44
agricultural labour 44
agriculture 1, 3, 14, 23, 45, 54, 58,
   68, 73
   debt bondage problem 82
   expulsion of labour from 37–8
   informal employment 24
   workers distribution in formal
      economy 24
All India Congress Committee,
   17 (see also National Planning
   Committee)
Ambani, Mukesh 109
Annavajhula, J.C.B. 136n
Annawadi slum in Mumbai, study of
   101–8
anthropologists 9, 27–8
Arunachalam, R.S. 43n

Babri Masjid demolition, in Ayodhya
   (1992) 71
badli (stand-in) 61
Banerjee–Guha, S. 86
Bangasser, P.E. 36
Basu, Kaushik 125
Baxi, U. 123
bazar economy 12 (see also traditional
   economy)

below the poverty line (BPL) census
   99, 110n
Bernstein, H. 31
Bhatia, B. 86n
Bhatt, Ela R. 130
Bhowmik, S. 131
Boeke, J.H. 12–13, 25n
bonded labour 79, 81–2, 111, 138
Bonded Labour System (Abolition)
   Act, 1976 82, 119
Boo, Katherine 101–3, 105–10
Breman, Jan xi, xii, 5–6, 8–9, 11n,
   15, 25n, 37, 40, 42, 43n, 57,
   60, 69, 72, 78, 82, 84, 86, 91,
   93, 99, 113, 119, 122, 128,
   141–2

capital
   accumulation 22
   in informal economy 55–7
   intensity in industrial production
      125
capitalism 2, 5, 10, 13–14, 100–1
capitalist globalization 14
cash crops cultivation 2
caste 48, 69, 78–9, 87, 100, 117,
   122, 129, 132
   access to work 98
   complaint from lower caste
      members 52
caste-cum-tribe order, 100
casual male workers, wage rate
   of 125

*Challenge of Employment in India:*
*An Informal Economy Perspective*
report, NCEUS 40
chawls 68
Child Labour (Prohibition and
Regulation) Act (1986) 119
children at work, in informal
economy 61
Chowdhury, S. 63
citizenship 85, 103, 139
Cohn, B.S. 16
collective action 4, 7, 15, 19, 34, 40,
72, 105, 107, 117, 122, 128–32,
224, 244, 252, 316–20, 378–9,
413–4, 425
colonial capitalism 15
Committee on Fair Wages (1948)
115
Committee on Unprotected and
Unorganized Labour (1972) 115
commodification 59, 109, 110
commodity production 31 (*see also*
informal economy/sector)
common people (*aam admi*) 94–8
competition 47–8
Congress party 112
consciousness 7, 53, 91
consumerism 40, 138
Contract Labour (Regulation and
Abolition) Act 1972 118
coolies 15, 19–20, 55, 142
*The Cost of Coercion* report, ILO 79
corruption 23, 27, 107, 119, 126–7,
209, 245
covert resistance 134–5
criminality 106
cultures
clash of 13
of informality 8
of poverty 90, 100, 122

daily commuting of worker 46
daily earnings of worker, in informal
economy 57–9

daily rhythm, of working classes in
informal economy 53
Dalit community workers 98
Das, Arvind 86n
Davis, M. 68
debt bondage 78–80, 82
Desai, K. 136n
Desai, R. 86
Deshingkar, P. 68, 93
development path 14–18
discipline 44
discrimination 59
dispute free products 40
domestic servants 46
dualism theory 12, 18
capitalist globalization process 14
demarcation between formal
versus informal sector 13

economic behaviour, of Western
man 12
economic freedom 39
economic necessity 6
economic recession 10
economic status 93, 100
*The Economic Survey of 2011* 135
economic transformation 5
employer–employee relationship 5,
32, 35, 38, 50
employers
advance wages for workers 78
primordial ties use by 135
employment
access to outside venues of 45
conditions in lower echelons of
industrial economy 48
congestion in labour market 42
contract 60, 80–1
economic policy impact on 6
in formal sector of economy 17
in informal sector of economy 53
security 25
Equal Remuneration Act (1976)
119

exclusion 20–1, 29, 58, 100, 110,
    123, 140

fallacy
    of binary division 18–20
    of self-employment 30–2
family wage 60–1
Fanon, F. 88, 110n
Farrington, J. 68, 93
females, engagement as domestic
    servants 46
flexibilization 48, 125
forced exit of workers, in Ahmedabad
    36
forced labour 79
formalization of labour 17
formal sector 13, 17
    legal recognition of 28–9
    regulations in 19
    security in 18–19
    workforce distribution in 23–4
free labour 79–80
free market doctrine 34, 41, 101, 128

Gandhi, Mahatma 37, 59–60
garibi hatao (remove poverty) 112
Geertz, C. 137
gender differentiation 59
Ghose, A.K. 38
Gill, K. 109
Global Hunger Index 128
globalization xiii, 14, 124, 140
global recession in 2008 41
green revolution 112
gross domestic product (GDP) 20,
    22
Gujarat Industrial Development
    Corporation 4
Gupta, S.P. 63

Haan, A. de 42
Harriss–White, Barbara 25n, 33
Hart, K. 26–7, 29–30, 33, 43n
Haynes, D.E. 4

Hazare, A. 126
head loaders labour (hamalis) 114
hetero- and homo-sexual abuse 72
heterogeneity 92–4
Hirway, I. 125–8
home-based workers 32, 49–50
housing cooperatives 68
human trafficking 79
illegal retrenchment 126
inclusion
    politics of inclusion 100
    politics of exclusion 20–1
The Indian Journal of Industrial
    Relations 28
The Indian Journal of Labour
    Economics 28
Indian Labour Conference (1957)
    116
Indian Society for Labour Economics
    95
individual-based labour contract 117
Industrial Disputes Act of 1947 36,
    126
industrial employers 37
industrialization process 15
    state regulation need in 21
Industrial Training Institute, 54
industrial workforce 15, 17–18, 49,
    68, 96
inequality 80, 95, 98–9, 99–100
informal economy/sector 4, 10,
    12–13, 91, 132 (see also peasant
    economy)
    accommodation of newcomers 42
    as commodity production 31
    definition of 26
    inspection in Gujarat under
        labour laws 127
    labour agitation in 122
    labour circulation facilitates
        activity of 70
    mode of payment in 50
    NCAER report on 20
    origin of 26

product of brand capitalism 21
size of 32–3
workforce distribution in 23–4
working hours in 50–3
World Bank role in 41
informalization 6, 22, 23, 36, 41–2,
   62–3, 92, 108, 125, 133, 140,
   141
informalized state 121–5
informal workers distribution, by
   socio-religious groups 97
informal worksites 6
insecurity, in job 25
'inspection raj' 125
Inspectorate for Rural Labour,
   Gujarat 119
International Labour Organization
   (ILO) 27, 38–9, 79, 82
International Monetary Fund (IMF)
   41
Inter-State Migrant Workers
   (Regulation of Employment and
   Conditions of Service) Act 1979
   118
intra-rural labour mobility 64–5
involuntary unemployment 38
Isherwood, C. 109

Jawaharlal Nehru National Urban
   Renewal Mission (JNNURM)
   86
jhopadpatis 71
jobbers 32, 72–7, 117
job(s)
   in government services 3
job security 37–8, 49
jobless growth 63

Kahn, J.S. 31
Kanappan, A. 27, 53
Kannan, K.P. 24, 42, 49, 84, 91,
   94–8, 100, 114, 124
Karnik, V.B. 37

Khera, R. 84
Kundu, A. 85

labour agitation 122
labour aristocracy 87–9
labour bondage 82, 134
labour circulation 66, 70
Labour Commissioner 126
labour contract 48–50
labour contractors 66, 73
labour elite 87
labour laws 35–6
labour market 100, 129
   congestion in employment 42
   dualism 35
   flexibility 54
   segmentation pattern in 66
   World Bank supports on dualism
      in 38
labour inspectorate 72, 126, 127
labour mobility 5, 64–8, 83
labour regime, in Western business
   15
labour rights 4–6, 16, 32, 35, 37–8,
   94
labour welfare 37
landless colonies 2
landless labour 2, 44
land-poor households 2–3, 67, 77
land reform 16
leisure 51, 61
Lerche, J. 80
Lewis, F.A. 13–14
Lewis, O. 90
Li, T.M. 143n
long hours of work 49
loss of job 129
low-caste workers, landless 78
Lubell, H. 36
lumpenproletariat 87–9
lumpenization 106

Mahadevia, D. 86

Mahatma Gandhi National Rural
 Employment Guarantee Scheme
 (MGNREGS) 84
*majuri kam* 46
Marx, Karl 88, 141
McGee, T.G. 110n
merchant capitalism 43
microcredit 30
migrants
 from Ahmedabad 76
 definition of 67
 loneliness among 93
 temporary and short duration 67
migration 6, 37, 66, 70, 83, 85
mills closure, in Ahmedabad 6
mill workers 37
 Gandhi's struggle in Ahmedabad
  for 59
 lifestyle, features of 51
Minimum Wage Act 113, 115, 122
minimum wages 21, 35
modernity versus traditionalism 20–2
Modi, N. 39, 135

National Commission for
 Enterprises in the Unorganized
 Sector (NCEUS) xii, 23–5, 31,
 40–1, 43n, 55, 58, 63, 81, 94–5,
 141
National Commission on Labour 18,
 117–18
National Commission on Rural
 Labour (NCRL) 67, 96, 119, 124
National Council for Applied
 Economic Research (NCAER) 20
National Planning Committee 17
National Sample Survey
 Organisation (NSSO) 8
National Sample Survey, 61st Round
 96
Nehru, Jawaharlal 17
neo-bondage 62, 77–81
neoliberalism doctrine 34, 39

new economic regime, in Gujarat
 39–41
New Trade Union Initiative (NTUI)
 132

occupational multiplicity 44, 48
occupational variability 19
Office of the Labour Commissioner
 115
Other Backward Castes (OBCs) 95,
 98
outsourcing 19, 29, 50
own-account work 31, 140

*pagar* (regular salary) 45
Papola, T.S. 33
parallel economy 28
Parry, J.P. 38
pauperism 101
pauperization 88
peasant household 3–4
Peattie, L. 137
petty bourgeoisie 89–92
petty capitalists 90
piece-rate payment system 117
*Planet of Slums* (David) 68–9
Planning Commission 63, 99
Polanyi, K. 14, 25n
policymakers, extension of attention
 to non-agrarian workforce 113–14
political economy, of post-colonial
 capitalism 20
poverty 3, 93, 97–8
 distribution of informal workers
  by religious groups 97
 distribution of population and
  informal workers by status 96
 economic transformation in
  1990s 5
 line 40, 95, 97–9
 among seasonal migrants 6
Pratap, S. 136n
primordial loyalties 129, 132

private capital investment 39
private enterprise 36
pro-free market media 41
proletariat 2, 47, 53, 122
public sector 3–5, 17, 36, 52
purchasing power, of proletariat 15
purchasing power parity (PPP) 98
putting-out system 50

quota system 3

Raveendran, G. 97
recruitment of labour 70
redundant labour 64
*Report Committee Unprotected and
    Unorganized Labour* 115
*Report of the National Commission on
    Labour* 114
*Report of the National Commission on
    Rural Labour* (1991) 67
reserve army 66
Right of Information Act 107
rotation of job and workplace 134
rural economy 7
    diversification of 44–8
Rural Labour Inspectorate, Surat 123
Rural Workers Welfare Board 127
Rural Workers' Welfare Centres
    (Gram Majur Kalyan Kendra)
    122

*sahukars* 43
Sainath, P. 85
Sanyal, B. 20–1, 30, 63, 89, 100, 137
Scheduled Castes (SCs) 3, 7, 95, 98,
    128
Scheduled Employment Act 114
Scheduled Tribes (STs), 3, 7, 95, 98
schooling, of children from landless
    households 54
seasonal migrants 118
    debt bondage among 81
    recruitment of 5–6
    in south Gujarat 72

Second Law Review Committee,
    Government of Gujarat 123
sectoral distribution, of workers 24
Sehgal, R. 136n
Self Employed Women's Association
    (SEWA) 130
self-employment 30–2, 45, 50
self-exploitation 50
semi-permanent migrants 66
Sengupta, A. 95–6
Sengupta, M. 108
Sethuraman, S.V. 27
sexual abuse 94
shadow economy 28
Shah, N. 125–8
shift work 50–1
'Shining India' slogan 40
Shiv Sena 105
short duration migrants 67
Singh, Y. 36
Sinha, A. 20
skill 28, 37, 55, 58, 59, 64, 72, 171,
    189, 195, 222, 225, 228, 232,
    252, 272, 275, 281, 316, 358
skilled workers 54–5
skilling 53, 54–5, 441
slavery 79
slum dwellers 102, 106
    difficulties to obtain urban
        citizenship 85
    disenfranchisement campaign
        for 86
slums 54, 65, 68–9, 101–2
small-scale employers 58
social consciousness 37, 122, 135,
    365, 381, 414, 424
social Darwinism 7, 140
social groups, population distribution
    and informal workers 96
social inequality 95, 113
social networks 44, 136n
social profile, of workforce 87
social question 15, 140
social security 15–16, 25, 37, 92, 127

social struggle, industrial proletariat
  against mill owners 15
solidarity 72
Sood, A. 40
Soto, H. de 32
south Gujarat
  anthropological research in 30
  daily earnings of workers 57
  informal sector activities in 55–6
South Gujarat University 123
Special Economic Zones (SEZs) 39,
  83, 126
Srivastava, R. 68, 93
state-sponsored relief 2
street vendors 51
strike 37, 59, 114, 123, 130, 132,
  134, 135
subcontracting, 19, 29, 32, 117
sub-proletariat 89–92, 101, 110n
subversion 123
Sud, N. 39, 136n
suffrage 15, 106, 112, 138
Surat
  abuse and violence against
    workers 72
  capitalist regime of 56
  doubling of population in 5, 56
  industrial work regime in 5
  informal sector activities in 55
Surat city Census 2011 42, 131
surplus people 140, 142
Swaan, A. de 15

Tabak, F. 137
technology 17
temperwalas 47, 48
temporary migrants 67
temporary relocation sites 86
Tendulkar Committee 99
Textile Labour Association (TLA)
  59–60, 129–30
Third World countries 14, 16, 27,
  88
Thompson, E.P. 53

trade unions 17–18, 34, 37, 40, 114,
  117, 131
traditional economy 12
traditionalism 20–2
tribal communities, workers from 98
tripartite formula 16

undercity 101, 103, 105, 106, 110
undercitizenship 101–10
underemployment 42
underground economy 27–8
unemployment 42, 48, 104, 132
  of footloose workforce 42
  increasing among agrarian class 2
  involuntary 38
unfree labour 79–80
United Progressive Alliance (UPA)
  125
unorganized workers 117
unprotected labour 18
unregulated capitalism regime 22–3
unskilled workers 26, 51
unskilled workers, in informal
  economy 51–2
urban casual labour market (nakas) 46
urban dualism notion 29
urban economy 7, 13, 28, 34
urbanization process 17, 36, 65,
  84–5, 99, 110, 140

Valsad town, field study in 4
Vijayabaskar 142n
village economy 37–8
violence 71–2
votes of landless 112

wage hierarchy 59
wage rates 41, 54, 57–8, 115, 118,
  121, 123, 125
waged employment 67
waged labour 28, 30–2, 65
Wallerstein, I. 141
Wall Street Journal (WSJ) 41
Weber, M. 18

Weisskopf, T.E. 99
welfare state 10, 15, 36
welfarist governmentality 21
Wertheim, W.F. 25n
Western economic culture 13
Wiradi, Gunawan 11n
workers
    in formal sector of economy 17
    need of shelter 68–70
    sectoral distribution of 24
*Workers in an Integrating World*
    report (1995) 35

working-class colonies 68
working day, in informal economy
    50–3
Workmen Breach of Contract Act
    (1859) 37
work security 25
World Bank 32, 35, 38, 41, 54,
    83–4
*World Development Report* (2009) 83
World Employment Programme, by
    ILO 27
Worsley, P. 110n

Selected Readings

# Publisher's Acknowledgements

The publisher acknowledges the following for permission to include articles/extracts in this volume.

Popular Prakashan for 'The Market for Non-agrarian Labour: The Formal versus Informal Sector', in S.D. Pillai and C. Baks (eds), *Winners and Losers: Styles of Development and Change in an Indian Region*, Chapter 6, Bombay, 1979, pp. 122–66.

Sage Publications for 'The Study of Industrial Labour in Post-colonial India: The Formal Sector—An Introductory Review', in Jonathan P. Parry, Jan Breman, and Karin Kapadia (eds), *The Worlds of Indian Industrial Labour: Contributions to Indian Sociology, Occasional Studies 9*, Chapter 1, New Delhi, 1999, pp. 1–41.

Cambridge University Press for 'Quality of the Labour Process', in Jan Breman, *Footloose Labour: Working in India's Informal Economy*, Chapter 5, Cambridge, 1996, pp. 109–40; for 'Neo-bondage: A Fieldwork-based Account', in *International Labor and Working-Class History*, vol. 78, no. 1, 2010, pp. 48–62; for 'Proletarian Life and Social Consciousness', in Jan Breman, *Footloose Labour: Working in India's Informal Economy*, Chapter 8, Contemporary South Asia 2, Cambridge, 1996, pp. 222–64.

Macmillan for 'The Expulsion of Labour from the Formal Sector of the Economy', in Sabyasachi Bhattacharya and Jan Lucassen (eds), *Workers in the Informal Sector: Studies in Labour History, 1800–2000*, Chapter 9, Delhi, 2005, pp. 177–209.

# 1

# The Market for Non-agrarian Labour

## The Formal versus Informal Sector*

The as yet scant literature on this topic focuses mainly on the labour system outside agriculture.[1] The term 'formal sector' is taken to mean wage work under conditions of regular employment, such as is characteristic of the modern private enterprises and of government institutions. In this, we are dealing with a labour force which is mutually related in a functional or hierarchical way with employment situations which can be traced in economic statistics and whose working conditions are controlled by law. Hence, it is also referred to as the 'organized', 'registered', or 'protected' sector.

Labour performed outside this set-up is grouped under the term 'informal sector', an euphemism for a wide range of economic activities often brought under the common denominator of 'self-employment'. These work situations manifest little or no interconnection, are difficult to register, and are not covered by laws controlling their working conditions. The description is sketchy, and in lieu of a precise definition, one often makes do with a lengthy, more or less arbitrary enumeration in order to give some idea of the breadth of variety. This simple division into two categories is not very precise and also unsatisfactory in other ways. It is thus not always clear if the distinction is relating to the means of production rather than to the labour force.[2] The two do not simply run parallel. For instance, it is not uncommon at all to find labour relations in modern enterprises which are typical of the informal economy. I

* Originally published as 'The Market for Non-agrarian Labour: The Formal versus Informal Sector', in S.D. Pillai and C. Baks (eds), *Winners and Losers: Styles of Development and Change in an Indian Region*, Chapter 6. Bombay: Popular Prakashan, 1979, pp. 122–66.

will deal with this in more detail at a later stage. Conversely, it would also be a misconception to assume that self-employment is restricted to the informal sector. In the *bazar* in Bulsar, one can find a great many shops and establishments, even one-man businesses, which indeed must be put under the formal sector. Compare this with the street vendors and craftsmen—for example, a carpenter without a fixed work base or someone working at home to whom jobs are subcontracted—who make their living in an irregular manner. In other words, the distinction between the formal and informal sectors is not tied to particular branches of economic activity or to particular occupations. It is more a case of the context in which the economic activities come about and of the way in which an occupation is carried out.

In attempting a more precise outline of the labour force of the informal sector, we must first look at the absence of security and regularity in working conditions and of the income derived from that work. In this respect also, attention has primarily been focused on the insecure and irregular existence of the self-employed, to the improvisation and scraping necessary in the rounds of the shoeshiner, the street vendor, the porter, the tinker—that is, those who do not maintain regular contact with employers or clients. The obscure nature of their existence is illustrated with references to illegal or semi-illegal practices such has begging, smuggling, distilling alcohol, or gambling. But work in the informal sector is also carried out, to a great extent, under terms of employment by others if indeed not on a continuous or standardized basis. Even activities within the illegal sphere are often carried out not on one's own initiative or risk but rather at the direction of an employer. Porter with a gang of smugglers, ticket seller for a big gambler, or servant to an alcohol distiller are just a few of the most common criminal types of labour relations to be found in the town of Bulsar.

In view of the preoccupation in recent literature with self-employment as an essential feature of the informal sector, I will limit myself in further discussion to a comparison of the labour relations in this and in the formal sector. In contrast to workers in the formal sector, who have a regular job and whose income and working conditions are standardized and controlled, the informal sector is characterized by the absence of formalized work relationships. Labour is an irregular commodity, both with respect to the personal traits of the labourer himself and the services he renders. Before subjecting the topic of labour relations to closer examination—an examination which will proceed from the premise that there are differences in the way in which work is obtained, in the conditions in which work is carried out, and in bargaining procedures—I shall first look at the composition and magnitude of the two sectors.

## SOCIAL COMPOSITION AND SIZE

We have already established that people working in the formal sector form a privileged category. The security of employment and income facilitate a regular existence; work is generally tied to a fixed location and the rights and obligations towards the employer are more or less established. 'Service' is attractive not because of the high level of income in itself but by virtue of the regularity and standardization of having a settled position. Apart from economic advantages, such an arrangement also offers protection against humiliating and arbitrary treatment. In a situation of work shortage, employment in the formal sector affords a guarantee of maintaining a reasonable degree of highly valued economic and social independence, together with the possibility, if one is employed at higher levels, of having other people as subordinates. These features are, in fact, considered to be the prerogative of high castes. Their disproportionate representation in 'service' bears witness to this fact, as indeed does their opposition to infiltration from the lower reaches of society. For the members of higher castes, this represents not only an infringement on what they consider to be their appropriate position but also on the exclusiveness of their style of life, of which their sphere of economic activities forms a close part. The very standing of one's work is being attacked. Their irritation is expressed in conceited terms over the quality of work of these outsiders, 'upstarts', who are charged with responsible work 'even though all they are capable of doing is signing their name with a thumb print'. Conversely, those from the low castes who have worked their way up to a 'service' position are very hesitant and diffident in their behaviour towards the '*moto manaso*' (big people), who leave no doubts about their feelings of superiority.

For members of higher castes, the insecurity of employment and the social dependence accompanying this are reasons enough to shun the informal sector. Many of them prefer long-term unemployment to taking the risk of being associated with a work environment which they consider to be the exclusive stamping ground of the low castes. The stigma of an unordered life, the absence of a definite work location, a varying but generally low income, and low-prestige work are the fate particularly of casual labourers leading an extremely precarious existence on the margin of society.

In order to gain an insight into labour relations in the informal sector, it is essential to undertake an analysis on the household level. Only by looking at the household, in which many if not all of its members are involved or do want to be involved either partly or completely in the labour system, can we begin to understand the relative elasticity with which they are able to counter unemployment, severe fluctuations in income, and other similar vicissitudes. It also explains that mood of resignation, so striking to an outsider, with which they abandon the chance of a position, or when the opportunity of a job is foregone, for seemingly irrational reasons.

In contrast, work within the formal sector is much more restricted to one or perhaps a few of the members of the household. It goes without saying that under these circumstances, the children are able to receive an education, as it is also economically feasible to avoid the women having to work outside the home (or even working within the home, if possible, by hiring outside help).

It is difficult to establish the magnitude of these two sectors, since they are simply not mutually comparable. It has already been mentioned above that the working population is composed in entirely different ways. In fact, this term cannot even be used to describe the informal sector. Here, we find many more children, women, aged, and infirm people. Their labour—and for that matter that of the men also—is not always of great use. The irregular and obscure conditions make it difficult for a researcher to collect data on the informal sector, a recurrent complaint made by authors working on this topic (see, among others, Dasgupta 1973: 57; Hart 1973: 70). The specific structure of the informal sector—dominated by exchangeability and discontinuity and knowing only a very slim margin between employment and unemployment—makes categorization according to the accepted concepts and problems defined in terms of the informal sector a rather dubious affair. Only in a formal set-up, and even here only to a certain extent, can labour relations be reduced to separate variables and components and these phenomena measured and counted. Outside this framework, any attempt at a similar break-up into formal units seems forced, a statistical exercise which violates reality. Hence, we can understand why sociological and economic analyses of the labour market focus predominantly if not exclusively on the formal sector, a preference which, however, can scarcely be justified. For, whether one takes either a wide or a narrow view, it does not alter the fact that a very large section of the population is thrown upon the informal sector for its living. Dasgupta posits a figure of 40–50 per cent of all income earners in the city of Calcutta, and Hart includes half of the working population of Accra in this category. There is reason to believe that for the non-agrarian working population of the Bulsar district, the figure is certainly as great and probably even as high as three-quarters of the total. The latter figure would include, under the informal non-agrarian sector, that part of the rural labour force which works in agriculture for only a relatively short period of the year, mainly before and after the rainy season.

Agricultural labourers and small farmers are recruited in large numbers by jobbers for gang work within the district or outside. These seasonal migrants from the countryside form yet another highly neglected category within the informal sector.

Wherever one draws the lines, the fact remains that it is essential to widen one's horizons in order to make a study of the similarities and differences in labour relations between the formal and the informal sector.

## RECRUITMENT AND ACCESS

In the informal sector, work is sought and found by means of personal contacts. This is especially the case with those who do not have any particular skill but seek casual work (*chhuta kam*); every single day, these odd-job men must look for new work and are directed in this by information they receive from their families, acquaintances, neighbours, or during casual encounters along the road. Their existence, full of improvisations, is illustrated by the variety of work they do in consecutive days or sometimes even during the same day. It is exactly this very short-term and precarious way in which they are incorporated into the labour system that compels them to maintain a wide network of contacts.

Although lacking a set work location, their daily attempts to earn an income do, in fact, follow a more or less fixed pattern. A labour market in the literal sense of the word is the Tower, a meeting place in the centre of the town where dozens of workers gather in the early morning. The following passage is taken from my diary:

It is 6.15 in the morning and there are about fifty workers here. M. tells me that they come every day from the town and the surrounding areas. Some of them have no place to stay and are sleeping here and there in groups of two or three. Both the old and the young are represented. Some look healthy, others thin and decrepit. They walk around or sit chatting on the ground, waiting for someone to come and hire their services for the day or for a particular job. A man comes up and asks five labourers to come with him to work on his land. What do they ask? No, Rs 4 is too much. His offer is Rs 3 and then he goes up to Rs 3½. When this is refused he walks away. 'Then you'll all just have to stay here'.

The next one arrives on a bicycle and shouts to them that he needs 10 workers. One of the men in the group asks what sort of work they have to do. A whole day of transporting goods. The spokesman says that they want Rs 4 per person for that and it must be paid in cash. Agreement is reached. The man selects the workers himself. He waves aside an old bent worker who has stepped forward, saying: 'Have you seen yourself in a mirror lately?' The old man shuffles back to the row of those still waiting. A quarter of an hour later another prospective employer comes and says that he needs 6 men to pack sodawater bottles. For how long and how much? Smiling he replies that this is hard to say, but that they will be treated well. The negotiations on his side remain rather elusive. Finally 6 men follow him hesitantly. M. tells me that many employers are very noncommittal about payment and the duration of the work. When the work is done they give less than the vaguely agreed price. But also not too little, otherwise they would not be able to get anybody the next time. A farmer in an ox-cart takes two boys with him to work in his mango garden for a month, picking the fruit during the daytime and guarding it at night. He offers a total of Rs. 40 as well as food and some mangoes every day. The boys try to work out how much that is per day. An older worker quietly warns them that they will probably only get enough food for one man.

Some one-day employers take particular men away for some work without negotiating. They are old acquaintances and so there is no need to reach an agreement beforehand. A man asks one worker to go with him but he says that he already has work for today. He has just come along for a chat. The man persists: 'I know you and I may require you again the whole of next week'. The worker still does not acquiesce but promises to send a friend whom he will vouch for. Five labourers are taken to work on a construction site but for a price of only Rs 3¼. They are conceding more easily now. It's getting late and they are afraid that otherwise they won't get any work today. At half past seven there are about 15 workers left. Some have left in the meantime but new ones have arrived in their place.

Many follow a fixed route in their daily search for work. First, early morning they stand in the queue at the railway workshop where casual workers are taken on. Then they go, for this effort is generally in vain, to the Tower, and if this is also unsuccessful, they try their luck as porters somewhere else in the town where there are concentrations of shops and commercial establishments. Some restrict themselves to carrying a load on their head, while others hire a 'lorry'[3] and wait at the corner of a street in the hope of getting enough jobs to be able to pay the hire fee of 50 paise and still net Rs 2–3 at the end of the day. The difficulty in selling his labour and in scraping together a daily income is illustrated in the following interview report with R.:

I am doing all kinds of odd jobs carrying goods from shops to houses, roadside labour, construction work, etc. Because of the monsoon it is very difficult now to find employment. Usually I sit in a corner near Machli market, waiting until a shopkeeper or his customer calls me. This morning I earned Rs 2 digging drainage trenches. One pipefitter told me that there was some work going on nearby in house construction. I went there and the contractor told me to come tomorrow and the next day. He offered to pay a rupee per day but this I refused. We finally settled for Rs 1.50. If I had not accepted and I had tried my luck elsewhere, I might also have lost that money. We are poor and can't raise ourselves; it is barely possible to survive. When I woke up this morning I didn't know whether we would have food for today. Just by good luck and the help of God I earned Rs 2 this morning. Of course, in the afternoon there is nothing to do now. But because of work tomorrow, at least I don't have to worry about food. After that the problem starts all over again.

While the casual workers are constantly on the search for work, they are also sought after. People who need labourers for one day, or a longer period, go to the settlements and the streets where they live in order to be sure of arranging sufficient and reliable manpower. Semi-fixed relations thus arise between 'temporary' employers and temporary workers; the services of the latter are available on call. Similar loose relations exist between craftsmen and their assistants, called 'begari'. Masons and carpenters work on contract basis at a construction site or somewhere else and require young women or men to assist them, doing the rough and heavy work and handing them the tools and materials. Those semi-skilled workers who wait for customers every morning with their tools at the Tower are also called 'begari'.

Not only is day-to-day labour variable in character, but several forms of longer-term work are also characterized by their exchangeability. Many economic activities are seasonally bound, and particularly the performance of casual labourers follows a rhythmical cycle. Cutting grass, transporting timber, working on roads and digging, as well as other forms of both agrarian and industrial work follow one another in a more or less seasonal pattern. However, the various locations are not freely open to those who want to work. Besides being familiar with the work, one must also command the proper contacts in order to be in the running. A lot of temporary and unskilled work is done in gangs which means that one has no choice but introduction to and collaboration within a team. Often, there is a small core of steady workers which can be expanded by the jobber, according to demand, by mobilizing additional labour from their families or circle of acquaintances.

Finally, a lot of the labour force in the informal sector is engaged on a semi-permanent basis, that is, they are employed with the tacit understanding that they are to make themselves available wherever there is a further notice, without however deriving any rights or guarantee of fixed employment. A career perspective is out of the question. Working together with a few others or completely alone, they go to make up the entire personnel that the employer has at his disposal. This category includes, among others, shop boys, loaders and unloaders in transport business, workers in small artisan shops, boys in 'hotels' and tea stalls, and of course, domestic servants (which includes many women). This loose and incoherent collection of semi-permanent labour is similarly engaged on personal recommendation and without any clearly defined terms of employment. Their services can be terminated at a moment's notice and the employer thereby sheds any further obligation. They, too, come under the category of 'chhuta'.

From the above, we can see that the decisive factor in getting employment in the informal sector is personal contact. The nature and extent of this network of contacts determines not only whether one is incorporated into the work process but also where, how, for how long, and for what type of work.

Personal intervention is institutionalized in the figure of the jobber (*mukadam*) whose practice is connected with the unskilled and irregular work carried out in gangs. We have already noted that this type of labour situation is inherent in the informal sector. The jobber acts on behalf of the employer, recruiting and dismissing workers.

Inevitably, he himself comes from their ranks. The 'mukadam' owes his responsible position to his relationship, often extending over many years, with the boss, his proficiency in the work, his command over other workers, and his ability to read and write. He is responsible for the day-to-day overseeing of the work gang; he divides the work, supervises it, and then is responsible for the end result. Although representing the workers in dealings above, he is, however, primarily the employer's agent. In addition to a limited number of gang workers, on whom he can count and who cannot work for others without his approval, he also maintains contact with a wider circle of workers whom he could possibly round up, and can quickly extend his recruiting domain with the aid of other 'mukadams'. As the link between supply and demand and the bridge between various fields and levels of work, he is highly sought after by both parties but is guided, first, by his own interest and then, by those of the employer. Both his base of operation and his style of recruiting characterize the informal sector for what it is—an unstable labour market with a high degree of obscurity and very sharp fluctuations, traits which are generally detrimental to supply.

Entry to the formal sector generally follows standard procedures, the starting point being that the most highly qualified candidates are selected. The course of events for appointments at a local postal service will illustrate the point. Periodically, once or twice a year, vacancies are made public through announcements on a board in the post office and advertisements in the local newspapers, while at the same time, the district labour bureau is also notified. Prerequisites are stipulated, such as the level of education required and age limits; all candidates who apply must fill out forms (available upon payment) and furnish a health certificate. Final selection is based on merit. Once a year, a written test is held in the district office for the position of postman and other lower personnel. The review of applicants for the post of clerk takes place one level higher (Surat Circle), the main standard of judgement being academic results. This was not the case previously. Older informants in this category related how they had been appointed by the postmaster himself through the intercession of their father or uncle. Close relatives could count on preferential treatment. A person leaving the service virtually had the right to recommend a close relative to fill his position. However, when giving this information, most people added that it had not been so difficult to find work at that time. The drastic change in this regard now means that outsiders have little chance, in practice, of gaining a vacant position. Preference is, in fact, given to people of a lower rank, provided that they meet the prerequisites and are of a sufficiently high standard. So great is the shortage of work that even educated people show interest in the very lowest positions, for example, that of A.D., a boy who empties the mailboxes and brings the mail to the village postal agents and so on, a part-time job for a wage of Rs 30 per month. Only after patiently passing through all the various scales of Class IV personnel, a matter of many years, is one finally in the running for the position of postman. Conversely, people of higher education apply for this latter position as a means of reaching, in a roundabout way, the post of clerk.[4] An extra disadvantage is that in all of these cases, appointment is only on a temporary basis; permanent appointment coming only after a period of time, at the earliest, three years.

The distinction between temporary and permanent employment is also of great importance at the railway workshop with its many hundreds of workers. Whereas technical personnel are generally accepted into the latter category shortly after their appointment, the former is predominantly made up of unskilled workers. It is a reserve of cheap labour which can be shrunk or expanded according to need. Money is made available for each particular piece of work and a notice is hung in the office for temporary work to the effect that interested parties should report the following morning. Already at an early hour, there is a long queue of people waiting. The surplus, and indeed there always is one, is sent away. Personal data of those remaining are noted down and their papers (references from previous employment which they have brought with them) are subjected to scrutiny. After a medical examination, those who have been accepted are given a temporary work pass. Also among these, some are kept in excess of the number required daily. The supernumerary workers have to report early in the morning together with the others, and are sent away, of course without any pay, when there are no absentees.

Upon completion of the work, all are dismissed. This procedure is then repeated the next time some work arises. Temporary workers can make the transition to fixed employment after a period of years, certainly no less than five, but only if there are vacancies available and if they have successfully passed a test. They are judged by a small commission on the grounds of the quality and regularity of their work in the past. Among my informants, there are some who are still temporary workers after 10 or 12 years of service, or even longer.

Finally, in the large private enterprises, there are no formal mechanisms of recruitment. This is the case with the workshops as well as the big factories such as Atul and its subsidiaries. According to a personnel officer I spoke to at Atul, the phase of industrial expansion has passed and so, there is now hardly any demand for an expansion of the labour force. Vacancies can easily be filled by selecting from the steady stream of applications which pour in unasked. Selection of new personnel is made by the head of the department concerned together with a personnel officer, the former having the final say.

The head of the District Employment Exchange office in the district town gave me a brief and terse explanation to the effect that this service exists to meet the demands made by employers. Labour mediation exists mainly on behalf of the government agencies working within the district. The mediation of the labour bureau is prescribed in case of vacancies within government institutions.

The supply of labour is so great that the private sector of the district has little or no need for the mediation of such a service. Of a registered number of 1,319 who were found work in 1971, 1,172 went into the public sector.

The labour bureau is not only responsible for mediation but also for keeping statistics concerning the size and development of the labour force. According to a report in the second quarter of 1971, the number of work positions was around the 45,000 mark, of which *c.* 30,000 were in the private sector and approximately 15,000 in the public sector. These figures, based on a total district population of some one-and-a-half million souls, are by themselves an indication of very substantial under-registration. It seems valid to conclude that the report was mainly based on the urban formal sector, although even the conclusion here is no doubt also incomplete and unreliable. This is equally the case with the assessment of unemployment. The figures are derived from the so-called Live Register, a list which notes all people who have reported to the labour bureau as seeking work. In the middle of 1971, there were 6,662 unemployed on this list, who can be divided as follows:

1. *Those who have worked previously:*
   a. in higher occupations (independent professions,
      highly qualified technicians, managers, etc.)          980
   b. in administration (clerical staff, civil servants)      402
   c. as skilled workers (craftsmen, drivers, etc.)           526
   d. as unskilled workers (night-watchmen,
      cooks, sweepers, etc.)                                  167

2. *Those who are seeking work for the first time:*
   a. with a college education (graduates, inter mediates)    707
   b. with secondary education wholly or partly
      (matriculates, middle sschool standard)               3,004
   c. literates (upper grades of primary school)              872
   d. illiterates                                               4
                                            Total           6,662

The summary clearly indicates that the bureau primarily extends its services to matriculates and graduates, a category which is representative for more highly qualified work in the formal sector. It is therefore no surprise that temporary and unskilled workers seem, by and large, unaware of the existence of the labour bureau. When I asked those who were, in fact, aware of its existence whether they had ever gone there, they reacted with the comment, 'that's not for type of people like us', or in similar words.

Everyday one can see groups of young graduates hanging around the labour office. They come to find out what their chances are of finding a job, which are usually negligible. In order to stay on the books, they must report regularly. People over the age of 24 are not considered for a government position. Many become tired of the endless waiting and after a while, do not come back—their names are taken off the register. To make the going even tougher, a further prerequisite is often demanded for the few positions offered, namely, that only those candidates who have obtained 'first class' will be taken into consideration.

The methods followed produce a statistical optimism which gives a totally misconstrued picture of the work opportunities and unemployment situation, a bias which is mainly caused by neglect of the informal sector both from the point of view of registration as well as labour mediation. While the availability of work is thus drastically reduced, we also find that private employers only call on the services of the labour bureau when they want specialized positions filled. It was recently proposed to set up, under the auspices of the labour bureau, technical courses in which only matriculates would be able to take part, without however sufficiently gauging the need for skilled labour. The above-mentioned quarterly report listed the following vacancies: chemist, medical officer, female health visitor, auxiliary nurse, sanitary inspector, high school teacher to teach special subjects like English, Sanskrit (trained and experienced), professor in Gujarati (experienced), lecturer in accountancy and commerce (experienced), stenographer (fast and accurate), tractor driver (experienced), jobber in loom (experienced), weaver (experienced), shaper-cum-miller (experienced), welder (experienced), refrigeration and airconditioning mechanic, boiler attendant, fire brigade superintendent (experienced), photographer (experienced).

However difficult access to the formal sector is, one can deduce from the above that entry into this labour force does, in any case, follow standard procedures. Interested parties must meet formal requirements and selection is generally based on merit and thus, given the inequality of opportunity that exists, there seems to be a substantial play of objectivity. There is, however, an important difference between theory and practice. The situation of shortage necessitates the use of influence along personal channels. Only through 'lagvag' can you get a fixed job, according to countless informants I spoke to.

This is certainly the case with government positions. People who themselves are already employed in a service naturally have a head start in their attempts to secure a position for their son or some other member of their family or a relation. The rule that the higher your own position, the greater the chance of success applies, especially so far as appointments being decided on the spot are concerned. If the position falls under the competence of a higher level, then one does not always have the contacts necessary for such far-reaching influence. This restriction is particularly relevant for the lower staff who are often dependent on protection by social superiors. Quite a few of my informants owed their position with the post office or the railways to the fact that their father or mother worked as a servant in the house of a higher official. Influence is also of crucial importance in trying to change one's position from a temporary to a permanent basis. For that, you need the help of '*mamas*' and '*kakas*' from higher circles, I was repeatedly told. This means that you work in the boss's house in your spare time, run errands for him, occasionally take him some liquor, a chicken, some mutton, or some other treat—in other words, you make your services available and behave as a 'chamcha' (literally, spoon), that is, you bow and scrape.

G. was asked to transport and afterwards clean the cooking vessels and utensils at the marriage party of one Desai's daughter. He didn't get any money for this work but he asked this man, who was a clerk in the railways, to help his son getting a job. By accident, because another labourer died, and because his son's wife worked in the household of one officer, he became permanent already after three years. Now, he works in the parcel van and earns about Rs 250.

The formal bureaucratic rules concerning employment do not appear to be followed in practice by the regional government agencies. This situation is even more apparent in local administration—the municipal apparatus, the district offices—where posts are more or less at the disposal of local politicians who court key members of their rank and file with favours of this kind.

Standardized procedures for securing personnel in the private sector are, as far as they exist, rendered completely meaningless, a fact usually not deemed necessary to conceal from the outside world. But in big companies such as Atul, a semblance is kept up. In addition to forms of favour such as those described above, we find here that even more so than in government institutions, positions are bought with either commodities (durable consumer goods such as a radio, a cupboard, or a refrigerator, but also a parcel of land, a mango garden plot) or with money. People are prepared to put themselves in deep debts for this, which, of course, only those households with greater financial means at their disposal can afford. However, this practice is generally restricted to those cases where there is some prospect of getting a fixed appointment. In small-scale enterprises, such as most of the workshops in the industrial estates near Bulsar town, new personnel are recruited from families or circle of friends of current personnel (the more skilled of whom are generally members of artisan and other intermediate castes) through the intercession of a third party or by direct request to the owner.

The hardly skilled nature of the majority of work and the absence of the security and protection which characterize the formal sector means that the method of employment differs only slightly from recruitment in the informal sector, as described in the previous paragraph. It is indicative that labourers in the workshops also call themselves 'chhuta', even if they have worked for the same employer for a long time.

Apart from the personal advantages derived by a broker exercising his influence, ranging from deference shown to him to more material benefits, it also is in the interests of employers to eliminate the impersonal mechanisms of selection. Following this procedure increases their hold over workers. In the first place, the newcomer is aware of the fact that he has been selected not because he had the best papers but rather because he had the best influence. Thus, he is tied up in his loyalties and is placed in a position of dependence. Moreover, the person who intervened on behalf of the newcomer is responsible to the employer for his work and behaviour. This element plays such an important role that several informants stated that they refused requests made to them to use their influence, expressing a disinclination which increased according to how far the favour seeker stood from his household. They were afraid that commitments of this type would reduce their own autonomy, and they wanted to avoid being held co-responsible if the work performance or behaviour were not up to the expected standard.

Above all, owners of workshops particularly try to systematically avoid any formal procedure of employment in order to maintain as much freedom as possible and to reduce their obligations towards their workers to a minimum. The limited size of the enterprise, haphazard and elusive management practices, fluctuations in production, and last but not least, the lack of efficient government control, all contribute to a type of employment which barely distinguishes this section of the formal sector from that situation which I have outlined for the informal sector.

## WORKING CONDITIONS

As we have already seen, casual labour is the rule in the informal sector. All those who fall in this category are grouped under the collective term 'chhuta'. This work is, in many respects, far from being specific in character, first, with regard to the context in which it is carried out. There is little task differentiation, a fact which facilitates mutual exchangeability, and the worker's position is weakened by the abundant supply of labour available. Second, the work is not specific insofar as labour may be spent in entirely different economic locations on consecutive days, although this does not substantially alter the nature of the work performance. Finally, casual labour is not bound by sex or age; both men and women, young and old, generally do the same work under approximately the same conditions.

As well as being exchangeable, this type of work is typically unskilled in nature. Most people under this category have had no, or at the most a few years of, education. They are illiterate or can only sign their name, an achievement which is very important because it implies that one is not dependent on a thumb print in order to establish one's identity. Even those who have a long record of employment behind them differ only insofar as they have experience in a greater variety of work but have generally not become more skilled through this.

Their extensive wandering, both inside and outside the district, fit into the total picture of a rambling irregular existence. The work of most personnel in the small artisan shops seems, in comparison, to be much more routine in character. A set number of manual functions can be acquired in a relatively short time but they do not allow any claim for payment higher than that of a day labourer.

Workers in shops and trades, although they cannot derive any rights from their fixed employment, are nevertheless assured of more regular work. Their work performance is less improvised in character and less subject to daily fluctuations. This difference, on the other hand, should not be overstated as indeed many small business enterprises also undergo severe fluctuations in production as a result of, for example, delay in the supply of raw materials or difficulties in marketing the final products. For instance, an embroidery shop may not be able to obtain gold or silver thread or in the slack season sales of their expensive hand-embroidered saris come to a halt. While they may reach their peak on the Bombay market around Divali or during the wedding season in spring, they will drop off and virtually cease during the rainy season. This stagnation and sensitivity to often uncontrollable circumstances which characterize production are countered in a very flexible manner, namely, by laying off the personnel (usually, only a few labourers per establishment), naturally without any compensation.

Working hours, especially those for day labourers, are not specified. These labourers are often engaged not on the basis of a day's work but on the basis that they must complete a particular job, a task which might take only a few hours or which might necessitate working until late at night. A lot of casual work, for example, digging a piece of land or transporting a load, is given on piece rates or on contract, so that the worker sets his own tempo. Doing heavy manual work at irregular points of time is inevitable for the existence of the day labourer. The disreputable nature of their work together with sometimes long periods of waiting and hanging around have earned casual labourers the reputation of being unmotivated and undisciplined, although, in fact, the discontinuity and unfavourable circumstances of their work are to blame for these supposed qualities. Workers in the small industries exert themselves no less strenuously but, on the average, they work for longer hours and in doing so, they do enjoy a greater degree of regularity. Still, rises and falls of a seasonal kind do occur and these result alternately in business closures and overwork. Thus, for the entire informal sector, there is little standardization of working times. In this connection, it may be stated that my fieldwork into these work situations did not follow a set pattern but was conducted either in the morning, afternoon, evening, or night.

Remuneration in the informal sector varies widely. Much casual labour is paid at piece rates or with a fixed amount for the completion of a particular piece of work. Calculated on a daily basis, casual workers earn an average of Rs 3, equivalent to the legally fixed minimum at the time of this research, and sometimes a little more. The law stating this minimum is not enforced for casual work and the assumption upon which it is based, namely, that this amount be earned daily, certainly does not apply in this case. Viewed over a longer period, the income of day labourers falls far short of the officially established minimum. If their low income is the result of the unskilled nature of the work they do, then the fluctuations to which their income is subject are due to the irregular demand for their services.

In the yard of Bulsar's large railway workshop, long-distance trains are loaded with coal brought from Orissa and Bengal. Coal loading is given out on tender to a dealer who, with the help of a jobber, has gangs of labourers continually at work. The day gang begins at eight in the morning, the night gang at eight in the evening; shifts are changed once a fortnight. Work is carried out according to various systems. One group of 20–5 men and women from Uttar Pradesh works on the basis of 1 rupee for every ton of coal carried. If there is enough work, together they can get through 80–90 tons per day. The other workers are recruited locally. They are divided into teams of six, men and women, several of whom are related to one another; they form the teams themselves. My information shows that they generally come from various castes, although these castes are inevitably low in the social hierarchy. The work is tiring and dirty. Two members of each team (usually men) shovel the coal into baskets; the others then carry it, at a trot, to the train and then empty them into the coal wagon via a running board. On the way back, they receive a 'chhapa' (a small metal disc) from the 'mukadam'. When the work is finished, the foreman of each team counts and notes down the total number of discs and then hands the result over to the 'mukadam', who likewise counts them. The payment for 100 baskets is Rs 2.25. Money is paid out once a fortnight when the shifts are changed over. The foreman collects the money and divides it among the members of the team on the basis of attendance during the past two weeks, every one person receiving the same amount. I recorded the earnings of one team over a period of 11 nights. During this period, three of the six members did not turn up at all. They were all members of the same household, who had to cut grass for the man who owned the land where their hut stood and to whom they were also in debt. They earn no more than Rs 1½–Rs 2 per day, cutting grass, but they could not refuse to fulfil obligations in this way. Of the remaining three, A. came ten nights, B. nine nights, and C. eight nights. Depending on the amount of work available and on the attendance of the team, their earnings over this period ranged from nil to Rs 7 per night. Trains loading coal come very irregularly, and during three nights, none came at all. At times when there is nothing to do, the members of each team sit or recline around a fire which, on winter nights, they set up along the railway track to drive away the cold. They chat, play cards, or just sleep. During the total number of nights that they were present, A., B., and C. earned Rs 2.10, Rs 2.60, and Rs 2.60, respectively, on the average. These notes concerning coal porters hold more or less true for gang work in other fields also. From the data I collected about transporting timber—the centre of the timber business is a village on the edge of Bulsar town—we find the same picture: minimal task differentiation, irregular working hours with severe fluctuation in earnings, periodic absenteeism of team members because of commitments elsewhere, and so on. The main difference is that at the head of each team—which are somewhat larger, varying from eight to 15—is a 'mukadam'. He supervises the work and receives the payment from the dealer at the end of the day, later distributing it among the team members at the bazar in town.

Workers in artisan business, small restaurants, trades, shops, etc., have the advantage of more continuous employment, but the price many of them pay for this advantage is generally longer hours of working for a lower daily wage. Although their wages are dependent up to a point on age and experience—the latter is especially relevant in piece work—these are not uncommonly lower than Rs 3 per day.

S. has worked in a grain business during the past two years, being paid Rs 2 for a 12-hour day. He could not support his family on this and so, about a month ago, asked for a rise. When this was refused, he left the job.

R. has been employed as a cook in a 'hotel' for the past 11 years, working from half past five in the morning until late at night. He now gets Rs 3 per day. His younger brother who worked as a waiter in the same establishment left when the boss refused to pay him more than Rs 2 per day.

L. has worked in a handloom shed since childhood. At first, he was only allowed to wind the yarn on the bobbins but later, he learned how to weave. He gets Rs 1.75 per yard, and can make one or two bedspreads, the product of the business, in a day. In other handlooms, payment is fixed at Rs 2½ per day. He himself is able to earn, by piece rate, about Rs 3 per day and thus, Rs 70–Rs 75 per month.

H. works in a furniture workshop for a monthly wage of Rs 75; his younger brother earns Rs 20–Rs 25 as apprentice to a carpenter. T., in contrast, receives Rs 10 per day from his employer for his work as a skilled mason but naturally, only when there is work available.

N. has been working in an embroidery business for ten years and, if there is enough work, earns from Rs 105 to Rs 110 per month as a skilled craftsman. There is no extra payment for overtime. His younger brother, who is around 18, has been taken on as an apprentice and receives 50 paise per day. His wage will be increased after longer service and greater experience. Craft enterprises such as these are 'sweatshops' in the classic sense of the word: the small staff, never more than five or six people, work with a few, generally simple machines in a small stuffy room with little light or ventilation. Finally, there are domestic servants, generally but not always women. These women work from 7 a.m. to 12 p.m. or 8 a.m. to 2 p.m., but also sometimes till the evening, and receive a monthly wage ranging from Rs 5 to Rs 15. In case a lower salary is paid, they receive one meal a day and get leftover food and cast-offs to take home, and sometimes a sari once a year (at Divali). Particularly young women, who are still strong, work in various households in one day but for a shorter period of time and less remuneration in each house. Girls up to the age of 14 are employed for light domestic duties such as filling water pots or looking after children. If they do this for the whole day, then they are given lunch and dinner and 1–2 rupees for the month.

We can again clearly see from the above survey that an analysis of working conditions in the informal sector can only be carried out on the level of the household. Establishing the nature of individual conditions says little of the life that these people lead. The household consists of a number of individuals, the greatest possible proportion of whom contribute to securing an income. Not all of them work continuously or full-time, but the consequences of temporary or partial unemployment are absorbed as much as possible by the household as a whole. Often, even after enlisting all available manpower, the household cannot raise enough money per head to subsist even at the minimal level.

By obtaining credit, they attempt as much as possible to cover this shortage, a rather loose concept indeed. Casual workers who must resort to day labouring suffer most in this respect. Perhaps they can try to get an advance from someone who employs them every now and then, but this will result in only a few rupees. For a larger amount—a wedding or sickness, for example, or for settling debts that run up too high—the women appeal to the higher-caste households where they work. This very relation can often be traced back to a debt to that family, sometimes even incurred in a previous generation. All members of the household are inevitably obliged to put their services at the disposal of this 'benefactor' and thereby, if necessary, to free themselves from other tasks.

Those labourers who work more or less continuously for the same boss likewise have a chance of getting credit, an advantage which partly compensates for their lower earnings. They would otherwise never be able to afford an expenditure of Rs 100 or more incurred through a major event or by an emergency. However, there is no question of their having a right to credit; indeed, one must literally implore the employer for it time and again. Generally, it follows that the looser the relationship with the employer, the less inclined he is to advance credit. He also tries to cover his risks by demanding a security or by supplying the money through a middleman. Thus, members of a labour gang can solicit an advance only through the 'mukadam'; in case of default, the latter is also held responsible. Providing credit is an excellent means of demanding labour under the most favourable conditions: the person in debt is bound to work whenever it suits the creditor best, and indeed not only he but also other members of his household must make themselves available, and finally, be satisfied with remuneration lower than that on the free market.[5]

Casual workers try to lessen the risks by spreading their sources of credit, but in this way, they are exposing themselves to the possibility of mutually conflicting claims on their labour, again a case in which the household acting as a unity can provide a means of escape. The selling of labour on credit, characteristic of the insecurity of the casual worker's existence, is a specific trait of the informal sector. As will be shown later on, payment in the formal sector, generally, is only attendant upon completion of the work.

In conclusion, working conditions in the informal sector have very pronounced personal overtones. The existing variations, even with respect to the one type of work, are great and the employer's treatment is highly arbitrary. Social security, government protection, and the assistance of other protective arrangements are absent for that section of the working population which is, in fact, the most vulnerable. Workers who generally work on a semi-permanent basis for one boss hope for the continuation of their work, for as long as possible, for as much credit as possible, and for as much consideration as possible, but they carry no hopes for fixed appointment or legal security and protection. In their circumstances, that would be highly unrealistic. Casual workers also try to diminish the insecurity of their living by establishing dependency relationships. Some of these households are tied to families of higher caste by paternalistic bonds, bonds which are utilized in finding work, perhaps in helping their children to receive an education, in confronting illness, unemployment, and other setbacks, in covering deficits in day-to-day expenditure, that is, generally gaining favours and assistance. In cases where this succeeds without too much difficulty and tension, it comes as no surprise to hear from an informant that 'it's good for the type of people like us to live in the shadow of a Desai family'. Members of work gangs also maintain relations with a 'mukadam' which bear a somewhat paternalistic imprint. Contract labour is made illegal since 1971, but indeed it would seem that, were this law enforced—which is far from being the case—working conditions would suffer rather than benefit. That vertical relations are personally coloured and contain affectionate elements does not detract from the fact that the inherent dependency results from the pressure of circumstances. Sometimes, workers in the informal sector are thrown upon the favours of a more or less feudalistically oriented patron, but more often they are at the mercy of employers who behave like ruthless exploiters.

The relatively rare occurrence of an independent, autonomous existence that is in any way commensurable with life on a reasonable level of material well-being and human dignity, is no justification for idealizing all kinds of dependent forms of existence.

Conditions in the formal sector should approximate the reverse of those dominating the informal sector. To what extent is this the case?

The first essential element is the establishment of regular employment, a labour arrangement which is definitive for, though limited to, employment in the government bureaucracy and in the larger private enterprises. Workers in the formal sector are less mobile, in the sense that they change jobs less frequently, which does not however necessarily mean that they are tied to the same work location year after year. In many government institutions, rules have been set up for the circulation of their personnel. Thus, in the postal service, lower functionaries like postmen are periodically placed in other departments, while staff from the rank of clerk upwards must be prepared, in order to get promotion, for transfers within or even outside the district. This does not detract from the fact that the employer does not change. Once in fixed service, one does not readily give up one's job.

This certainly applies to government positions in particular, which, by virtue of the employer, afford extra protection, but is also true of the private sector. Labour turnover in an enterprise such as Atul is negligible, a fact which is easy to understand given the security attendant upon permanency. These are, in fact, the prebends in today's hierarchy.

Work in the formal sector is more specific in nature. To begin with, it is more or less an easily distinguishable dimension of social existence, generally tied to a fixed time and place. A random example of what I mean by this is the distinction between working days and free days (Sundays and holidays), a contrast which has little or no significance for many workers in the informal sector. Overtime, that is extra work which is paid for, is an indication of formal labour relations.

Also indicative of the greater specificity is the more rigid standardization of tasks and the specialization of work performance within narrow limits. Exchangeability is not within the natural order of things but is rather dependent on training and experience. The majority have at least passed primary school (PSC). Higher prerequisites, namely, secondary school certificate (SSC) or a college degree, are established for typical 'service' positions. Manual labour is less dirty and more skilled in nature, moreover implying a greater use of machinery, in the formal sector.

Finally, there is much greater task differentiation in the work process, the various functions being attuned to one another without being identical or mutually exchangeable. The greater variety in work also opens up the possibilities of a career perspective. By attending courses and training programmes, whether or not given in-service, a worker can qualify for a higher position. Promotion is possible on the basis of merit. The government bureaucracy, in particular, has a very fine gradation into scales and ranks, the latter being graduators for the evaluation of the relative social distance both inside and outside one's sphere of work.

H., after 12 years of temporary service, has passed the exams for postman and in acquiring this post, has passed through all scales. He would like to have a try at becoming a clerk but he cannot read or write well enough. Some of his colleagues who have already been promoted had taken private lessons but he can't afford this. Also, he can see no possibility of learning any English. He wants to try to learn by heart the five stories on the test, which have been the same ones for years now, and also the questions on them, which are also invariably the same. He is relying on a combination of swotting and 'lagvag'. However, his chances of successfully crossing this barrier are doubtful, especially since there are better qualified people climbing the ladder from below all the time.

It has already been described in detail earlier how far from truth is that all workers in the formal sector have a fixed position. This is true both inside and outside the private sector. In spite of what I was told by an Atul official, not all new employees are made permanent after a relatively short time (3–6 months). The staff of some departments is virtually entirely made up of temporary personnel. The actual conditions differ from the formal sector's concept of them in other respects also. Especially in the lower echelons, work is less specific and less skilled and the worker is thus easily replaceable. Similarly, work is not restricted to a fixed time or location, especially for temporary workers.

The post office was once called '*Desai na raj*', the exclusive realm of the Desais. All of the higher personnel belonged to this caste, and postmen and other subordinates had to work in their houses as well. At least that time has gone, was the comment of the informant who told me about it. But he is not aware that for his colleagues working in temporary service, the situation has not changed. Outside working hours, they do small jobs for their boss and other superiors, hoping for their mediation in gaining a permanent position.

Also, gratitude for a service rendered, for example, being given a job, necessitates making one's free time available to a benefactor, doing odd jobs, running errands, and so on. People at this level have little else but their labour with which to reciprocate.

About 8 years ago, D. got a job in a rice mill through the help of a Parsi to whom his father was a domestic servant. Even now, he works every morning from 4 to 8 in this Parsi's house before going to his job, his wife then taking over until 5 in the evening. Also, in the evening, he must return and do the chores. Together they earn Rs 25 per month for this. One hears more or less identical tales from many workers whose hut stands on a piece of land which they do not own and who must therefore carry out services for the landowner, sometimes even during the time reserved for working for an employer in the formal sector.

Employment in the small metal, textile (power looms), plastics, and chemical enterprises designated as workshops and having no more than a few dozen workers means working conditions similar to those I have called characteristic of the informal sector. Of their personnel, only those with administrative, technical, and supervisory functions—if indeed these are not united in the person of the owner or a member of his family—can regard themselves as being more or less fixed in their positions; only more or less, since many workshops have a rather precarious existence. Production is either maintained or then falls off for perhaps a long period of time depending on market conditions and the availability of raw materials and electricity. Regular employment says very little under these circumstances. The flexibility characteristic of the owner of such a factory under these conditions is made possible by laying off his personnel which has temporarily become redundant. Their ingenuity in coping up with this situation is more remarkable than the flexibility shown by their boss, which is so often praised in literature on entrepreneurial behaviour.

Schooling and/or occupational skill are demanded for the generally limited number of specialized functions in the work. Thus, it is mainly members of intermediate and higher castes, of the former, especially the artisan castes, who come under consideration. The remaining workers belong to the category of 'helpers', a rather vague term signifying those who, on the basis of experience and capacity, are given somewhat more specialized tasks, as well as those doing unskilled work for which experience and skill are not necessary. The latter are easily replaceable but indeed, all those who do not belong to the higher trained core remain outside industrial legislation concerning the wage level and social security, regulations covering dismissal, work safety regulations, etc. Thus, by splitting the enterprise into small, seemingly independent units, each with no more than 10 labourers, the rules and regulations under the Factory Acts can be circumvented.

The law stating that temporary workers must be appointed on a permanent basis after a set period of time can also be skirted by regularly firing and hiring part of the labour force. This is but one instance of regulations which, though meant to provide protection, produce, in practice, the reverse effect for exactly those workers who are in the weakest position. It also happens that the owner of a workshop entrusts all dealings with personnel, including recruiting, to a reliable member of his staff. In this case, a *'mehtaji'* takes charge and deals with the workers, dismissing them at his discretion, any time. In keeping with this, the turnover of unskilled personnel is high.

Regular working hours are adhered to. Office work, in particular, has a uniform rhythm, although this is less true for lower personnel such as messengers, sweepers, and watchmen who, besides their actual work, have to do all kinds of odd jobs. Industries also have fixed working times, for example, 8 a.m.–12 noon and 1 p.m.–5 p.m. Some factories and some departments of the railways work continuously on a shift system. For example, the factory personnel at Atul are divided into three shifts: 7 a.m.–3 p.m., 3p.m.–11 p.m., and 11 p.m.–7 a.m. Smaller workshops that work round the clock and which employ labourers on a temporary basis manage with two shifts of 12 hours each.

Not everyone can stand up to this. M. worked alternatively on day and night shifts at a power loom, doing 12 hours straight on piece rates. He received 10 paise per metre and could earn Rs 4–5 per day if he worked hard. He stopped doing it a few months ago. The combination of long hours and strenuous work, together with the long distance he had to cover every day—walking there with a lame leg one-and-a-half hours each way—proved too much for him.

One of the reasons why performance in the formal sector is characterized by greater regularity also within the hours of work is that labour is usually attuned to machines. Further, there are regulations concerning time off in the government bureaucracy and large private enterprises. Thus, post service personnel can have one free day per 11 working days, and also have the right to 20 free days per year on half pay. The immediate superior considers this type of regulations more as favours he can grant at his own discretion rather than as something which must be adhered to. This arbitrariness is, however, still less than in the case of temporary workers in government institutions and in small workshops where similar regulations are not applied at all. In these cases, requests from workers for time off are either refused ad hoc or granted, naturally in the latter case without remuneration. It is less risky to simply stay away without having asked for approval beforehand. A high degree of absenteeism results, which is, once again, interpreted as a sign of irresponsibility and lack of discipline among these labourers. The greater regularity of work, even of shift work for that matter, allows workers in the formal sector to follow a fixed daily schedule. As a consequence, they are able to lead more orderly lives.

Workers with a fixed income, this being typical for conditions in the formal sector, are paid every month or every fortnight. In the public sector, this income is not only dependent on the rank or grade but also on the number of years of service, a small rise being periodically given until the maximum for that scale is reached. In addition, those who are employed on a permanent basis also receive a dearness allowance.

A few random examples: G., a postman, has a basic wage of Rs 85, to which is added his dearness allowance (DA) of Rs 100. V. is a skilled worker in the railway workshop and earns Rs 159 per month plus Rs 122 DA. S., peon in a bank, earns on the average Rs 175 per month, a little more with overtime. B. is a cleaner with the state bus service and, as unskilled labourer, gets only Rs 110, including DA. T. is pointsman in the railway traffic division and nets a total of Rs 150 per month, or somewhat more if he works on night shift once a fortnight (12 a.m.– 8 a.m.). H. has reached the position of cabin man with the railway and earns a total of Rs 258 per month. An unskilled worker at Atul has an income from Rs 225 per month upwards.

Calculated on daily basis, the incomes of established workers are generally much higher than in the informal sector. To a large extent, this difference is based on the size of the dearness allowance. This amount is attuned to the cost-of-living index, and the steep price increases over the past years have meant that this allowance is sometimes higher than the actual wage. Permanent labourers in large private enterprises have the right to an annual bonus: 2–4 per cent or more of their annual basic income. At retirement, for which fixed age limits are set—58 years of age in the postal service—a lump benefit is given from the so-called provident fund. Workers pay a monthly premium for this, which is deducted from the above-mentioned wages. Sickness expenses are paid, and in addition, large enterprises such as Atul and the railways also have their own dispensaries for the treatment of personnel and their dependents.

Finally, there are various other facilities such as the provision of work clothes and, as in the example of the railway colony, private housing, and a cooperative store selling the basic necessities which are priced somewhat lower and which can be bought on credit, payable at the end of the month.

One must keep in mind, however, that these facilities are exclusively for workers in permanent employment. Even labourers who have, for example, worked for many years for the railway on a temporary basis have no right to a dearness allowance and indeed, some of them are even not covered by the Minimum Wages Act. They can only claim medical treatment when their illness is due to some accident which has occurred during working hours. In small factories, we find that both the conditions and the ratio are even more unequal. Only a small established core is able to bring in a daily wage of more than Rs 5–6, whereas the great majority earn far below this figure, and also do not profit from the extra facilities designed to promote social security.

On the other hand, the security and protection enjoyed by the most favoured should not be overrated, since their advantage is only relative and can easily disappear. During the course of my research, production at Atul was cut drastically time and again over a period of months—this was due, first, to excessive stocks and then, later, to power restrictions introduced by the government to cope with shortage of energy. This was accompanied by wage freezing, all kinds of curtailments, and by large-scale laying off of personnel. There are also various cases of permanent workers losing their job as a result of sickness.

N. was a postman but was dismissed when he contracted tuberculosis. G., a welder at the railway workshop for 18 years, was troubled by weak eyes and, after a medical examination, was instructed to undergo an eye operation. When this failed, he was dismissed with Rs 1,500 from the provident fund. Now, he is dependent on what his wife earns working as a maid.

Workers in the formal sector have more avenues of credit at their disposal; their social security, although much better, is not so great that many of them do not have to resort to credit. First, they may, after a number of years, draw on part of the amount which they have paid by way of premium into the provident fund. These loans are used to finance larger expenditures and are paid back by reductions to the monthly salary on an instalment basis. Further, there are mutual credit clubs which have a limited number of members who contribute every month to a common fund. An informant told me that the club he belonged to has a total of 25 members, all of whom worked in the same department of the railway. They each pay Rs 5–10 per month and the funds are controlled and administered by a clerk. Everyone trusts him, and also one another. Those who draw a loan must pay interest of 2–4 paise per rupee per month and two or three other members must stand as guarantors for him. At the bottom of the formal sector, workers with low incomes also try to make loans for which they approach personnel in higher ranks, but this is almost always only limited to small amounts of 3–5 rupees, intended only to cover a daily shortage or a sudden expense. Workers in the small establishments of the private sector, and in workshops, must fall back on their employers for larger loans. However, only those who have served for a considerable period of time and proven themselves reliable workers (the standards for judging this being diligence, competence, and meekness), can hope to receive loans. Such loans are prudently and scantily given and are recovered in instalments by periodic deductions from the wages. The debts are seldom completely paid off, as before this stage is reached, there usually arises some new emergency necessitating, at the very minimum, postponement of final payment. These tried sources of credit have the advantage that at least the interest, as far as it is demanded, does not prove to be an insurmountable obstacle to settling the debt. What we are dealing with, in fact, is loans and advances which stand in close relationship to remuneration for the work done and which sometimes are even viewed by the parties concerned as an integral part of wage payment. In spite of their generally higher pay and thereby greater access to credit facilities, workers in the lower categories of the formal sector also find that all of the financial means which are actually or potentially at their disposal are not sufficient to counter all eventualities. H., for example, has a permanent position with the railway and receives a net monthly wage of Rs 131 (Rs 142 minus Rs 11 premium for the provident fund), out of which, however, Rs 34 per month are taken to cover debts. He can, of course, borrow the money from usurers at an interest of 12–24 paise per rupee per month. Some moneylenders do this to supplement their income, while others make a career of it. H. tells me that you can even wake them up in the middle of the night, 'but every knock on their door has already cost a rupee'. He has borrowed Rs 100 from one of these moneylenders and is trying to pay it back in monthly instalments of Rs 2–5. Every pay day, the creditor or his agent is waiting outside the office. However unattractive a loan made under such circumstances is, at least it affords permanent workers another possibility of countering a crisis. The regularity of their work makes them eligible for credit, as opposed to the 'chhuta' categories who live from day to day. The only thing that these people have to offer as security is their labour. And there is too much of that already.

The greater social security, the establishment of legislation, and the provision of facilities resulting from this, clearly explain why the formal labour system is also designated the 'protected sector'. There is a greater degree of occupational security, which is the result of the more specific character of tasks and positions and the lesser exchangeability of more specialized labour. Relations with the employer are less personal in nature than those in the informal sector. The worker's obligations and rights are clearly defined.

The more precise definition of rights and responsibilities and the greater objectivity do not, however, take away the fact that workers are under the control of their immediate superiors, who put their own interpretation on the rules and regulations and thus create a personal dependence on them. However, this arbitrary exertion of individual power has certain limits. Thus, the conclusion that labour relations in the formal sector are more standardized remains valid.

Moreover, this standardization is controlled by the government. A government labour officer is stationed in Bulsar who is responsible for seeing that labour legislation is indeed adhered to in the district.

Workers covered by the various Factory Acts can direct their individual or collective grievances to him. He also visits industries to check whether the minimum wage is being paid, whether the obligation to pay annual bonuses is being enforced, and so on. His colleague in Navsari is responsible for checking whether the more technical regulations are being followed: safety requirements, a working day of no longer than eight hours, rules concerning the amount of light and ventilation in the work location, and so on. In cases of labour conflict, the help of the government labour officer is enlisted to settle disputes. If an agreement cannot be reached between the parties here, then the case goes to the Labour Court in Surat; appeals can be made to the Industrial Court in Ahmedabad.

The government labour officer, during an interview in his office, rattles off the various labour laws, stating the year and number, the jurisprudence, and on further enquiry, even the clauses giving exceptions, all as if he were reciting holy passages from the Mahabharata. He could rightly be called the Brahman of the labour system and indeed, his behaviour is commensurate with this. He is a Brahman also in the sense that he caters only for a small section of the population, namely, those permanently employed in the formal sector, the top of the hierarchy;

he is also mostly concerned with the larger enterprises. He considers labour relations in the small industries, the workshops, and other small establishments to be outside his competence, a domain that is difficult to survey and control. Quite rightly so, since as we have already seen, the majority of personnel in this domain are temporary workers to whom industrial legislation does not apply. This is also true of temporary personnel in government institutions. Conditions considered to be characteristic of the formal sector indeed do not apply for most of these workers. The very slight difference between workers in the formal and informal sector is also apparent in their method of employment. Influenced by the abundant supply of labour, the minimal skill required for much of the work, and the invalidity of protective measures laid down in legislation, a substantial part of the labour relations in the formal sector has undergone a process of informalization.

## INTEREST BARGAINING

Summing up, we can say that government regulations concerning labour structure have a bearing on roughly only one-quarter of the working population. This is only a rough estimate, as official data concerning temporary workers on daily wages—household servants, personnel in shops and small establishments, work gangs under jobbers—is incomplete or entirely missing. This is indicative of the lack of real interest in exercising any control over the conditions under which the largest and most vulnerable categories of the population work. It is not difficult for employers to skirt even those regulations which are more general in scope—to a certain extent, this applies to the Minimum Wages Act, for example—because of the many loopholes, conditional clauses, and the half-hearted implementation of these regulations in the case of unskilled and low-paid labour. When no external guarantees are given for even the most minimal protection and security, we find that bargaining for interest occurs mainly on an individual basis.

Workers in the informal sector attempt to make their existence more secure by means of vertical relations. Contacts with employers are particularistic in nature. Employment is dependent on the momentary inclinations and impulses of those who use or hire labour. Working conditions also present a high degree of variety, and the provision of extra facilities depends on the whim of the employer—the worker cannot refer to standard custom or to what has been given to others. One does one's best to put the boss in a good mood and to arouse in him a feeling of leniency, so that he will give more than he would otherwise consider to be his minimal duty. Whatever he gives may vary from case to case, but it is usually very small.

For the same reason, namely, the need for assistance and protection, contacts with social superiors are also sought. These serve as an umbrella under which one can find shelter. Strong ties with a family of high caste afford a degree of protection which would be impossible to achieve on the basis of one's own status. These ties are not of an individual kind but rather embrace several if not all members of the household. In return for the services they render, they are granted a whole range of favours: land for a hut; mediation in finding work; assistance in the event of illness; a loan for a wedding; protection in conflicts with third parties; and acquiring any leftovers from the household of the high-caste family.

Ever since he was a child, D. worked for a Parsi household where his father also served. He used to drive the family's 'ghoda-gadi' but then, 15 years ago, he contracted elephantiasis and since then is unable to do regular work. Now and then, when his leg allows him, he does casual labour for Rs 2 or Rs 3 per day. But he also still works in the Parsi's house, cleaning pots and pans, for example. His wife and an unmarried daughter work for the whole day in the Parsi's house. His daughter is sexually at the beck and call of the Parsi. D. lives at some distance from the Parsi house and must come when he is called for. The land on which their hut is built belongs to the Parsi. In a small shed, built as an extension of the roof, they keep a cow, given to them by the Parsi when it was sick. After good care, the cow survived and its milk is now sold to the neighbours, although a certain amount must first be given to the Parsi every day. D.'s oldest son living at home has found a job at a rice mill through the Parsi. Before leaving in the morning, he first works for a few hours for the Parsi and also does the necessary chores after he comes home from work. His wife works as a casual labourer in construction, but if needed in the Parsi household, she must stay there. Another son is house servant to a related Parsi family in Bombay. Both D. and his married children were given money by the Parsi for their wedding. It is impossible to settle their debts; in fact, it increases from year to year. The only thing they can do is work for the Parsi's family for the rest of their lives.

Until his death, R.'s father was in the service of a Desai with whom he had moved from a village to Bulsar some 35 years ago. At that time, R. was 7 years old and he has worked for the Desai's family ever since. Behind the Desai's property was a stable where R. was allowed to live after the horse died. This accommodation is better than the average for unskilled workers of low caste. The Desai gave R. 200 rupees for his wedding and this debt has steadily risen over the years. He does not know how high the amount is now. He doesn't have to pay it back as the Desai knows that he simply isn't able to. But he has to work for the Desai whenever he needs him. His wife works full-time in their house and receives two meals in return. Because of the Desai's encouragement, R.'s three children have been able to receive an education. His two daughters still attend school. His son, who has already got his SSC, is employed on a temporary basis at Atic (a big industrial concern) through a nephew of the Desai who is a supervisor there. In cases of difficulty, R. can always turn to the Desai for help.

People try to accommodate themselves in these hierarchical, patronage-like relationships in order to secure work and the income necessary for supporting themselves. In doing this, they recognize the many and various obligations towards those people to whom they owe their survival, these commitments generally if not exclusively being realized in the form of labour. Dependency and the realization of it by all parties concerned is also a source of satisfaction for the benefactor. This type of relationship strongly resembles the 'hali pratha', the institution which formerly controlled relations between large farmers and agricultural labourers in the agrarian system (Breman 1974a: Chapter 4 especially).

Contact can also be made with employers through jobbers, and for those working regularly in labour gangs, this forms an important link in the promotion of their interests. The 'mukadam' is almost always from the ranks of workers themselves and belongs to the same low castes; thus, dealings with them are less hierarchical in nature. He pleads for their interests with the 'seth' and tries to persuade him to give a small advance (a 'khavti', literally, 'in order to eat') in slack periods, particularly the monsoon months, and acts as a go-between for the core members of the gang in their efforts to secure a larger loan. However, his power is largely derived: first and foremost, he is the agent of the 'seth'. Several 'mukadams' told me that they prefer not to recruit labour from their immediate social environment. Family members, for example, could make too many claims on him and also would be hard to call into line if their work performance was not satisfactory.

Casual labourers working on a day-to-day basis have even less chance of bargaining for their interests. To survive days or weeks of unemployment and to counter illness and other blows on their existence, they must have recourse to the artisans, shopkeepers, jobbers, contractors, and others who use their labour incidentally. But, as we have already seen, their solvency is virtually zero. They can only use cash to pay for their daily needs. They are virtually devoid of any contacts with possible benefactors. They have nobody to turn to and lack any props to fall back upon in times of minor or major crises. Their lack of connections means that they lead a threatened existence, absolutely and permanently. As the most obscure category in the informal sector, their size is often underrated and indeed, their very existence sometimes goes unnoticed by the upper strata of society. However, it would be misleading to describe their conditions purely in terms of isolation. In fact, they constitute a solid section of the social system, their function with this system being that of a reserve. Their function as a buffer is also definitive for the dependency characteristic of other categories. They do not form a secluded, self-contained segment of the labour force; on the horizontal level, a multitude of intensive relationships are maintained. This leads to the following question.

In the informal sector, is it possible to assume a stand on the basis of common interests? At first sight, the answer would seem to be 'no'. Largely because of their low education, people in the informal sector have a very restricted view of society. Illiteracy is the cause of much of their helplessness and their inability to act. The victims of these circumstances do not know what is going on in the world, except for what they might happen to see and hear at places like the bazar, and are unaware of either the existence of facilities designed to help members of low castes or of the means of gaining access to these facilities. Often, it is social superiors who 'show them the way', in exchange for tacit or explicit commitments. Thus, those very means which should be leading to the promotion of common interest are, in fact, used in such a way that vertical dependence on an individual basis is intensified. People seeking a living in the informal sector are naturally competitors in the struggle for the same scarce commodities, namely, employment and its resultant chance of making a living. In view of the abundant supply of labour, it is inevitable that conflicts of interest, both on an individual and institutional level, soon manifest themselves, for the very reason that labour relations are not standardized and protective measures are either lacking or not enforced.

Under these circumstances, there can be little stress on solidarity. Conditions for organization on a common basis are extremely unfavourable. Not a single informant in the informal sector was a member of any form of trade union. A researcher soon becomes accustomed to the conditions determining his theme of study and so it was that, after a while, I no longer asked these informants if they belonged to a trade union, since this question turned out to be totally unrealistic in the informal sector. In addition to the strong vertical ties binding many workers in the informal sector, there are also many other factors which hinder organization on a horizontal basis:

1. The non-specific, temporary character of much of the work, which makes it necessary to carry out a wide variety of activities on successive days and under widely divergent conditions: self-employed, working for a temporary employer, working on a contract basis, and so on.

2. In connection with this, great fluctuation in the work location and the mobility of labour virtually excludes the possibility of forming a common front.

3. A limited number of personnel is engaged in many work situations. Especially in the distribution sector (shops, small trade, 'hotels', etc.), and also in small industrial establishments, the number of workers varies from only one up to no more than a few, a fact which restricts the possibility of joining forces collectively.

4. The improvised nature of the existence, the result of trying to scrape some money together one day after the next, leaves little time or energy for a behaviour that is oriented to a long-term perspective.

5. Finally, there are sufficient sanctions to neutralize the effect of those who dare to stand up and act as spokesmen of collective interests. Claims, made either on themselves or their direct social environment (member of their families or of the same household), see to it that such 'nuisance' is called into line. Leaders who arise in certain cases to defend the interests of the luckless almost always come from higher social strata and are often self-motivated in what they do.

As we can already discern from the above-listed factors, poverty itself restricts the manifestation of solidarity. The provision of mutual aid is limited, and when exchange among social equals becomes lopsided over longer periods, the stronger party which emerges generally tends to loosen the relationship.

This also happens among members of one family and even members of the same household.

The following passage from my diary is based on information from my wife who helped in undertaking research into the daily budget of low-caste workers:

Today she visited L., a widow who works as a coal-porter. She can never be found at home at the same time. L. has two saris which, because of the dirty work she must do, she has to wash every other day without any soap. Her daughter occasionally gets cast-offs from the family for whom her husband used to work as a carpenter. The son is about 15 years old and earns good money as a porter with a smuggling gang. Today L. was sitting in her hut crying, beaten black and blue. Her son had done this to her when she asked for some money to make a meal.

Actually it's no longer possible to determine the daily earnings and expenditures of S. who lives on Halar Road. It is monsoon season and the rain is coming through the flimsy roof. Little can be destroyed inside. Through the outside wall you can look right across the hut to the other side of the street. S. is already old and also blind in one eye; he has been sick for some time now and can no longer do his work as a gardener. He has an argument with his wife, complaining that she hasn't given him anything to eat for weeks. He now confines himself to one side of the 1½ X 1½ m. hut while his wife and daughter sit on the other side sharing between them food she got from her household. A second daughter, who has a live-in job with another family, occasionally brings her father something to eat.

Squabbles between neighbours and quarrels between man and wife, or between parents and their children, are an integral part of poverty and of the contrasts and conflicts inherent in this wretched situation. But the notion of a state of mutual warfare is equally as inaccurate as the reverse concept of stereotyping the weakest categories of society as living together in natural harmony and sharing each other's lot. The latter is naturally out of question, but the fact still remains that there do exist considerable cementing forces.

This is primarily true at the household level. While the household may well disintegrate as a result of old age, long illness, or death of an important breadwinner, we find in the majority of cases that the members of the household are guided by the conviction that, acting together, they increase their capacity to survive and decrease their social vulnerability.

Outside the household, there is also the notion of relying on one another for information concerning work and income, that is, chances in life in general. This mutual dependency necessitates great tolerance and we find that conflicts only seldom harden into lasting, insurmountable oppositions. The lowest categories of the working population are bound to one another by contacts and activities which, existing as they do under the most unfavourable circumstances, nevertheless afford a minimum of orientation towards a social life.

Most work situations and locations do not generally act as crystallization points from which a common stand could be taken. Similarly, caste ties do not easily create feelings of solidarity in an urban environment of poverty. The multitude of castes, all of which are low in the social hierarchy and which are not spatially segregated, hinders the joining of forces on this basis.

The situation is different for both rural labour[6] as well as higher strata of the urban milieu—for these people, caste is a significant base for the organization of promoting interest.

The most important framework for integration among the urban poor is the neighbourhood. It is interesting to note that many informants when asked how they spent their leisure time, answered that they did not bother with other people, denied that they had any friends, and declared that they limited themselves to contacts within their own household. However, once my research moved further into those localities where workers live together, the presence of a 'we' feeling became more evident. In the evening, they sit together in groups, or in winter around the fire, and review the events of the day: what happened to someone, what somebody else heard, and so on. They ridicule and defame the behaviour of their social superiors and this acts as an outlet for their unrest and as a symptom of passive resistance. There is a general agreement as to who is to be blamed for the insecurity and dependency that characterize their existence. What unites all categories of the informal sector is their impotence and the feelings of consciousness they thus share.

Standardization of labour relations in the formal sector implies that one's rights and responsibilities are more or less precisely defined. The generally higher level of education means that workers are more familiar with the rules and regulations and know how to make use of them in cases that arise. Greater protection of rights cannot however provide any watertight guarantees against the arbitrary use or abuse of power by superiors and other people in high positions. Particularly the lower regions of the formal sector, used as they are to getting the rough end of a bargain in their social existence in general, simply have to put up with such treatment. This is an unfavourable basis for showing resistance, making an appeal, or asserting one's right. Obviously, it is better to try to maintain good individual relationships with people placed higher in the labour hierarchy. It is no surprise then to find that vertical ties of a personal nature are not restricted to the informal sector. Also, many people who have a permanent job owe their appointment, their promotion, or other facilities to the personal protection of their boss or employer, or to the intercession of an influential third party. Especially in cases of great social distance between benefactor and worker, this debt is settled in terms of displaying obedience and subservience. But the younger generation who have risen socially through the help they got in education and also through 'lagvag' in their employment, are inclined to refuse to carry out reciprocal services which may vary from working in that person's household to an explicit display of gratitude. Their parents, who are still strongly bound, bemoan this fact and fear the patron's displeasure. However, these observations do not detract from our assertion that the conditions for promoting interest on a collective basis are much more favourable in the formal sector than in the informal sector. To what extent is this reflected in the activities of trade unions? The rest of this section will be devoted to answering this question.

The various government institutions have their own unions and sometimes more than one in the same unit when higher and lower personnel are organized separately. In the postal service, only the clerks are covered by a union, the district branch of the postmen's union having ceased to function some years ago. I was told that this is the result of the failure of a national strike of lower personnel in 1969 which had been called to support the claim for an increase in the dearness allowance. The higher officials exerted great pressure among the rank and file so that they did not take part in the action; many of them remained at work merely out of fear of reprisals from their superiors. According to the former branch secretary, himself a postman, the strike failed because of the lack of unity. There have been no local activities since then and the union fees are no longer paid. The Western Railway Employees' Union, an affiliate of the Indian National Trade Union Congress (INTUC), is the largest union of railway personnel. When I asked an informant if he was a member, he replied: 'Why should I be, I've got a permanent job after all'. Many of his colleagues seem to agree with him. The monthly fee of one rupee brings few, if any, advantages. Many members themselves were of the opinion that the leaders of the union did nothing for them, only listened to what the 'big officers' said; they also showed other similar symptoms of dissatisfaction. One of the members who registered a complaint two years ago with the union concerning a transfer he did not want is still waiting for an answer, and he bitterly speaks about the high-handed behaviour of union officials who have never shown any interest in his case. One explanation for the lack of faith in unions and the lukewarm response to their activities by government personnel is that most negotiations are held on a national level. Local branch offices are not supposed to be active in promoting collective interests. The lower officials are faced with limitations in what they can do and are under strong pressure from the local management, sometimes giving in to them extremely easily.

Workers are thus quite justified in thinking that it is better that they themselves promote their individual interests in contacts with their superiors. It goes without saying that temporary workers in government institutions do not join trade unions. Their interests are not recognized and therefore, can hardly be promoted in any organized way. Also, in the large private concerns, the existence of a formal system of work regulations seems to impede rather than promote organized action among labourers. The trade union at Atul, for example, is not very active. The proposals of members, mostly factory personnel, concerning time-off or leave regulations, shift work, canteen facilities, uniform allowances, and so on are presented to the labour welfare officer. Important issues such as dearness allowance, bonus and gratuity, and so on, being covered under the law, are not subjects for local negotiation. The officials, themselves Atul workers, have been allotted a small office on the site in which to hold their meetings. I was assured that the management has established very harmonious relations with them. It is true that the government has introduced a formal framework regulating labour conditions and relations but a very important function of the trade union is to ensure that these regulations are, in fact, enforced. After further investigation, it became clear that this counterbalancing function is rendered impossible by the Atul management. The company was established in 1949 and production began in 1952. During the first years, there was no form of organization whatsoever, but in 1956, a company union was formed mainly from the skilled and unskilled workers, which then joined the INTUC. In 1958, a strike was called for the improvement of the poor working conditions of factory personnel.

The management agency in Bombay refused to give in to the strike and it lasted from May to October. That many of the strikers had the stamina to survive six months' loss of income can be ascribed to the fact that, as members of rural households in most cases, they could fall back on the yields from agriculture. Though production certainly fell off, it was however maintained by enlisting the services of white-collar personnel and by bringing in labour from elsewhere, who could be quickly fitted in because of the relatively high degree of mechanization. The management seemed to command better reserves and when a shift of newly hired workers was attacked while leaving the factory one night and some of them killed, the INTUC, in true Gandhian tradition, lifted the strike. Workers who had played an active role in the strike were dismissed. All parties concerned clearly felt that all the tensions and the sacrifices of workers had been totally in vain. For several years, every union action was 'doomed to failure'. But then in 1964, two skilled workers, chemists, took the initiative and set up a new organization, the Atul Kamdar Sangh (AKS), this time seeking to join the Bombay union for workers in the pharmaceutical industry. The response from the personnel was encouraging. At the first meeting, several hundred interested workers turned up and many of them became members. Learning from experience, the two initiators strove to get staff members and office personnel as well to join their organization. The popularity of the new organization was further enhanced when, through arbitration, several demands which had been rejected by the management previously were now conceded to. Then, the two leaders were accused by the management of encouraging communist infiltration in Gujarat, and when efforts to exert pressure on them to cease their activities failed, the management succeeded in setting up a new, more cooperative company union.

Department heads issued (and then collected again) forms saying that the undersigned had given up their membership of the AKS and joined the new union. The company paid the membership fees for the new union. In 1966, the two leaders of the AKS resigned from Atul. Since then, only the company union has functioned, 'a puppet union run by yes-men', as I am told by my informants in confidence.

My earlier conclusion—namely, that there is relatively little need for organized action in the formal sector since standardized labour conditions, guaranteed by legislation, allow the promotion of interest on an individual basis—can only remain intact if we ignore the political economy in which trade unions must operate in an area which is only lightly urbanized and industrialized.

This situation is even more apparent in the organization of collective interests in small industries in the private sector. The main factors hindering organization are the dispersed location of the factories and workshops; the limited number of personnel; the low level of education of workers; the predominance of temporary employment with a concomitant high degree of labour mobility; and the countless possibilities of escaping labour legislation.[7] On the basis of a description of two labour conflicts, I will deal with various aspects of the work of trade unions and their leaders, and with the way this work is balanced on the line dividing the formal and informal sector. The two strikes in question occurred during the period of my research.

While cycling to a nearby village, I passed factory A. situated on the highway from Bombay to Ahmedabad. About 15 men and women are standing in front of the gate shouting slogans. Under an improvised lean-to made of wooden sticks draped with cloth, a few workers are playing musical instruments to accompany the songs that are sung at regular intervals by the people standing around. Flags are hung on the fence running alongside the building and a board announcing the demands has been posted. The strike is already four days old and the strikers take turns in maintaining a round-the-clock picket. The strike is obviously not universal. There are workers inside the grounds doing their work as usual. The strike leader, a skilled worker from a high caste, explains that the owner has divided the factory into several units and that the personnel in departments other than his are too afraid to join in. This is already the second strike this year; during the monsoon, they had stopped work to press for a wage increase and for more favourable terms for gaining permanency. He is a rank member of the trade union, Valsad Jilla Kamdar Sangh (VJKS), which is affiliated to the Majur Mahajan Sangh in Ahmedabad, the famous textile workers' union formed on Gandhian lines. A week later, I met him again in the VJKS office at the bazar. The government labour officer had intervened in the conflict and the strike ended while they waited for a decision. But then, the owner first sacked 19 temporary workers and thereafter another 23 permanent workers, including the leader himself and two other union cadre members (both belong to intermediate castes and also skilled workers). This step, which is in violation of the rules of arbitration, is designed to frighten the workers. If the management won't revoke these measures within a few days, the action will be resumed. The next morning, the secretary of the VJKS is also at the office. From his base in Surat, he gives guidance on behalf of the INTUC to all activities of industrial trade unions in south Gujarat (Bulsar, Navsari, Surat, and Broach). His union has considerable political influence in the Congress party, a fact which can also be utilized in settling this dispute. Yesterday, a cabinet minister, himself coming from Bulsar, had a meeting with the labour commissioner in Ahmedabad. The commissioner immediately sent his second-in-command to Bulsar and today, a compromise will be reached which has already been accepted in advance as binding by the parties concerned.

A strike in factory B., on the outskirts of Bulsar town, on the road to Dharampur, lasted 31 days. When I visited the spot for the first time in the initial stage, the union leader who had organized the action was addressing about 40 men and women in front of the factory. Small groups of workers were taking turn in holding 24-hours hunger strike in order to lend weight to their demands. The yellow-orange flags over the main gate lend everything an almost festive air, but the atmosphere is tense. The factory owner refuses to give in or even to discuss the demand. He has threatened to have the strike declared illegal and to sack the workers.

The union leader quite rightly points out that many employers would rather spend more money to break the union than it would cost to make a few minimal concessions, merely out of annoyance that their otherwise undisputed lordship is being challenged by organized and collective opposition. Here also, not all personnel have joined the strike. The Bharatiya Mazdoor Sangh (BMS) is a relatively new union and one that is closely aligned to the politics of Jana Sangh, although this is vigorously denied by B.D., the strike leader. A year ago, the workers of this factory were organized by the VJKS. After some labour unrest, this organization had concluded an agreement with the owner which was to remain valid until 1976 and under the terms of which, the wage scale was to increase every year by an amount of no more than 30–70 paise. There was absolutely no mention of other facilities. B.D. utilized the dissatisfaction, which had steadily increased because of the rapidly rising cost of living, proposing his own union to the workers with the promise that he would really fight for their interests. He believed that the union leaders and the government labour officer had been handsomely paid to side with the management against workers. He kept harping on this theme in his address in front of the factory gates, and the strikers agreed in a chorus. They have a whole list of grievances, all of which boil down to evasion of industrial legislation. There are 29 women working in the factory who were hired through the 'mehtaji' to work for a daily wage varying from Rs 2 (the majority of them) to Rs 2.75 (only one woman in this category). Though called packers, in fact their work consists of preparing the acid baths and cleaning the boilers. The acid is so corrosive that it leaves white spots on the women's hands and they have to buy a new sari every month. Most of the 80 men working in the factory receive a monthly wage ranging from Rs 80 to Rs 115. I could see from the pay sheet that I was shown that even the most highly trained workers earned no more than Rs 5–6 per day. It is no secret that higher wages are recorded in the 'whitewashed' administration and that all kinds of amounts are entered which are, in fact, not given. A part of the profits from this is used to bribe government officials and trade union leaders. The official who goes round on inspecting tours is usually friendly enough to announce his arrival in advance, so that anything not in order can be temporarily removed from his sight. Furthermore, he is given only the 'whitewashed' administration—that is the bookkeeping, based on the rules of the formal system, which is specially maintained for the government—to check. This is then solemnly approved, of course, with a few marginal comments.

There is a law stating that a list of labour regulations must be hung up in the factory to inform workers of their rights. If during inspection visits, it is noticed that this is missing, the official is paid some 'hush money'. In order to keep wages down and to avoid having to employ people on a permanent basis, part of the labour force is periodically dismissed, but of course, not before their successors have been sufficiently trained. Time-off is given only as a favour and even absence due to illness is frowned upon. Indeed, there are many other complaints. In a letter to the factory management, B.D. has demanded the enforcement of the laws concerning remuneration, time-off, and other facilities which exist for this branch of industry, as well as the regulation governing the appointment of temporary workers to permanent positions. There was no reply—instead, one of the BMS active members within the factory was sacked on the spot. B.D., his reputation as a union leader being at stake, is forced to call a strike the very next day. The owner retaliates by requesting the government labour officer to declare the strike invalid. The labour officer maintains that the labour contract signed by the VJKS half a year ago is still valid. Moreover, B.D. has not conformed to the regulation stating that a strike must be announced well in advance. When I speak to B.D. again a fortnight later, he complains about the opposition he has met from other local trade unions. Also, other employers in the district have urged the factory owner not to give in to the BMS, whom they do not want to grow too powerful. A week later, it seemed that the end was in sight. He had managed to get a letter to the Minister of Labour, through a Member of Legislative Assembly (MLA) in Ahmedabad, in which he accused the government labour officer of partiality, but both this and his visit to the capital had produced no result. The owner has asked for permission to dismiss 16 permanent workers, all union members, on the grounds of absence from duty.

After a few days of negotiations back and forth, this number is reduced to five, all active union members. B.D. has no choice but to give in, for the workers are on the point of ending the action without his approval anyway. The strike has failed.

Trade unions complain about the lack of unity and awareness among workers in small factories and workshops. When it is difficult enough to unite workers of one factory, to bring about a sense of solidarity among different enterprises within the district is almost unthinkable. The position of the workers is determined not only by the difference in personal relations with the owner—he has several trusted hands who inform him about what is going on among the personnel—but also by caste, level of education, and of course, the type of employment (permanent or temporary). The differences arising from these factors can turn into conflict of interests. An important point in this connection is the extent to which workers are dependent on their work in the factory for their existence. Many labourers, especially those in workshops outside the town, belong to rural households and are thus landowners at the same time. Their work and income from agriculture is not enough to form the base of their living, but still it prevents total involvement outside it. Although they have a greater capacity to survive a strike (naturally, no strike pay is given by the unions), it is these very farmer-workers who balk at forming a united front against the employer. Relationships in small industry are characterized by both 'petty bourgeoisie' as well as by 'petty labour'.

Yet, notwithstanding these discord-inducing factors, it would indeed be shortsighted to cite the lack of solidarity as the main cause of the indifference to joining together in organizations that we find among lower categories of the formal sector. It is a question of whether the trade unions fulfil their set task, the promotion of workers' interests, in a manner that is both maximal and systematic. We can see from the two cases given above that there is intense competition between the various trade unions. As a Gandhian union, the VJKS is guided by the principles of conciliation of differences and consultation, and adheres in general to more established procedures. Thus, it carries more weight and influence with the government.

The BMS, on the other hand, is more radical, makes more far-reaching demands, and does not balk at head-on conflicts at the expense of arbitration regulations. This new union promises more for less, that is to say, it charges a monthly fee of only 50 paise instead of the usual one rupee.

The main issue in the mutual competition is the total number of members, which is the decisive factor in any exertion of power. The VJKS claims a total district membership of 3,000 and the BMS, 2,250, figures which are improbably high. The BMS claim, especially, has no base at all, but the VJKS figure is also much too high. When I was given the membership list to look at, I came to a total of 1,389 registered members spread over 46 enterprises throughout the district; 32 of them have less than 20 members. Even this figure is a little high since not all registered members still pay their fees. But then trade union leaders have the understandable tendency, when speaking about membership, to point out the imminent assimilation into their ranks of a large number of workers from several factories, which is going to bring about a drastic revision of their numerical importance.

In order to search for reasons why demands are not conceded to or only partly conceded to, and why decisions reached through arbitration are so slow to be implemented (it takes a long time to set the government machinery in action) and are often to the detriment of the workers, we must also look at the subject of corruption. One of the countless stories I heard about this topic concerned the role of government labour officers. Soon after a new official arrives in the district, he is still doing his rounds on a bicycle. A year later, he has already a scooter and in the end, when he is due to leave, he drives his car around the factories to introduce his successor and to tell him what his leniency would earn him from each owner in the way of 'haphta', a periodic bribe.

In view of their own experience, workers do not find this hard to believe but then, they have good reason for suspecting that trade union leaders are just as corrupt and serve their own interests by reaching a secret agreement with the factory owner. The attitude of most workers is also entirely pragmatic and is in no way dictated by ideological motives. They remain loyal to that union which they feel adequately represents their interests and are prepared to change over to any other union which seems to be able to achieve more. In contrast to the VJKS, which takes a moderate line and only succeeds in negotiations for marginal improvements in working conditions as a result, the BMS must show itself to be more aggressive. Things have gotten out of hand this time.

B.D. exposed himself too much and too quickly and, when his most important active member was dismissed, he was forced, in order to save face, to risk an unexpected strike. The negative outcome was a personal setback for him and was greeted with delight by the competition.

In fact, trade union leaders operate as entrepreneurs on the labour market in which they try to organize the supply side on the basis of their familiarity with labour legislation and with their knowledge of the channels on how to enforce the various rules and regulations and to make bargains with parties in demand of labour.

B.D. is the prototype of the union man, capable of gaining the trust of workers through his knowledge of the laws and regulations, which if needs be, he can rattle off mixing his quotations with English idiom. He is well abreast with the political and economic situation in the district, has gradually built up a reputation as a local politician, and has all sorts of links with higher levels for getting things done. At any rate, he likes to give the impression that he is part of a wide-reaching and influential network. Unlike most other leaders, he does not come from a high caste and thus cannot mingle with government officials on the basis of social equality, as can most others. On the other hand, B.D. is very close to the workers with whom he mixes on an equal footing and has considerable talent in public speaking. In addition to his union activities in the small factories and workshops, B.D. is also secretary to the municipal workers' union in the district town. However, both functions are not enough to keep himself busy, and to add to his income, he also recruits labour for temporary employment in Madhya Pradesh and Maharashtra, on behalf of a friendly relation. At the moment, his political affinities are with Jana Sangh. Until a few years ago, he worked for Brihanmumbai Electricity Supply and Transport (BEST) in Bombay, where he began his trade union activities as a front member of INTUC. Later, he went over to the Praja Socialist Party (PSP) union as a cadre member. After returning to Bulsar, he started out on his own. Two years ago, he took over the leadership of the Bulsar Municipal Employee's Union from a PSP man and substituted the connection with the INTUC with an alliance with the BMS, for which he is now the local man.

The entrepreneurial functions of this type of trade union leaders do not remain limited to interest bargaining in the labour market. Their following is also offered for sale in the political market, although dealings to this effect are comparatively more flavoured by ideological overtones. Political connections and the possibility of a change in loyalties are, of course, both part of a more general pattern. Particularly surprising was the defection, during the time of my research, of the leading union man of Bilimora, who controlled a large number of unions, from the Communist Party of India (CPI) to the New Congress Party. The former party, whose following was already feeble, had reached the end of the road. Also, in Bulsar, there are other examples of trade union officials shifting their political affiliations: previously, there used to be mutual shifts between the PSP and the Congress party; more recently, it has been shifts from the old to the New Congress Party. Union officials are also local politicians at the same time. This is partly due to necessity, since the exertion of pressure via political channels, or at least being able to threaten to exert this pressure, is an important factor in negotiations. By mobilizing a following, a leader can sell this scarce commodity to the highest bidder, but the gains must not fall below a certain minimum if the rank and file is to remain content.

Conversely, it is very important for political parties to secure strongholds in a society where the principle of organization is rather weakly developed. The area of formal labour is thus an important basis for gaining and exercising power.

The size and composition of the labour market must also be taken into account when assessing trade union activities in small industries. These organizations concentrate mostly on permanent workers since their rights are outlined most explicitly, at least on paper. This can even lead to a 'closed shop' mentality. Thus, the Dharampur Majur Mahajan union, when concluding an agreement with the owner of a large tannery in one of the centres, insisted on including a clause to the effect that the annual bonus should only be paid to those employed on a permanent basis.

The virtual absence of any government protection for temporary workers means that it is not very profitable to focus on this category. In their function as bargaining for interest, union leaders are, first and foremost, brokers who try to press for the enforcement of established labour regulations. Their attempt to organize as many workers as possible is balanced by the pains they must take to avoid, as best as possible, the informalization of labour relations.

By way of a concluding remark, I would like to reaffirm the fact that the peace and harmony supposedly characteristic of labour relations in Gujarat are certainly not apparent, at least in the southern part of the state. Factory owners from Bombay and other more turbulent areas are lured to south Gujarat by this stereotype image of peace and harmony, and also by the low level of wages. The latter is certainly true but the docility of the workers is partly fiction, partly resignation to the highly unfavourable circumstances of the moment.

No proof, however, is there of accepting and internalizing existing conditions. There were other strikes and labour conflicts during my stay besides the two I have mentioned, but I found out about these only afterwards. There is little publicity given to them and the contacts between workers are restricted by distance, illiteracy, and poverty. The exchange of information is not so much scarce as fragmentary in nature, the decisive factor in this being the many obstacles to a mutual joining of forces on a horizontal level.

## NOTES

1. One of the first publications to use this term is the report made in 1972 by the International Labour Organization (ILO) concerning the employment situation in Kenya. See also, E. Thorbecke (1973). Insofar as these are explicitly cited, labour relations in agriculture are included under the formal sector, generally without any further explanation. But if there are sufficient grounds for making a distinction, between a formal and an informal sector, then this is also very relevant for the agrarian economy—a relevance that is becoming steadily greater in view of the transformation in production methods under the influence of capitalistic tendencies.

2. In the first case, there is similarity to the contrast between the modern and the traditional sector, a contrast which was first constructed in the theory of economic dualism and then later, sharply criticized, quite justifiably so.

3. A vehicle consisting of a large wooden frame mounted on four bicycle wheels.

4. The head office and branch offices employ a total of 57 clerks, which I have divided according to caste, with the help of a few informants spread over various departments. Leaving aside the nine cases which cannot be considered because there was no information or at least no unanimity of opinion about their caste, I have divided the remainder into high, middle, and low. 19 clerks belonged to a high caste, including many Anaval Brahmans and other Brahmans, a few Baniyas, and Rajputs. Clerks belonging to intermediate castes numbered 16, most of whom were Kolis, followed by Mochis, Kumbhars, and members of other artisan castes. All 13 clerks from a low caste were Dhodhiyas. It thus seems that in the case of the clerks (who come under Class III), the regulation stating that 40 per cent must come from 'backward communities' has not been adhered to, while on the other hand, the percentage which has been attained refers to only one tribal caste which has a virtual monopoly in occupying these reserved posts.

5. For similar conditions concerning agricultural labour, see Breman (1974a: Chapters 7 and 8).

6. Lack of space prevents any elaboration of this difference. For mobilization of agricultural labourers on the basis of caste, see Breman (1974b).

7. Illustrative of the way in which an apparent victory can turn into the exact opposite is the case of one informant who worked in a small factory where the union finally managed, after great effort, to have the regulation introduced that workers must be taken on a permanent basis after six months of service. As a consequence, he was recently thrown out into the streets after five months' service.

# 2

# The Study of Industrial Labour in Post-colonial India

## The Formal Sector—An Introductory Review*

## CONSTITUTING LABOUR

In post-colonial India, labour began to signify work in *industry*; the 'worker' worked in the modern economy, towards which development would be rapid. The agrarian–rural order would soon be replaced by an industrial–urban one; labour economics was consequently closely associated with industrial employment, and the authors of authoritative textbooks on the shape of the working class and the trade union movement (for example, Crouch 1979; Pant 1965; Sen 1977; Singh 1971) felt able to largely ignore the vast majority of the working population.

The National Planning Committee, set up in 1940 by the All India Congress Committee and chaired by Jawaharlal Nehru, formulated policies that would be executed after independence. The Gandhian doctrine of small-scale village development was completely ignored. One of its working groups was on 'labour', but the only subjects it discussed were concerned with *industrial* relations, and the regulations it proposed were modelled on those in the already industrialized world. One major reason for this circumscribed focus was the fact that only the industrial sector had an established trade union movement.

Even more important than the unions was the leading role which the state would play in the transformation to come. A modern industrial

* Originally published as 'The Study of Industrial Labour in Post-colonial India: The Formal Sector—An Introductory Review', in Jonathan P. Parry, Jan Breman, and Karin Kapadia (eds), *The Worlds of Indian Industrial Labour: Contributions to Indian Sociology, Occasional Studies 9*, Chapter 1, New Delhi: Sage Publications, 1999, pp. 1–41.

infrastructure would require huge investments which could not be mobilized by private business alone. The active participation of the state in restructuring the economy was therefore essential, and met with the unreserved approval of private enterprise (Ray 1979). Public and private sectors would reinforce rather than compete with each other, and the strategic role of the state would facilitate the public regulation of the terms and conditions of employment in the new and modernized sectors of national economy. The labour legislation that was soon introduced gave the government considerable power over industrial procedures and dispute settlement, and this led to the creation of a massive bureaucracy charged with its policing.

At the start of the post-colonial era, India had fewer than 10 million industrial workers, of whom considerably less than half worked in factories (in 1950, a mere 2.5 million, according to Ornati 1955: 9). But even on the higher figure of 10 million, industrial labourers formed less than 6 per cent of the total workforce; of the *non-agrarian* sector, it was barely 17 per cent (Pant 1965: 12). This small minority was nevertheless regarded as prototypical of the labour force that would determine the future.

... their importance does not lie in numbers ... (but) because growth and expansion of the economy depends, to a large extent, upon its attitude towards industrialisation. It being the only section where labour organisation exists and can grow easily, it can influence the pace of change. It is this section which along with its problems will grow with the progress of industrialisation. (Pant 1965: 12)

But attention was focused on industry not only because of its future dominance but also because of its political significance. The post-colonial economy would be planned and socialist in orientation; industrial employment would shape a future in which employers, workers, and the state would accommodate their separate interests for the common good.

Even when the industrial breakthrough failed to materialize, when planning became far less significant in policy execution, when the goal of a socialist ordering succumbed to other interests, and the emphasis shifted from public to private sector expansion, 'labour' retained its connotations of employment in the organized sector of the urban economy. The implicit assumption was that a social system would eventually emerge similar to that which had already developed in the West. K.N. Raj, the economist, referred approvingly to a statement made before independence by Zakir Hussain, the future President, to the effect that Indian capitalism would differ little from that of the West

(Raj 1993: 211). Little thought was given to the way in which local and historical conditions had shaped the working class in that part of the world; and it was the evolutionary schemes which dominated the social science theory of the time which provided the point of departure, rather than the more recent exceptionalism of Chakrabarty (1989), whose critique of the universalist view of working-class dynamics elaborates on the specificities of the Indian case.

The accelerated migration of labour from the countryside to the cities seemed to herald the approaching transformation. Between 1901 and 1961, the urban population rose from 4 to 18 per cent of the total. But still only a tiny portion of the working population was employed in modern factories, and little consideration was given to how the much larger remainder managed to earn a living, or to the huge number of labourers who worked for big industrial enterprises in the rural hinterland. Mine workers and plantation coolies constituted a far bigger workforce than that of the factories of Mumbai and Calcutta. Among the exceptions were Mukherjee (1945), who discussed working conditions in mining and the plantation corporations, and Chandra (1966). But neither paid any attention to waged labour in agriculture.

The preoccupation with industrial employment diverted attention not only from the large segment of the urban population that earned its living in other ways, but even more from the social relations of production in agriculture. Iyer was one of the few who specifically drew attention to agricultural labour as a separate social formation, commenting at the start of the twentieth century on the miserable plight of the landless (Iyer 1903, in Chandra 1966: 762). Post-colonial policymakers only very slowly came to realize that agricultural labourers constituted the largest single section of the labour force (Thorner and Thorner 1962: 173). Nationwide investigations in the early 1950s showed that this rural underclass included roughly one-quarter of the agrarian population. The industrial proletariat, even on its broadest definition, was far smaller in size. This systematic neglect had begun in the colonial era and was related to the stereotyped image of the rural order as made up of fairly homogeneous communities of independent peasant producers. Case studies, such as that of Lorenzo (1943), were barely noticed.

Reacting to the received wisdom in nationalist circles, represented by writers like Patel (1952) who saw the growth of a class of landless labourers as the product of the break-up of the old village community of peasants and artisans under alien rule, Kumar (1965) was able to establish its significant presence in early colonial times; to show that this class was overwhelmingly made up of people of low caste and was subjected to servile labour arrangements based on bondage. Widespread use was later to be made of indebtedness in recruiting rural workers, not only to the coal mines and tea plantations but also to harbours and factories. The classic thesis that industrial capitalism only comes about when the transition to free labour has occurred—in the dual sense of workers detached from the ownership of means of production and able to decide for themselves how and where to sell their labour power—is not applicable to the colonial situation (Breman 1985: 59–77; see also Robb 1993). But in the final chapter of this volume, I will argue that the neo-bondage of contemporary industry is fundamentally different from the bondage of the old agrarian order.

For present purposes, the point to stress is that in the post-colonial literature on labour, the focus of attention was not on the rural economy per se, but on the labour surplus that had accumulated in it, and would have to flow towards the real poles of economic growth. But did these supernumerary rural masses match the requirements of modern industry?

## A DEFICIENT WORKFORCE

The emphasis on the rural origins of the working class dates back to the colonial period and was coupled with the notion that early generations of factory hands refused to sever their ties with the hinterland. The industrial worker as peasant *manque* was a principal motif of the *Report of the Royal Commission on Labour in India* (GoI 1931: 26), which reiterated the conventional view that economic necessity forced the migrants out of their villages, to which they remained socially and emotionally bound (cf. Ornati 1955: 36). This explained the lack of enthusiasm with which they subjected themselves to the demands of the industrial regime. Their disappointing quality was shown by their slovenly work pace (loitering was an ever-recurring complaint), the ease with which they changed jobs, and their high rates of absenteeism which were linked with their perfidious habit of returning to their villages and of staying away indefinitely. At heart, they were still peasants and their labour discipline was seriously defective. Moreover, the suspicion grew that this was not a transitory phenomenon that would be corrected as workers grew accustomed to their new world.

This image was reinforced by the social science literature of the 1950s and 1960s on the modernization process. The capacity of non-Western peoples to internalize the behavioural norms required by an industrial way of life seemed at issue. For Feldman and Moore, as for Kerr, industrialism imposes a set of conditions that must be met before economic transition can be considered complete. The key question was therefore how, as economic development progresses, the obstacles that hamper the quantity and quality of labour could be overcome (Kerr 1960; Moore 1951; Moore and Feldman 1960). Ornati spoke of a dislike for factory work and doubted that the industrial worker, in the proper sense of the term, exists in India. Violations of industrial discipline, including damage to goods and machinery, protracted inertia, and other forms of 'unsuitable behaviour' were persistent. Shows of defiance were symptomatic of the worker's inability to adapt himself to the new working conditions. 'Occasionally, the worker leaves the factory not to return to the village but to rebel against being forced into what might be called the "factory norms": time discipline, the limitation on leisure, the confines of the machines, the toil of learning, and the like' (Ornati 1955: 47). It was their peasant background which explained why workers preferred the more irregular and risky, but less self-disciplined, existence of the self-employed. The life of the 'peanut entrepreneur' was, in social and psychological terms, more attractive.

In 1958, the American Social Science Research Council sponsored a conference on how to motivate labour to perform non-customary tasks as a precondition for economic growth. Moore and Feldman edited the subsequent volume, *Labour Commitment and Social Change* (1960). 'Commitment', as they defined it, 'involves both performance and acceptance of the behaviours appropriate to an industrial way of life' (Moore and Feldman 1960: 1). Kerr's contribution distinguished successive stages, culminating in the willingness to conform permanently and unconditionally to the demands of the new mode of production (Kerr 1960: 351–2); while Myers had elaborated on the conditions necessary before one could speak of a stable and dedicated labour force:

... when workers no longer look on their industrial employment as temporary, when they understand and accept the requirement of working as part of a group in a factory or other industrial enterprise, and when they find in the industrial environment a more adequate fulfilment of personal satisfactions than they enjoyed in the village or rural society. (Myers 1958: 36)

Indian factory workers were, at best, only partially committed. Though keen to have fixed employment, they had few scruples about deserting the job in order to visit their village. They want, as Myers (1958: 45) put it, 'to have their cake and eat it too'.

To protect themselves against such unpredictable desertion, the factories set up a reserve pool of casual labour on which they could draw when necessary. James saw in this provision of *badli* (substitute) labour the good sense and tolerance of the employers. Recognizing that their workers found it difficult to adjust to an industrial existence, and drawing on long experience, they refrained from harnessing their permanent workforce too tightly (James 1960: 100, 104).

The high rate of absenteeism was not the only reason why Myers placed Indian factory workers so low on the ladder of commitment. 'Commitment to industrial employment implies more than the presence of workers on the job, however. It involves also their acceptance of industrial discipline and the performance of tasks under supervision' (Myers 1958: 53). The self-discipline of committed workers was required if they were to keep up with the tempo of the machines. But it is important to remember that they operate machines which do not belong to them; and it is possible that their resistance to machinery might be due to their rejection of the property relations intrinsic to the industrial mode of production. As Moore and Feldman (1960: 19–26) recognized, we must therefore ask about their ownership notions. Until we are informed about these, it seems premature to pontificate about their capacity for, or commitment to, modern machine production.

Lack of commitment narratives slide seamlessly into complaints about lack of discipline. Workers are reported to be unwilling to accept managerial authority, in particular the control of shop-floor supervisors. What is initially explained as non-internalization soon becomes a question of the employers' failure to gain an adequate grip on the behaviour of their subordinates. Loitering and leaving machines unattended are the most innocent examples of behaviour which shades into sabotage, physical violence against management agents like timekeepers or *gherao*ing the company offices (Myers 1958: 48).

What seems to be forgotten in these discussions is that commitment to industrial labour and commitment to managerial practices are not the same thing. Rather than insufficient engagement, much labour unrest can equally and perhaps more justifiably be described as an index of the opposite. What is more, the lack of commitment is always that of the working class. Kerr is explicit that it does not apply to the management (Kerr 1960: 358)—a diagnosis flatly at odds with the findings of research in a West Bengal factory where supervisors charged with disciplining the workers did not themselves have the necessary discipline to fulfil their task (Chattopadhyay and Sengupta 1969: 1209–16). Invariably, the problems are *with* labour, not *of* it—not those it experiences but those it causes. With Myers, this bias seems to be closely connected with the way he did his research. He held discussions with management; his Indian research associate reported on the unions. In addition to 125 officials in 49 enterprises, he spoke to leaders of employers' organizations and trade unions, government officials, academics, and representatives of international agencies (including the International Labour Organization [ILO] and American technical missions). Workers? It is not clear that he met any (Myers 1958: xvi).

## REJECTION OF THE COMMITMENT CONCEPT

Morris's historical study of labour and the growth of cotton mills in Mumbai, supplemented by briefer and less detailed research into the development of the Tata Iron and Steel Company (TISCO) in Jamshedpur, brought him to conclusions that were in many respects diametrically opposed to the prevailing orthodoxy. In response to the thesis that urban industry had initially suffered from a lack of labour, Morris showed that it had never been difficult to recruit workers for the textile factories, although the distance they came from increased over time. Simultaneously, however, a working class had evolved which closely identified with Mumbai's industrial sector and had renounced its roots in the rural milieu (Morris 1960, 1965). Workers were not irredeemably mired in traditional institutions or incapable of cutting their umbilical ties with the village. So why the vast army of migrant labour? To understand it, we first have to distinguish between large- and small-scale industries, and between enterprises that produce only seasonally and those that produce the whole year through. In short, circulation between city and village was a product of the nature of economic activity rather than of the ingrained habits of workers (Morris 1960: 175). In the end, Mumbai's cotton mills got the workers that they wanted: temporarily employed and dismissed without notice; and their productivity remained low because of a lack of investment in training and management:

These practices made it possible to use very large amounts of minimally trained labour, precisely the sort that was easy and cheap to obtain in Bombay. But the work schedule also made it necessary to employ enough labour to permit workers to take breaks while the machines were running, to develop what in effect amounted to an informal shift system.... There is no question that employers could have initiated a tighter and more precise system of labour utilisation and discipline had they so wished. But such an approach would have required more expensive supervision than could be obtained from the jobbers.... (Morris 1965: 203)

The psychologizing interpretations of writers like Kerr and Myers were well off the mark. Industrial work did indeed subjugate the workforce to fairly rigid rule-by-the-clock, but there was no question of a sharp break with the labour regime to which rural workers were accustomed; and in fact, the majority of factory workers had no contact with machines (Morris 1960: 188). Nor did labour unrest indicate lack of commitment. Willingness to strike meant just the opposite—adaptation to the industrial way of life.

Again, Lambert—a sociologist, who in 1957 had investigated the origins and identity of the workforces of five factories in Pune—reported that he had found no confirmation of the 'recruitment-commitment problem' (Lambert 1963: 6). Some of the workers he interviewed (a stratified random sample of 856 chosen from a population of 4,249) said that they would probably return to the countryside when their working life had finished. But one-third of his respondents had been born in Pune, an unspecified percentage in other urban localities, and the majority was certainly not recent rural migrants. Further, three-quarters of his respondents could be classified as 'committed' in Moore and Feldman's sense of the term (ibid.: 83–4). But Lambert was clear that he found little utility in this modish concept.

Notwithstanding that scepticism, he was clearly also dubious about the transformative effects of the industrial–urban system. The transition from tradition to modernity had been very partial; and factory organization had features derived from the social institutions of caste and the village. In particular, the *jajmani* system gave members of the local community the *right* to a job and a livelihood which the patron could not unilaterally abrogate. Employer–employee relations in the factory were based on the same principle. The worker regards his job as his property of which, he assumes, his employer cannot deprive him as long as he behaves as a duly deferential client, and fulfils all sorts of obligations that have nothing to do with work performance. As far as the latter is concerned, it might be better if the workers were less committed to the secure niche to which they believe themselves entitled irrespective of their competence and work discipline. In the early phase of industrialization, the employer's only escape from these claims was to use labour contractors and jobbers who profited from a constant rotation of workers. When those practices disappeared, the factory job became a more permanent form of property. Employers reacted to this limitation of their powers to discipline and dismiss their workers by making it more difficult to obtain fixed employment. They did so by forming a pool of reserve workers who were available when needed and who had far fewer rights than permanent employees (Lambert 1963: 91–4). In

India, the transformation from *Gemeinschaft* to *Gesellschaft* still lay in the distant future.

More nuanced was Sheth's (1968) study of labour relations in a modern industrial enterprise in Rajnagar, a fictionally named medium-size city in western India. No confirmation was found for its working hypothesis—that traditional institutions like the village community, the caste system, and the joint family had obstructed progress towards industrialism. What Moore, Kerr, and others had characterized as 'industrial society' was actually an ideal–typical construct for a great variety of social formations which did not, in reality, approximate to it at all closely. It was equally impossible to reduce the 'pre-industrial' society to a single uniform type. Neither were the two types of society polar opposites and nor did the new technology preclude continuity with the traditional social system. Moore (1951: 124) was in error to suggest that sluggish economic development was to be blamed on the tenaciousness of traditional social patterns, of which idea the commitment concept was simply a development. There is no radical rupture between relations in industry and those in the wider social environment; and factory managements make use of ascriptive and particularistic norms in their dealings with the workforce. Was that not also characteristic of Japan? Between the tradition-oriented social life of the worker and his rationality-based work in the factory, there was no conflict. What we have rather is 'a coexistence of the two sets of values and neither seems to hinder the operation of the other' (Sheth 1968: 203).

Sheth's study had affinities with Lambert's. Both denied that industrial employment is a watershed in the worker's attitudes and behaviour. Neither discussed the social life of the workers or the way in which they spend their income and leisure time outside the factory gates. On the other hand, Sheth points out that his methods were different from Lambert's, who had focused on questionnaire data and had paid no attention to interpersonal relations in the factory. But even more than Lambert, Sheth failed to give the pool of casual labourers (in both cases, about one-fifth of the total factory workforce) the strategic significance that industrial reserve army undoubtedly deserves (Lambert 1963: 94–104; Sheth 1968: 56–7).

Other authors rejected the commitment thesis on other grounds—Sharma on the basis of socio-psychological research on the attitudes and behaviour of workers in a car manufacturing plant in Mumbai; setting out to test the thesis through 262 in-depth interviews. The factory appeared to prefer educated workers over the non-educated, urban born over the rural born, and workers with industrial experience over those with no experience or with a background in non-industrial occupations (Sharma 1974: 14). But workers of rural origin had *better* attendance records than those who had grown up in the city (and trade union members were less likely than non-members to absent themselves). There was apparently no evidence of alienation and anomie to which the labourer from the countryside stereotypically fell prey in his new environment, and of which lack of discipline was an important symptom. The conclusion was that: '... traditional Indian culture appears to present no serious obstacles to the workers in either accepting factory employment or in becoming committed to industrial work. Moreover, the commitment of workers seems to be influenced not by their traditional backgrounds but by work technology within the factory' (ibid.: 48). The last point is clearly important. Commitment varies according to the nature of the industry, the technology used, and the demands regarding training and skills made at the time of recruitment.

Holmström's (1976) monograph on industrial workers in Bangalore was based on more anthropological methods of data collection. His fieldwork concentrated on workers in four factories, two in the public and two in the private sector; his focus was on the residential milieu rather than the factory itself; and the findings were based on case studies of 104 workers, selected to provide a cross-section of educated–uneducated, young and old, members of diverse castes, and so forth. Holmström's point of departure was that the significance and impact of urbanization should not be confused with those of industrialization and that it was senseless to assume a simple linear dichotomy between tradition (rural–folk society) and modernity (urban–industrial society). His principal questions concerned the social identity of the factory workers and what distinguished them from the majority of city dwellers who had not found access to modern and large-scale industrial enterprises. And how did members of this industrial vanguard think about their work and careers? The commitment issue was bypassed as largely irrelevant to the workers he studied.

In an overview published in 1977, Munshi concluded with a devastating judgement on the utility of the whole concept, again rejecting the opposition it postulates between modernity and tradition and the implicit assumption that industrialization would follow the path that it had followed in the West. Failure to do so had come to be seen as the inability of the working masses to meet demands dictated by the logic of industrialism, and a lack of awareness of the strategic significance of a management style attuned to industrial relations in American industry (Munshi 1977: 82). As Holmström later summarized it:

Foreign writers, and some Indians, wanted to find the formula for successful industrialisation, the ingredients missing from the traditional society which must be added to make India an industrial country: entrepreneurship, efficient management, changes in social values, 'achievement-orientation' or a committed labour force. The problem of supplying the missing ingredient or ingredients was believed to be common to non-industrial countries which lagged behind, at various points, on the great highway of development marked out by the west and Japan. (Holmström 1984: 28)

But at least the new variant of the old colonial dogmas acknowledged that non-Western peoples did have the ability to follow that highway. The bad news, however, was that this was likely to be a slow process since the industrial mentality took more than a generation to instil.

Kalpana Ram was one of the first to attempt to put the discussion on a new footing by drawing attention to the ways in which the capitalist work process manifests itself in India. Its specific nature, she argued, lies in the interconnection between rural and industrial labour. In the coal and iron mines of West Bengal, Madhya Pradesh, and Orissa, for example, workers did not have the chance to cut their ties to their villages of origin. This also applied to many migrants who found more permanent employment but had neither the accommodation nor the income that would allow them to maintain their family in their new location. The migration system 'allows employers to transfer the costs of reproducing and maintaining workers' families, and even of providing for the worker himself in times of illness and old age, on to the villages' (Ram 1984: 182). It also results in an extremely unequal distribution of work between the sexes. The Indian pattern of industrialization and urbanization has largely been based on women's exclusion from industrial employment; and Ram rightly points out that the theoretical literature has paid much too little attention to the very biased gender composition of India's industrial economy.

## FACTORY WORKERS AS A DOMINANT CLASS IN THE URBAN ECONOMY

The growth of India's modern proletariat was largely an urban phenomenon. The new towns and cities, as well as existing urban centres, became the sites of a great diversity of industrial enterprises. Jute and cotton mills had long been of vital significance to Calcutta, Mumbai, and Ahmedabad. Of much more recent origin was the emergence of heavy industries in the public sector economy, in particular the manufacture of iron and steel for the production of capital goods—for machine and construction workshops, petrochemical enterprises, cement factories, the manufacture of cars and other forms of transport, military equipment, shipbuilding, etc. The Second Five Year Plan, implemented in 1956, had prioritized the expansion of the industrial infrastructure.

The new public sector industrial workforce soon acquired a distinct character. The benefits of jobs within it included security of employment and various social provisions—like housing, health, and education—which were often the envy of workers in private enterprises. It is therefore hardly surprising that such workers became the reference point in the collective actions of industrial labour at large; while the relations of production initiated in these new government enterprises helped to give labour a new dignity. The 1969 *Report of the National Commission on Labour* elaborated on the characteristics of this new type of factory worker:

The social composition of labour is undergoing a change. Labour is not restricted to certain castes and communities.... [S]ocial mobility today accounts for the emergence of a mixed industrial work force. While in traditional industries this change is slow, one cannot escape noticing it in sophisticated employments such as engineering and metal trades; oil refining and distribution; chemicals and petro-chemicals; machine tools and machine building; and synthetics and in many white-collar occupations. The background of the intermediate and lower cadres in the latter industries is overwhelmingly urban: their level of education is higher. They come from middle or lower middle classes comprising small shopkeepers, petty urban landlords, lower echelons of public service and school teachers and professional groups. They have a pronounced polyglot character. (GoI 1969: 33–4)

In what follows, I will look in turn at the recruitment, mode of employment, and the social composition and lifestyle, of this segment of the working class.

### Recruitment

According to the colonial stereotype, the workforce which flowed straight from the villages to the factory gates had little, if any, direct contact with management. Workers were recruited by jobbers who were frequently also charged with control on the workfloor. Combining the functions of recruitment and supervision, the middleman was sometimes also responsible for housing and feeding his workers. The physical, economic, and social gap that had to be bridged was so crucial that the jobber is justifiably described as the midwife of India's industrialization. But one of the first changes to occur, starting around the turn of the century, was the transfer of recruitment from the hinterland to the factory itself. Increasing pressure on subsistence resources as a result of population growth and land alienation accelerated the flow of poor farmers and non-agrarian workers to the cities where industrial employment gained new impetus during and after World War II. The role of the jobber declined. From being an intermediary between worker and management, leader of a gang of workers whom he had himself brought together, he became a foreman charged with implementing orders from above. 'The hiring of workers is becoming the responsibility of the employment office, and the "labour officer" is beginning to take over the welfare and service activities of the sirdar' (Ornati 1955: 40). The decline of the jobber went hand-in-hand with the introduction of new rules which obliged major industrial enterprises to professionalize their personnel practices, and which eventually led to his disappearance (Papola and Rodgers 1992: 27).

But if selection procedures become more impersonal, can we infer that qualities based on individual achievement—experience, training, social skills—have replaced those based on ascription? Economic logic and the interests of the employer would suggest that they should. Thus, Papola (1970: 182) dismissed the suggestion that caste, religion, custom, or tradition might be crucial. But, in fact, it is clear that they continue to play a very large part. From the employer's point of view, recruitment mediated by existing workers helps to stabilize performance in daily production.

Recruitment through present employees continues to prevail. According to the evidence before us, employers prefer this method to improve the morale of workers. In some companies, labour–management agreements specify entitlement to a percentage of vacancies to close relatives of senior employees. In a few cases, both the employer and the union maintain rosters of people so eligible for employment. Recruitment through advertisement is restricted mainly to supervisory and white-collar employments and is being increasingly used to tap skilled labour. For occupations which do not require skills, an arrangement by which workers appear at the factory gate in the hope of getting employment still operates. (GoI 1969: 70)

The widespread use of relatives, neighbours, and friends in order to influence those who have jobs to bestow testifies to the enormous disparity between supply and demand. So great is the latter that applicants without such contacts stand no chance at all (Holmström 1976: 42–54; U. Ramaswamy 1983: 18–19). Some authors have seen the vitality of such particularistic mechanisms as a carry-over from the traditional prescriptions of kin solidarity; and Sheth noted the continuity between the patronage found in the factory and the values of the world outside it. But in any event, it is now hard to believe that particularism can be simply equated with an 'earlier' or 'lower' stage in a unilinear transformation along a continuum that eventually culminates in a universalistic and globalized civilization. The Japanese example is instructive. Rather than emphasizing its continuity with older social and cultural forms, others—myself included—would see such behaviour in more universalistic terms as a common response to a situation of extreme scarcity which prompts people to put pressure on kin who are more favourably placed. But whichever way it is, the facts are not in doubt. Papola summarized a series of studies from different parts of the country as follows:

In over two-thirds of cases, the workers got information about the availability of jobs from friends, relatives and neighbours. Employment exchanges were the source of information to a very small extent ranging from 1.5 per cent in Bombay to 10.6 per cent in Coimbatore, though 20 per cent of the workers in Ahmedabad and 25 per cent in Poona had registered with the exchanges. Newspaper advertisements provided information about their jobs to 1.5 per cent of workers in Bombay, 2.2 per cent in Poona and 10.6 per cent in Coimbatore. Jobs were secured on the basis of recommendation or introduction by friends, relatives and persons of the same region and caste, generally employees of the same factory, in 67 per cent of cases in Poona and in 61 per cent of cases in Ahmedabad, Bombay and Coimbatore. Placement through employment exchanges accounted for 2 per cent of jobs in Poona and Ahmedabad. (Papola and Rodgers 1992: 27)

Many factory workers attribute their access to the coveted arena of employment, in more veiled terms, to 'coincidence' or 'good luck'. Such terminology, quite incorrectly, gives the impression of an unexpected windfall, a mere stroke of fortune. It is a euphemism for claims made on their more fortunate fellows for help.

## Mode of Employment

Much of the work on Indian industry has been based on survey data, questionnaires, and formal interviews. In earlier studies, there was seldom much personal contact with the workforce. On Myers (1958), I have already commented; while Singer's essay on 'The Indian Joint Family in Modern Industry' was based on the family histories of 'nineteen outstanding industrial leaders in Madras City' (1968: 433).

The next generation of researchers did actually descend to the level of the workers, but their contact with them rarely went beyond brief one-off encounters. The exceptions were studies of a more anthropological nature—like that of Uma Ramaswamy (1983: 14) who lived in an area populated by factory workers during her fieldwork. To my knowledge, however, no researcher has ever actually worked in a factory. What is also lacking is documentation that originates from the workers themselves—diaries, biographies, or even oral histories.

Nor has research usually focused on the workplace, often no doubt as a consequence of management suspicion combined with some scepticism about its tangible benefits to the company. The researchers too have had their prejudices and inhibitions—one reporting that questions regarding trade unions were avoided 'because these excited the workers too much' (van Groenou 1976: 175). Sheth is still unusual in having managed to move freely inside the factory, to ask whatever he liked, and to observe the daily work cycle—all on the understanding 'that I would stick to my academic business and would cause no trouble in the administration of the factory'. But the blessings of management may, of course, result in antagonism and distrust among the workers. One told Sheth that:

It is all very well. You are doing good work which may benefit us in the long run. But you don't know our employers' tactics! You will now write down your report and publish it. But I am sure that if your book contains anything against the interests of these masters, they will buy up all the copies of your book to prevent others from reading it. And they are so rich that they can buy any number of copies that you print. All your labour will then prove futile. (Sheth 1968: 8)

That the majority of accounts of factory labour are based on contacts with employees outside the factory explains why ethnographies of the work process and hierarchy are still comparatively rare.

The social mobility mentioned in the 1969 National Commission on Labour (NCL) report assumes the possibility of progress up the occupational ladder. The picture presented by most studies, however, is one of little task differentiation. Lambert found that in the five factories he investigated, 75–90 per cent of all workers were rated as unskilled or semi-skilled, and the majority were doing the same jobs as they had started with. The unskilled category in particular, varying from one-third to three-quarters of the workforce, was distinguished by an almost complete lack of mobility (Lambert 1963: 131). It is therefore hardly surprising that roughly three in five workers did not expect any promotion and considered their present position to be as high as they would get.

As this suggests, the idea that factory work is skilled is only to a very limited degree true. In many enterprises, roughly one-quarter of the workforce belongs to the supervisory and maintenance staff. The former act as bosses on the workfloor and do not directly participate in the production process. The maintenance staff are indispensable but not important. As cleaners, guards, messengers, or general dogsbodies, they occupy the lowest ranks in the factory hierarchy. Between these two poles are the production workers, about three-quarters of the total workforce, who are split into two sections: 'operators', who are assumed to be the skilled workers; and the subordinate 'helpers', who function as their less skilled sidekicks and substitutes. The progressive mechanization of production means that a higher percentage of workers than in the past now regularly or continuously handle machines to whose regime they have to subject themselves. But this does not necessarily mean that their work is more skilled. Much of it is monotonous and makes no demands of craft competence. In fact, induction into the factory workforce may even result in a loss of skills.

If the prospects of promotion up the factory hierarchy are limited, we might expect workers to try to realize their aspirations by moving sideways into other enterprises. But by contrast with the lack of commitment stereotype, the great majority show extreme entrenchment. None less than Myers discovered that they tend to cling at all costs to the job they have got. Absenteeism is high, but horizontal mobility is rare—by contrast with the USA (James 1960: 103; Myers 1958: 47). Or as Lambert put it in terms that will by now be familiar: '... a factory job is a form of property to the worker.... [H]e will seek to retain, but not improve it.... [T]he worker's status in the general society seems not to be increased by upward occupational mobility within the factory' (Lambert 1963: 179). While the early literature complained about lack of commitment, the problem was now defined as one of workers who behaved as though they were clients who could not be dismissed by their patron–employers, and who showed no inclination to either work or find another job. Undercommitment had mysteriously metamorphosed into overcommitment.

Uma Ramaswamy reached a more balanced conclusion. On the one hand,

... most workers expect to retire in the factories they first joined unless better opportunities present themselves elsewhere, which is unusual. They increasingly look at their jobs not only as a right but also as property to be passed on to their children through warisu [a hereditary transaction]. All these find their reflection in the low turnover in the work-force. (U. Ramaswamy 1983: 145)

But she is, on the other hand, clear that this is not a simple product of the power of custom or of inescapable cultural determinism. It is rather the consequence of a quest for maximum security in an insecure world in which it is the lack of permanent employment which is the norm (cf. Holmström 1976: 139–40).

The attributes of factory workers in permanent employment have to be seen in the context of the very substantial labour reserve retained by most enterprises. What is striking is how many researchers have focused on this rather peripheral category of badli labour (regular substitutes who report to the factory daily) while largely ignoring the much larger numbers of floating casual workers. A United Nations Educational, Scientific and Cultural Organization (UNESCO) survey of factory employment in various Indian states unblushingly says that 'the short-tenure factory workers and the non-factory workers had to be left out' (Versluys et al. 1961: 7). Though the badlis' presence is required to replace permanent workers who are absent, this does not always mean that management is able to send them away again when they report at the stipulated time and there is no work. Their more or less continuous involvement in the flexibly organized work process, long beyond any reasonable trial period, is often essential to management. Their lack of formal work contracts, however, gives employers the freedom to minimize their rights. In south Gujarat, I repeatedly encountered people who had worked for the same boss on a temporary basis for more than 10 years, without ever giving up hope of eventually being rewarded with a permanent job in return for their 'loyalty'.

The size of the labour reserve varies by enterprise. In the five factories studied by Lambert, 10–20 per cent of the workforce belonged to that category; in Sheth's study, almost one-fifth, though this did not include the casual workers who were hired and fired according to need. Two subcontractors were charged with hiring these casuals. Each morning, the manager gave instructions as to how many extra workers were needed that day, and the two labour contractors would admit them at the factory gates. On average, they numbered 70 or 80 men, representing another 10 per cent of the total labour force. The contractors were paid piece rates; and neither they nor the gangs under them appeared on the factory's books. First, the contractors deducted their own generous cut and then paid their teams. This floating reserve, completely without rights, was not only called upon for all kinds of odd jobs but also to take the place of regular labourers who had not reported for work (Sheth 1968: 56–7).

Holmström's Bangalore study revolved around the idea that those fortunate enough to have found factory employment had crossed the threshold to a secure existence. The contrast was with the precariousness of life outside. 'Once inside the citadel, with a job to fall back on, improving one's qualifications and getting promotion becomes a gradual process, a matter of more or less, faster or slower progress, rather than simply of having a permanent job or not having one' (Holmström 1976: 41).

In my view, however, Holmström pays too little attention to the considerable and often lasting gap between temporary and permanent workers, appearing to suggest that passing from the former to the latter category is, in most cases, nothing more than a matter of time and patience. 'Even educated Brahmans will take unskilled casual factory work in the hope of permanent jobs. Once inside the citadel, a man can look around for alternatives, if he wants' (ibid.: 137). The idea that upward mobility is a common career pattern is not confirmed by other studies. In fact, temporary workers often get no further than the bottom of the work hierarchy. Although better off than the labour nomads beyond the factory gates, they can make no claim on the secure conditions of employment enjoyed by permanent hands, and are usually assigned the lowliest and most unskilled chores. Even when their work is the same, they are paid far less than permanent employees (Lambert 1963: 99–100). Further, Lambert noted a tendency to lengthen the term of temporary employment. '[I]t does appear that the average time spent in non-permanent status is increasing in all the factories, and that the two older companies using the badli system have a non-permanent labour pool that is tending to become stabilized' (ibid.: 102).

I would make that conclusion dependent on business cycles. During periods of rapid growth, when existing factories expand their production and new ones are opened, permanent employment becomes more quickly and easily available. The reverse happens in recession. It is probably no coincidence that Uma Ramaswamy—whose fieldwork was conducted at a time when the local textile industry had just passed through a decade of massive retrenchment—described a residual category of workers who had sometimes been registered as temporary hands for over a dozen years. They were not only much cheaper, but factory management expected them to be far more tractable—which is not surprising given the following account.

There are about seventy temporary workers in our mill. They were made to give their signatures on blank sheets before being taken for work. They have to report for work ten minutes before the others and are sent out ten minutes after the shift is over. The idea is to prevent them from mixing with permanent workers. Management fear that association with permanent workers might cause discontent in them. If a temporary worker is found sitting at the back of my cycle, he would be immediately denied employment. The blank sheet with signature would be used to write out his resignation. (U. Ramaswamy 1983: 21)

In general, labour productivity remains low. Management publications attribute this to worker and union militancy. What with the numerous holidays and days off, this means that a quarter to almost half of all days in the year are, according to some sources, lost to production (Papola *et al.* 1993: 294–325). But from an entirely different perspective, low productivity is also blamed on the owners' refusal to invest. Rather than technological improvement, the emphasis is on increasing productivity by intensifying labour. Women are frequently the victims. Fearing a loss of income, they are prepared to do work that is customarily carried out by men, to allow themselves to be illegally included in night shifts, and to work overtime without extra payment (U. Ramaswamy 1983: 23).

Skilled factory work remains the preserve of only a tiny portion of the total workforce. In recent times, surplus labour, which has acquired enormous proportions in the countryside, has looked en masse for work away from the village and agriculture. Those of this surging army of migrants who manage to reach the urban economy for shorter or longer periods, are rarely able to penetrate the strongly protected bastions of secure factory employment. And even if they are, the security of a permanent job is often beyond them. It is those fortunate enough to have such a job, more influential than might be supposed from their numbers, who have acquired a vital significance as a truly dominant class in the urban–industrial landscape. What are the principal social characteristics of this elite among the working population?

## SOCIAL PROFILE AND LIFESTYLE

Rather than a rural migrant, the majority of studies show that, today, many if not most workers have lived in the city or its immediate environs for many years, if not since birth (cf. Holmström 1976: 28; Lambert 1963: 7; U. Ramaswamy 1983: 12; Sheth 1968: 79–82). Those who have only recently settled in urban locations would generally be only too grateful for factory employment, but lack the experience and contacts needed to compete for it. E.A. Ramaswamy's report from the mid-1970s is by no means exceptional: 'The textile industry in Coimbatore is near saturation from the employment point of view. Even with the creation of additional capacity, jobs are too few in relation to the number of aspirants, particularly considering the low skill requirement' (E.A. Ramaswamy 1977: 175). Literacy rates among workers in large-scale enterprises are quite high. Although it is not really essential for unskilled work, practice shows that the ability to read and write is a minimum qualification for even a temporary hand. Over time, educational qualifications for recruitment to permanent jobs have been continually upgraded. Candidates without a secondary school certificate are no longer considered (Holmström 1976: 38; U. Ramaswamy 1983: 20).

The old wisdom held that the first to report for work in the modern urban industries were landless and land-poor farmers from the countryside (for example, Buchanan 1934: 294; Ornati 1955: 29), the social complement to their economic vulnerability being their low caste. But as industrial employment gained in respectability, the higher castes also began to show interest (Myers 1958: 39–40). Morris was amongst the first to reject this view, which he traced back to Weber's claim that a significant part of the emerging industrial proletariat stemmed from 'declassed and pariah castes' of rural origin. In Mumbai's cotton mills, Morris found that caste was not a relevant—let alone a primary criterion—of recruitment, and that untouchables were not discriminated against (Morris 1965: 200–1). But

it is interesting that this distinctive institution of caste has been almost entirely ignored in connection with Indian industrialization. No detailed study of the relation of caste to industrial work is available. In the vast array of official investigations into the conditions of industrial labour, virtually the sole reference to caste relates to caste dietary restrictions, which employers claimed prevented them from establishing factory canteens. The institution has been treated mainly by anthropologists, and almost entirely in its rural setting. Those who have studied caste have ignored industry, and those who have studied industry have ignored caste. (Morris in Moore and Feldman 1960: 182–3)

Little of this disregard is noticeable in later research, and we now have a considerable body of data on the relationship between caste and factory employment (for example, Holmström 1976: 32–4; U. Ramaswamy 1983: 102–14; Sheth 1968: 73–5). The general conclusion seems to be that the caste composition of the workforce broadly reflects that of the urban population as a whole, though the middle and higher castes are over-represented in the higher echelons of the industrial work hierarchy (Sharma 1970: 13), while the bottom ranks have high concentrations of lower-caste workers—a correlation which is strongly affected by differences in educational levels. But has the growing discrepancy between the limited supply of industrial work and the enormously increased demand for it led to exclusion of the socially deprived categories? Harriss, amongst others, offered evidence which pointed in that direction (Harriss 1982: 999). Moreover, in capital-intensive, technologically advanced industries, particularly corporate and multinational concerns, staff are almost entirely recruited on the basis of requirements that show a strong bias towards the higher social classes. On the other hand, positive discrimination in public sector employment has prioritized the recruitment of candidates from the Scheduled Castes and Tribes. But however one assesses these contradictory currents, no demonstration that caste still operates inside the factory gates should be taken to mean that it must still retain its old ideological salience.

[C]aste is no longer plausible as a thorough-going religious ideology, justifying all social and economic relations as parts of a divinely established hierarchy. The main public ideology—not just the language of politics and unions, but much ordinary talk—tends to stress moral and social equality. The status inequalities that count depend on jobs, income, life style, manners and education. Where these things go with caste rank, this is usually because some castes had more access to education and good jobs in the past—a situation that will not last, because effective caste job-finding networks are not stable or confined to high castes. (Holmström 1976: 80)

More generally, Sharma's conclusion of 25 years ago seems to stand: that factories prefer 'educated workers over the non-educated, urban-born over the rural-born, and those with industrial experience over the ones having no experience or with a background in non-industrial occupations' (Sharma 1974: 14). But what is still missing from this profile is its gender dimension. Early studies give the impression that women were rarely found in factories. Their apparent absence prompted Kalpana Ram to comment that 'the virtual exclusion of women from the Indian industrial working class has drawn little theoretical comment' (Ram 1984: 182), particularly in the light of their far higher participation in the early industrialization of the West as well as in various contemporary Third World societies. Her formulation needs some qualification, however, in that in Mumbai's cotton mills at the end of the nineteenth and in the early twentieth century, for example, women made up one-fifth to one-quarter of the workforce (Morris 1965: 65). Although that was far less than in the early Western textile industry, it was certainly not negligible.

So, how are we to explain the fact that the steady expansion of the industrial sector brought a fall rather than a rise in the percentage of female factory workers? The primary cause reported is that factory legislation restricted the use of the far cheaper labour of women and children in the first few decades of the twentieth century. More important, in Morris's view, is that women's reproductive role causes them to absent themselves more frequently. It is not clear, however, how this argument squares with huge local variations in the employment of women in textile industries throughout the country. For Morris (ibid.: 69), the marginalization of women substantiates his thesis that there was no lack of male workers who were ultimately preferred by the industry.

By the mid-twentieth century, industrial work was more than ever a male preserve. The prototypical factory worker was a young man of no more than 30–5. Official reports confirm the decreasing participation of women.

This decline has been more marked in the textile and basic metal industries. In both cotton and jute textiles ... [it] is attributed mainly to technological changes rendering the[ir] jobs ... redundant. Fixation of minimum work load and standardisation of wages in the cotton textile industry necessitated retrenchment of women workers who were working mostly as reelers and winders where the work-load was found to be lower.... Rationalisation and mechanisation schemes in the jute industry eliminated some of the manual processes which at one time were the preserve of women workers. Certain occupations giving employment to women in the jute industry earlier were found to be hazardous and are therefore closed to women now by Rules framed under the Factories Act. (GoI 1969: 380)

Rationalization of production and the weaker sex being relieved of labour considered too strenuous for them—whatever the pretext, the fact is that the progressive elimination of women from the workforce has further strengthened male dominance of economic life.

In factories where machines are not only used but also made, women seem to disappear entirely. While Sharma (1974: 7) at least reported that only males were employed in the car plant he studied, Sheth totally omits any mention of the fact that the workforce of Oriental did not apparently include a single woman. Where both sexes are employed, women are invariably in a small minority. In 1956, women formed only 11.7 per cent of the workforce in manufacturing industries in India, and were concentrated mostly in medium-sized to large enterprises (Lambert 1963: 23). They were present in only two of the five Pune factories which Lambert studied, and his sample was 96.6 per cent male—which under-represented their average in the enterprises in question. The same applies to Holmström's Bangalore study: 5.6 per cent of his sample were women, compared with 15 per cent of factory workers in Karnataka as a whole (Holmström 1976: 19). The bias is not unconnected with a code of social conduct which makes them less easy to approach not only by male researchers but also by male co-workers.

[T]he one woman 'draftsman' says the men in her office treat her as a sister, but she never goes among the men on the factory floor to discuss design problems, and so she cannot get promotion. Women keep to themselves in the canteen, play a minor part in most clubs and then only in the shadow of their husbands, and take little part in the union beyond attending general meetings and voting. (Ibid.: 65)

It is no accident that women workers have a higher profile in Uma Ramaswamy's research. They formed 15 per cent of the total workforce but their participation, in absolute as well as relative terms, was declining (U. Ramaswamy 1983: 22). Again, this was part of a trend towards mechanization by which they in particular were victimized. At the time of the study, the output of one woman equalled that of five a few decades earlier. Their employment was falling even though their productivity was higher than that of male workers. Why? The answer boils down to the fact that in practice, it is easier to let men take the place of women than vice versa. In addition to all manner of inhibitions connected to the employment of women, and regardless of their willingness to work night shifts, they have to be paid for maternity leave. Factory regulation had also helped to reduce the differential wage level which meant that the attraction of women as cheap labour was reduced.

'Supernumerary' women are dismissed or transferred to unskilled work with lower earnings. It is repeatedly shown that they are invariably the lowest paid workers. Insofar as they have not been completely ousted from the industrial labour process, women seem principally or exclusively to be assigned tasks which need no special knowledge or skill and which—thought often monotonous—require precision and alertness.

When a certain job requires, in the employee's eyes, delicate handling, or when the work is time-consuming and tedious, women are called upon to do it. Thus, women are favoured in the electronics industry, for jobs which require tiny parts to be handled gently and carefully, and where fine wires have to be twisted and wound. In the textile industry, women have traditionally been employed as menders, spinners, winders, reelers, folders and cottonwaste pickers. In the pharmaceutical industry, women are generally employed as packers. (Quoted in Holmström 1984: 227)

Far more than men, the jobs they can get keep them riveted to the bottom of the work hierarchy without prospect of promotion.

## *Lifestyle*

Despite their considerable social heterogeneity, factory workers in the organized sector share a number of characteristics that have to do with the industrial culture in which they work and live, and which distinguish them from other components of the labour force. The expectation that a more homogeneous lifestyle would eventually emerge prompted various researchers to investigate the effect of the industrial–urban setting on household forms. In much of the literature, the industrial worker is a man living apart from his family and leading a bachelor's existence in the city (Das 1984: 165). Only when thoroughly established there, would he be joined by his wife and children who had been left behind in the village. But in southern India, labour migration was far less likely to lead to family separation. The worker was either accompanied by his family or was joined by them at the first opportunity (Holmström 1984: 68). As Kerr saw it, family reunion at the place of employment marked the transition to 'commitment'. The worker

... is fully urbanized and never expects to leave industrial life. His family is permanently resident in an urban area, and it is not unusual for the wife also to enter the labor market. In fact, one good test of the degree of commitment of a labor force is the percentage of it comprised by women. An uncommitted or semi-committed labor force is predominantly male. The committed worker depends for his security on his employer and on the state, not his tribe. His way of life is industrial. (Kerr 1960: 353)

Low female participation in the industrial labour force is held, in short, to be symptomatic of low commitment. What this wholly implausible proposition ignores is that it is not that women are unwilling to take factory work, but rather that they cannot get it. Those who do, make use of precisely the same channels of influence and personalistic links as men. This explains why factory women are frequently close relatives of a male employee in the same enterprise. The greatest favour that a worker can hope for from management or union is a job for his wife (U. Ramaswamy 1983: 25). If both work, they have an income that many middle-class households would envy (cf. Holmström 1984: 227–8).

In the early literature on factory labour, the transition from caste to class—not whether but when—was widely discussed. So, too, was the break-up of the joint family given its supposed incompatibility with industrial–urban life (for example, Goode 1963). Both caste and the joint family represented the traditional culture and social structure which would be progressively transformed by the new economy. The much smaller size of the average household in industrial areas looked like confirmation. But faith in this theory that development would follow the same course as it was supposed to have taken in the West was gradually undermined. The realization dawned that for a very large segment of the rural population, the joint family had not been the only or even most common unit of cohabitation. Further, Singer (1968) described the preservation of the—albeit streamlined—joint family among the industrial elite of Chennai; and showed how 'the home becomes the sphere of religion and traditional values; office and factory become the sphere of business and modern values'—the phenomenon which he called 'compartmentalisation' (ibid.: 438). 'Modernisation' was a much more complex and uneven process than was often supposed—in one sphere, 'tradition' might rule, in another, the values of modernity.

With regard to the joint family, however, I find the argument unconvincing, not least because it was entirely based on the households of Chennai's captains of industry. Lambert, however, develops a similar thesis for industrial workers. Though their households were not very different from those of other segments of the city's population as a whole, they did on average include more members, being frequently supplemented by all kinds of relatives (Lambert 1963: 56). This seemed to contradict the supposed transition to the conjugal family form. It is by no means certain, however, that this should be taken as evidence of the persistence of the 'traditional' joint family. I would rather agree with Holmström that, for the average factory worker, '... the earning and spending unit is the nuclear family settled in the city, depending on one main earner, which expands to take relatives in need and then goes back to its normal size; linked to relatives elsewhere by bonds of duty and sentiment which are sometimes expensive' (Holmström 1984: 274).

This alternation of expansion and contraction is based on obligations towards relatives—cramped living space limiting the possibility of housing them indefinitely, and the inclusion of additional members partly arising from the necessity of broadening the household's economic base by increasing the number of workers. To contrast the 'traditional' joint family with the modern nuclear family is to ignore the fact that the predominant working class household in the industrial–urban milieu belongs to neither. It is rather a unit of cohabitation forced into being by low earnings and by specific conditions of employment (see Report of a Survey 1978: 1169).

The NCL report observed that the quality of accommodation for industrial labour had improved since the first generation of *ahatas* in Kanpur, labour camps in Mumbai, shanties in the south, and *basti*s in eastern India, which, over time, had become even more miserable and congested. New urban housing colonies have been constructed, though they rapidly tend to be burdened by overcrowding. Some large industrial enterprises have their own quite respectable housing estates, but these cater to only a small fraction of the working class. The greater proportion have to make do with primitive and confined living quarters in neighbourhoods that are mostly dilapidated and sordid. 'Real change is seen inside the tenement. Earthen pots have been replaced by aluminium or brass-ware; pieces of crockery are not an unusual possession. There are also items of furniture, such as charpoi, a bench or a chair and a mosquito net. Radio/transistors/watches are often the proud possessions of not a few' (GoI 1969: 33).

This list of consumer goods, now 30 years old, would today include a sewing machine, a bicycle, or even a Hero Honda, a fan, refrigerator, and television. Most would have access to tap water and many to a toilet. The NCL report also comments on new consumption patterns in food and clothing. Regional specialities are now common throughout the nation, for which factory canteens are partly responsible. Some foods are now bought pre-prepared. Clothing and footwear have increased both in quantity and quality. Many labourers now wear overalls in the factory, and gone are the days when they went unshod and garbed only in short baggy trousers and a vest.

A composite portrait of the average factory worker is difficult because the differentiation is so striking. The upper bracket consists of employees in capital-intensive multinational corporations who should be included in the expanding middle class, not only because of the nature of their employment but also due to their lifestyle. At the bottom is a colossal army of unskilled and semi-skilled workers in industries that lack almost any advanced technology and have far less attractive working conditions. Comparatively, these workers are not badly paid, but they are threatened by continual demands that they increase their low productivity and have more difficulty passing their jobs on to the next generation.

However great the distance between these two poles, they also share some crucial characteristics. In the first place, they are all in regular employment and the great majority receives a wage that fluctuates little. This is based on the hours they have put in, which in turn implies a clear distinction between working and non-working times. Finally, their conditions of employment—not only of appointment, promotion, and dismissal but also a great diversity of secondary provisions regarding illness, vacations, pensions, dearness allowance, bonuses, etc.—are governed by well-defined rules laid down in legislation and partly brought about by trade union pressure. It is this combination of features which leads me to consider workers in medium-sized and large industries as the dominant fraction of the working class in the industrial sector of the modern economy. Their lifestyle, culture, and consciousness reveal their commonality.

They belong to a distinctive Indian industrial culture, with typical assumptions and expectations and tastes which cut across divisions of skill and age and origin. They share a common situation. They act, and sometimes think of themselves, as a group (if not a class) different from peasants, workers in the 'unorganised' sector or in older factories with different technologies, from casual labourers, shopkeepers, professional people and so on. (Holmström 1976: 27)

But they are only a small minority; and it is their high social, political, and economic profile—rather than their numbers—that makes them dominant and a model for emulation amongst other segments of the working class. Should they therefore be regarded as a privileged elite who—like the dominant caste in the agrarian–rural sphere—have appropriated a disproportionate share of scarce goods at the expense of other groups? Opinions differ.

Their basic wage, which increases with the number of years worked, is supplemented by a dearness allowance and other benefits. Their total earnings are significantly higher than that of other sections of the proletariat without formal labour contracts with their employers; and various social provisions—which also benefit their families—insure them against risk and uncertainty. They know that they are privileged, but are reluctant to share their advantages with the far larger mass of workers without them, realizing that their extension to others might well result in their dilution. Lowering the citadel wall, or building more entrance gates, would threaten inundation. So according to some, this industrial vanguard has developed into a class that is solely concerned with strengthening its own interests.

[I]t is the organisational strength of industrial labour that prevents the transfer of resources from urban to rural sector and thereby to agricultural labour. If the power of the industrial labour is curbed and it is prevented from exploiting its strategic location in the growth of the Indian economy, efforts can be made to improve the lot of the rural poor. (Sinha 1993: 271)

Sinha here summarizes a standard argument, though his own views are different. Arguing that industrial wages have only risen in reaction to increases in the cost of living, he rejects the suggestion that capital accumulation has been delayed by draining off profits to organized sector labour for consumption. But other authors continue to see them as a labour aristocracy whose privileged position explains why, all over India, the gap between their income and the wages paid to agricultural workers is now far greater than ever.

## THE ASSERTION OF DIGNITY

What further marks factory workers in regular employment out as a special category is that they have amalgamated into trade unions to negotiate improvements in their conditions of work and to defend their rights. In both, the state has also played an important role. The labour legislation introduced after independence has operated primarily, if not exclusively, to the benefit of this segment of the working class. Nor should it be imagined that the protection of the state was prompted by pure benevolence. It was a concession to the power built up by the factorized proletariat, and the inevitable consequence of the commanding role which the state had assumed in managing the transition to an industrial order in which these workers were considered so vital.

At stake in the discussions of the National Planning Committee in 1940 was the creation of an industrial machinery like that which already existed in Europe. Coupled with this was the introduction of extensive legislation on conditions of employment, including delimitation of the working week, prohibition of child labour, provisions for sanitation, health, and safety at work, the fixing and implementation of a minimum wage, equal pay for equal work, the right to a paid vacation, maternity benefits, housing quarters, procedures for settling conflicts, and compulsory arbitration by government (necessitating the establishment of a Conciliation Board and an Industrial Court). The creation of a system of social security was also discussed.

A system of compulsory and contributory social insurance for industrial workers should be established directly under the control of the State to cover the risks of sickness and invalidity other than those covered by the Workmen's Compensation Act. Schemes for providing alternative employment to those involuntarily unemployed, Old Age Pensions and Survivors' Pensions, and also Social Insurance to cover risks of sickness and invalidity for all, should be established directly under the State. These schemes should be extended by stages, priority being given to particular classes of workers, with due regard to the relative urgency of their needs, facility of application, and to the ability of the community to provide for them. (National Planning Committee 1940)

The last sentence was intended to check exaggerated expectations. During the deliberations, however, Ambalal Sarabhai, President of the Ahmedabad Mill-Owners' Association who acted as the employers' representative, asked whether it was really intended that the entire package should be introduced in the short term. The Chairman, Jawaharlal Nehru, explained that it represented a coordinated scheme which did not allow for piecemeal selection, but was vague about the timing of its implementation which would anyway have to wait until after the transfer of power.

The nationalist leadership realized that the mobilization of industrial workers, which had started in the colonial era and had expressed itself in strikes and other forms of protest, might gain new impetus after the liberation from alien rule; and therefore recognized the need to pacify labour. In 1929, the number of registered trade unions in India was 29; in 1951, it was 3,987 (Ornati 1955: xi). Economic policy obviously had to come to terms with this institutionalized interest. Although the unions cared for the interests of only a tiny minority of the labouring classes, that minority formed its most vocal and most militant segment. The hope was that, in exchange for special treatment, this vanguard of 'the dangerous classes' might be induced to abandon more extreme demands. Peasants and workers were ad nauseam told to sacrifice their own interests for the good of the nation. One member of the National Planning Committee suggested that there should be no room for industrial unrest in the planned economy. But fear of the radicalization of the factory proletariat, whose numbers were bound to increase rapidly, was nevertheless great (for example, Kanappan 1970: 315).

Faced with this threat, the politicians adopted various strategies. First, they successfully encouraged the rise of trade unions that were linked to different political currents and whose mutual rivalry prevented the labour movement from forming a united front. Second, every effort was made to avoid or defuse direct confrontation between employers and employees. The priority given to harmony and reconciliation, with arbitration prescribed, meant that the state itself became a principal party to negotiations. Third, through the carrot of benefits and facilities, they sought to detach the industrial elite from its links with the far greater mass of workers. This enormous army of underprivileged labour was excluded from formal wage negotiations, and there was no institutionalized mechanism for the promotion of their interests.

A Fair Wages Committee was given the task of finding out how much an industrial worker needed to provide for himself and his immediate family (significantly identified as a unit of man, wife, and two children): '... not merely the bare essentials of food, clothing and shelter, but a measure of frugal comfort, including education for the children, protection against ill health, requirements of essential social needs and a measure of insurance against the more inevitable misfortunes including old age' (Loknathan 1993: 51).

The employers argued, however, that even 'a measure of frugal comfort' was too heavy a burden and that they could only grant a fair wage if labour would agree to increase production and maintain industrial peace. This was not unattractive in that the wage set was far above that on which the greater part of the working population had to survive. Until the beginning of the 1960s, the illusion was maintained that industrialization would be instrumental in the transition towards a socialist society. In addition to a fair wage and bonus policy, and the acceptance of collective bargaining, industrial socialism would also mean workers' participation in management and eventually, profit sharing (Joseph 1978: 123–39; Mukherjee 1993: 109)—but this, of course, was never achieved, nor even seriously attempted.

The class consciousness of factory workers is demonstrated by their willingness to organize, and union membership is conventionally taken as evidence of their readiness for collective action and as an index of their solidarity. In fact, by no means all workers in the formal sector became union members. Even on the grossly inflated membership figures provided by the unions themselves, less than one out of three workers were registered; and if regular payment of union dues is the yardstick, the proportion shrinks much further. The hard core of trade unionists is actually a small minority; and as we have seen, this 'vanguard' of the working class shows no inclination to join the struggle for improving the plight of the non-organized masses.

Evaluation of this rather pessimistic picture must be on the basis of empirical research on the relations between workers and unions. The best study undoubtedly remains that of E.A. Ramaswamy, already more than two decades old. This showed that Coimbatore mill workers keep a sharp eye on whether the union's cadre exert themselves in caring for their concerns; but are also acutely aware that their existence is far more comfortable than that of the great mass of workers who have no one to defend their interests. As one senior member remarked:

There is a limit to what we can ask from the millowner. I get four times as much as my neighbour who toils in a field all day, and yet my job is easier and not very much more skilled than his. Unless conditions improve all around it is difficult to get us to ask for more. (E.A. Ramaswamy 1977: 182–3)

Despite Ramaswamy's title (*The Worker and His Union*), trade union membership includes women. Hastening away at the end of their shift to do their household chores, they are said to be generally quite passive in union affairs and to do no more than pay their contributions. But if their jobs are endangered, or if other problems arise, they are extremely militant. At the time of the research, they had every reason to assert themselves because women were particularly threatened by redundancy.

We have earlier seen that women are concentrated in the lowest ranks of the labour hierarchy, and often get no further than casual work. Whatever their sex, casual workers have greater need than regular workers of the help and protection of a union. Not only is their unionization opposed by the employers (U. Ramaswamy 1983: 21), but union leaders show little zest for—and even some hostility to—it. Can they be blamed? Holmström takes a charitable view, pointing out that consolidating their gains is difficult enough without having to defend the interests of a mass of workers who are far more vulnerable. Even more than the badlis, who have at least been able to join the pool of reserve labour to await their turn for a job, that vulnerability afflicts the infinitely greater mass who have not yet found their way into the waiting room.

Many unions are overwhelmingly defensive. They are there to protect jobs first, then the real value of wages against inflation, with safety and working conditions a poor third, rather than to win more than the members have already. They know their bargaining power is weak; noisy militant demands for more are a tactic to hold the line, something to be bargained away when vital interests are threatened. The union has a hard enough job protecting its own members without worrying about outsiders. (Holmström 1984: 289; see also Das 1984: 174)

Other authors, like Mamkoottam (1982), are far more critical. The leaders are manipulative and corrupt, more concerned with their own interests than in caring for those of the rank and file. Workers react by making their support for them contingent on the results they achieve. If these are disappointing, they have no hesitation in defecting to a rival union. It is not a question of ideology but a pragmatic choice of who offers the most for the lowest price. According to such authors, trade union bosses operate as brokers, like the earlier jobbers, and use their mandate to enter into deals with employers, politicians, and rival unions. It is perhaps not surprising that the unionization of the factorized workforce remains quite limited.

The battles which had to be fought in order to break through the employers' resistance to the formation of unions and to the first collective actions is perhaps the principal reason why the present generation of factory workers have any faith in these organizations. The memory of champions in the fight for a better life, who often had to pay a high price for their ideals and dedication, still lives on. Sheth, who concluded that the union had only marginal significance for the workforce he studied, nevertheless added the qualification that:

... workers realised that though the union achieved precious little for them, they could achieve even less in the absence of a union. Individual workers could make a comparison in retrospect between 'union days' and 'unionless days' and found that though the union got them hardly anywhere in relation to the demands it made on the management, it was necessary for systematic dealing with the management. (Sheth 1968: 159–60; see also Sharma 1978: 1239)

This seems to be a common view amongst organized labour whose lack of a more embracing sense of solidarity I see less as the product of a short-sighted aristocratic mentality than as of a quite realistic fear that the cake may be too small for all comers.

In my view, however, the Indian trade union movement has played an emancipatory role. Perlin is quite correct in pointing out that little if any improvement has been brought about in the more deplorable working conditions. In a great many enterprises, these are injurious not only to health but also to human dignity (Perlin 1979: 457). The complacent opinion of the NCL report, that industrial workers become inured to such hardships and can more or less ignore them (GoI 1969: 35), fails to grasp the sense of resentment, ill-being, and pollution to which such conditions often give rise. But this does not alter the fact that factory workers' in regular employment have made great progress, particularly in their own self-esteem, and that this has been significantly due to the protection offered by membership of a trade union. Conversely, self-esteem encourages them to organize themselves, even when this is likely to arouse the displeasure of their bosses. As the NCL concluded, 'the industrial worker of today has acquired a dignity not known to his predecessor'—or, as the employers saw it, 'a greater measure of defiance towards his superiors'. The new assertiveness was based on a new awareness: 'a worker today is more politically conscious than before, more articulate of the existing order and more sensitive to his conditions and hardships' (GoI 1969: 35). And it was the charismatic role models provided by the cadre members which induced the less active and less conscientized factory workers to assert themselves, even if only temporarily. The research of E.A. and U. Ramaswamy illustrates this well:

[They] describe in detail—with sketches of individuals and their life histories and thoughts—a world of the union activists ... held together by an ideology of working-class solidarity cutting across barriers of caste and employment. By their personal example, they carry along the mass of ordinary workers who are moderately apathetic about wider issues, but still loyal enough to strike, demonstrate and perhaps vote when asked by those they respect. The union provides a service when needed; in return it sometimes asks for sacrifice and enthusiasm. (Holmström 1984: 294–5)

Wage increases have undoubtedly been the most urgent demand of the trade union movement since its inception. Its programme of action soon broadened, however, into a more general protest against the hierarchical order, not only of industry, but of society as a whole. While that hierarchy instructed labour to resign itself to its own subordination, the ideology of the unions nurtured the principles of equality and social justice. Corruption of those ideals was linked to everyday party politics, in which the unions were deeply embroiled; and also resulted from contradictory currents that prevailed among the working masses, a great proportion of whom originated from a world that was by no means impervious to distinctions of caste, class, ethnicity, religion, and gender. It is thus all the more significant that 'the main public ideology—not just the language of politics and unions, but much ordinary talk—tends to stress moral and social equality' (Holmström 1976: 80). Assertions of dignity were also a denial of dependency and inequality, and were met with considerable oppression from the employers who attached great significance to the recognition of their traditional authority, and who quite rightly saw industrial agitation as undermining their claim to respectful obedience. Consider the following appeal with which, at the start of the 1950s, one employer called his striking workers to order:

Your illegal and indisciplinary ways distress me. I am tired and will be compelled to take action.... My advice to you as your elder and wellwisher is work wholeheartedly and maintain discipline.... [I]f you do not follow my humble advice you will compel the company to dismiss all those who act illegally as we have waited patiently for long.... (Cited in Ornati 1955: 15)

Three decades later, such language would have been greeted with utter hilarity.

During the 1970s and the 1980s, drastic changes took place in labour relations as a result of the restructuring of the industrial economy. Rationalization of production became a major trend, first in private business, but subsequently also in public sector enterprises, and resulted in significant 'downsizing'. Between 1968 and 1984, the average number of production workers per factory declined from 75 to 61 (Papola and Rodgers 1989: 46). Technological change played some role, but many more workers were replaced by cheap casual labour than by machines. Exit policies in the guise of 'voluntary' retirement schemes reduced the size of the permanent workforce in both large and small companies. The efficiency drive met with the wholehearted approval of the state bureaucracy which increasingly shared the employers' view that the maintenance of existing labour rights was a major obstacle to economic growth. The inevitable outcome of the 'flexibilization' of industrial work has been a contraction of production in the formal sector, and a further expansion of the informal sector economy.

In this scaling down, the job security of the permanent workforce was nevertheless reaffirmed and they may even have improved their bargaining position—suggesting a direct link between the privileges granted to a tiny section of the workforce and the marginalization of a much larger segment. But, however this may be, lower manning levels meant heavier workloads for those who remained. In return for higher wages, they had to commit themselves to higher production targets.

These changes gave rise to a new type of trade union leadership, exemplified by Datta Samant in Mumbai. The style of negotiation was confrontational, demands were immoderate, and legal niceties were ignored. The leader insisted on a united front and demanded total obedience, but also promised no compromises. Direct action had only one aim: monetary gain. The relationship between leader and worker is essentially contractual and does not bind them beyond the duration of the strike. The union boss is more the leader of a campaign than the head of an enduring organization. He neither bothers about the problems, complaints, and requests of individual workers, and nor is he deeply interested in ideological issues or the working-class movement at large. If the strike fails, he simply moves on to the next target, which may be a different industry. Before the start of any action, the financial standing of the company is carefully assessed in order to calculate the level at which the union's demands should be pitched. When labour costs are not critical to the total cost of production, management is much more eager to settle the dispute than in industries where wages are pegged at one-fourth or one-third of manufacturing expense. The failure of the huge textile strike in 1982–3 in Mumbai, which lasted for 18 months and in which more than 200,000 workers took part under the leadership of Datta Samant, should be seen in this light. The defeat certainly affected his reputation, but only for a short time and not in more capital-intensive branches of industry.

Aggressive leadership of this kind stands in marked contrast to the less militant and more legalistic leadership of the conventional unions. Mavericks, like Datta Samant, are accused of luring workers away from established leaders who best know how to take care of their real interests. They antagonize employers and rural workers with deals which are bound to turn sour. But, as several authors have argued, this representation does little justice to the sense of disillusionment and resentment which many organized sector workers had developed towards their erstwhile representatives. The new combination of working-class radicalism and businesslike unionism is indicative of a new stage in industrial relations in which wider solidarities are sacrificed to narrower and more short-term interests. To dismiss such behaviour as apolitical would be to misread the assertiveness and self-consciousness of these militant workers whose social identity differs markedly from the older generation of factory hands.

The traditional stereotype of the industrial worker as an illiterate low-caste migrant, pushed out of the village by unemployment, was dubious at the best of times. Now it is becoming more untrue with each passing day. Most enterprises in the organised sector would not consider for employment anyone without a school leaving certificate, and the presence of graduates and post-graduates in the blue-collar workforce has long ceased to be a novelty. For the skilled trades, a technical diploma from an industrial training institute is an additional advantage. With wages so attractive and employment so scarce, the blue-collar workforce too become[s] a polyglot mix of workers from various castes and religious backgrounds. (E.A. Ramaswamy 1990: 170; cf. Heuzé 1990: 177).

As for management's reaction to this new radicalism, much depends on their readiness to adjust to the new times. Some took offence at being addressed in a manner which did not acknowledge their authority and superiority. Others responded in a businesslike fashion and clinched deals which still gave them the upper hand. In exchange for an increase in the wage packet, they insisted on including clauses on heavier workloads, incentive schemes, and lower rates of absenteeism. It was not at all rare for the union which had called the strike to be held responsible for the worker's fulfilment of these conditions. By allowing the likes of Datta Samant to operate on their premises, the employers not only hoped to buy industrial peace but also a more productive workforce. The other side of the story is, of course, that ever-increasing benefits were placed in the hands of ever-shrinking numbers. As Ramaswamy has astutely noted: contract work, casual labour, redundancy, and voluntary retirement schemes create the surplus that is passed on to those left behind in permanent employment. The flow is from one segment of the workforce to another rather than from capital to labour. If not from ideology, then at least from self-interest, the unions will eventually have to organize the unorganized—if they are to be left with a constituency at all (E.A. Ramaswamy 1988: 74).

Employers who initially did not know how to cope with the phenomenon of independent unions have grown to like them. What they want for their enterprise is not representation by several unions fighting with each other over the spoils, but a strong leader able to instil discipline among his clientele. The industrialists' organization has consistently argued in favour of the 'one factory, one union' principle (Heuzé 1990: 185). That preference is strongly inspired by the perception that plant-level associations do not have a wider agenda and are wary of joining national federations which are hand in glove with political parties. This trend is also in line with World Bank recommendations. In its 1995 annual report, negotiations at plant level are praised as the most appropriate framework in which to achieve positive economic effects. Positive for whom? Does the Bank's recipe for 'responsible trade unionism' take cognizance of the vast army of casual and contract labourers moving around as wage hunters and gatherers in the lower echelons of the industrial economy and who are the subject of my end-piece to this volume?

# 3
# A Question of Poverty*

## DEBATES ON DUALISM, OLD AND NEW

The state of deprivation, which is the essence of poverty, easily conjures up an image of helplessness, of people who are failing in the universal human urge to live in dignity and are a burden both to themselves and to others. This need not necessarily suggest that the blame for their inadequate existence lies with the poor themselves, in the sense that they are primarily responsible for their dismal fate. The misery in which at least one-fifth of humanity lives—a figure that rises as high as a third or a half in some regions[1]—is, after all, associated with lack of access to the basic resources that could free them from poverty. Aid from the non-poor can help the poor in their efforts to achieve progress and can even be of critical importance. The idea of development aid—transfer of capital, mainly, from the rich North to the poor South—bore witness to this sense of generosity in the second half of the twentieth century. The economic policymakers of the new world order that now exists have also committed themselves to reducing poverty as part of their strategy aimed at perpetual growth. However, it looks like the World Bank, the International Monetary Fund (IMF), and the World Trade Organization will succeed in their pro-poor mission only if the remedy suggested wins the approval and support of all concerned, beginning with the target group itself. Enlightened self-interest activated through market forces is the undisputed cornerstone of the neoliberal policy.

Does the habitus of the poor really conform to that golden rule of the globalized economy? The long-cherished argument that poverty is mainly a question of insufficient or inadequate economic activity—whether

* Originally published as 'A Question of Poverty', in Jan Breman, *The Labouring Poor in India: Patterns of Exploitation, Subordination and Exclusion*, Chapter 6, New Delhi: Oxford University Press, 2003, pp. 194–220.

voluntary or imposed—has become less convincing since the 1970s, when case studies on what is known as the informal sector in various parts of the world began to reveal the highly active existence of men, women, and children crowding at the bottom of the urban economy in Third World countries. This insight has given rise to a new platitude that unemployment is a luxury poor people cannot afford. I believe the term 'labouring poor' is entirely appropriate for the unregulated and complex community that populates the informal sector.[2]

A stream of empirical micro-studies, mostly undertaken by anthropologists in urban locations within the Third World, has expanded our knowledge of how workers succeed in living on the fruits of their labours outside the formal sector of the economy. In an early paper (Breman 1976a), I maintained that the formal–informal dichotomy could be regarded as a new variation on the dualism theories of the past. In his classic exposé on the nature of the colonial economy, J.H. Boeke examined the contrast between an invasive Western capitalist commercial sector and an opposing Eastern non-capitalist people's economy. In post-colonial development theory, the concept of dualism was applied to the dichotomy of traditional and modern. In this view, the rural–agricultural order was pre-capitalist and contrasted with the urban–industrial economy, which was described as capitalist. In the most recent phase of the dualism doctrine, an advanced segment that bears the mark of capitalism is identified within the urban milieu: the formal sector. The modes of production in the lower economic terrain, with their non-capitalist stamp, are characterized as the informal sector.

While the scope of the dualism model became narrower and narrower—from Western versus Eastern, via industrial–urban as opposed to rural–agricultural, and finally, formal–informal as distinct circuits in the urban system—this historical development did nothing to change the idea that the two economic segments, which are placed in opposition to each other, can be identified as capitalist and non-capitalist respectively. In operationalizing these variations on dualism, it is the contrasts we must rely on to clarify matters, rather than the specific characteristics of each moiety. For instance, it is entirely normal to describe the informal sector by summing up the absence of elements found in the formal sector and explaining how difficult it is to gain access to this elevated part of the urban economy, which is disciplined by all kinds of government regulations. In the absence of a stricter, more analytical definition, the landscape of the informal sector becomes synonymous with the kaleidoscope of unregulated, poorly skilled, and low-paid workers that the observer encounters when walking through the streets. It was in depicting just such a chaotic assortment that Hart coined the term 'informal economy' in his famous paper of 1971, based on fieldwork in the Ghanaian city of Accra.[3]

## Rise of the Informal Sector

Sometimes, the term 'informal sector' refers to a certain modality of employment and sometimes, it refers to the organization of economic activity as a whole. My own research is based on the first definition: the income from work, performed either on one's own account and at one's own risk or as waged labour, for which no explicit written or oral contract stipulating the rights and obligations of the parties has been agreed, where there is no legal protection for the conditions of employment, and the activities are only sketchily recorded in the government's accounts, if at all (Breman 1976a, 2001a). Focusing on the organization of activity emphasizes characteristics like the small scale of enterprises, the predominance of familial employment and property, low capital intensity and simple technology, fluctuating production, easy entry to and exit from the lower echelons of the economy, the preponderance of local markets, and the lack of government recognition and support. In the former case, the dualism is attributed to the nature of employment and labour relations, while in the latter, the economy is split into two circuits, each with its own modality of production methods. The assumption that the dichotomy is parallel is incorrect in both senses and has led to much misunderstanding in both theory and practice. The criteria do not produce a clear and consistent classification. The resulting confusion stems from the tendency to incorporate elements of both definitions in the analysis. The hybrid often chosen seems to arise from the fact that informality is frequently associated with self-employment. This was also how Hart initially described it:

The definitional distinction drawn here is between activities classified as formal, i.e. wage-earning employment, and informal, i.e. self-employment. This parallels that drawn between the unorganized and organized sections of the urban labour force, common synonyms for the latter being 'the reserve army of underemployed and unemployed', 'those who are self-employed in small enterprises', etc. Often one is talking of those workers who are enumerated by surveys of establishments and the remainder who are not. (Hart 1973: 66)

Despite the ambiguous and overlapping criteria, the duality of the urban order is explained in both definitions with reference to the nature of government intervention. The rules applying in the formal sector refer to both the proper use of labour and the environment, for instance, and set quality standards that the goods and services offered must meet. The informal sector is less burdened by this kind of public regulation, if at all, partly because of the authorities' inability to get a grip on the wide range of activities through conditions and licensing, and partly as a result of resistance, by the economic actors concerned, to registration, inspection, and taxation by the government.

Since the introduction of the informal sector concept, opinion has been divided as to its social impact. Some authors, inclined to a more positive assessment, have pointed to the accelerated shift in livelihood patterns away from agriculture and villages to cities and towns that has occurred in large parts of the Third World since the mid-twentieth century. Even if the masses of migrants flooding into urban areas were lucky enough to find their feet, the vast majority of them could gain no access to the formal sector. It was still too small to cope immediately with the continuous influx of newcomers. Under the circumstances, the informal sector acted as a catchment reservoir for the job seekers who had been forced out of their rural–agricultural existence. In this interpretation, the emphasis is on the stamina, the flexibility, the will to adapt, the ingenuity, and the attempts made for upward mobility of the footloose workforce flooding into Third World cities. The more integrated they became in their new milieu of work and life and the more skills they acquired, the better qualified they would be for the formal sector of the economy. In making this leap forward, they would form trade unions to strengthen their bargaining power with both employers and the government.

The more critical analysis of researchers, who have observed that the formal sector remained inaccessible for reasons other than the inferior quality of the new urbanites' labour and their other defects, contrasts with this optimistic view. The failure of the newcomers' efforts to find stable and reasonably paid work was due mainly to a development strategy that, in the face of excess supply, sought to keep the price of labour as low as possible, allowed no room for collective action to reduce these people's vulnerability, and refused to provide this footloose workforce with government assistance. In short, the lack of registration, organization, and protection does not have its origin in the free play of social forces but is the product of economic interests that benefit from the state of informality in which a wide range of activities in all branches of the economy are kept, systematically and on a large scale, through evasion of labour laws and taxation.

I share this last interpretation, and I have documented my view in various publications based on repeated fieldwork in west India (for example, Breman 1994, 1996, 1999). To start with, I strongly resisted the temptation to present the informal sector as a separate and closed circuit of work and labour. To fully understand the mechanisms that underlie economic transfers, we must focus on the interaction between the formal and informal sectors, and particularly on the dependence of the latter on the former, and its subordination to it. My arguments refute the long-held theory that the informal sector is a characteristic feature of urban economic activity. To the extent that there is social duality, the tendency to split into two sectors manifests itself in a way that transcends the dynamics of the urban economy. By drawing the same distinction in the rural economy, it is possible to identify the ties between formal and informal segments in town and hinterland— manifested in the circulation of both labour and capital—and include them in an analysis of the economic order as a whole.

Finally, I reject the view that informality refers largely or exclusively to self-employment. What often appears to be own-account work is, in fact, some form of wage labour, for orders contracted out by intermediaries such as (sub)contractors or jobbers. Both in small-scale enterprises and in the chain of dependency made up of brokers and ending with homeworkers, wages are paid not on an hourly basis but by piecework. To record this as self-employment is to overlook the fact that such labouring modalities actually bear the hallmark of an employer–employee relationship expressed in the form of wage payment. The different views on the informal sector did not stop most studies focusing, until recently, on its time-bound nature. Whatever the school of thought authors adhered to, they almost always felt they could assume that informality was a temporary phenomenon born of the slow expansion of the formal sector economy. The acceleration that would inevitably happen would lead to a simultaneous shrinking of the informal sector. This prognosis came from the assumption of parallel development whereby the process of transformation seen in the Third World in the second half of the twentieth century would essentially follow the same route already travelled by developed societies. The formalization of industrial activity was bound to lead to technological modernization and organizational expansion, while the productivity of services would also increase as capital was added. This transformation should be accompanied by growing state involvement designed to increase public control over the use of capital, labour, and other resources. The silenced informal sector workers would gain a voice in society by taking collective action to represent their own interests. These analyses, made in the 1970s, seem to have lost more and more of their currency over the years.

The fact that the informal sector has continued to grow rather than decline in magnitude and significance is undoubtedly the most obvious indication of this reverse trend. The earlier estimates, that less than half the working population lived on the proceeds of the informal sector, have since been revised to include more than three-quarters of all those who are gainfully employed. A complex of economic and social mechanisms has led to a rapid fall in the volume of labour in agriculture. Displacement to other areas of economic activity, in both urban and rural areas, has occurred under conditions characteristic of work in the informal sector, which I have summarized as sustained mobility, not stable but casual employment, and piecework rather than time-rate work (Breman 1996). The growing pressure in the bottom layers of the economy outside agriculture has not been relieved by the expansion of formal sector employment. There are, in fact, signs that this segment has shrunk over the past few decades.

## Decline of the Formal Sector

The recognition of this unexpected dynamic has led to a reconsideration of the view that the process of economic growth in the Third World is essentially a delayed repetition of the industrialization and urbanization scenario that laid the foundations for the Western welfare state in the early twentieth century. This critical review of the initial notion of an evolutionary development process based on the Western model has major policy implications. It has increasingly become politically correct to believe that efforts should no longer focus on formalizing the labour system. By way of an explanation for the essential reversal of the previous development trajectory, the suggestion now is that the privileges enjoyed by an exceedingly small proportion of the working population must end. The protection enjoyed by the elite within the workforce—who, in Third World countries, represent no more than a tenth of the total population living on the fruits of its labour power—is detrimental, according to this argument, to the efforts of the vast majority to improve the conditions in which they live. This 'unfair' competition could be avoided by abolishing security of employment, minimum wages and maximum working days, and numerous other labour rights that used to apply in the formal sector. Should we not then worry that things will get even worse for the quality of the labouring existence? No, those who call for flexibility to give employers a free hand to hire and fire as they please suggest that this approach would actually lead to more, and better work, and a rise in wages in real terms.

The World Bank has been a leading proponent of the process of informalization, as we might refer to the erosion of the rights of formal sector workers. This was the basic message of the 1995 *World Development Report* (World Bank 1995), which looked at the position of labour in the globalized economy. In a critical review of this ground-breaking document, I summarized the World Bank's proposed policy on Third World countries as follows.

I myself have conducted several empirical case studies of the progress and impact of the informalization process in recent years. After the Asian economic crisis broke in mid-1997, I was able to observe its impact on work and welfare during a visit to Jakarta that autumn. Both national and international policymakers responded to the loss of jobs in the formal sector of the urban economy by suggesting that these workers who were 'temporarily' superfluous would easily find other work in the informal sector. The extent to which this was based on wishful thinking became clear when, between 1998 and 2000, I and an Indonesian colleague did research in rural Java on the impact of the loss of urban employment and the income it provided for a considerable proportion of the workforce in the two villages where we located our investigations (see Breman 2000; Breman and Wiradi 2002). Recently, I undertook another study on the loss of jobs in the formal sector in the west Indian city of Ahmedabad. The closure of more than 50 large textile mills meant that, from the early 1980s onwards, some 100,000–125,000 factory workers lost their jobs. On the basis of anthropological fieldwork in the mill localities where they resided, I studied how their households fared after they were forced to join the informal sector (Breman 2001a; Breman and Wiradi 2002). My findings unmistakably show deterioration in the living standards of the many workers who were no longer covered by the regulations applying in the formal sector.

The results of my research in Ahmedabad must be viewed in the light of the fundamental change in the labour policies of the Indian government. This turnaround came about not least as a result of pressure from transnational institutions like the World Bank and IMF. The idea that efforts should no longer be focused on increasing formalization of the labour system appears to have gained the status of political correctness. H. Lubell, who has written on this subject in the past, observed in his last publication, that 'the informal sector is here to stay' (1991: 111). His inclination is to emphasize the benign effects of this dynamic. Analyses focusing on the positive side of the regime of economic informality are designed to refute the idea that anyone leaving the formal sector and joining the informal sector will automatically experience a deterioration in their standard of living. This is based largely on the argument that working on one's own account and at one's own risk is the best route to development. Such a view often tends to culminate in an ode to the virtues of microenterprise. Lubell summarizes his discussion of the debate with the conclusion that:

ILO and other informal sector surveys showed that many informal sector participants who had worked in the formal sector before going into the informal sector shifted to the informal sector not because they were redundant to the formal sector but because they chose to be self-employed, using skills acquired in the formal sector to establish themselves as independent producers or traders; they were small scale entrepreneurs who chose self-employment because they could capitalize on skills (and savings) acquired in the formal sector. (Ibid.: 112)

The voluntary transfer suggested here is an option that very few of the former mill hands in Ahmedabad, or sacked formal sector workers in Jakarta, would support. As I have explained, the choice was not theirs. It was forced mobility, and downward mobility at that. As soon as they lost their jobs, they realized that their lives were set to become much worse.

## ON POVERTY AND PROPERTY

### A Mystery Unveiled

Can poverty best be solved by the formalization of economic activity and labour in the global economy or should the solution be found in a policy of informalization? In 2000, a book that offered a crystal-clear answer to this question was published. The author is Hernando de Soto, whose *penchant* for publicity has previously brought his name to the attention of a wide audience. In 1989, this Peruvian economist published *The Other Path: The Invisible Revolution in the Third World*, in which he presented himself as the self-appointed spokesman of the informal sector in his native country. From his base in the Institute of Liberty and Democracy in Lima, founded and directed by him, de Soto drew attention to the creative manner in which the urban poor resisted their exclusion from the social order as dictated by capitalism. The World Bank was among the donors that provided this institute with substantial funds. The action-oriented research instigated by de Soto over a period of many years resulted in a range of concrete proposals. His mission was to persuade politicians and policymakers to introduce the reforms necessary to assure the informal sector of the respectability and recognition that it had until then lacked. The experience gained during his sustained campaign for a better deal for the mass of people forced to live in the shadow of the formal economy formed the raw material for a new publication that has brought him even greater international acclaim. Why capitalism triumphs in the West and has failed everywhere else: this is the rather provocative subtitle to de Soto's book, *The Mystery of Capital*, published in 2000. The failure should be not taken too literally because everywhere in the Third World, a segment of the formal economy has emerged which is capitalist in every sense of the word. The problem is that the visible and invisible activity outside this circuit—in which an estimated half to three-quarters of all workers are engaged and which accounts for more than two-thirds of gross national product— is conducted without regard to the legal rules applying to the formal sector. Instead of losing ground, this underground extra-legal economy is displaying a tendency to expand.

De Soto's study has been received with great admiration in neo-conservative circles, and sometimes outside them.[4] *Time* magazine went so far as to call him one of the most prominent Latin American thinkers of the twentieth century, while the *The Economist* said that his institute is the world's second most influential think tank. These praises are reproduced on the book cover, together with warm recommendations from a number of dignitaries, including Francis Fukuyama, David Owen, and Margaret Thatcher. How can we explain such enthusiastic acclamation?

One major reason is that all of these opinion leaders have little difficulty in recognizing in de Soto a like-minded soul, an undiluted advocate of the idea that capitalism is not the cause of poverty but a condition for assuring escape from it. The Third World and its new variant, the ex-communist countries, are suffering from not too much but too little capitalism, and it is this which prevents an increasing proportion of the population from taking the salutary step towards greater prosperity. De Soto's optimistic message is that poverty is not as widespread and intense as we tend to believe. The majority of the people in the enormous and still expanding informal sector of those countries do not as much suffer from a lack of savings or property as from the opportunity to make the capital that they do have more productive. The remedy that de Soto claims to have found to this unfortunate situation has undoubtedly enhanced his popularity among Western neo-conservative thinkers and politicians even further. In his view, poverty will solve itself without aid from external sources. Poor countries should stop their desperate search for capital outside their own economies and devote their energies to accessing this enormous reserve of untapped wealth and making it profitable:

Leaders of the Third World and former communist nations need not wander about the world's foreign ministries and international financial institutions seeking their fortune. In the midst of their own poorest neighbourhoods and shanty towns there are—if not acres of diamonds—trillions of dollars, all ready to be put to use if only we can unravel the mystery of how assets are transformed into live capital. (De Soto 2000: 30–1)

For de Soto, seeing poverty as destitution erroneously diverts attention from the heroic achievements of the multitude of petty entrepreneurs, the countless men and women who, through hard work and a frugal lifestyle, succeed in saving enough to build a house and start a small business. In this hopeful view, the poor, with their micro-workshops, are not the problem but the solution. Most of them find a way to overcome their setbacks and to generate the means of production that enable them to escape from the state of underdevelopment. In this milieu, which is almost exclusively described in terms of misery, enlightened self-interest is more than a doctrine. It is a way of life.

What is sure to enhance the neo-conservative approbation for this constructive analysis even further is that it makes development possible without a supranational or even intra-national redistribution of the sources of wealth and prosperity. In de Soto's scenario, the poor are no longer outcasts but heroes, in that they generate capital and property as it were out of nothing. This is, after all, completely in keeping with the history of the people-oriented capitalist development in Western societies: '... much of today's surplus value in the West has originated not in the scandalously expropriated labour time but in the way that property has given minds the mechanism with which to extract additional work from commodities' (ibid.: 198).

Lastly, the delight with which supporters of the free-market ideology advocated by de Soto have greeted his inventive solution to the mystery of capital should not, in the last instance, be attributed to his observation that government presents the greatest obstacle to the expansion of popular wealth and prosperity. Such expansion can be achieved only by giving social and economic forces a free hand. A certain amount of regulation by the state is, of course, necessary to guarantee the owners of capital sufficient profit and legal certainty. The withdrawal of the state from the economy is beneficial and desirable—except when it is counterproductive to the further development of capitalism.

## The Representation of Capital

The starting point for de Soto's study is the radical transformation that the Third World has undergone in the past half a century. In a historical sketch that is a simple summary, he describes the past of these societies as an agrarian order that is feudal in character. The peasantry in the countryside lived and worked in a state of bondage tied to an aristocracy of indigenous landowners or colonial planters. The cities were small and functioned as trading centres under the control of a small but powerful merchant class. After 1950, an industrial revolution gained momentum, which was a repeat of that in the West two centuries earlier, but at a much faster rate and affecting a much larger mass of people. The transition from agriculture to industry was accompanied by an exodus from the country to the cities—a phenomenon which, according to de Soto, in an incomprehensible manner, has been as good as neglected—causing such a shift in the dynamics of Third World societies that their institutional structures were unable to adjust. What de Soto means to say here is that those who were pushed out of isolated, small-scale rural communities failed in gaining access to the legal mechanisms of regulated economic activity once they arrived in the cities. The absorption capacity of the formal sector economy is insufficient to deal with such an enormous volume of migrants and the reform of the legal order that might have offered a solution is not implemented. The newcomers have no other choice in protecting the savings they accumulate than to make up their own rules. This self-devised code functions adequately within its own sphere but is not recognized by outsiders.

The failure of the legal order to keep pace with this astonishing economic and social upheaval has forced the new migrants to invent extralegal substitutes for established law. Whereas all manner of anonymous business transactions are widespread in advanced countries, the migrants in the developing world can deal only with people they know and trust. Such informal, *ad hoc* business arrangements do not work very well. The wider the market, as Adam Smith pointed out, the more minute the division of labour can be. And as labour grows more specialized, the economy grows more efficient and wages and capital values rise. A legal failure that prevents enterprising people from negotiating with strangers defeats the division of labour and fastens would-be entrepreneurs to smaller circles of specialization and to low productivity. (De Soto 2000: 62)

To acquire a perspective on property formation among this poor mass, de Soto commissioned a large team of local researchers in Haiti, Peru, the Philippines, Egypt, and Mexico to conduct a thorough study of the value of real estate that does not appear in any official records. Empirical investigations were carried out in five specific locations—Port au Prince, Lima, Manila, Cairo, and Mexico City—and resulted in a detailed mapping of landownership. On the basis of the findings, it can be estimated that 85 per cent of all urban lots and around half of land parcels in rural areas of the Third World are in the hands of people who have no form of legal proof of ownership whatsoever. De Soto calculates that the value of this property amounts to a total of some US$ 9.3 trillion. This is the equivalent to twice the total money in circulation in the United States, more than 20 times the combined investment in the Third World and the former communist countries since 1989, or almost 100 times the volume of all aid provided by developed countries to developing countries in the past 10 years.

In short, the under-capitalization of the informal sector is the crux of the development problem. The poor lack the capacity to reap the economic benefits of their property, since it remains outside the formal accounts and registers. They lack the capacity to represent their assets and create productive capital. They have houses but not titles, crops but not deeds, and businesses but no articles of association. The accumulation of wealth is, therefore, not hampered by the absence of property or of an entrepreneurial spirit. 'The poor have accumulated trillions of dollars of real estate during the last 40 years. What the poor lack is easy access to the property mechanisms that could legally fix the economic potential of their assets so that they could be used to produce, secure or guarantee greater value in the expanded market' (de Soto 2000: 40).

The gigantic volume of property possessed by the poor remains dead capital because they lack the proof of legal ownership required to allow them to take out mortgages, arrange loans, and conduct other financial transactions. Only by doing this can the real value their property represents be employed productively for investment in new economic activity. In this view, the poor remain outside the formal sector because they have no access to the legal procedures integral to it. The difference with the road to development followed in Western societies is that, in the latter, property rights were confirmed over time in such a way that the poor were integrated into the national economy. According to de Soto, the triumph of Western capitalism is due to the formalization of capital, in the same way as he attributes its failure everywhere else in the world to the refusal to legalize the immense property of the mass of people in the informal sector of the economy. The consequence of this failure has been the consolidation of underdevelopment and poverty on a large scale.

If this is indeed the path to prosperity, why then is the transition from informal to formal, which in this analysis coincides with the replacement of extra-legal with legal ownership of property, hampered in the Third World rather than encouraged? De Soto makes it clear that there is no question of a monopolistic conspiracy. His explanation is much simpler: collective amnesia. The path to development followed in the West is seen as so self-evident that Westerners are no longer able to explain their own success. De Soto claims to have solved this riddle. In *The Mystery of Capital*, the rediscovery of the history of property registration plays a key role. By way of explanation, de Soto investigated how a large army of migrant squatters managed to take possession of land when they entered the plains of North America around the middle of the nineteenth century. The opening up of these 'empty' lands occurred outside the existing rules and laws. In the frontier society they created, the settlers operated at their own risk and on their own account. This made them, so the argument goes, the early predecessors of the self-employed masses who now populate the informal sector in the cities of the Third World. The American government eventually had little other choice than to legalize the arrangements that the colonists had established amongst themselves. The adoption of the Homestead Act in 1862, which gave the settlers the right to 160 acres of free land simply for agreeing to live on it and cultivate it, was less an act of official generosity than the recognition of a fait accompli. Americans had been settling—and improving—the land extra-legally for decades (de Soto 2000: 95). That de Soto takes the Wild West as his example in unravelling the formalization of common law in the developed countries is, of course, no coincidence. His illustration is entirely in keeping with the tendency to see the US as the heartland of capitalism and helps to support the author's claim that property acquisition is essentially a matter of individual entrepreneurial spirit. In this interpretation, land becomes property through settlement and then acquires a value it never had. Much can be said about this explanation of the 'mystery'. It is contestable that the lands into which the colonists streamed en masse were empty at all, unencumbered by the ownership claims of the indigenous population. Even more dubious than the denial of large-scale land theft in the history of the US is the suggestion that the early colonization of the thinly populated American plains in the middle of the nineteenth century can be compared, in any way, with the manner in which, a century-and-a half later, the migrant masses in the Third World left the countryside and took possession of the space they found to inhabit in the cities.

## A Moralistic Discourse

Rejecting the relevance of the historical example presented by de Soto does not affect the importance of his question as to why legalization of property in the informal sector of the economy has not yet occurred. De Soto himself lays the blame primarily with governments in the developing countries. Their failure to address the persistent and continually expanding regime of economic informality is founded on misconceptions and a political and administrative unwillingness to apply the rules of the formal sector to the economic activity of the population as a whole. The advantage of having to pay little or no taxes is, according to him, offset by the much greater disadvantage that an enormous amount of real property falls outside the capitalist circuit. This exclusion is counterproductive not only for the owners but also for the national economy. De Soto has unravelled the mystery that none of us understood. That in itself should be enough to earn him our thanks. The recognition he so richly deserves is, however, enhanced by his offer to call to order all the indifferent bureaucrats, reluctant legal professionals, and blind political elite in the Third World and to exercise pressure on them to take proper action in the process of capitalization. It is a script for politicians and decision-makers that they can use as a manual to embark on the road to legalization, the conversion of informal property into formal capital.

By way of experiment, de Soto and his staff set up a garment workshop with two sewing machines in a slum locality in Lima to experience the countless obstacles to legalization at first hand. They kept an accurate record of the time and costs involved in acquiring an official licence for their microenterprise: in a procedure that totalled 728 bureaucratic operations, it amounted to 300 days and at a cost of 32 times the minimum monthly wage. Their recommendation that the road to legalization should be shorter and cheaper comes as no surprise.

What happens if vested interests keep refusing to put the capitalist handbook into practice? De Soto makes no threats but does remind us of the acute resentment that micro-entrepreneurs at the foot of the economy feel regarding their legal apartheid. The longer the rightful expectations of this substantial underclass are frustrated, the more fuel it will provide for those opposed to capitalism and to globalization. Marx was mistaken in as much as he failed to realize that the phase

of primitive accumulation was already as good as over in his time and
that having no means of production is not the real problem of capitalist
transformation. After Marx's death, the West finally managed to set up a
legal framework that gave most people access to property and the tools of
production. Marx would probably be shocked to find how in developing
countries, much of the teeming mass does not consist of oppressed legal
proletarians but of oppressed extra-legal small entrepreneurs with a
sizeable amount of assets (de Soto 2000: 198).

The policy of tolerance that the authorities in the Third World
have pursued so far means that they have accepted informal property
accumulation without allowing the real estate and the small-scale
enterprises that have evolved in the informal sector to realize their full
value by recognizing them as formal capital. In the same way, land reforms
in many developing countries have remained restricted to handing out
land to poor peasants. They remain unable to increase the yield of the
land because they have not been issued with the corresponding title
deeds. It is a state of exclusion that invokes anger among the victims.
In de Soto's view, *la classe dangereuse* is not a horde of dispossessed
and uprooted paupers but a huge mass of petty property owners who,
indignant about their extra-legal status, are prone to resort to crime or
prove susceptible to political extremism (to be read as leftist radicalism).

De Soto's argument has a number of positive elements that I should
not fail to mention in my largely critical appraisal. He rejects the view
of the poor as a parasitical and unproductive class that prefers doing
nothing to hard work. He also clearly does not support those who see
poverty as a question of choice, which is part of the pattern of culture
of many non-Western societies. Entrepreneurial talents are by no means
the monopoly of countries that have spearheaded the development of
capitalism. But the capabilities that can lead to higher production and
productivity will only develop under favourable social conditions. De
Soto appears to believe strongly in progress and refuses to accept that the
misery in which a large part of humanity in the Third World lives is a
situation that they themselves would not change if they were able to do
so. This, however, is about the extent of my appreciation for his analysis.

Before elaborating on my substantial objections, I would like to make
a few comments on the methodology and style of de Soto's work. It is
telling to see how he himself describes his modus operandi.

But no one had any exact idea. No one even knew how to measure what the
poor were doing or precisely how much they owned. And so my colleagues
and I decided to put away our books and academic journals, not to mention

our reams of government statistics and maps, and visit the real experts on this problem: the poor themselves. Once we went into the streets to look around and listen, we began stumbling across surprising facts. (De Soto 2000: 66–7)

The research leader and his team of associates took it upon themselves to collect the information that could not be found in the literature. The story is told as a quest for the key to the mystery—the complete lack of documentation on the scale of property owned but not registered legally as such—in a way that is not free of conceit. To perform this operation successfully, de Soto explains how he acquainted himself with the anthropological technique of participatory observation. There is, however, little evidence in the book of this in-depth method of collecting data in the field. The poor remain at a distance, an anonymous mass about which the author writes with a show of sympathy but who he clearly has not met in their own milieu. 'You need only open a window or take a taxi from the airport to your hotel to see city perimeters crowded with homes, armies of vendors hawking wares in the streets, glimpses of bustling workshops behind garage doors and battered buses crisscrossing the grimy streets' (ibid.: 23).

The reader is better informed of the author's discussions with intellectuals and political leaders—including Suharto's generals in Indonesia—than about his fieldwork in the slums of the Third World. 'After thirteen years, thousands of miles and little more grey hair, I had visited just about every property-related organization in the advanced world', de Soto (2000: 93) informs us, but only to discover that they had nothing to tell him. There was little else to do than to go out and seek the answer for himself, to spend thousands of days measuring and counting what was not recorded anywhere in the official property registers and settlement reports. Considering the emphasis de Soto places on empirical investigations, it is surprising to observe that his book is extremely vague about the way in which these were conducted and the problems he encountered along the way. Nor is there even a general appraisal of the findings of what in the last decades has become a substantial pool of knowledge on the origins, workings, and dynamics of the informal sector economy.[5] De Soto's references to the work of others are limited to an august batch of classical and modern thinkers such as Plato, Kant, Wittgenstein, Foucault, and Derrida, to mention but a few. He clearly feels that he is at home among such illustrious scholars and seems to consider himself of equal rank. This claim is even more remarkable in that *The Mystery of Capital* is written in *Reader's Digest* style. An example is his observation that if all the street vendors in Mexico City were placed side by side, they would form a line no less than 210 kilometres long. I include his anecdote about the dogs on the island of Bali in the same category of platitudes. Walking through this earthly paradise, he finds himself unable to distinguish where one plot of land ends and the next begins:

> But the dogs knew. Every time I crossed from one farm to another, a different dog barked. Those Indonesian dogs may have been ignorant of formal law, but they were positive about which assets their masters controlled. I told the ministers that Indonesian dogs had the basic information they needed to set up a formal property system. (De Soto 2000: 146)

By explaining his mode of thinking in such simple terms, de Soto clearly wishes to reach out to a wide audience. This in itself is praiseworthy but not when it affects the persuasive power of his analysis and his argument loses its value due to oversimplification. Mario Varga Llosa, once a great admirer of de Soto and author of a glowing foreword to the latter's first book, later spoke of his former friend in damning terms, describing him as vindictive, a man with more ambitions than principles, whose integrity should be called into doubt.[6]

This prima donna conduct, which Llosa also observes, comes clearly to the fore in de Soto's writing style. To avoid any misunderstanding, the nature of the man's character—pleasant or otherwise—plays no part in my opinion of his work. My criticism applies solely to the lack of theoretical depth and the lean empirical foundation of his main hypothesis. He presents it as a social–scientific analysis, but it is much more an ideological statement intended to advocate capitalism as the only true path to development. 'As all possible alternatives to capitalism have now evaporated, we are finally now in a position to study capital dispassionately and carefully' (ibid.: 11). De Soto does not fulfil this promise in any way in his book. Although he claims to use a research technique meant to bring the researcher closer to those he or she is researching, he continues to look down from above. His perspective is not so much populist as elitist. This is not only because of the company de Soto seeks but, even more so, because he chooses a method of elucidation in which poverty disappears from view entirely, to be replaced by property—which proves to be present among the common people in much greater quantities than those in power ever imagined. No wonder that his message was received by such as Suharto's generals as the word of an apostle. The final section of my argument is intended to correct de Soto's strongly biased portrayal of social reality on a number of essential points.

## Mystery as Fable

The first misconception that must be rectified is that the informal sector exists as a separate and closed circuit with its own logic and game rules.[7] In de Soto's interpretation, it is an economic segment that not only operates extra-legally but is also non-capitalist in nature. As I have already observed in the first part of this essay, in my view, the existence and working of the informal sector can be understood only by tracing the lines that connect it to the formal sector. It is true that precious little information is to be found on the economic activity in the lower echelons of the urban and rural economies in official statistics and records. However, both the way in which property is formed and the structure of the relations of production display the same capitalist characteristics as occur in the formal sector. In other words, the poverty that manifests itself so explicitly in the informal sector is not a survival from a pre-capitalist social order but a consequence of the processes of change that de Soto has chosen as the starting point for his study. Nor is he consistent in his opinion that there is a fundamental distinction between the two sectors. After first typifying the dualism in the economy as a system of apartheid, a few pages later, he points out that informal sector workers also supply a wide range of goods and services to clients in the formal sector. This apparent contradiction disappears when we realize that, even in apartheid South Africa, the black majority was closely linked in all manner of ways to the white minority. This interaction was expressed in the dependence of the majority on the minority, a situation which is paralleled by the way in which the informal sector functions: not separate from but subordinated to the dominant circuit.

Second, I would like to distance myself from the tenaciously held opinion, which de Soto shares, that the informal sector economy rests purely on self-employment. In this view, the actors in the informal economic landscape are small, self-employed entrepreneurs who work on their own account, at their own risk, and do not employ others. Where there is a need for additional labour power, it is provided by other family members. The informal sector is seen as an infinite reservoir of one-man businesses run by what are, in essence, petit-bourgeois entrepreneurs who create their own means of production and who use the resulting revenue to lead a modest but not poor existence that enables them to accumulate property. This is an extremely distorted view of reality that, to start with, does no justice at all to the fact that a high percentage of informal sector workers are labourers who work for informal or formal employers, sometimes on a regular and sometimes on a casual basis. Moreover, so-called 'self-employment' is often thinly disguised work performed for others. Goods and services are produced, frequently by means of contracting and subcontracting, which are paid for on a piecework rather than a time-rate basis. To classify those who earn their living in this way as own-account workers is to deny what they really are: hired labour.

Third, and closely linked to the previous point, in solving his mystery, de Soto has created a new myth: that the informal sector consists largely of people who own property. They are not poor in the sense that they lack the basic means of production. In his words, 'most of the poor already possess the assets they need to make a success of capitalism' (de Soto 2000: 5). In the course of his long-lasting fact-finding mission, de Soto appears to have landed in very different slums and shanty towns in the Third World from those that I have studied. The findings of my fieldwork, conducted in India and Indonesia, show that the abject poverty in which the mass of those in the informal sector live is clearly a direct result of their lack of means of production and other forms of property, combined with the low return they receive on their labour.

Fourth, de Soto's analysis completely ignores the fact that property is not necessarily owned by those who use it as a means of subsistence. Land, buildings, tools, or means of transport often have to be hired or leased. The costs of such sharecropping arrangements account for a disproportionate part of the total earnings. The surplus, therefore, goes to the rent-seeking supplier of such capital rather than to the user. By ignoring all kinds of transactions flowing from the unequal distribution of property, de Soto suggests that the surplus value generated by the wide range of activities performed at the foot of the economy makes the poor less poor. But this is not the way in which the process of accumulation usually works. De Soto claims that what Marx called the primitive accumulation of capital no longer exists in today's world. He is referring here to primitive accumulation in its classical forms: plunder, slavery, and colonialism. It will be clear that I do not share his optimism. My empirical findings show that the term primitive accumulation is very appropriate to many of the facets of the informal sector economy. Much of the economic activity in these quarters is founded on capital from the formal sector and—given the low cost of labour and taxed minimally or not at all—returns to where it came from with a tidy profit.

Fifth, de Soto's explanation of the trend towards informalization is only partly correct. He is right to note that the expansion of the informal sector is paralleled by a contraction of the formal sector. He attributes this to the high costs inherent to legitimate economic activity. Doing business legally has become the exception; extra-legal business the rule. He adds to this observation that underground economic activity is not without cost. Non-official levies account for 10–15 per cent of the annual income of informal sector workers. They include bribes to the authorities to ensure exemption from a wide range of regulations. This shows that many in the formal sector, not least government officials, seek to benefit from the sparsely recorded activities in the informal economy. Bureaucrats and politicians—those in prominent positions as much as their inferiors lower down the hierarchy—use their public office to supplement their official income with varying degrees of discretion. These multifarious illegal practices can be understood only in the light of the collusion between the more powerful actors at both ends of the informal–formal spectrum. The preservation and even expansion of this social segregation, rather than its dissolution, is in both their interests.

Sixth, the notion that people in the informal sector are outside the law is as absurd as the reverse claim that the formal sector provides guaranteed protection and government control. The transfer of capital to the hidden side of the economy is an essential component in the informalization process and is a direct expression of the desire among capital owners to be free to organize production as they see fit, without undue interference from authorities which force them to pay taxes, not to mention their urge as agents of 'free enterprise' to minimize labour costs. It is the informal sector again, where there is no protective legislation and where workers are not in a position to organize and engage in collective action, that provides these favourable conditions. De Soto's claim that the owners of businesses in the formal sector, for the sake of enlightened self-interest, have no other choice than to contract their production out to informal workshops in the suburbs makes them the victims. In fact, it is they who can be blamed for the excesses of capitalism, for the way in which they manage to evade both their fiscal obligations and the rules governing the humane treatment of labour. By equating the distinction between legal and extra-legal with that between formal and informal, the author of *The Mystery of Capital* creates more confusion than clarity.

Now that the mystery has been solved, de Soto believes that it should be a simple task to put into practice the remedy he recommends. Is this really so? The objections I have raised against the way in which he poses the question, validates his assumptions, and verifies his data, conclusions, and recommendations can be summarized under the observation that de Soto's analysis has a one-sided bias in favour of capital and ignores labour as a factor of production entirely. His conclusion that the expansion and dissipation of Western prosperity was the result of a process of legal property formation in which the whole population took part is founded on preconceived ideas rather than on historical facts. Labour has achieved value and dignity in Western societies through a political and economic process of emancipation that entailed the curbing of capitalism. This meant bringing the unrestricted quest for profit and the free working of the market under public control and entrusting the responsibility for a wide range of care tasks to the state. The result was a social order based on equality. Capitalist development as described by de Soto, 'the only game in town', boils down to the formalization of the factor capital in such a way that the trend towards informalization of labour relations can continue unabated. The solution he offers is no solution, and to continue along that road will not bring to an end the poverty in which a substantial part of the world's population is forced to live.

## NOTES

1. The figure of 1.2 billion in 1998 is based on the well-known criterion of an income of less than 1 dollar per capita per day. The huge scale of poverty in the world has seen little change over the past two decades. See *World Development Report, 2000–1* (World Bank 2000).

2. This was the key message of several contributions to the Sephis workshop held in Mexico City's Centro de Estudios de Asia y Africa, El Colegio de México, on 27 and 28 June 2001.

3. The reader is referred to the abridged version in the *Third World Employment* collection edited by Jolly *et al.* (1973: 66–70).

4. Strikingly enough, the social–democratic strategists of the 'Third Way' are no less enthusiastic about de Soto's ideas than the select company of right-wing economists and politicians. Geoff Mulgan, Tony Blair's economic policy advisor, has called the author of *The Mystery of Capital*, a 'genuinely radical thinker' (see *New Statesman*, 4 September 2000).

5. In a devastating review of de Soto's first book, Bromley wrote: 'From an academic standpoint, De Soto's most irritating tendency is to reinvent the wheel without acknowledgement. He scrupulously avoids mention of prior work by other researchers or of models, ideas and policy recommendations previously developed by others' (Bromley 1990: 334).

6. See *El pez en el agua* (The Fish in the Water), 1993. My comments are based on the Dutch translation, *De vis in het water* (1994), in which pages 162–5 are devoted to de Soto.

7. According to my Oxford Dictionary (Indian edition 1992), a fable is an 'untrue statement or account'.

# 4

# Quality of the Labour Process*

## INFORMAL TRAINING FOR WORK

The main characteristic of the work done by the majority of workers in whom I am interested is that they lack skills and have to depend on little more than their own physical strength. Learning by doing is common practice from early age onwards. This type of training is standardized, particularly in the case of those who are taken on for an indefinite period but who at the start lack the necessary knowledge that will help them in due course to become experienced workers. One of the workers already employed—perhaps the same one who mediated in finding employment—will then show the newcomer the tricks of the trade.

Apprenticeship in the diamond industry is undoubtedly the longest, that is, six months, but still too short to teach the newcomer how to use the lathe and all stages of diamond cutting. Old hands at work told me with pride that their generation needed two years in which to become fully skilled. It will be clear that only young males who belonged to a household already firmly above the poverty line went for that training. For the landless, it would have been impossible to carry the subsistence burden of adults or adolescents who, instead of contributing to family income, invested in their own future. Nowadays, instruction is restricted to a single part of the cutting process. Most of those who finish this short training period are not given, or do not take, the chance to expand their knowledge to other parts of the work process. At the time of my fieldwork in 1986–7, a boy had to pay Rs 500–Rs 700 to the workshop

* Originally published as 'Quality of the Labour Process', in Jan Breman, *Footloose Labour: Working in India's Informal Economy*, Chapter 5, Cambridge: Cambridge University Press, 1996, pp. 109–40.

owner if he wanted to learn how to cut diamonds. That charge was said to be to compensate the employer for the devaluation of stones that became damaged during the learning period. This explanation is not at all convincing, nor is the argument that it costs time and money to supervise the pupil. For an experienced worker, it is an investment that will begin to show profit after only three months. That is, when the trainee is considered to have learned the cutting technique. The full wage for the stones that he processes during the following three months is paid to his instructor, who is thus generously compensated for the loss of income suffered during the time that the pupil demanded his constant supervision. A more plausible argument is that the obligation to pay a tuition fee discourages those who show little interest and patience in becoming proficient diamond cutters. One result, intended or not, is that the charge for entering the profession inhibits youths from the lower social-economic milieux. To members of the tribal castes, payment of such an amount is almost equivalent to the amount of dowry: '[A] woman who offers her future husband the chance to become a diamond cutter is a good match and on that basis can enter into marriage with the son of a large farmer; in addition, she then marries a man with the prospect of earning a good income' (Koelen 1985: 83; see also Kalathil 1978: 99–100).

The modest number of Halpatis who have entered the diamond-cutting profession usually have to thank a beneficent atelier owner for their induction. Instead of paying the fee in cash and in advance, he might permit them to pay it in arrears by working for a longer period for nothing or for a nominal wage. From the viewpoint of labour attachment, this is an attractive arrangement for the patron. It means, however, that the parents of these young adolescents must have sufficient means to maintain the favoured son or brother for even a longer period than that of apprenticeship. In the preceding chapter, we have seen that for the landless labourers and marginal landowners, this depletion of meagre reserves is an almost impossible burden to carry. Job training without pay is usually beyond the capacity of such households. A Halpati friend of mine in one of the fieldwork villages had run away from home as a young boy because his father forced him to leave school to help him in his daily work as bricklayer.

The textile industry lacks proper training facilities for beginners. According to some sources, textile workers from Andhra Pradesh are brought to Surat owing to their traditional experience in weaving, particularly in the Warangal region. That reputation was probably the reason for importing labour from those parts, but it does not signify that the young men who come to Surat have ever worked in that industry. This background does not apply to the greater flow of migrants recruited from a peasant caste in the countryside of Orissa. Their acquaintance with weaving looms starts only when, after reaching their destination, they first enter the factory to learn the work. One researcher reports, as follows, on industries in Surat where woven cloth is dyed and printed: 'that new workers learn only by working with experienced workers. An unskilled worker is known as *begari* who in course of time becomes semi-skilled and is a "helper". As he gains more experience he becomes skilled and he is taken up as a "printer" in the printing section when a vacancy arises' (Desai 1981: 115).

It is just the same in the power-loom workshops, as I observed. A beginner can only enter the industry and learn the trade by literally standing next to an experienced worker. He is present only in a marginal sense and has to make himself almost invisible where and when the manufacturing process takes place. The night shift is ideal for the purpose because the workplace is then peaceful. The surreptitious manner in which skill is passed on is characterized by the fact that the patron often does not know what is going on, or at least behaves as though he does not. His deputy, the weaving master, is in close touch with the workers and it is impossible to avoid him while teaching a skill to newcomers. His silence and collusion have to be bought because the errors that an apprentice makes cannot be hidden from him. There must not be too many errors, however, because then the prospective weaver is irrevocably shown the door and his instructor must take care not to suffer the same fate. Why, then, are the experienced workers prepared to accept such a burden? Apart from social obligations, that is, to help a relative, caste fellow, or inhabitant of the same village, financial gain is the principal motive. Actual apprenticeship lasts no more than a few weeks but it is continued thereafter for some time, varying according to the nature of the relationship, in order to compensate the instructor. The latter shares the yield of the production of his pupil with the weaving master. This state of affairs again emphasizes the principal reason why members of the landless castes are under-represented in the weaving industry. Men of these households cannot permit themselves to work for longer than a few days without wages. If an opening becomes available in the workshop, the apprentice may show that he has become a fully qualified worker. If this takes too long, then he may seek an opening in another establishment.

Halpatis from Gandevigam and Chikhligam who travel daily to the industrial sites of Bilimora are, at first, paid as 'helper' for activities that require neither training nor experience. In fact, the nature of their occupation differs little from that of long-term workers. In such cases, the term 'helper' indicates that he has been employed for only a short time, a sort of trial period during which output is remunerated at a lower level than the wage paid to older workers. Although there are no formal entrance requirements for this sphere of employment, my fieldwork data show that in practice, employers only take on young workers who have attended at least some years of elementary school. This information seems to conflict with the assertiveness with which employers claim that they have no need for literate workers. Certain employers whom I met expressed that they considered the ability to read and write a handicap rather than a recommendation. Similar pronouncements are found in other studies concerned with my research area. For example, on textile workers in Surat: 'Seven entrepreneurs informed us of having caught raw hands from nearby villages and of having trained them gradually. This took some time but entrepreneurs felt that old workers were trouble creators due to their contacts with trade unions and labour leaders. So they preferred raw hands from villages in spite of their limitations' (Bhatt 1979: 167). On diamond cutters in the countryside of south Gujarat: 'A few owners will find a couple of years of schooling favourable, but of secondary importance. An owner in Bajipura, on the other hand, found even the slightest amount of education to be disadvantageous because, in his opinion, it destroyed any ambition to do manual work; he gave preference to dexterous boys without any education' (Koelen 1985: 78).

The reasons vary, but in both cases the meaning is clear: education results in a mentality which, in the eyes of the employer, reduces rather than improves the quality of labour. The argument underlying the first quotation will be discussed more extensively in a later chapter. The veracity of the second quotation is doubtful. The statement ignores the fact that factory labour demands a certain amount of discipline and a sense of time that are difficult to adjust to for a Halpati boy accustomed to grazing the cows of a local farmer. Even a few years of schooling will teach, in addition to elementary literacy, a feeling for order and regularity, acclimatization to a rhythm based on the division of the day, week, or month into permanent reiterative time periods. To work under a roof, to find shelter from the elements among four walls, in itself gives a higher status to the work that has to be done. But not all those who are privileged to penetrate such an environment are able to adapt to the demands that go with it. Not without gloating, farmers in Gandevigam told me about local landless youths who had fruitlessly tried their luck in the factories of Bilimora, but who soon had to resume their existence as agricultural labourers because they could not stand the rigour of industrial discipline. This encourages the local elite in their conviction that members of this lower caste are suited for little other than work on the land. And even in that respect, according to Anaval landowners, the Halpatis who formerly served them as *halis* compare badly with the harder-working migrants now coming to the village. A preoccupation with those who manage to work their way upwards from a situation of extreme poverty should not lead us to overlook those who are forced to drop out from this steep and slippery path to a better and more dignified life. They just seem to fade away in due course.

An Industrial Training Institute (ITI) has been set up in Bilimora, for imparting training in various trades and crafts. Students admitted to one of the vocational courses are given a certificate which gives them access to jobs in the formal sector of the economy. In my fieldwork villages, a few youths from higher castes and more from the middle castes (Anaval Brahmans and Koli Patels respectively) have qualified as mechanics, motor mechanics, turners, or fitters. But they include no Dhodhiyas, let alone Halpatis. Dhodhiya youths are increasingly exposed to secondary education but mainly to seek employment in the public sector where the government's policy of positive discrimination gives them more chances than in the private sector. Halpati children rarely attend even primary school and many of them drop out even at this elementary level (Breman 1993b: 345–6). In many cases, their parents realize quite well the value of education but are simply not able to bear the cost of such an investment in the next generation. Even in villages located at a stone's throw from the town, disappointingly few children from the landless quarters ever attend school. When people are questioned about this fact, their replies are often quite bitter.

If our children are uneducated how can they hope to get better jobs outside in the city? People say that we Dublas are careless and irresponsible. We send them to field or tobacco factory or to *chayno larigallo* [tea stall] rather than send them to *balmandir* [kindergarten] or primary school. We force them to work and live on their earnings, they say. It is a cruel joke they are heaping on us.... We also have fatherly sentiments and we also know value of education. But when I am refused work in the field and my old mother comes back saying she too has no work on that day, we momentarily cease to be fathers and against our wish ask our children to go out and work. That is what is happening in Halpativas. (Cited in Punalekar 1992: 252)

The few craftsmen that I encountered in the Halpati quarters of Chikhligam and Gandevigam have to be satisfied with on-the-job training, under the supervision of their father or uncle. In view of the few tools at their disposal, they are only able to perform fairly simple and crude work, cheaper, and inevitably of poorer quality than that of skilled craftsmen from intermediate castes who have gone through formal technical schooling.

Children born to landless households seldom have the opportunity to gain any knowledge of a trade at school or even in practice. The route through education is closed to them. Even the apprenticeship which they ought to undergo by an employer if they are to acquire technical or trade skills assumes that their parents or other guardians are willing and able to provide for them during that time. This is usually out of the question as can be seen from the report on an enquiry among children found working on the streets in four towns of Gujarat, including Surat:

Some car cleaning boys do try to learn servicing and repairing of two-wheeler auto [rickshaw]. Not many of them are always successful though. Servicing and repairs carried out at known garages require sufficient training background. That training is given without wages. Training period is at least three to six months. What would they eat during this period? (Punalekar 1993: 106)

Non-specialization, that is, to avoid concentrating on and trying to learn a single trade, is the most commendable strategy for those who exist on the broad underside of the labour hierarchy. There are many slum dwellers who seem to have drifted along a large number of employment sites on which they get information from neighbours, friends, and their temporary workmates. Lobo has described such wandering occupational histories in his research on one particular Surat slum (Lobo 1994a: 45–65). Progress in the art of survival is determined by success in the constant search for new sources of income. Street children, in an effort to scrape a living, learn that lesson at an early age.

Car cleaning activity [at the crossroads of busy streets,] is a transit occupation for many [boys]. They try to learn and do other jobs like selling dusters, flowers, etc. or do cycle repairing, coolie work, etc. (Punalekar 1993: 106)
  Rajesh and Ramesh live on the platform at Surat railway station. The young boys, one from Bihar and the other from Maharashtra, clean railway compartments and are given small tips by the passengers. Both travel daily from Surat to Bulsar, and then Bulsar to Baroda. They prefer Gandhidam Express. Because, in this train they are sure to earn good money. All the same, they are not too happy with their life. They do remember their parents. But they do not want to go back home. They feel that once they are grown up and become

adults then they have to change their occupation. That is why both are saving for buying shoe-shine kits. (Punalekar 1993: B-5)

Their sheer survival is dependent on their will and ability to be as flexible as possible, to take on or to search for anything that offers. By preference, they work close to home, but if there is no alternative, they go farther or even far away. Such work is by definition unskilled, not requiring any experience; in short, work that everyone is able to do without having done it before. This is the commonly held opinion but it needs adjustment.

In the first place, not everyone has the physical strength to do hard, strenuous work. During my fieldwork, I repeatedly met people who found it impossible to continue in the brickworks, cane cutting, quarries, or salt pans. They simply could not keep up with the killing work tempo, were unable to cope with working during the night or for more than 12 hours at a stretch, and suffered too much from the abominable conditions in which they were forced to live and work. It was easy to see from their experience that complaints were by no means always due to weak physical stamina or to unsuitable age, that is, either too young or too old. Some people had literally fled from such work because they obviously lacked the mental toughness that would enable them to acquiesce to the demands of the production process. Second, the fact that jobs in specific branches of industry as also the slum habitats are broken up in distinct social collectivities to which people belong with a shared identity along regional, communal, or religious lines, conflicts with the notion of a total state of flux and an unstructured heterogeneity at the bottom of the urban economy. Ethnic segmentation is even an organizing principle of the urban labour market. The customary as well as superficial explanation given for this is that some people are traditionally familiar with particular work. Kathiawadis and Kanbi Patels in particular, for example, are deemed to be more suited than any other for the diamond-cutting trade; Khandeshis have long been accustomed to cane cutting; tribal workers from the Panch Mahals are known for their dexterity in road building; and in Bombay, but not at home, Halpatis maintain a reputation as brick makers. My own interpretation of the division of the mass of unskilled labour into several segments, already discussed, will be examined further in a later chapter.

Members of the rank and file in the informal sector, which to an outsider seems to be an undifferentiated mass, have a strongly developed sense of their own diversity, which is expressed in a high–low interrelationship. The inclination of the toiling mass of street workers to place one another in a ranking that runs from untouchable to high (self-)respect, as though on a caste ladder, is learnt at an early age.

A female street child working as a domestic servant considered herself higher than a rag-picker.... Nature and status of each street activity was judged by them and accordingly ranked socially. This is also true for male activities on the street. Male beggars were treated as lower in status by the male coolies or compartment cleaners working on a railway platform. The latter in turn were looked upon as inferior by shoe shine boys who in turn were rated low in status by teashop/ hotel servants. Boys working in a garage or a small workshop on a road side took immense pride in their job and considered themselves higher to everyone else engaged in other street activities. They called themselves as 'skilled workers', 'technicians'. (Punalekar 1993: 153)

The unskilled labour scene is thus much less uniform than it might seem at first sight, while within each branch of industry, the division of tasks is far more complex than an outsider might assume. A telling example is the elaborate work organization in the somewhat larger brick-fields. The man who makes the bricks is surrounded by a group, called *patala*, made up of adults and children who each have a specific task: to knead and mix the earth in a pit with water; to dig it out in heaps that are deposited in front of the *patavala*; to give him a ball of mud which he smacks into a mould; to snatch the brick that he has formed from the slab under his feet; to carry away this raw product; and to lay it in rows further away to dry. These are all separate activities that are allocated among 9–11 different men, women, and children. In addition to this, there are other work gangs as well: to bring earth to the worksite; to stoke the kiln; to carry the bricks to the kiln; to pile the bricks on top of one another; and after baking, to empty the kiln again. These are all tasks carried out by the people concerned for an entire season and already specified in the contract when they are hired.

In the lower economic echelons, the labour scene is thus characterized by strong differentiation which is horizontal in nature. The landscape is rather flat, by which I mean the absence of vertical stratification. As a result, the great mass of people are trapped in a work environment that offers almost no prospect of improving their position. The chance of obtaining employment that is a cut above that of others in terms of skill, esteem, and income, is minimal. An exceptional case, for example, is that of a seasonal worker in the brickworks who, sitting next to the one skilled man on the job, learns how to drive the lorry and later has the chance to get the driving licence which makes him a licenced driver. A great deal is necessary for such social mobility, however: not only a cordial relationship with the tutor and the owner of the brickworks, but also good luck or just bad fortune. An obvious example is that of the *mukadam*, the jobber-cum-gang boss who is close to the workers whom he mobilizes but at the same time, stands head and shoulders above them.

Finally, although there is very little vertical differentiation among unskilled labour, there is one type of distinction that is noticeable all along the line: that between man and woman. The former is invariably the focal figure: the cane cutter, quarryman, road worker, brick maker, and, not to be forgotten, the overseer in all his variations. The woman, on the other hand, fulfils the classic role of 'helper', although the severity of her work gives no reason for that subordinative term.

It is definitely not profitable for informal sector workers to delay ingress into the labour process until after having completed lower and continued education, perhaps followed by some sort of vocational training that would eventually enable them to cross the threshold into formal sector employment. The minimum training that they need in order to find work is a question of practical experience, of imitating others, a manner of learning which soon enables them to earn an income. This can be further illustrated by considering the highly skilled personnel employed by two high-tech firms forming part of the petrochemical industry in the coastal town of Hajira, west of Surat.

Larsen & Toubro (L&T) is a heavy engineering plant which specializes in factory equipment and offshore installations. At the end of 1992, one-third of the almost thousand employees belonged to the managerial and supervising ranks, and there were 676 labourers. A man starting in this lowest rank had a beginner's wage of Rs 1,800–1,900 per month. This is preceded, however, by a long qualifying period as apprentice. To be accepted as such—there were 50 trainees at that time—aspiring hopefuls have to have a secondary school diploma and an Industrial Training Institute (ITI) diploma. This is followed by a three-year industrial training during which they receive a modest monthly allowance which just covers their cost of living. Only those who are prepared to subject themselves to this lengthy training—in effect they work as mature but low-paid labourers—can be given a permanent job afterwards, always provided that places are available. Kribcho is an extremely modern plant in the co-operative sector, daily producing 5,000 tons of artificial fertiliser (urea). Its employees, numbering 1,400 at the end of 1992, consist for 75 per cent of people appointed to the higher ranks as manager or officer, in salary scales that reflect their college or even more advanced education. Kribhco, whose administration is computerized and production is automatized, has little need for unskilled labour. Workers who are employed as operators, only 25 per cent of the total workforce, have completed Polytechnic School (Diploma Engineer) or at least have an ITI certificate. The latter have to work a three-year apprenticeship before being given the chance of permanent employment. During that time they receive a meagre monthly allowance ranging from Rs 675 (during the first year) to Rs 725 (subsequently), free hostel accommodation, medical care, home leave, work clothes, and a few other facilities. The rank of operator provides a starting wage of Rs 2,300 per month. (Fieldwork notes)

In view of the high demands for preparatory training and the low wage paid during the long induction period, it is clear that members of the proletariat have no chance at all of penetrating to this arena of formal employment. It is neither possible nor attractive for them to take even a step in this direction. Such an inclination does exist at a higher social level, however. Not because the wage paid to lower-ranking workers is so generous, but because of the security, the protective working conditions, and the prestige that accompany permanent employment.

The extensive industrial terrains formerly belonged to inhabitants of surrounding villages. To persuade them to relinquish their land, the enterprises promised to reserve workplaces for the farmers' sons. To the intense indignation of the local population, however, little has come of that promise. The industry's management defends itself with the argument that local people were not sufficiently qualified for this work when the factories were opened. The village youth lacked the necessary training even for a job as operator. For the same reason, they were quite unsuitable for the less numerous but more lucrative officer ranks. Moreover, it is customary for such big corporations, with branches throughout India, to recruit their higher cadre on a national rather than a local basis. This explains the noticeable presence of non-Gujaratis in these enclaves of economic modernity. In the meantime, interest in advanced technical education has increased greatly in the villages. In most cases, however, the factory gates remain closed even to young men who have the necessary papers, due to lack of suitable vacancies. It is rarely that anyone with a permanent job will give it up, nor is there much scope for expansion of present capacity in these capital-intensive enterprises. Apart from lack of capacity, there seems to be some degree of reluctance on the part of employers to meet the reasonable wishes of the local people. I deduce this from the fact that non-technical personnel are also brought in from elsewhere: for example, the factory police who guard the gates and patrol the grounds, as also the cleaners and maintenance workers.

## USE OF TECHNOLOGY

Hajira is a model for the high-grade industrial sector in which labour almost disappears from sight in a landscape dominated by capital. On the broader underside of the economy, the opposite is true in the relationship between these two factors of production. The majority of the workforce do what is demanded of them each day with no other means than their own physical strength. Working principally with their arms and legs, but with the additional use of head, shoulders, back, and hips, their work posture shows evidence of physical motions that demand much energy: various combinations of hauling, pulling, pushing, carrying, lifting, bending, and squatting. In their research among women who sell their labour power each morning at the urban markets, Punalekar and Patel ascertained that 90 per cent of them have no other means of production than their own bodily strength: 'They went to the casual labour market bare handed. Some of them felt that they should have had some tools like sickle, hammer, axe, etc. of their own. [Thus equipped] they could possibly have had an edge over other persons in getting work' (Punalekar and Patel 1990: 136).

Most of the rural army of labourers also have to do the work that is daily demanded of them with no other means than their crude labour power. Only a minority make use of tools, usually no more than one: a machete for cutting the sugarcane; a pickaxe with which the road worker can break up the ground; a wicker basket or iron tray in which the woman can carry soil on her head or hip; a crowbar and sledgehammer with which the quarryman may dislodge chunks of rock; a two-handed hammer with which his wife can break them into smaller pieces; a spade for a navvy; a mould in which the man may form bricks; a small iron or wooden plate on which women and children may carry the wet or dry bricks away. The meagre range of tools used by craftsmen is their own property. Labourers are usually lent them by their employer. But if the cane cutter's machete should break, anything but a rare occurrence in its use during the many months of the campaign, the cost of repair or replacement is deducted from his wage. It also happens, however, that people who own nothing have to provide their own tools. Road workers take a pickaxe and basket with them, a mukadam will only recruit a man as brick maker if he has his own mould and forming plate, while many quarries will not take on labourers who do not have their own crowbar and hammer.

The new owner of the quarry in Pardi explained this by saying that people who own little if anything are careless in their use of other people's property. In the past his workers left the tools lying around or took them home and then tried to get him to give them new ones. He had not been bothered in this way since he introduced the rule that workers who used tools could get them from him, but only on payment. (Fieldwork notes)

At a slightly higher level of production in the informal sector, more progress has been made with the use of modern means of technology. This applies, for example, to the industrial workshops such as diamond ateliers and power-loom sheds which were the focus of my research in Surat. Nevertheless, even this environment seems to be dominated more by labour than by capital. Owners of such workplaces can manage with a limited assortment of tools and equipment. Their limited stock is usually, however, very intensively utilized. Labour is made to work for long hours and also the shift system is practised to maximize the exploitation of the capital invested.

The labour intensity of the sort of industries covered by my research is illustrated by the fact that only a small minority of the workers come into regular or even sporadic contact with machinery. They include diamond cutters and operators of power looms. Owners of such workshops can also make do with only a modest capital investment. A small diamond atelier requires nothing more than a turner's lathe, an electric motor, a couple of workbenches, and a number of clamps with which to hold the diamonds. At the end of the 1980s, this involved no more than some tens of thousands of rupees. In the same period, a power loom cost Rs 20,000 at most. More important than the small size of this investment is that after only a year, profits will equal the total investment cost. This does not alter the fact that the starting capital needed for acquiring these more advanced means of production is prohibitive for those who own little if anything at all. The yield of their labour power does not allow them to accumulate even the modest sum that would enable them to cross the threshold towards entrepreneurship. Nevertheless, the minority of workers who use tools or who operate machines are paid for their skills to handle such equipment a higher wage than the majority who have no assets other than their own bodily strength. It may be added that women are strongly under-represented in the first category and over-represented in the second. But even at that more inferior level, there are signals of further marginalization. In her case study of gender employment in Surat's art silk industry, Agrawal has observed that women have not been able to become loom operators. On the other hand, however, the abundant supply of alien labour has resulted in male migrants taking over jobs which used to be reserved for female workers: 'Thus, for women it is difficult to enter into traditionally male jobs but men have sought an easy entry into traditionally female jobs' (Agrawal 1992: 258).

The technology used in the informal sector is generally not only of a fairly simple nature but also is rather obsolete. The first generation of mechanical looms to be installed in Surat, mostly still in use, were bought second-hand from traders who had retrieved them from shut-down factories in Bombay and Ahmedabad.

For the weaving industry in Surat, it can be said that the technology employed is conventional, may be obsolete. Almost all the units use only plain looms even though they produce expensive synthetic fabrics. It goes to the credit of the workers and entrepreneurs that even on plain looms, they are able to produce fabrics of acceptable quality. Loom speeds are low compared to other countries such as Japan, for similar fabric using filament yarn both as warp and weft. Even simple attachments such as electronic weft feeders which have a short pay back are used by only a few units. Preparatory machines likewise are cheap and conventional type and no attempt has been made to use high speed, semi-automatic machines. (Mehta and Gandhi n.d.: 24)

The authors comment that the backward technology is all the more surprising since the industry is relatively young, and more advanced machinery was already available when production started to boom. The abundant supply of cheap labour which can be trained at no or minimal cost to the employer is, in my opinion, the main reason why industrialists are reluctant to replace this factor of production by capital. As has been pointed out before, labour constitutes only 10–11 per cent of the sale value of grey fabrics. At the same time, however, power-loom owners are prepared to accept that wages are a major or even the most important part of the total cost of production.

In the diamond business as well, wages paid to the cutters make up 87 per cent of all costs borne by the atelier owners (Desai 1985: 2). In these workshops, the same modest range of instruments is used that I already came across during my fieldwork in the early 1970s. The only innovation is the recent introduction of a semi-automatic *ghanti* (an iron workbench around which four diamond cutters sit on the floor). Few owners have so far acquired this new equipment because, in their opinion, it is only advantageous for the cutting of larger stones for industrial use.

The brick-making industry is a perfect illustration of the way in which employers have, for many years, persisted in handmade production. The way in which this business used to be run at the beginning of the 1960s had undergone no change in later years, as spokesmen of the manufacturers' union in Gujarat acknowledged in front of a committee set up by government: 'At no point in the process of making bricks any machinery, operated with or without power is used. All sorts of work are being done by human labour. Thus brick industry is a labour oriented industry' (Government of Gujarat 1975: 29).

On the basis of data compiled during the past 15 years, I have no reason at all to overrule this statement. The technological stagnancy is all the more surprising in view of the enormous increase of production during the intervening years. This can be illustrated with the aid of a step-by-step description of how things are organized in the brickworks:

When earth at the worksite becomes exhausted it is brought in by truck or tractor from a distance of five to ten kilometres. Members of the gang who are charged with the transport use only a spade with which to fill the container with *mati*. Larger clumps are passed by hand or headload to a mate who stands in the container. Unloading is just as laborious. On the worksite the earth is distributed in piles at the places where the brick-making gangs are at work. The amount needed for a day's production is thrown into a pit filled with water. The two to three men whose chore this is have to mix the earth with water, coal dust and rice husk. For hours at a time they knead the mixture with legs and hands, standing in the pit from which they remove stones, pieces of wood and other flotsam. Two other men and/or women dig the resulting mash out of the pit with their hands and knead it once again. The partner of the brick-maker squatting next to the pile, seizes a ball of mud with both hands and passes it to the *patawala* who puts it into the mould. This linchpin of the group then smooths both sides of the mould, an action that he has to repeat 2,500 to 3,000 times each day. When the mould is lifted off, the wet clay remains in the form of a brick on the steel groundplate. Two or three children, dependent on their age, take turns to lift the plate with the brick and to run with it to an older child who carefully lays the bricks next to one another. The rows that are thus formed are left to dry for half-a-day. But then the occupied space has to be emptied for the next series. Members of the same gang carry the bricks a little farther away to pile them in rows so that the drying process can continue. Another work gang, almost all girls and women, then carry eight or ten bricks together on their heads to the kiln, where they are taken over by one or two men who specialize in the correct stacking of the half-product for the firing process. They also take the fired bricks out of the oven and pass them to the waiting women bearers. These then carry their heavy headload to the stockpile from where the end-product is transported away, or directly to a waiting lorry. (Fieldwork notes)

Are the entrepreneurs not aware that machines are available that wholly or partially replace the human labour power on which the production process now depends? Owners of small brickworks showed little if any interest in the question, but larger manufacturers were usually prepared to give a more detailed answer. A few had heard about a semi-automatic kiln in Ahmedabad. Others told me that a few years earlier, a machine had been tried somewhere in the neighbourhood of Vapi which delivered the raw material ready-made. The bricks that were made with it fell to pieces during the drying process, however, and the experiment was soon stopped. I was told repeatedly that human hands were simply indispensable for the making of good quality bricks. This argument is easily refuted, as shown by the kneading machine that I found in 1962 in a brickworks on the banks of the river Tapti in Surat:

The Parsi owner proudly showed me around when I visited the works to meet a gang of brick-makers from Chikhligam. The motor-driven mixer stirred the earth with water, coal dust and rice husks in a large cement tank. Workers used their hands to pull the compound away from under the mixer and threw it by the armful from bins into tipper carts. These were pushed along rails through the yard to the place where the brick-makers and their gangs were busy. I found the innovations which I saw and the large scale of the production process very impressive. This entrepreneur was certainly taking the lead in a modernization process that would be followed by more and more owners. However, this was not the case. When I visited the now aged Parsi for the last time in 1984 I found him in his office enraged about the *mukadams* who could not be trusted. They always wanted a large advance in cash but at the start of the season they came with less workers than they had been paid for. He also vented his spleen about the authorities who sent him far too little coal with which the two chimneys had to be kept burning. He had had enough and was going to stop the work that year. When I returned two years later, I realized that that decision was connected to the old man's illness. After his death last year, a daughter and a son took over management of the business. (Fieldwork notes)

In 1985, after a great deal of trouble, I eventually managed to speak to the chairman of the *Surat Jilla Int Utpadhak Mandal*. Members of this local association of brick manufacturers, set up in 1974, are almost all owners of large businesses. The association looks after the interests of its members and mediates in the supply of coal which is available at fixed minimum price only for holders of an official licence. The chairman appeared not only a warm champion of the industry but also one of the very few who were familiar with the machines used in Western countries. A couple of years earlier, he had taken part in an international congress of brick manufacturers held in London. He had a photograph in his office of the mechanized firm that he had then visited in the United Kingdom. He was all praise for what he had seen. But according to him, there is little chance of introducing that technology into south

Gujarat in the near future. Why that should be so was concealed behind a stream of words. Apart from the extremely low wages, a subject dealt with in the next chapter, this seemed to be due to the manufacturers' wish to conceal their production from government as much as possible. This would be out of the question if they changed to a production system which demanded more fixed capital. In some way, machines are easier to register than working people. At any rate, owners would then be far more vulnerable to numerous legal or illegal depredations on their profits by government officials. Nevertheless, a point can be reached where it is economically unwise to continue production on a manual basis only. One example that has been discussed already is that of a number of road builders who started to mechanize the exploitation of the quarries for which they have a bought a licence. In seeking an answer to the intriguing question why the power-loom workshops and diamond ateliers dominating the industrial landscape of Surat continue to run on the basis of a backward technology, I earlier referred to the ready availability of cheap labour. However, the reluctance to go in for more capital-intensive industrialization may also have to do with fluctuations in the demand for the commodity produced. Most power-loom entrepreneurs have no or only minimal control over the source, quantity, and price of the raw material their patrons are willing to deliver, while they also have to accept whatever conditions are imposed on them for marketing the grey fabric. In the same way, the owners of diamond ateliers are bound hand and feet to traders who supply them with the stones, dictating the price of processing, and who may at any moment and quite arbitrarily decide to discontinue the business relationship. Such structural constraints, which were already a feature of the pattern of industrial development in colonial India, are not really favourable for persuading industrialists to invest in more advanced technology. It is not that the actual producers do not get a proper price—as a matter of fact, profit margins are usually very high—but that they have to operate in an unregulated and unsteady market. Given these conditions of uncertainty and dependency, it becomes attractive to pass on the entrepreneurial risk and to keep a less costly and more variable production factor than capital unstable, that is, to expand or contract the workforce according to the need of the moment. It sometimes happens that employers bring up the mechanization argument as a threat with which to reject demands for higher wages or, more generally, to nip in the bud any attempts that are likely to result in increased labour costs. In south Gujarat, the management of the capitalist agro-industry uses these tactics to bring pressure to bear on government (Breman 1990: 605). Spokesmen for the brick-making industry in the state use the same argument. To members of a government committee charged with fixing a minimum wage, they had declared a long time ago that any increase in cost price caused by a wage increase would make it necessary for them to introduce machinery (Government of Gujarat 1975: 33). In the intervening years, as noticed, that threat has not been put into practice. In view of the increasing irritation shown by employers with regard to what they see as fickle and dishonest behaviour on the part of their workers, however, I do not consider it out of the question that such a trend will yet arise.

Together with his brother, J owns a tile-making workshop, one of such enterprises for which Bilimora has long excelled. Increased prosperity has caused many large and medium landowners to decide to modernize their houses into bungalows with the help of interior decoration, more specifically, by having the floors and walls of their rooms tiled. J has no lack of orders, but he has a great deal of trouble in keeping up the size of his workforce. At first he employed almost only local Kolis, but they took too many holidays or even stayed away without asking his permission. A couple of years ago he changed to using *bhaiyas*, the generic term given to people from Uttar Pradesh. These outsiders are hard workers and are always available. During the summer they sleep somewhere on the worksite—J nonchalantly pointed out of the window—and in the winter he allowed them to sleep indoors. The problem is that these workers, whom he has trained himself, return to their homes once each year and then he never knows whether they will come back. They could find similar work in Kashmir where the wages are higher. J is fed up with always having to instruct newcomers how to do the work. He wants to bring in machines as quickly as possible, though his brother is still against the idea. (Fieldwork notes)

## WORKING HOURS

For the large mass of people who earn their living with unskilled labour, standardized working hours are an unknown luxury. The casual use of physical power is characterized by uncertainty as to when the working day actually begins and ends. Calculating according to number of hours is not so important as making sure of the income that the physical effort will provide. Factory labour brings an end to the unpredictable rhythm of daily workers who, each day, have to roam restlessly seeking work and trying to contact employers who will pay them a wage. Just as work performed under a roof increases a worker's prestige, the marking of a day into a regular and clear-cut pattern of work and non-work increases the dignity of labour. When, in addition, the work is interrupted once each week by a free day with pay, and a longer leave even is given once a year, working life takes on the character of formal sector employment. Such a situation is approximated by workers who serve the power looms in Surat. However, they lack all those restrictive and protective conditions that make employment in the formalized sector of the economy so attractive. It would seem that the long hours of work in the weaving units go back to the time when this industry was still run as a family business and the monopoly of local craftsmen. All members of the household used to participate in the production process which went on in an uneven rhythm all hours of the day and night. A report describing the artisanal style of operation also draws attention to the importance attached to ownership of the means of production in this petit bourgeois milieu which prevailed:

All members of the family irrespective of age and sex participate in weaving as and when they get time. The single condition of work is that weaving is their bread and butter. Thus in the case of small units weaving is a way of life. It could be that the girl who is adept at weaving is a better qualified girl as a bride. She won't be a burden to the family, either as a daughter or as a wife. Perhaps the worth of a family might be measured by the number of looms it owns. (Mehta and Pathak 1975: 100)

The work regime has since become more capitalistic. The workers do not belong to the family or even the same caste anymore, and the intimate relationship between capital and labour that earlier existed has been clearly cut. The loom operators are hired hands only who, however, have not been given the type of protection enjoyed by the workforce in the formal sector of the economy.

Although the Factory Act expressly stipulates a working day of no more than eight hours, almost all employers give their weavers no other choice than to stand behind the machines for 12 hours at a stretch (South Gujarat University 1984: 42). These conditions do not only prevail in the power-loom sheds of Surat, as is made clear in a report on the regime in the same industry in Ichalkaranji, a town in Maharashtra.

'The twelve-hour shift is a real bitch. Gnaws at our lives it does!'...'Twelve-hour shift? Not eight?'...'Oh no! 8–8 full twelve hours. And you can't go off like in other factories because all pay is by piece-work. 13 paise per metre. We have to keep the loom going till the other shift arrives. Then we put our mark on the cloth and get up.' Another, a little older, said, 'That twelve-hour shift kills a man. By the time we get home after the shift we are like zombies. Some get drunk on the way home, some not. Put some junk in the tummy and go out like a light. Get up and come to work.' (Awachat 1988: 1733)

And if a member of the next shift does not turn up to take their place, then the workers have to continue operating the looms until they are relieved 24 hours later. Such an extreme lengthening of work time is not disagreeable to the power-loom operator. In line with the law of self-exploitation, he makes use of each and every opportunity to maximize his income. This is naturally impossible without one or two brief intervals, but it is typical of the industrial climate in the informal sector that most workshops have no formal rules regarding intervals. The weaver who rests a little, eats something, or has to go to the toilet, remains responsible for anything that might go wrong during his short absence. Shortage of electrical power makes it unavoidable that workplaces in Surat close down for one day each week. That is the only reason, caused by the interrupted use of capital, that the workers are given a day off. It is a matter of fact that they are not paid on the day that the looms have to close down (South Gujarat University 1984: 44). This also applies when workers take any leave, which they have to do on their own account and at their own risk. A weaver is fortunate if, on his return, he does not find that his place has been taken by another.

The better life of the diamond cutters is also expressed in the greater latitude they are given in performing their daily task:

Diamond workers start and stop at their convenience. Workers who stay in the town may commence work as early as 7 a.m. Those who stay in the surrounding villages commute to work by cycle, bus or train. Buses and trains are not noted for their punctuality and travelling by cycle is problematic during the monsoon months. These workers report for work by nine or even ten o'clock in the morning. Workers also have their lunch break or noon rest at a time convenient to them. By five o'clock in the evening workers begin to leave, but some may continue working up to seven or eight o'clock in the evening. (Kalathil 1978: 100–1)

At first sight, this relaxed manner of employment, certainly as regards its flexibility, compares favourably even with the more comfortable working conditions that characterize formal sector employment. Piece-work payment plays an important role, however. It sometimes leads to this type of more skilled labour taking an attitude that I am inclined to associate with the work mentality of petit bourgeois behaviour. Diamond cutters are paid per stone. The work tempo that they maintain—that is, to come or not, to start and finish earlier or later, to work harder or more slowly—determines the amount of their earnings. If the work will not go right, if a stone is difficult to cut, the worker may decide to chuck it in for the day.

He may quit work early to watch a movie or roam about the market place. In the matter of leave too there are few restrictions on the workers. While some are considerate enough to inform the *karkhanedar* in advance, others fail to do so. In the agricultural harvesting season some workers who come from villages absent themselves to engage in harvesting. They say that this arrangement works out to their advantage financially. On the whole, the workers do not like a lean pay packet, and this is what keeps them on the job 6 days a week. (Kalathil 1978: 101)

This last remark is not in the least superfluous, even if only to avoid the impression that diamond workers form the sort of labour aristocracy that can be found in the formal sector of the economy. The owner of the workplace accepts such behaviour only from his best workers whom he does not want to lose. The others not only work long hours if the patron so wishes, but are also given little latitude to regulate their own presence or absence.

Piecework is generally the customary method of payment of labour throughout all layers of the informal sector. It also applies to the power looms, without even a small percentage of the workforce being granted any discretion as to their obligation to report for work. Weavers are paid per metre of woven material, and management bases itself on an average daily production per machine. The amount is based on what a hard and skilled worker can produce in 12 hours. If the output of a newcomer or an older hand remains below that norm, not incidentally but systematically, then he is discharged by his employer who thus puts an end to the underutilization of his capital investment.

The large number of workers used in all sorts of seasonal rural or semi-urban industry are also paid on the basis of piecework: in cane cutting, fruit picking, paddy harvesting, quarries, road building, brickworks, and salt pans. An important difference with the textile worker or diamond cutter is that all these occupations usually have to be carried out by more than one person. All kinds of combinations occur, varying from work teams consisting of a few family members, to larger groups of adults with children.

1. *Cane cutting*: The gang led by a mukadam which stays in the plain of south Gujarat for the sugarcane harvest is made up of 20–50 members. They are subdivided into smaller units, called *koytas*, usually made up of a man, woman, and often a child. At the start of the working day, the gang boss lines up the koytas at the beginning of the field. The members of each team have to cut the rows of stalks in front of them, remove the leaves, cut them into pieces, and bundle them. The area that all cover working in

this way is the same, but the tempo depends on the labour power. This means that one work gang will finish its daily task earlier than another. The norm is high: approximately three-quarters of a ton, which demands an effort lasting 9–10 hours. Weak teams need so much time that the gang boss may decide to transfer part of their task, and its payment, to other teams that have extra capacity.

2. *Brickworks*: A gang of brick makers consisting of 9–11 members is expected to produce and stack 2,500–3,000 bricks per day. The amount of earth and other raw materials (coal dust and rice husks) with which they are provided at the start of the work day is attuned to that number. In my experience, the time in which the quickest and slowest gangs manage to process this quantity varies from 10–14 hours. Gangs that systematically fail to produce the required number of bricks are penalized for their shortcomings by reduction of the weekly allowance on which they depend for their sustenance.

The above examples show that the norm is based on an uninterrupted workload, of which only the strong are capable. Those who have difficulty in keeping to that tempo and in maintaining it until the end of the day, are discharged in due course. They have been judged and found inadequate, unsuited to take further part in the production process. The workers have their own unwritten rules, however, with which they try to defend themselves against their exploitation as a result of the piece-rate method. That defence is the subject of constant complaint by the employers to the effect that labourers absent themselves without valid reason and without making it known beforehand. Such behaviour, considered reprehensible by employers, is due to the long and severe work days and nights that are made even more taxing by the lack of any regular and paid intervals. Under such circumstances, absenting oneself from work is one of the few effective means by which to avoid complete subjection by the employers. The latter react angrily to the unexpected breach of their authority, thinking, often correctly, that it is due to sabotage by the workers. What is known in the employers' jargon as 'lack of discipline' is a logical consequence of the workers' lack of alternative for avoiding total hegemony over their labour power in any 'civilized' fashion.

There is yet another reason for scepticism about the indignation with which employers react to the unpredictable conduct of their subordinates. Employers do not show the slightest scruple in victimizing the workers for the many work stoppages that occur. The working rhythm is, in fact, very irregular. Therefore, the employers ensure availability of reserve labour which is not paid in the case of underutilization. This applies both to all sorts of tasks that take place in the open and to manufacturing processes in a closed space. The entrepreneurial risks and the resulting costs are thus transferred from management to labour.

1. *Cane cutting*: Day and night, a fleet of vehicles—lorries, tractors, and bullock carts—comes and goes to bring cane to the factory. Management is in constant contact with the field staff so as to accelerate the work if the supply is insufficient, and to slow it down if the factory becomes congested. Cane cutting repeatedly has to be stopped because of machine defects in the mill, a transport breakdown, or other technical flaws. It means that, on the one hand, the army of cutters has to be constantly available but, on the other hand, it is not paid when breakdowns occur in the process.

2. *Transport*: Loaders riding with the lorries are paid per run at rates that fluctuate according to distance. Like the lorry owner, they are concerned with loading and unloading as rapidly as possible because the number of runs they make will determine the wage they get at the end of the day. Sometimes, however, they just have to hang around for hours on end if the arrangement to pick up a load falls through or if the lorry breaks down. That enforced idleness is their problem and bad luck, according to the employer.

3. *Weaving*: The patron who yesterday had given a weaver a scolding due to absence without leave, now explained patiently why workers have no right to an income when production is interrupted. That this occurs fairly regularly can be seen from the underutilization of the looms, which run at rather less than three-quarters capacity (South Gujarat University 1984: 13). Confronted with complaints from his impatient workforce, the employer replied that he couldn't help it if yarn was not delivered, if there was a power cut, or a machine broke down. And what could he do other than to send his workers away temporarily, with instructions to report daily, if he could not sell his product for a decent price?

Apart from staying away from work now and then, the mass of unskilled workers have no other choice but to subject themselves to the dictates of the production process in which they have to earn their livelihood. Their submission is so complete that outside the work sphere, they have

almost no say even over their private life. The cane-cutters' working day
is extended into the night by another three or four hours if they have
to return to the fields to load onto lorries the cane that they have cut
during the day (Breman 1990: 586–7). The same story of suffering can
be told about labourers in the brickworks. Their work starts between two
and four o'clock at night and continues until the end of the morning.
They then have a break, when the women prepare a meal and do other
household chores. In the afternoon, it is time to clear the workplace for
the ensuing night. Bricks that have been laid out to dry are stacked in
rows a little further away. In the evening, the water-soaked earth is taken
out of the pit and heaped up close to the spot where the brick maker will
sit or squat a few hours later.

Altogether, the result is a working day lasting 14–16 hours, but
that duration does not sufficiently illustrate the burden of the job.
Unconditional surrender by labour is manifested in the complete subjection of the rhythm of life to the demands of the job, for 24 hours at
a stretch. The smooth and efficient organization of agro-industry forces
cane cutters, at night, to load the amount of cane that they have cut
during the day, because the mill's machines run continuously. But why
is it necessary that the purely manual production of bricks should start at
night and in the early morning? Brickworks owners were not unanimous
in their reply to such questions. Many just said that this was customary in
their branch of industry. The majority argued that drying is a very gradual
process. If wet bricks are immediately exposed to the glaring sun, they
would break easily even before being put in the kiln. Some employers say
that workers are less distracted when it is dark, that they work harder in
winter in order to keep warm, and that in summer they work at night to
avoid the day's heat. Productivity certainly shows some fluctuations. In
both cane cutting and brick making, daily production is highest between
November and February. From then on, the amount of cane cut by a
koyta drops to little more than half-a-ton every 24 hours and the number
of bricks made by a gang falls to substantially less than 2,500. The heat
during the day undoubtedly plays a role, but more important is the
exhaustion caused by the production process itself. The decline in performance does not mean that working hours become any shorter. Only, the
effort put into the work slows down towards the end of the season.

In general, the labour regime in the informal sector seems, over the
years, to have been intensified. Women who wait long hours in the
casual labour markets until someone may need them insist that they
have to work both harder and longer now than ever before. They are

expected to work until after dusk if necessary to complete a job. In most cases, the greater effort is not compensated by extra payment. This is a hidden wage reduction which indicates the increasing inequality between supply and demand.

> Previously the contractors used to take work for 8 hours from the labourers. Now they take work for 9 to 10 hours a day. Many a time, they are not allowed to go home till the cement concrete mixing work is completed. The labourers engaged in slab-filling work usually start working in the morning and work till 7 p.m. Sometimes, this work is extended to midnight also. (Punalekar and Patel 1990: 126)

A common complaint is that members of the lower castes who come straight from the countryside into an industrial environment are not able to work attentively and regularly for hours at a time. This stereotype is further accentuated in the case of labour from a tribal background. Of them it is said that, as carefree children of nature, they lack the self-discipline that is the basis of any successful performance in modern methods of production.

> In their traditional economic activities, the tribals have never been bound to work in a routine manner. After doing some hard labour, they used to have relaxation for as much time as they wished. Now in their new occupation it is required for them to work for hours with a small break. They have not yet fully adjusted to this sort of routine and hence some of them clamour for more recess hours. (Lal 1982: 83)

The essay from which this passage is taken is concerned particularly with Dhodhiyas and Halpatis who have penetrated to the industrial sites of Vapi in south Gujarat from their nearby villages. Their employers were dissatisfied about the lack of a steady work rhythm among these newcomers, a recrimination that I see as a variant of the lack-of-discipline complaint. As stated before, informal sector workers sometimes leave unexpectedly, and inopportunely for their employer, in order to escape the extremely heavy workload and other pressures. It would be misleading, however, to attribute erratic working behaviour at the bottom of the economy exclusively to a more or less veiled refusal to toe the line. A more important explanation is the lack of regularity inherent in the labour process itself. The regime of the informal sector is characterized by the sudden and unexpected alternation of peaks and falls, not only per season but even in daily activities. Hours and days of almost unbroken drudgery make way for shorter or longer periods of imposed idleness.

This contrast between maximum effort and forced inactivity reflects the logic of informal sector business and is not the manifestation of an uneconomic idiosyncrasy which disqualifies the worker from a better existence. This mass of men, women, and children has to be present wherever, whenever, and to the extent that there is a need for their services. A child working on the streets expressed this as follows:

I have no fixed timings for my work. I go to Sardar Baug in the morning for selling balloons, plastic toys, etc. In the evening either I do the same thing or engage myself in selling water in an earthen pot. I am not always lucky. Often times, the policeman or sometimes the garden watchman drives us all away. On some days the area is cordoned off by the policemen if the procession (*julus*) has to pass that way. So though we are ready to work all days, the situation is not always in our favour. (Punalekar 1993: 127)

What seems at first sight a disjointed and irregular schedule, is not due to unwillingness or carelessness. Such an outlook does not do justice to behaviour that shows the greatest possible flexibility in systematically attuning labour supply to the strongly fluctuating demand. Of relevance here is the point made by Thompson about the need of disciplining a labour force which is only partially and temporarily 'committed' to an industrial way of life (Thompson 1993: 352). However, time- thrift and a clear demarcation between 'work' and 'life' seem to presuppose an industrial environment in tune with the factorized urban capitalism that emerged and became dominant in the Atlantic world during the nineteenth century. It does not mean that lack of time consciousness is characteristic for the rural and urban proletariat which I have researched in India towards the end of the twentieth century. The daily rhythm of informal sector working classes is conditioned by the need to surrender completely to the unreserved claim made on their availability at all hours of the day or night, in all seasons of the year. That this potential demand is only partially and temporarily actualized has to do not so much with their faulty time-thrift but with the low and irregular demand that is made on their labour power.

Far more than in the countryside, the urban lifestyle is now regulated by time. A Koli woman from a village that has recently merged into Surat and which has long been exposed to the impact of its proximity, has expressed that type of pressure as follows:

Because of urbanization, our domestic tasks have become more complex. We have to take care of so many things in an orderly manner. Thirty years ago, we did not even care to have a wall clock. And when we purchased one, its novelty did not last long then. If it went out of order, we did not much bother to get it repaired. But now the situation is different. We have five wrist watches and two alarm clocks. We feel uneasy if we get up late. That upsets our routine for the whole day. Not only that, we cannot spend much time with our relatives and friends if they happen to visit our house on working days. That has created some misunderstanding among my relatives living in Olpad villages. They say that I have become *pucca* Surati and deliberately neglecting them. That way they are carrying wrong notions about me and my way of hospitality. How can I convince them that Piplod is not much different from Surat and our life must be run in clockwise precision? It is very difficult to convince them. They will only realize if they live in places like Piplod. (Punalekar 1992: 402)

However hectic daily life may be, the disciplined handling of clock time apparent in this quotation is, above all, the prerogative of that small portion of the working population, to which this Koli household belongs, which may boast of subjection to punctuality in which formal sector activity is said to excel. However, time is also a strategic good in the hands of those whose intention it is to aggravate the task of informal sector workers by extending its duration. It is no coincidence that mukadams, as leaders of work gangs, are easily and immediately identifiable because they wear a wristwatch. It is an article that forms part of the standard equipment for their profession.

## DEGRADATION IN THE LABOUR PROCESS

In most branches of industry covered by my fieldwork, the labour process has such a degrading effect that, for that reason alone, employers feel forced regularly to replace and replenish their workforce.

This is, however, less applicable to diamond workshops. The term 'sweatshop' perfectly illustrates my immediate and principal impression gained from visits to these establishments in Surat, Navsari, and Bardoli. In a small room with no ventilation, well-lit with neon tubes but without fresh air, 10 or more young men sit cross-legged and close together on the floor around ghantis, workbenches, closely watched by the owner from his air-conditioned cubicle. A towel hanging around the worker's neck is used to dry hands and face of sweat that runs profusely, particularly in the summer heat. The boss does not tolerate any fresh air to come into the atelier out of fear that his workers might rob him of diamonds by throwing some of the valuable stones given to them for processing out of the window or use any other opening to the outside world for that purpose. The textile workplaces occupied by power looms are larger, but the people working among the machines have hardly space in which to move. The enormous noise of the looms and the heat under the corrugated zinc roof are also sources of discomfort. Even employer-biased reports are somewhat critical of the appalling work conditions to which the industrial proletariat is exposed, resulting in a 'balanced' picture like the following:

… largely due to insanitary living conditions, the health of the workers is affected and absenteeism from work is noticed. It is difficult to attribute all health problems to the working conditions or long hours of working as most diseases are not work-related. Diseases like chronic head-aches, stomach problems and skin affections could hardly be work-related. These are more likely to be due to lack of nutritious diet and maybe, to drinking habits. For hearing problems or deafness in the weaving industry, there is no solution. It is, however, true that if safety precautions are observed, problems like electrical shocks, chemical burns, physical injuries due to fall, etc., could be prevented. It is sad to note that, in the majority of factories, even first aid facilities are not provided. (Mehta and Gandhi n.d.: 128–9)

However bad conditions might be in the factories, those who work there find it rather less uncomfortable than most forms of industry that occur in the open air. Employers of the latter type frequently disagree. The manager of a sugar mill whom I accompanied on his daily round through the fields was quite convinced that the much lower wage paid to fieldworkers was compensated by their stay in the countryside. 'During the campaign they live in similar fashion to the sort of picnicking and camp life that you westerners enjoy in your leisure time,' he commented when we passed a cane-cutters' bivouac along the roadside (Breman 1978/1979: 66). This opinion was surpassed by the way in which the owners of salt pans boasted about the beneficial effect of this habitat on the physical well-being of their migrant workers. Their evidence before an official committee gave the impression that workers from south Gujarat came there every year to enjoy the delights of a health cure: 'The employers further claim that the workmen who work in an atmosphere saturated with salt are generally free from attack of cold, rheumatism, neurology and similar other troubles. The preservative qualities of the salt account for a long life among these workers' (Government of Maharashtra 1976: 13)

I have seldom seen a more inhuman work environment from the climatological point of view than these salt pans during my fieldwork. Nature does not tolerate any living organism above water other than human workers. On the bare plain, not a single piece of shade can be found against the burning sun, and the saltish soil reflects the fierce light on the body. At the end of a day, my eyes were rimmed with red.

During the hot summer months, the morning temperature rises to such a high level that work has to be stopped at noon for a couple of hours. The work gangs who stamp down the soil of the pans at the start of the season accentuate their work rhythm with songs in which they sarcastically praise the mercy of the bosses who enticed them there, far from home, with their cash advances.

The stone quarries are just as ruthless. The workers who quarry the hills in the middle of the plain do not even have water nearby in which they could, once in a while, seek cooling during the hot summer months, as do the men who work in open mines along the river banks.

The work is done in the open air without any form of shelter. In the morning hours they work in the shadow of the rock wall; after about 1 p.m. this shadow disappears and work stops until 4 o'clock. Even then, it is exhausting just to stay in the quarry without working, with the sun reflecting on the now heated rock face. The men keep fit by regularly taking a dip in the river. (Koelen 1985: 104)

Not only adults but also children are victims of the miserable working conditions in the brickworks. Their labour power becomes indispensable while they are still quite young, and from the age of six they are wakened during the night to carry the fresh bricks made by their father. While wet, those bricks weigh roughly 3 kg. The little children run with one brick each, away from the base plate and into the darkness. When they reach the age of about nine, they are promoted to carrying two bricks. Sometimes, their parents wake them up crying from the rags that form their beds. But at night, they are the only ones who sing, trying to give themselves courage. If they run back quickly, they can warm their hands for a few seconds by the wood fire which provides the patavala and *patavali*, the brick maker and his female mate, with light and warmth in the cold winter nights.

Last night, while the parents were at work, a toddler was badly burned. The little boy, not yet three years old, had scampered to the kiln to seek warmth. There he must have fallen against the hot bricks in his sleep. Wet rags did little to stop the lad's screaming and crying.

A couple of days later, in another brickworks, I found a girl of about fifteen years old who lay on the ground under a couple of jute sacks, shivering with fever. Her younger sister came now and again and shook her gently, trying to get her to go to work, because she was unable alone to carry all the bricks away from the base plate. The labour power of her sick sister is needed to eliminate the backlog. When that has been done, she can lie down again although for no longer than ten minutes. (Fieldwork notes)

The sources of employment in which the toiling mass at the bottom of the economy is imprisoned not only provide poor earnings but also cause damage to health in ways that are obviously linked to the appalling work conditions. Independently or in combination, heat, cold, dampness, noise, dust, and stench are noticeable risk factors in this debilitating working environment. Of all categories of labour to which I have directed my attention, the diamond cutters are undoubtedly the most fortunate. Although they complain that the constant peering through the magnifying glass is damaging to the eyes and that the diamond dust released during grinding eventually causes breathing problems, I have found no tangible evidence of these occupational diseases whether in practice or in the reports of other researchers.

On the other hand, I had no difficulty at all in corroborating the complaints of power-loom operators about their working conditions. Noise is the greatest evil. When streets are quiet at night, the continual rattle of the machines in buildings in many parts of the city is all the more noticeable. Investigations into conditions in this industry showed that 78 per cent of the respondents suffered from fairly serious health complaints, particularly hearing disorders, eye disease, bronchial complaints, and chronic pain in the head or limbs (South Gujarat University 1984: 79). Even worse than the situation of weavers is that of workers in the dyeing-and-printing mills who have to handle dyes often with their bare hands and inhale the noxious smells of chemicals. And then there are those who, in a closed space with very high humidity, operate a machine with a high piercing sound, which treats artificial silk yarn in such a way that the threads are loosened and curled. Listening to the shouted explanation of this treatment and profusely sweating over my whole body, I have never been able to stay in such a workplace for longer than a few minutes. Reports which are the outcome of employers'-sponsored research quite blatantly hold these industrial workers responsible for their poor health condition. Both statistics and research on work hazards, industrial injuries, and occupational diseases which disproportionately afflict people in the informal sector, are sadly lacking.

The industrial townships on the edge of Surat, in particular Udhana and Pandesara, are bad places in which to stay, let alone in which to work. Environmental pollution, of air and water, is unimaginable. Dense smoke, soot, and dust make it difficult to breathe, and I have often left this jungle of modern industry with my eyes watering and nose running. The same applies to industrial sites in other places along the main road and the railway, which form the connections with Bombay in the south and Vadodara/Ahmedabad in the north. Farmers in south

Gujarat's western coastal plain complain about the damage to their crops and land caused by the chemical industry that has been set up here. Employment in any of these industries entails a considerable health risk, as labourers from Gandevigam and Chikhligam have experienced. They have to handle corrosive salts and acids without any protection at all for face, arms, and legs. 'I can show you the wounds on my hands,' a Dhodhiya man said to me, 'but not the pain that I feel inside my body'.

Workers in the open air are perhaps less exposed to modern industrial pollution than are the factory workers, but they run other risks that may result in temporary or permanent harm to the body. Industrial accidents are a common occurrence on work locations in the informal sector. Building sites, in particular, are notorious for risks to which casual workers are exposed. The contractor refuses to accept any liability for injuries resulting in temporary or even permanent disability, and it is equally futile for the worker to seek redress from the mukadam. On the contrary, it is quite normal for the victim to be instantly dismissed without any form of compensation. Men and women frequently fall victim to the primitive modes of extraction that are still practised in the majority of quarries:

… the feet and lower legs are particularly at risk because the labourers work with bare feet and legs. The greatest risks occur when large rocks have to be hacked into more manageable pieces with a sledge-hammer; the pieces are rolled into position and held there with the bare feet. There is always a great danger of rebounding hammers and mis-hits. (Koelen 1985: 104)

The arms and hands of the cane cutters are not protected against the knife-sharp top leaves or against slips with the machete. On their bare feet, they have to carry their heavy headloads out of the stubble that they leave in the fields after harvesting. The primitive or even non-existent medical care means that wounds on arms and legs, hand and feet, easily become infected. In the brickworks, precautionary measures of any kind are conspicuous by their absence. Injuries of all kinds are common occurrences in the handling of raw materials, operating the kiln, and humping the bricks in the successive processing stages. The workers who stand in the mixing pits for hours at a time, the women who carry the bricks on their heads 10 at a time with a total weight of about 25 kilos, the brick maker and his partner who sit in a squatting posture for hours on end—they all complain about pain in their backs and other parts of the body. While discussing health hazards with a Halpati from Chikhligam, who has taken part in the seasonal migration for many years, he pointed out many knock-kneed children, a defect that is certainly caused by a combination of poor food, long working hours, and too heavy burdens at a young age. Brown lung disease seems to be another complaint peculiar to this branch of industry. It applies particularly to the *chapavali*, the women who each day and all day carry the baked bricks out of the kiln. By evening, their faces are like masks, entirely covered in dust. Using an edge of their sari, they do their best to cover their mouth and nostrils. But the stone dust even penetrates that veil.

As a result of the poor hygienic conditions under which seasonal migrants in particular are forced to live, they fall victim to all sorts of chronic disease, for example, dysentery, tuberculosis (TB), and malaria, and take them home. An impression of this can be gained from the following description of conditions found in cane-cutters' camps by a committee appointed by the High Court in Gujarat:

> Being compelled to use highly polluted, non-potable water for drinking purposes many a time, it is not surprising that there were large numbers of cases of workers suffering from dysentery and diarrhoea ... it was obvious that the workers live in total destitution without even a minimum facility for staying, clothing, and nothing to sleep on, children of tender age without clothes were a common sight at the camps. Pregnant and nursing mothers also sharing the same conditions, all left without any clothes to protect themselves from the winter cold. (Breman 1990: 585)

'The Crushing of Cane and of Labour' was the subtitle that I gave to my first report on the employment of the huge army of migrant harvesters in the fields of south Gujarat (Breman 1978/1979). Similar circumstances dominate most other branches of seasonal industry. From the mass of men, women, and children who participate in this mobile workforce each year, a number always return back home blind, deaf, crippled, or bent double with rheumatism. In discussing secondary labour conditions in the next chapter, I shall further examine the fate of the workers who are forced to live a circulatory existence, temporarily or semi-permanently. Adults older than 40 years migrate less and less frequently. Not because they can permit themselves the luxury of staying at home, but because their lack of sufficient fitness in mid life makes them the last to be considered by jobbers. As the owner of a brickworks told me: the replacement of old labour by young costs nothing, but the replacement of old by new capital is expensive.

A well-known doctor in Valsad, whom I met occasionally during my fieldwork, has his medical practice in a neighbourhood populated by unskilled labourers. He attributes the poor health of the majority of his patients to the conditions under which they have to work.

How will they be able to do normal work when they have to inhale dust particles? They take cold and insufficient food. Over and above that they consume liquor to relieve themselves of tensions and exhaustion. Their lungs become weak and they begin to suffer from incurable diseases like TB and asthma. They suffer from sunstroke as they have to work in a scorching heat. There are some cases of cholera too. They suffer from boils because they sit in dirty, insanitary places. Some female labourers are compelled to have sexual relations with people in order to get work and other favours. That leads to venereal diseases. (Punalekar and Patel 1990: 101)

The brutal labour regime imposes an even heavier burden on women and children than on men. Boys and girls of 10–12 years of age frequently have to work the same long hours as the adults, but at their tender age, they are less able to withstand fatigue. Their pace of strenuous work is not always adequate, and it is quite customary for employers and overseers to be harsh in disciplining them. Their greater vulnerability makes them an easy target for verbal or physical violence and for the continual threat of dismissal due to default (Punalekar 1993: 134). The same author states that three out of every 10 children who earn their living on the streets suffer from hunger. Although extreme poverty is undoubtedly the principal reason why they have to seek work at such an early age, many, obviously, earn too little even to assuage their hunger. Nevertheless, even the most deprived among these young people maintain a work code of regulating what is decent or improper. The latter category includes the acceptance of free food (ibid.: 161). Mutual solidarity among fellow sufferers in miserable conditions helps them to cope with extreme adversity. Children who not only work in the streets but also have to do so without adult protection will share the food that they earn and look after their sick mates. Street wisdom teaches them that help and distrust are not far removed from one another.

Pick-pocketer could be any of us standing here. How do we know? When living is expensive and when there is too much competition in earning money, some of us end up by earning only a paltry sum of Rs 5 or Rs 10 by evening. Day's expenses including tea–bread, potato, wada etc. cost us more than Rs 10 per day. When we earn less, we request our work mates to lend us money or food. Sometimes they oblige, sometimes they do not. In such eventualities, anyone of us can be tempted to steal away money even of our close friend. (Ibid.: 146)

The women usually have to cope with a double burden of work. A few hours before starting their paid labour, they are busy with all sorts of domestic activities: preparing meals, caring for the children, washing, and cleaning. They are the first to rise in the morning and the last to go to bed at night. The men come back tired from their work, demanding rest, care, and attention. The women, who are equally tired, are expected, as a matter of course, to continue their work in the private sphere.

> When we come back home, we feel already tired and exhausted because of factory work. We need some respite and rest. But our husband, children and in-laws, all expect that we must begin our domestic work as soon as we enter the house. They have little understanding of how much fatigue we experience in the factory. They think as if we come back from movie or marketing. (Punalekarv 1988: 76)

We have already seen that working girls and women run the risk of sexual abuse. This may be forced on them in the household where they work as domestic servants, for example, by the mukadam who can select or ignore them for employment, by an employer or his foreman who can dismiss them if they refuse a wide range of sexual intimacies, including rape. Usually, the only protest possible against such treatment is to leave the workplace. In order to avoid risks of this nature, which bring the whole family into disrepute, people are quite anxious to find out about employment opportunities for female household members in advance. This is the practice in the case of Surat's *jari* workers:

> The women workers who are ignorant about all other things are very conscious about their safety. The mother will check whether a place is safe before sending her young daughter for a job. When a woman wants to change her place of work, the men in her family first check whether the new place is safe or not and then only the woman worker is allowed to go there. (Soni 1990: 145–6)

Those who are at the bottom of the informal sector cannot always afford to safeguard themselves against attacks on their code of sexual honour. I found, for instance, seasonal migrants going to the brick kilns to be quite helpless in resisting mukadams and employers who took advantage of young girls or married women even when fathers or husbands of these victims were around. Similarly, young children scraping a meagre living on the streets are without protection against sexual assaults. A quarter of the street children questioned by Punalekar had been forced to have intercourse or named their friends who had experienced this (Punalekar 1993: 170). This is an alarmingly high figure for a subject that is taboo and regarding which the researcher gets to know little even after long acquaintance.

Informal sector workers have to survive in extremely cruel conditions. It needs all their resilience to cope with a continual series of setbacks. It is inadvisable to express anger and disappointment during working hours, but their bottled-up aggression regarding their miserable circumstances has to find an outlet. It is hardly surprising that the weakest members in their milieu are then victimized, as one regular customer to an urban labour market acknowledged:

Since last one month, we have been passing through very difficult times. We are not getting work. It has become difficult to buy even a cup of tea, not to talk of snacks or regular food. If the children cry due to hunger, we beat them and force them to sleep. What else to do? (Punalekar and Patel 1990: 141)

# 5

# The Expulsion of Labour from the Formal Sector of the Economy*

## MILL CLOSURES

The closure of nearly all the textile mills in Ahmedabad in the last quarter of the twentieth century led to the dismissal of more than 125.000 workers. The textile industry in Ahmedabad was so important that the city was known as the Manchester of India. In western India, Gujarat was traditionally a leading centre for growing cotton. For many centuries cotton processing remained a cottage industry, with spinning and weaving done by hand in the home in small towns and spread over the rural hinterland. But from the mid-nineteenth century onwards, the production process was mechanized. Bombay grew to become the prime centre of the new industry, with mills which were owned and controlled by British capital. The success of this technological transformation encouraged Gujarati entrepreneurs in the old trading centre of Ahmedabad to follow their example. After the opening of the first mill in 1861, and then a second in 1867, the number of locally financed and run companies increased rapidly during the later colonial period. This labour-intensive industry acted as a magnet and, in the first half of the twentieth century, the city expanded to become the largest population centre in western India after Bombay.

The reputation Ahmedabad acquired as a prominent modern industrial centre was underlined by the advanced organization of labours, which reflected the large-scale capitalist structure of production. A strike

* Originally published as 'The Expulsion of Labour from the Formal Sector of the Economy', in Sabyasachi Bhattacharya and Jan Lucassen (eds), *Workers in the Informal Sector: Studies in Labour History, 1800–2000*, Chapter 9, Delhi: Macmillan, 2005, pp. 177–209.

which started at the end of 1917 resulted in the establishment of the Majoor Mahajan Sangh, a trade union which received the support of Mahatma Gandhi. The large majority of the workers in the textile mills joined this new organization. In addition to defending the interests of their own members, the leaders of what became known as the Textile Labour Association (TLA) played an important part, through their close ties with the Congress movement and later the Congress party, in the creation of legislation on industrial labour at both state and national level in the late colonial as well as the post-colonial era.

According to the annals of the Mill Owners' Association, in the mid-1960s, Ahmedabad had close to 70 textile mills[1] which provided around 130,000 jobs. In 1981, the workforce in the city amounted to nearly 750,000 men and women, with a total urban population of over two-and-a-half million in that year. At least two-thirds of those who were economically active were, however, forced to work in the informal sector, either as casual labourers or as self-employed at their own cost and risk. Consequently, the formal sector at that time comprised only 250,000 workers. A different source relating to the situation in the early 1970s calculated that the cotton mills accounted for three-quarters of the 150,000 workers in all employed in organized industry.

Nearly all of these factory workers lived and worked in a crescent around the old city centre, located on the east bank of the Sabarmati river. This part of Ahmedabad was dominated by these industrial districts, a densely populated landscape, where in the first half of the twentieth century, dozens of factory stacks reached skywards as beacons to the labour that toiled below them. But no smoke has billowed from the stacks for many years, and the sirens that used to call the workers from the surrounding communities to their machines, divided into three shifts around the clock, have been silenced one by one.

The progressive closure of the mills since 1980 has a variety of causes: the switch from cotton to synthetic yarns; the refusal of the owners to invest in new technology; low productivity combined with failing management; the separation of the composite phases in the textile production process; and the relocation of weaving in small workplaces with no protection at all for the workers involved. These dramatic changes in the organization of the industry took place within the context of a government policy that was introduced in 1985 and which gave priority to liberalization of the economy and increasing the flexibility of the labour system. There is, of course, much more to be said about these factors and how they are related, but this is not the place to do so.[2] My concern here is the mass dismissal of the mill workers and the changes this has brought about in their lives.

The decline of the large-scale textile industry in India was not restricted to Gujarat and Ahmedabad, but nowhere else in the country was the impact as deep. Of the total workforce of 158,713 engaged by 64 textile mills in late 1979 in Ahmedabad, 122,580 were permanently and 36,133 casually employed (Sharma 1980: 4). During the first wave of closures in the early 1980s, 40,000 labourers lost their jobs. The start of a new industrial policy in 1985 gave rise to a second and even more substantial round of retrenchment. Towards the end of the last decade of the twentieth century, 52 enterprises had stopped their operations or were on the verge of closing the mill gates. By the end of 1996, the earlier workforce had shrunk to 25,000 at the most. But whereas the first wave of closures in the early 1980s had generated great indignation in Ahmedabad, public attention gradually waned. In the 1990s, each new closure and the ensuing loss of hundreds or even thousands of jobs invoked little response outside the immediate circle of those directly affected. Media reports were restricted to bare facts and politicians appeared to have lost their earlier interest in the issue. There are no recent figures available on the size of this army of rejected mill workers, but it must have risen to above 125.000 during the final quarter of the last century.

One possible explanation for the waning interest in the dramatic decline of the textile industry is that it was not caused by a more general economic crisis. The closure of the cotton mills was accompanied by the advent of other branches of industry, such as petrochemical and pharmaceutical companies, diamond-polishing workshops, and cement manufacture. Even more important than that was the shift in the city's economic balance from the secondary to the tertiary sector, that is, from industry to trade and services. By 1991, the population of Greater Ahmedabad has risen to 3.3 million, of which a little over a million were registered as workers. Published statistics do not immediately suggest that deindustrialization has led to a decline in the standard of living of the working classes. According to the figures, the percentage of men with regular paid work even increased significantly between 1987 and 1994, while the percentage of casual labourers fell from 20 per cent to 13 per cent during the same period. Kundu (2000: 3172–82) concludes from these data that the closure of the textile mills did not lead to the predicted and feared transition to a labour system largely based on casual work.

The fact that regular employment generally pays better than casual labour or self-employment reinforces Kundu's assumption that the standard of living of the working population has not declined.

Furthermore, unemployment in Ahmedabad is not excessive compared to that in other urban centres in Gujarat. And there is even more good news: between 1985 and 1995, the percentage of households in the lowest income category decreased from 35.2 to only 11.3. These observations led Kundu to conclude that there appears to be no pronounced trend towards informalization in the economy of Ahmedabad. More permanent than casual employment, a reasonable wage, low unemployment, and, to cap it all, a clear fall in poverty as shown by the sharp decrease in the number of households in the lowest income category (Rs 18,000 or less per year), which is much better than the average for urban Gujarat as a whole in the early 1990s. But do these favourable indicators also apply to the 125.000 mill workers who have lost their jobs?

The answer to this question is based on the research that I carried out in the textile mill districts of Ahmedabad.[3] In analysing the situation as it has developed in the past 20 years, I was able to make use of a large volume of published and unpublished documentation, most of which deals with the events that led up to the mill closures and their direct effects. Much less is known about what happened to those who lost their jobs and the long-term impact on the households to which they belonged. This became the subject of a study I carried out in 1998 and 1999 in close cooperation with Dr B.B. Patel, who is associated with the Gandhi Labour Institute. Our quantitative analysis was based on a survey of 600 ex-mill workers between March and July 1998. Since there was no source of data on the total size and composition of the population affected by the closures, it was not possible to compose a representative sample. The initial criteria for selecting households was to choose respondents who has worked in mills that had stopped production in successive years. Consequently, we interviewed respondents from 33 mills, from which a total of 59,746 workers lost their jobs. Seven of these mills closed between 1980 and 1985, 13 between 1986 and 1990, four between 1991 and 1993, and nine between 1994 and 1998. The fact that the closures were spread over a considerable period allowed us to take account of the time required to come to terms with the shock of dismissal and to shed more light on the problems associated with seeking new employment. A second significant variable was age. We divided the respondents into those younger or older than 49 at the time of the survey. We also categorized them according to what they had done in the mills, basing the categories on the consecutive phases of the labour process—spinning, weaving, and the further processing of the textiles (bleaching, dyeing, printing, and packaging)—or support functions such as technical, supervisory, catering, security, or cleaning staff. Our reasoning here was that the work experience and training in the mills would determine the kind of employment sought. We ensured that the selected households reflected more or less the same balance of castes and religious groups as earlier studies had shown pertaining in the mills. As we shall see, these varying social identities (which we categorized roughly as: coming from within or outside Gujarat; membership of a higher, middle, or lower caste; Hindu or Muslim) were closely related to the kind of work performed in the mills and the position in the mill hierarchy.

To supplement the survey of 600 former mill workers, I selected 60 households for more detailed investigations on the basis of the same criteria to talk with the ex-mill workers and family members about their experiences during and since the closures in more detail. During this fieldwork, which took six months in total during 1998 and 1999, I further met many informal leaders who had emerged from the ranks of the former mill workers, usually during the struggle generated by the mass redundancies, as well as cadres and officials of the TLA and some other unions, to obtain a clearer idea of the role played by these institutional representatives. For the same reason, I also met officials in government agencies who could tell me the outcome of the various benefit schemes and retraining programmes. I spoke to several dozen people who had taken part in these short courses. Lastly, I visited the Labour Welfare Centres located in most of the industrial districts, to gain first-hand information on the activities organized to tackle the problems encountered by the textile workers and their families. These neighbourhood-based investigations, conducted in the spring and autumn of 1999, also included health care staff at a hospital and several dispensaries, and teachers at a number of primary schools. Building on the results of earlier studies (Chowdhury 1996; Jani 1984; Masihi 1993; Mehta and Harode 1998; Noronha 1996, 1999; Patel 1988), this combination of sociological and anthropological research methods produced a widely varied collection of data which enabled us to determine whether the former mill workers and their families had succeeded in maintaining their standard of living after the sudden and dramatic change in their working and living circumstances.

## PROFILE OF THE EX-MILL WORKERS
### Origins

Four-fifths of the dismissed workers originate from Gujarat. Three-fifths were born in Ahmedabad or have lived in the city from a very young age. These figures confirm that the majority of the workers in the textile industry had strong ties with the city (Table 5.1). Family histories

was able to complete secondary school. A higher professional or university education is much more exceptional, but these very low figures may be affected by the fact that our survey included almost no former members of the administrative, higher technical, or management staff (Table 5.4).

Most of the lower ranks in the mill hierarchy, in which the majority of the workers found themselves and stayed for the duration of their working careers, received on-the-job training. Workers were in effect assigned jobs according to their social identity: in the spinning shop, the weaving shop, or one of the departments where the textiles were processed further. It took several months to learn the job, the newcomers learning from an experienced workmate. This was usually a member of their family or of the same caste, quite often the same person who had helped them get the job in the first place. The process of finding a job in a mill entailed several stages. The first stage was to be registered as a reserve worker or *badli*. This meant reporting for work every day but only actually working in the absence of one of the regular members of the shift. To be considered for a permanent job, candidates had to keep this up day in, day out, and even then, sometimes after many years, they only succeeded with the help of someone on the inside. Once they had found a permanent position, upwards or horizontal mobility was more the exception than the rule. The opportunities for promotion never extended further than foreman or supervisor, and the number of these somewhat elevated ranks were limited. Transfer to a different department meant leaving the familiar surroundings of one's own caste, a prospect which appealed to neither the worker himself nor his colleagues. A move

TABLE 5.4   Education

| Level | Number | % |
|---|---|---|
| Illiterate | 91 | 15 |
| Primary school to 4th year | 125 | 21 |
| Primary school completed | 186 | 31 |
| Secondary school | 153 | 26 |
| Higher secondary school | 34 | 5 |
| College not completed | 4 | 1 |
| Non-technical degree | 6 | 1 |
| University Education | 1 | – |

*Source*: Survey, Breman and Patel, 1998.

to another mill was also quite rare and was usually instigated by external factors, such as transfer of part of the operation due to rationalization, or total closure. It was perfectly normal for a worker to stay at the same mill for the duration of his working life. Memories of their former workplace often invoked strong emotions among our respondents. One man told me, not without pathos, that the sound of the mill whistle was forever engraved in his memory as the cry of a mother calling her children home.

Spinning, which was known traditionally as an unclean activity, was almost exclusively the domain of the Dalit castes, as were many of the tasks that preceded it (working the frame and throstle, reeling). In the same way, a number of steps had to be taken before the actual weaving started (winding, warping, sizing, and drawing-in). The specialists in these tasks were largely Baxi Panch and Muslims. Weaving and further processing of the textile up to the final phase in the production process (batching, cropping, shearing, singeing, designing, bleaching, and lastly, dyeing and printing) were the responsibility of the middle and higher castes. This also applied to the finishing work, which was much less labour intensive (drying, stretching, damping, calendering, folding, and packing). This long chain of activities was based on a complex division of labour, within which three-quarters of the mill workers were engaged in spinning and weaving and related tasks. This work can be considered reasonably skilled for two reasons: it entailed the use of machines; and the rhythm of the work was closely linked to the preceding and subsequent phases of production. Punctuality, regularity, and precision were, therefore, required. The spinners and weavers did not, of course, receive as much training as the technical and administrative staff, who accounted for less than a tenth of the workforce. On the other hand, they required more professional skills than the considerable numbers of workers employed in support functions, such as messengers and guards, cleaners, and catering staff. The close correlation between social identity and the performance of tasks in the mill resulted in a segmentation between the various departments which closely resembled the model of communal segregation.

It is a unique feature of the Ahmedabad mills that each function in the production process is divided according to the caste of the worker. Thus, all spinners are Harijans; weavers are Patels, Muslims, UP bhaiyas, or Andhra Padmashalis. The frame department is manned by Vagharis and so on (Jhabvala 1985: 27; see also Masihi 1985: 211).

This division along caste and religious lines was further accentuated by a hierarchical structure which reflected the pattern of stratification in wider society: a very broad base where Dalite castes, Baxi Panch, and Muslims lived and worked in close proximity, with the middle and higher castes above them engaged in 'cleaner' and more respected work.

## Wages and Secondary Provisions

We based our estimate of the pay received by mill workers on the wage level of 175 respondent who were made redundant in the four years leading up to our study. They were part of a group of 15,766 workers from nine mills which were closed between 1994 and early 1998. For this category, it is possible to make a meaningful comparison not only between their incomes while working in the mills but also between what they have earned since being dismissed.

The wages in the cotton mills were standardized on the basis of an agreed minimum, a dearness allowance, and an annual bonus equal to one month's salary. In 1996, a shift worker working an eight-hour day for six days a week would earn an average of Rs 90–100 a day. The least skilled workers could earn as little as Rs 60 a day, while the highest scale, for which technical specialists were eligible, was Rs 175 a day. The wages of experienced spinners and weavers, who made up the mass of the workforce, varied from Rs 2,000–2,500 a month. Until the early 1980s, the textile workers were among the best paid industrial workers in India. This had much to do with the strong position of the trade union movement which had developed in the textile industry in the early twentieth century. The crisis which swept through the whole country from the late 1970s and which caused such a dramatic decrease in the number of people working in the textile industry, did not result in a real fall in wages in the sector but did mean that the lead it had previously enjoyed in terms of wage levels was wiped out. Within a comparatively short time, wages were lagging behind those in other sectors, specially heavy industry, such as metal and machine manufacture. This relative deterioration did not change the fact that, right up to the time that the mills closed, the textile workers enjoyed a much better standard of living than the large majority of the people of Ahmedabad, who had to survive outside the formal sector of the economy. This gap was not only a matter of actual earnings per day, week, or month. There was also a whole range of perquisites that entitled the mill workers and their families to low-cost or free provisions, including medical insurance, sick pay, paid leave, a saving scheme in the form of a provident fund to which the employer contributed a half and which was used to finance the workers', pension, and cheap credit from the mill's own credit bank to help cover major expenses. Lastly, the mill owners provided some workers with free or low-rent accommodation, usually in the immediate vicinity of the mill.

From the above, we can construct a profile of the average textile worker, typical of the thousands who have lost their jobs in recent years as a result of the closure of the mills. This would be a male between 30 and 45 years old, mostly born in the city or at least with strong roots in the urban milieu, married and the head of his household, literate and possessing skills acquired on the job, a member of a lower caste or religious minority giving him a vulnerable social identity, with a permanent job contract in the formal sector of the economy, providing a reasonable to good wage and a range of secondary provisions, and a member of a powerful trade union to defend his interests.

## THE RISE AND DECLINE OF COLLECTIVE ACTION
### Paternalistic Protection

The terms of employment of textile workers with permanent jobs in the cotton mills protected them against dismissal, bargained for wage increases and compliance with the agreements reached, limited the length of the working day and the working week and ensured the payment of overtime, enforced safety and hygiene in the mill, regulated leave entitlements, recognized seniority as the basic principle for the division of labour, and established procedures for airing grievances and settling disputes, including the right of appeal. All of these provisions were embedded in industrial legislation and an institutional framework for arbitration between specially set up government bodies and organizations representing employers and employees. The acceptance of these tripartite procedures for representing the interests of the various parties was due to the advent of the trade union movement. As mentioned above, the TLA—the union that was originally founded in Ahmedabad—became one of the largest in the country and played a leading role in the struggle for improved labour condition which was waged throughout the twentieth century.

The TLA was founded as the outcome of a strike which broke out on 4 December 1917. This date was commemorated as *majoor din* (labour day) ever since. The struggle started when the employers rejected the claim of workers for a pay rise. In the course of the agitation, an angry worker attacked the secretary of the Mill Owners' Association. When he heard of the incident, Gandhi imposed a fine of Rs 10 on the man

(Karnik 1967: 92). As a result of Gandhi's involvement, the labour union which was subsequently set up adopted non-violence as one of its basic principles. In spite of its militant origins, the organization—which was led for, rather than by, the people—preferred cooperation with the employers as its main means of representing the interests of its members. This choice was a consequence of the fact that the movement was based on the teachings of Gandhi, in which reconciliation of differences through arbitration and a willingness to make concessions played a central role. The quest for compromise and the rejection of confrontation on principle meant that strikes or other forms of direct action in order to place the opposing party under pressure would be resorted to only if absolutely necessary. In the movement's long history, it has indeed rarely employed such drastic measures to achieve improvement or avoid deterioration in its members situation. This paternalistic approach was accompanied by an unquestioned acceptance that labour was subordinate to capital. The corporate philosophy in the mills demanded that employees behaved towards their superiors as children to a father. Gandhi liked to use familial language to describe this relationship, which he saw essentially as one of guardianship. But he did not criticize owners who wanted to preserve the distance between themselves and their subordinates for not showing the same trust, respect, and subservience that labourers in the traditional economy were expected to show towards their masters (see Lakha 1988: 102). In 1919, the mill workers took to the streets again to protest against the colonial administration. The lesson that Gandhi learned from the nationalistic fervour of industrial labour was to exercise great caution in mobilizing the working masses and to educate them in the principles of satyagraha (Gillion 1968: 169). '

Over the course of time, many other industrial unions were set up, including a few whose member came from a very distinct category of workers, for example, a small organization which exclusively recruited its members from among the Muslims working in the weaving department of the Ahmedabad mills, or other with a distinct socialist agenda advocating a more radical strategy. The Lai Vavta (Red Flag) union repeatedly urged it rank and file to adopt hard confrontational tactics, with little success. Right up to the time of the closures, the great majority of the workers were united in the TLA (Masihi 1985). The union itself claimed that membership was as high as 90 per cent, but this was probably an exaggeration considering the stubborn survival of the smaller unions and the minority of workers who chose not to join an union at all. But even then, some 70 to 80 per cent of workers in the largest trade union, according to our estimate, the level of organization was very high.

The TLA members were grouped according to the kind of work they did in the cotton mills. There were eight subsidiary unions for workers in the various stages of the production process—four for the spinning shops, two for the weaving shops, and two for the finishing stages— and four others for, respectively, foremen, clerks, technicians (such as engineers and electricians), and support staff (canteen workers, guards, and cleaners). Each of these sections chose a number of representatives, depending on their size, to sit on a council which, in turn, appointed a central committee. It was via this hierarchy that membership contributions were collected and contact between the shop floor and TLA headquarters was mediated. In addition to the core union tasks related to industrial relations in the mill and, as an extension of that, defending the interests of its members in negotiations with employers, the TLA also developed a wide variety of welfare activities in the districts around the mills in which the workers lived.

## Improving the Quality of Life

It would be no exaggeration to say that the foundation of the TLA had its origins in the social care in areas such as health and education, the initiators of which were by no means from a working-class background. After a stay in Britain during which she had become acquainted with the ideas of the Fabian Society, Ansuyaben Sarabhai—whose brother Ambalal was head of a leading business family in Ahmedabad—had taken it upon herself to improve the living and working circumstances of the labour force employed in the mills. She set up an organization known as *Majur Mitra Mandal*, which undertook social work and tried to promote basic schooling in the residential districts of the city during the time of the World War I. Within the mills, attention was initially focused on simple facilities such as clean drinking water, toilets, and canteens. Activities in the slums included creches for the children (the mothers had not yet been forced out of the mills), campaigns to improve hygiene, reduce alcohol abuse and gambling and curtail the illegal practices of loan sharks, and pressurizing the mill owners to improve the wretched living conditions of the working people. As a result, to replace the self-built mud huts that stood in chaotic confusion throughout the districts, industrialists and landlords financed the construction of *chali*s, rows of terraced low-rise dwellings consisting of a living room-cum-kitchen with a veranda and back-to-back facing a narrow alleyway that ran into a street. These densely populated colonies continued to dominate the districts around the mills, but were later interspersed with residential blocks two or three storeys high which were built by cooperatives.

As time passed, the TLA accumulated more political power and this was reflected at the local level by the gradual improvement of public facilities in the residential districts, including pavements, electricity and water supply, and sewers. Cheap bus services increased mobility and made the city centre accessible for mill workers and their families. At the start of the 1970s, the TLA management and staff (office and field) totalled 200 full-time and 135 part-time employees, who provided members with a wide range of services relating both to work and their lives outside the mills. There were a large number of specialized departments to deal with complaints, help with problems related to housing, promote health care and schooling, set up youth clubs and libraries, provide credit from the union's own cooperative bank, run courses for the whole family, and stimulate members to spend their free time constructively, for example, by engaging in sport and recreation. The two-weekly paper, *Majoor Sandesh* (Workers' News), informed the rank and file of these activities, reported on success stories, and denied rumours or reports that might have been misleading. This even went as far as actively discouraging people from deserting the union to join another.

'There were two women in our *chali* who left the TLA and joined the Red Flag Union,' says Ratanben. 'We boycotted them. One woman had to get her daughter married but we said come back to the TLA then we will give our sons. Finally, she married her to a boy from out of town, but we did not go to the wedding. Later, they left the Red Flag and came back to the TLA. (Jhabvala 1985: 36)

The union agenda also included social reform outside the workplace. This desire for emancipation was focused, in particular, on combating the excesses of the caste system. In practical terms, it aimed to end discrimination against the untouchables, who were a large part of the workforce, by running campaigns to give them access to Hindu temples and public transport and to allow them to be served in teahouses and other public places. Completely in accordance with the ideas of Mahatma Gandhi, the actual division of the population into higher and lower castes was not disputed. The TLA never spoke out against the division of labour among the various departments in the mills according to caste and religion. The preservation of what had become 'customary' meant acceptance of the fact that Dalits drank from different pots and beakers and had their own canteens, while the small altars near the machines or in places in the workplace set aside for prayer reflected the separate identity of the workers in the department concerned.

Kankuben describes the 1940s:

When I was young we openly use to be called bad names like '*dhed*' by the higher castes. We always had to eat separately and they tried to avoid touching us. When we went to meetings in the TLA, the Patels and other high castes would sit far from us. Whenever the TLA organised a feast the high castes refused to join if we were there. Some Patels also left the TLA because of us. (Jhabvala 1985: 34; Parmar 1989)

This segregation extended to beyond the mill gates. Most chalis were the domain of the scheduled and other backward castes. Muslims used to have their own quarters and the weavers, who belonged to slightly higher castes, lived in accommodation provided by cooperative housing societies, and later in blocks built by the State Housing Board. These neighbourhoods were all in close proximity to each other and, as in the mills themselves, there was sufficient opportunity—despite the segregation—for workers from different backgrounds to mix with each other and even strike up friendships. Stories of visits to each other's parties and family events show that such interaction was fairly common. It is my conclusion that the trade union movement was not only important in representing the interests of the mill workers in the workplace, but it also played a significant role in the social struggle for the emancipation of the working masses and their acceptance as full-fledged citizens in the urban community. As the twentieth century progressed, the workers succeeded in acquiring a way of living and working that offered a reasonable level of stability, security, and dignity compared to the first generations who had flocked to the cotton mills. Above the entrance to the large union office (*Majoor Sevalaya*) completed in 1960, a bronze relief depicts the way in which this struggle was fought: a male and female mill worker look up at Mahatma Gandhi with adoration as he points the way to a brighter future.

## DISMISSAL AND REACTION

The mill closures in the last two decades of the twentieth century came as a great shock to the workers. Even among those who had lost their jobs sometime ago, the memory of this turning point in their lives invoked deep emotion. But was their dismissal really a bolt from the blue? This is very unlikely. In addition to the fact that many others had suffered the same fate before them, the writing had been on the wall for their own mill for a long time, in the form of a negative annual balance of accounts year after year. These persistent losses interrupted the rhythm of production and suppliers were only prepared to deliver raw materials on a cash basis. Workers were sent home for days or weeks on end because there was nothing for them to do, and were told there was no money to pay their wages. Vacancies as a result of natural wastage were not filled, the third shift was discontinued, and whole departments closed for an unspecified period or for good. These measures were obviously a cause of concern but, since such interruptions or reductions had occurred for longer or shorter periods in the past, it was perhaps understandable that it still came as a surprise to many when production stopped for good.

The final curtain fell when electricity was cut off because the bill had not been paid, or when a creditor had the mill declared bankrupt. In either case, it would be the owner himself who provoked this intervention to evade his legal obligation to give sufficient advance notice of his intention to close the mill. His standard reaction was that he had not made the decision himself and of his own free will. By claiming force majeure, he could defend himself against accusations that he had not fulfilled his legal obligations. These included primarily, a fair redundancy scheme based on years of service and other agreements with the now superfluous workforce. The closure came at a time that the owner had already withdrawn the capital he had invested in the mill during the preceding period. In many cases, the management also tried to transfer the administration elsewhere, take away any remaining stock and raw materials, and dismantle the looms and other machines to be sold for scrap. For their part, the alarmed workers tried to prevent these secretive and illegal practices by picketing the mill gates and searching all vehicles. Did the union also take action? Certainly in response to the first wave of closures in the early 1980s. There were large protest meetings at mills threatened by closure, marches through the city centre drew a lot of public attention and politicians and government were called upon in no uncertain terms to intervene. As the year passed and it became clear that the entire branch was in a deep crisis, this initial fighting spirit dissipated and each subsequent closure affected only those directly involved. Their reaction was as predictable as it was futile and seemed to have lost its power to arouse public opinion.

And yet, there was still hope for a return to better times. Within the context of the centrally planned economy, the state and its agencies in the 1970s showed themselves willing to prevent the shutdown of 'sick' private industries. The strategy was to inject new capital and to rationalize production, so that companies could continue as a viable concern with a smaller workforce. This policy of industrial reorganization through nationalization led to the setting up of the National Textile Corporation (NTC) in 1974. Ample funds were allocated to effect the necessary modernization and streamlining operation. In 1986, the Gujarat State Textile Corporation (GSTC) was launched under the Gujarat Closed Textile Undertakings (Nationalization) Act, with a mandate to restructure 12 closed mills into five or six revitalized operations. Both public corporations failed in their primary objective: to save at least a part of the jobs lost through technological and operational modernization. But the workers who eventually lost their jobs under this regime, at least, had the advantage that their redundancy rights were complied with. They received all their back pay, the money had built up in the provident fund and via other claims laid down in industrial legislation, and a small redundancy bonus of Rs 1,000 if they left voluntarily. This explained why the workers in mills threatened with closure hoped that the company would be taken over by NTC or GSTC. They might then lose their jobs, but they would be assured of receiving the savings and other money owed to them. At the start of 1997, the GSTC controlled over 19 mills employing 22,000 workers. Of these, almost 8,000 had taken voluntary redundancy between 1991 and 1996, while the remaining 14,000 lost their jobs between late 1996 and early 1997. This, too, was officially on a voluntary basis, but in reality, it was because the Board of Industrial and Financial Restructuring (BIFR) refused to allow the GSTC to continue operating, after it had exhausted its funds at a rate of Rs 600 million a year. The NTC controlled 10 mills employing 23,200 workers. Of these, 12,800 had taken advantage of the voluntary redundancy scheme between 1991 and 1996. The remainder of 10,400 received what was called 'idle wages': although production in these mills had come to a halt, they continued to be paid, albeit irregularly and not in full.

The industrial economy, which since independence had been largely based on central planning, had gradually made way for a policy in which production and distribution were increasingly determined by the workings of the free market. Liberalization of the flow and use of capital was accompanied by increasing flexibility in the labour system. This turnaround, which peaked in 1991, was followed a year later by the setting up of a National Renewal Fund. The aim of the fund was twofold: to cover the costs of benefits for, and the retraining of, workers who had become superfluous in certain branches of industry, such as textiles; and to finance the creation of new jobs (Hirway 1995; Mehta 1985). However, instead of being used to achieve these objectives, the largest part of the budget for the fund was spent on the voluntary redundancy of workers in mills that had been taken over by the government. But even among them, the programme was not received with great enthusiasm. Those who were targeted were put under pressure by the TLA leadership, who warned them that they were running the risk of losing all their acquired rights (Chowdhury 1996: L12; Mehta 1995: 605; Noronha 1999: 99; Patel 1997: 21). Because the amount of redundancy pay was linked to years of service, it was only the older employees who were tempted to go for voluntary redundancy. What had been announced as a social safety net was seen by the recipients as little more than meagre compensation for the loss of their protected right to income from paid work. Yet, the few tens of thousands of workers who were eligible for redundancy schemes from mills operated by the GSTC or the NTC were in an enviable position. A much larger group who had worked in companies that had remained in private hands not only received no compensation at all for their redundancy—which should have been equal to between a quarter and three-quarters of their last salary for a three-year period—but were often dismissed without even being paid the full amount they had saved as they worked. Mehta and Harode made a rough calculation of how much the dismissed textile workers in Gujarat missed out on in total:

... 72,840 workers of 46 mills have not received their statutory Rs 228 crore. This works out at Rs 31,293 per worker. The dues include wages, bonus, gratuity, retrenchment allowance and some others. These dues might not have been paid since many mills were closed way back in the 1980s. This is their lifetime earnings. (Mehta and Harode 1998: L79–80)

Such unequal treatment made the shock of dismissal even more intense. The amount of redundancy pay—indeed whether they received payment at all—was in no way related to the service record of the textile workers. A small minority were 'lucky' and received what they were entitled to, but the large majority who were unlucky enough not to be dismissed in the last instance by the government got too little or nothing at all. This is an injustice of which the victims are fully aware, which they cannot understand and which they experience as extremely unfair.

Table 5.5 shows that almost a third of the workers included in the survey received compensation of between nothing and Rs 25,000, and two-thirds less than Rs 50,000. A little over a tenth worked in mills operated by the GSTC or NTC. Most of the respondents were unable to give any accurate information on the composition of the payments they

TABLE 5.5    Compensation Received

| Amount | No. of Workers | % |
|---|---|---|
| No compensation | 39 | 6.5 |
| < Rs 25,000 | 141 | 23.5 |
| Rs 25,000–50,000 | 201 | 33.5 |
| Rs 51,000–75,000 | 76 | 12.5 |
| Rs 76,000–100,000 | 54 | 9 |
| Total | 600 | 15 |

*Source*: Breman and Patel (1998).

received, but said that the largest part (or the entire amount) came from the provident fund. At the time of our study in 1998–9, the conflict surrounding redundancy payments was still raging. For example, several dozen redundant workers continued to meet every Saturday morning in the Ahmedabad Advance Mill, which has been closed since 1995, to hear whether there is any news on the court case against their former employer. The leader of the action committee maintained contact with a lawyer who had agreed to represent them in exchange for a percentage of the compensation they were demanding. They assemble in a small temple in the factory grounds, close to a statue of the mill's founder, Jamshedji N. Tata. The bust was presented to the company in 1953 on the occasion of its golden jubilee, as a token of the workers' gratitude.

## THE FAILURE OF UNION AND GOVERNMENT

The former mill workers primarily hold the industrialists responsible for what has happened to them. The latter had discovered that it was cheaper to close their companies and transfer production to small-scale workplaces where they did not have to comply with labour legislation. Although the closures were therefore a direct result of a strategy of cheap labour, both government and the trade union did not oppose the transfer of production away from the mills and were, therefore, docile accessories to the mass redundancies.

I can fully understand the complaints of the former workers. After all, more than any other organization, the TLA professed to have fought to improve the lot of the working masses in the cotton mills. It was the only union authorized to negotiate with the employers on terms of employment. This mandate as 'representative union' was laid down in the Bombay Industrial Relations Act of 1947. The authoritarian manner in which the TLA was governed was in keeping with this hegemonic position. During his study of the union movement in Ahmedabad, Masihi observed that none of the union's leaders had worked in the mills themselves or even came from that background (Masihi 1985: 209). The shop-floor members chose a representative—known as a *pratinidhi*—from within their ranks, who would sit on a council which would, in turn, put forward candidates for a central committee. This was the highest level to which direct representatives of the rank and file could penetrate, and in practice, the union leadership often decided in advance who was to occupy these lower cadre positions. Gandhi introduced the name *mahajan*, in the sense of a guild, but it was also used in terms of an exclusive elite who made all the important decisions affecting their clientele amongst themselves.

In the eyes of the workers, this top-down way of operating has, from the very beginning, been a style characteristic of the TLA's management. The General Secretary whom I met on several occasions during my fieldwork between 1998 and 2000, occupied his chair for some 30 years, and the other senior members of the union board had been there just as long. Together they determined the policy of the union, acted as its representative in dealings with outsiders, and were accustomed to informing, instructing, and directing the rank and file. This model of leadership left no room for accountability or even the minimum of participation on the part of the members in appointing, promoting, or dismissing their highest officials. Together with the ideological choice to avoid militancy in favour of harmony and cooperation with the captains of industry, and for compromise as the basic means of settling disputes, this explains the detachment and the conspicuous lack of decisiveness with which the TLA responded to the mass redundancies among its members. At an early stage, after the first wave of mill closures between 1982 and 1984, Joshi produced a scathing criticism of the TLA's inertia:

The prime objective of a union is to struggle for security of service, wages and emoluments. When composite textile mills were being closed down and nearly 50,000 workers were made jobless, the representative union kept a low profile and agreed to the plans like restructuring of mills, early and premature retirement of workers, opening of just seven mills and rehabilitation of only 5,000 workers. It was a mute spectator when old machinery was being shifted to new sites. It did not struggle of workers rights. It agreed to almost all the plans of the management and the Government. (Joshi 1987: 155)

An ex-member of the Second Labour Law Review Committee writes, 'In addition, the phenomenon of company union is not unknown in India. As a member of the Second Labour Law Review Committee of the Government of Gujarat, I was astonished to find verbatim similarity in the representations of the Majoor Mahajan and Ahmedabad Textile Millowners' Association (ATMA)' (quoted in Joshi 1987: 155).

There was very little evidence of even a reasonably effective defence of interests safeguarded under industrial legislation. This neglect of its primary task by the TLA leadership seems to be coming to an end as this union—with such an illustrious past—now faces extinction. Towards the end of my fieldwork in early 2000, the membership had dwindled to 15,000, and even this number may have been exaggerated. The rapid decline from 1979 onwards, when the TLA counted 135,445 members, was a source of acute embarrassment in conversations with the remaining office bearers. These are all elderly men in the final years of their life who have to accept that annual expenditure of the union is now higher than income, which forced them to sack the administrative staff, while the large head office stands empty.

It would be grossly incorrect to attribute this sad collapse solely to the crisis in the textile industry. The advent of the TLA was irrevocably linked to the Congress movement, a political alliance which continued after independence. This changed in 1969 when the party that had essentially forged the national state became divided, and a minority, led by Gujarat politicians inspired by Mahatma Gandhi's thinking, split off from the mother party under the leadership of Indira Gandhi. The TLA leadership aligned themselves with the Old Congress branch but neglected to first consult their members. As a consequence, they found that they had manoeuvred themselves and the union in political isolation. In an attempt to break away from the conservative camp, the leaders, together with other unions from various part of Gujarat, decided to set up their own political party, the National Labour Party (NLP), which aimed at steering an independent course that was apolitical but based on Gandhi's principles.

The TLA has thus sought to forge for itself an identity that would distinguish it from the communist parties, from Congress leftism, and from party-based politics in general. One of the foundational concepts around which the formation of the union was forged was in Gandhi's distinction between 'sewak' and 'sardar', the sewak acts like a mother and attends to cure the ailment and even gives bitter medicine: while sardar acts like a politician and does all sorts of manoeuvres to keep up his position. The trade union leader should act like a sewak and not like a sardar' (TLA 1977). Thus, not only should a trade union not engage in politics, but in a sense it must stand above those whom it represents. (Chowdhury 1996: L11)

Just how much the TLA leaders had underestimated the submissiveness of their rank and file emerged during the next elections, when none of the NLP candidates who had concentrated their campaigns in the textile districts of Ahmedabad won a seat. Even more revealing was that the mill workers saw the defeat as a victory. The political chasm between the leaders and the union membership could not have been expressed in clearer terms.

My informants told me in no uncertain terms that they were very disillusioned and bitter about the refusal of the TLA to take a more decisive stand to prevent the redundancies, or at least to ensure that they received all the compensation and other payments to which they were entitled. There was great consternation when, as early as 1984, workers who had lost their jobs besieged the union office for days on end to express their displeasure at the passive response of the leaders and to demand a more resolute opposition to the high-handed activities of the industrialists.

Under the leadership of a technician, Mahendrabhai Shah, three of the technical workers went on fast until death at the gate of the TLA office. It caused a stir amongst TLA workers and the leaders.

Fasting technician, Mahendrabhai Shah, during talks with him said, 'On the very first evening of fasting, TLA president Arvindbhai Buch had come to meet us. He was very angry. He immediately asked me: 'Why have you gone on fast, here? I said, We are members of TLA, where else can we go? Arvind Buch: Are you members of any Party? It seems that somebody has misled you. What kind of farce you are staging here? I said: We do not belong to any party. We want that at any cost, mills must be re-opened. Do you consider this as a farce? To us, it is a question of life and death and you think that it is a farce! In fact, you should cooperate with us! (Jani 1984: 20–1)

In a half-hearted attempt to regain the initiative, Arvind Buch, the veteran TLA president who had led the 'just struggle' for many decades, decided to adopt a form of direct action. On 1 May 1994, he set himself up on a platform in front of the union office as a show of public support for the dismissed workers.

The instrumentalities of the demonstration were defined strictly in accordance with the Gandhian methodology of resolution of political conflicts, i.e. as peaceful, non-violent agitation, designed to generate moral pressure on the central government and to raise public awareness of the plight of the jobless workers. The specific modality adopted by the organisers of the *satyagraha* was to construct a makeshift *pandal* outside the TLA premises in the crowded Lal Darwaza area of the city; Buch shifted his office from the TLA premises to this location. Jobless textile workers gather and sit around on *charpoys*; at infrequent intervals, someone gives a short speech, or there is a recital of an inspiring song or verse. There are no provocative political speeches. The *dharna* starts at 10 a.m. and is over at noon. While in the initial weeks, a fairly impressive crowd had gathered at the site, and prominent labour leaders had shown up to address the workers, both public and worker enthusiasm over the *dharna* subsided fairly quickly. At present only a handful of workers (never more than 20 on a typical morning) appear at the site. The elderly and ailing Buch spends much of the morning writing letters, and part of it talking to the workers. (Chowdhury 1996: L11)

The author adds here that, in spite of the fact that the union formally supported the satyagraha, the other leaders kept their distance from Buch's peaceful agitation. Their refusal to join their president was an indication of divisions in the union leadership and was one of the main reasons why the protest made little impression. Even the workers who were drummed up to appear in front of the office every day lost interest, because they saw the ritual as serving no other purpose than that of a joint mourning session. The members' mistrust of their leaders was fuelled by the understanding and consent with which the latter responded to the mill closures. In the early stages of the decline of this large-scale branch of industry, Arvind Buch had written a memorandum on behalf of the TLA entitled, 'Scrapping Without Tears', which proposed the setting up of a tripartite council of representatives of employees, employers, and the government to ensure that the inevitable process of cutting back and trimming down of companies that found themselves in a state of insolvency proceeded with the minimum of problems. His plan assumed that the employers and the government would provide the money necessary to finance the rationalization process and ensure that the workers' rights were respected, in exchange for which the latter would voluntarily give up their jobs at the mills (Mookherjee 1987: 137–8). In 1994, Sanad Mehta, another pillar of the labour movement and a former Minister of Finance in Gujarat, launched a similar plan aimed at reforming the urban economy of Ahmedabad. The plan included taking out a loan from the National Renewal Fund to compensate the redundant mill workers and to create alternative jobs. This loan was to be repaid by selling the land, buildings, and equipment of the closed mills. The peaceful protest initiated by Arvind Buch was intended to pressurize politicians and the government to adopt this plan for a small-scale industrial development model built along corporative fines (B.E. Mehta n.d.; S. Mehta n.d.).

The fundamental change in economic policy that occurred during the early 1990s meant that these blueprints for the future, as envisaged by the labour movement, were doomed in advance. State intervention made way for the free market. This not only put an end to the state taking over 'sick' companies but also meant that bodies such as the NTC and the GSTC could no longer depend on public funds to rationalize the nationalized companies and were disbanded. During the first wave of closures, ministers and prominent politicians would appear at the mills to address the massed workers. They promised that the mills would be reopened or, failing that, full redundancy pay and new jobs. But as the dismantling of the industry progressed, these VIPs showed their faces less and less frequently in the textile districts of the city.

The flexibilization of the labour market that accompanied this policy of deregulation meant that employment was no longer governed by the industrial legislation that had been put in place during the second half of the twentieth century, after independence. I have elaborated on the impact of this change in industrial employment on the dismissed mill workforce in Ahmedabad in another publication. For the purpose of this essay, I have focused on the government's steadfast refusal to ensure compliance with the body of legal provisions that safeguarded the rights of the workers up to the time that they were dismissed. State agencies systematically failed to exercise political and bureaucratic pressure on the mill owners to fulfil their obligations towards their employees. I have already referred to the illegal manner in which most of the closures took place, but in almost none of the cases were the captains of industry prosecuted, let alone punished, for their illegal actions. I should note that the TLA leadership made a resolute effort to ensure that its members received all the money owed to them and full redundancy pay by taking owners who were in default to court. This was a slow and costly process that usually ended with a settlement and payment of a much lower sum than had been claimed. And the costs of legal assistance also had to be covered from the meagre fruits of this victory. Rumours were rife in the textile districts that union leaders were in cahoots with the bosses and were putting part of the redundancy money shelled out into their own pockets. Their suspicions were fuelled by the fact that the TLA asked a fee to finance the dispute with the employers. This commission—1 per cent of the final payment received—was the cause of much controversy and, according to one calculation, earned the union some Rs 16.5 million (Howell and Kambhampati 1997: 45).

Takeover by the NTC or GSTC was a precondition for the success of workers' claims against reluctant employers. The chances of this happening were greater in the early years of closure. Workers who were lucky enough to gain public employee status before losing their jobs could count on a redundancy payment from the National Renewal Fund. But even then, and contrary to earlier promises, the majority of them did not receive the full amount that was due to them. This privilege was restricted to the managerial staff members in the company concerned, whose dismissal was accompanied by a golden handshake (Howell and Kambhampati 1997: 40).

The lower one's position in the hierarchy, the greater the chance of being put out on the street with little or nothing. This state of affairs confirmed my conclusion that the excessive inequality in the treatment of the redundant workers, both between and within companies, considerably intensified the misery of the loss of job and livelihood. One indication of the scale of this failure to pay redundant workers their full dues was provided by the general secretary of the TLA, who told me during a conversation at the end of 1999 that the former mill workers had received no more than a fifth of the total compensation and other payment to which they were entitled.

## NOTES

1. Mills owned by the same company were counted separately (Papola and Subrahmanian 1975: 119).

2. The complex causes of the decline in the industry will not be considered further here. The principles and considerations of the new textile policy introduced in 1985 can be found in a government policy document included as Appendix 2 in Leadbeater (1993).

3. The empirical research was funded by the Indo-Dutch Programme on Alternatives in Development (IDPAD). I would like to express my gratitude to Kiran Nanavati who assisted me during the fieldwork and who also supervised the survey which I carried out in collaboration with Dr B.B. Patel. I am grateful for their insights and support which helped me in writing this report.

# 6

# Neo-bondage

## A Fieldwork-based Account*

Over the last half century, I have conducted anthropological fieldwork in the state of Gujarat, situated on the west coast of India. My first round in the early 1960s, when as a young student I was charged with collecting data for writing another village study, focused on the fading away of a system of agrarian bondage as it had been practised from generation to generation. I analysed the relationship under which agricultural labourers, with their wives and children, were attached to the households of the big landowners in the localities of my research in terms of patronage and exploitation. I followed up my fieldwork findings by going back to the archives, in India as well as in Britain, to learn about the historical antecedents of bondage: the social, political, and economic context in which the system of bondage, known as *hali pratha*, operated and the reasons why it started to disintegrate in the late colonial era.[1] More recently, I published a study in which I described in greater detail how bondage under the *ancien regime* came about, how colonial policymakers reacted to this institution of unfreedom, and which parties were at work during the struggle for national independence to try to dissolve the state of attachment in which agricultural labourers were forced to live (Breman 2007a). Below, I will summarize some of my findings.

While my basic argument is that the type of bondage that used to exist has disappeared, in my ongoing field-based investigations in west India in subsequent decades, I have often found practices at the bottom of

* Originally published as 'Neo-bondage: A Fieldwork-based Account', in *International Labor and Working-Class History*, vol. 78, no. 1, 2010, pp. 48–62.

both the rural and urban informal sector economies that restrict labour's freedom of movement. Indebtedness is invariably what causes labourers to comply with a condition of employment that keeps them entrapped at the worksite. Employers use the payment of advance wages ('earnest money') as a mechanism of attachment: the recipient has to repay the provider in labour if and when desired, for a price lower than the going market rate. The account that follows does not refer to sources other than my own writings, but the relationships I describe are, of course, also reported in many other publications that discuss ongoing practices of unfree labour in South Asia at large (see, for example, Breman *et al.* 2009; Prakash 1990; and Ramachandran 1990).

Employers who recruit migrant workers for an entire season are an important source for binding labour in a relationship of indebtedness. A wide variety of economic activities that take place in the open air make use of such 'footloose labour' tied down in a cycle of production that begins at the start of the dry season and ends before the first rainfall. The seasonal migration of labour has been a worldwide phenomenon for quite some time. The transition to a capitalist mode of production put a premium on mobility, resulting in an increase in both the scale of migration and the distances covered. However, as the transformation of Western economies progressed in the late nineteenth century, the circulation of labour declined. On the one hand, increased and more regular employment reduced the pressure to migrate temporarily to work elsewhere, while on the other hand, industrialization made it possible for rural migrants to settle down in towns and cities. The mobility of labour in India, both rural-to-urban and intra-rural, started to gather momentum in the second half of the twentieth century. But the annual trek from village to distant worksite and back has not resulted in permanent settlement. The circulation of labour is going on, with no end in sight, as described in two case studies relating to the villages of my recurrent fieldwork in south Gujarat.

## THE ANNUAL TREK TO THE BRICK KILNS

In the vicinity of Chikhligam, labour from far away is mobilized for a variety of activities, including the sugarcane harvest, road building, sand digging, and working in stone quarries. But large groups of labourers from south Gujarat go in search of work elsewhere, mostly in brick kilns. For many years, middlemen acting on behalf of brick manufacturers have recruited members of the land-poor and landless castes from Chikhligam. I have defined the modality of employment to which they are recruited as neo-bondage. Let me first explain why I see this arrangement as a form of labour bondage. During the monsoon, when the subsistence deficit in the landless neighbourhoods is at its most urgent because of lack of work and income, the recruiting agent arrives to hand out earnest money that commits the recipient to leave the village two or three months later to go work in the brickfields. When the migrants arrive at the worksite, the jobber or labour recruiter (*mukadam*) becomes the foreman of the gang he has contracted. The manner of recruitment is the same as that of the earlier *hali*, who was not forced to become a farm servant but offered his services 'voluntarily' to a master who was prepared to pay him an advance, usually to enable him to marry. The bondage relationship usually started with a debt, which is also true of the labourer nowadays, who surrenders his freedom of movement at the moment he accepts an advance from the jobber. Just like the hali—the bonded farm servant who had to work for his master until the debt was paid off—the seasonal worker cannot leave the brick kiln until he has worked off the advance payment. Once the debt has been cleared, he should be free to leave, but his wage is then held back after a deduction of a weekly amount to cover his daily requirements, and paid in a lump sum when he returns home at the end of the season. If he leaves the kiln prematurely, he loses the net balance of several months' work. He can ask for a new advance in the meantime, but if he does, too often he may have very little left at the end, perhaps just enough to pay for the journey home. Sometimes the migrant may even leave the kiln with a debt if he has received a large advance from the owner or the mukadam—for example, to arrange for his own wedding or that of another family member—an advance that cannot be paid off with one season's work.

I refer to this situation of indebtedness as *neo*-bondage because despite its resemblance to the previous practice of hali pratha, there are significant differences. Both situations lead to loss of freedom of movement, but in the case of the seasonal migrants, the advance they receive binds them only for the season. The agreement is not, as with the halis, the start of a relationship that often lasts for life or is even kept intact from generation to generation. Second, it applies only to the labourer, whereas when a hali was employed, his wife and children were usually in the master's service, too. That is not necessarily the case for the brick makers. The jobber pays earnest money for the wives and children, depending on their productive capacity. Sometimes, members of the same family even hire themselves out to different mukadams so that they can obtain a higher advance payment. Lastly, seasonal migrants are hired purely on the basis of a labour contract. The non-economic aspects of patronage that were so characteristic of hali pratha, the halis' function as an indicator of their masters' power and prestige, play no part in the kiln owners' decision to hire labour. They are not feudal patrons who surround themselves with clients but capitalist entrepreneurs who satisfy their time-bound demand for labour by recruiting workers in the rural hinterland. They do this with the aid of jobbers and in such a way that the army of migrant men, women, and children is immobilized as long as their presence is needed and sent back when the season is over. If they lose their productive capacity, they are a burden to the employer. Their temporary employment entitles them to no additional benefits. While the halis' masters were willing to provide support in cases of illness or old age, the kiln owners resolutely refuse to provide any guarantee of survival for their employees.

It is certainly not my intention to exaggerate the extent to which halis could solicit support and protection under the old system of patronage, but the seasonal migrants are not better off under a labour regime in which they are treated as commodities. Being unable to work affects not only those suffering from illness but also the other members of the team because the work is based on the active participation of men, women, and children in the production process. One evening, I was taken to a brick kiln that had been opened in Chikhligam—which, of course, used labour from elsewhere—to see a young girl of about 15 who had symptoms of malaria. I found her lying on the ground under a couple of jute sacks, shivering with fever. Her younger sister came now and again and shook her gently, trying to get her to go to work because she was unable to carry all the bricks away from the base plate by herself. The labour power of her sick sister was needed to eliminate the backlog. When she had done this, she could lie down again, although for no longer than 10 minutes (Breman 1996: 135; also see Figure 6.1).

The relationship between the jobbers and the labourers is contractual, but they are relatively close to each other. There is no great difference in social identity, such as that between the *dhaniyamo* (master) and the halis (servants). The labour contractors come from the same background as the migrants. They are part of the footloose army for many years until the kiln owner asks them to act as intermediaries and gives them a sum of money to recruit labour. To be eligible for the position of jobber, they must have experience with the work, possess the qualities required to act as an intermediary, and have a certain amount of property that can be

FIGURE 6.1    The More Bricks This Young Girl Can Carry, the Higher Her Weekly Advance Will Be
*Source*: Photograph by Ravi Agarwal in Breman and Das (2000).

used as security in the event that the agreed number of migrants do not show up. These criteria explain why outsiders cannot be middlemen. How completely wrong things can go is shown by the case of D., an Anaval Brahman and former village head of Chikhligam, who saw labour contracting as an attractive source of additional income. For many years he had witnessed the departure of seasonal migrants to the brickworks, whose owners regularly visited the village to gain information from him about the reputation of recruiters and workers. D. reckoned that he was better qualified than anybody else to streamline this demand for temporary labour according to the requirements of modern times. After all, members of the low castes in the village trusted him, and a man of his social background would find it easy to convince distant employers of his integrity and intelligence. D. took up matters in a big way and, according to him, entered into contracts to supply some thousands of workers to the brick-making industry of Bombay and south Gujarat from Chikhligam and adjacent villages. He even accompanied the first contingent of some hundreds to Bombay. However, the factory owners there, who had indeed provided him in good faith with a large amount of credit, were dissatisfied with the poor quality of the workers with whom he arrived. When these bosses continued to refuse payment of the commission he had been promised on deliverance of the gangs, D. loaded all his workers into lorries one night and took them to other brickyards in Surat. My landless informants burst out in laughter as they told me about this adventure (Breman 1996: 99).

Nearly all jobbers are Dhodhiyas, a tribal caste of land-poor peasants, who have first worked in the kilns themselves. They are therefore thoroughly familiar with the situation in the kilns, know what work to give to whom, and how to make sure it gets done properly. They are appointed as middlemen because of their good service record and their willingness in preceding years to act as an agent in the village for their own jobber. They give him information on suitable candidates, who will come with their wives and children, for recruitment and act as witnesses when the earnest money is paid out. In this way, they show their suitability to act as jobbers themselves and are eventually promoted. The Dhodhiyas have the advantage of owning some property—land and cattle—that they can offer as security against the debt the seasonal migrants have entered into. That is why very few jobbers are Halpatis, a tribal caste of agricultural labourers. In Chikhligam, L. succeeded in being promoted to the position of jobber, but he was unable to sustain it. At the time, I noted the following:

L. is again working as brick-maker having acted as jobber and gang boss for two years. He was ruined by a couple of migrants who had agreed to go with him at the start of the second season but failed to show up at the time of departure. At that late date, he was unable to find replacements, according to him due to lack of solidarity of Dhodhia *mukadams* in the village. They are prepared to help one another, but they spread a rumour about L. that the brickworks' owner had no faith in his ability as a gang boss. The patron was angry when L. arrived with fewer workers than he had promised and deducted the advances given in the monsoon to the missing workers from his commission. But this was not all the damage. Two members of his gang returned home early due to illness with the result that the output of the others was reduced. The upshot was that at the end of the second year he was indebted to the owner of the brickworks. According to the calculations of the latter at least, with the result he had to return to the village without a penny in his pocket. (Breman 1996: 97–8)

Jobbers are the guardians of the routes leading from the village to the outside world. They know how to deal with employers and to make sure the members of their gang do the work they have agreed to do, to pay out the weekly living allowance, to keep production going until the end of the season, and to mete out punishment in the knowledge that they will be backed up by their principals. The debt the migrants enter into commits them to obedience and a show of deference in the same way that the halis had to respect their dhaniyamo. The migrant workers, however, have much more opportunity to escape the grips of the jobber/gang boss, and this is perhaps the greatest difference between traditional bondage and neo-bondage. Often, they are cheated by one or the other. They are not able to check the balance of pay they take home with them at the end of the season. Protesting against maltreatment or underpayment when they leave is ineffective. All they can do is choose a different jobber the next season and go to work at a different kiln.

The reserve army of underpaid and underemployed labour has to stand by in the hinterland until the time comes to leave, but this does not mean these workers behave as a docile and helpless mass who, having received their advance, have no other choice than to accept their bondage from the moment they leave the village to the day they are sent home again at the end of the season. The jobbers have to keep a constant eye on them to ensure that they actually stick to the agreement to leave when the time comes. Some labourers accept earnest money from more than one jobber. The jobbers protect themselves against such deceit or disloyalty by keeping in contact with each other and drawing up a blacklist of clients who do not honour their contracts. When I came back to Chikhli in 1986, I was foolish enough to accept a ride in a jeep. Vehicles rarely enter the isolated landless neighbourhood, and when the inhabitants saw the dust cloud announcing my arrival, they fled into the fields, thinking that it was the mukadam who had come, together with the brick owner, to pick up those who had not turned up when the migrants left for the kiln a couple of weeks earlier. Complaints of ill health are not accepted as a good excuse for not turning up. The least these no-show cases could expect was a beating, and if they still refused to go, they would have to find a replacement. There is no point in demanding repayment of the advance, since the landless have hardly any property that can be confiscated in place of payment. What is often presented as deceit on the part of the migrants, however, can be fraud by the jobber, who has kept back some of the credit for himself rather than paying it out as an advance. The employers are aware of such practices and replace the mukadam if the scale of 'bad debts' becomes too high. The jobber is a necessary evil but needs to be kept under close surveillance, according to a kiln owner with whom I have remained in contact for many years.

An example is a jobber I had known for some time, whom I met again during the 1986 monsoon when he was staying with the owner of a petrol pump sited on the main road from Chikhli to Valsad. Here he meets the migrants recruited for him by a new gang boss. In exchange for placing their thumb print on a paper, they are given the first instalment of the promised cash advance. But the patron has armed himself against the deceit by which he had formerly been victimized. He takes a photo of each contracted worker. The flash that accompanies the making of the portrait is not really necessary, but its use dramatically stresses the importance of the proceedings. In a loud voice he then says that this evidence will be a great help to the police if the workers try to defraud him. In an aside, he tells me that he turns down anyone who refuses to follow his order to look straight into the camera when he is taking the photograph (Breman 1996: 107).

But the seasonal migrants do not allow themselves to be intimidated by these threats. Both parties are fully aware that trying to get compensation from them for failing to keep their part of the agreement is doomed in advance. The workers toe the line as long as it is in their own interests, but do not hesitate to back out if that suits them better. Nor do they let their indebtedness stand in the way.

## HARVESTING SUGARCANE IN NEO-BONDAGE

For many years, the Bardoli sugar cooperative recruited the majority of its cane cutters from Khandesh in the neighbouring state of Maharashtra. During the monsoon, a staff member of the cooperative management was stationed in Dhulia town to recruit cutting teams from the surrounding villages. He did that by taking on jobbers, who each received a sum of money for putting together a gang of work teams and contracting them by giving them an advance. This earnest money was paid in several instalments and came at a time when the village economy offered little work or income for the majority of land-poor farmers and landless labourers. This desperate situation was even worse in years when there was insufficient rainfall and going into debt was the only way that these households were able to survive. The jobbers had to sign written contracts that they had to follow to the letter: to leave when they were told to, to be at the designated locations with their gangs from the beginning to the end of the harvest campaign, and to supervise the work and ensure that it went as instructed. There were two kinds of teams. The *gadavala*s took an ox cart with them to transport the cane to the factory themselves. Four or five workers were needed for each cart:

two to take the fully laden cart to the factory, while the other members made sure there was a new load of cane ready to load when the cart came back. Much more numerous were the *koytavala*s.[2] These were minimal cutting teams consisting of two members, usually a husband and wife. Children from the age of eight would also often take part in the work. These gangs did not transport the cane themselves but loaded it onto tractors and lorries sent by the factory. The gadavalas received higher advances than the koytavalas, but both groups were forced to sell their labour in advance to enable them to survive the slack season.

The army of harvesters increased in size from the 1960s onward, when the expansion of irrigated land allowed the agro-industry to spread on the central plain. New cooperatives were set up in neighbouring sub-districts. They built their own factories and modelled their activities on the formula that had proved so successful in Bardoli. They, too, chose not to employ local landless labour and recruited work gangs from the far-off hinterland, using the routes that the pioneers from Bardoli had opened up. The intermediaries who form the link between the cooperatives and the migrants are crucial to the recruitment process. They come from the same background as the cane cutters, have worked as cutters themselves for many years, and therefore know what is expected of them as a jobber: they must be sufficiently creditworthy; know when, how, and whom to recruit; direct the work during the campaign; and settle wages with their gang. Being too accommodating to either side can get the mukadams into trouble, but being unwilling to take risks or refusing to pay out more earnest money than the factory agent is willing to supply can also be costly. The labour brokers are in competition with one another and often have to take out high-interest loans from private moneylenders to make sure their teams are complete. But this does not mean that they have no sanctions at their disposal to make sure the seasonal migrants do as they say. These are applied with customary brutality when making up a gang of cutting teams. It is found wholly in order, even by their victims, that the mukadams should demand and eventually force their rights. The factories discharge the recruitment risks onto the labour brokers, who consequently shift these further down onto the actual workers. The cane cutters have no means of defending themselves against unjust or unreasonable claims and resign themselves to their fate or are at least not in a position to come out in open protest against it (Breman 1994: 152).

Upon arrival on the central plain, the army of thousands of cane cutters is immediately divided up among the various zones demarcated by the cooperative, an area within a radius of 20–30 km of the factory.

The gadavalas teams are sent to locations up to a distance of 10 km, while the koytavalas work in the fields further away. For their tent-like shelters, the migrants are issued a few bamboo poles and three mats or sheets of blue canvas. They erect these less than a yard from each other, leaving no room for the cutters to retreat in a niche of their own or to sleep in the intimacy of their family. After the evening meal, they sit together around the fire on which the food is prepared. In the winter months, they warm themselves against the cold evening air. These compact colonies, ranging from a few dozen to several hundred men, women, and children, are set up in open spaces on the roadside or at the edges of villages. They are temporary settlements, which take no more than a couple of hours to erect and can just as quickly be dismantled when all the fields in the immediate vicinity have been harvested. The removal to a new location takes place as quickly as possible, so that the cutters do not lose a working day. There are usually several gangs in each camp. The teams are clustered around their mukadam for protection and to ensure that they are always at his disposal. They lack even the most basic facilities, such as a latrine, and often have no drinking water. The migrants have to wash themselves and their clothes in the irrigation channels, which are badly polluted as a result of the excessive use of fertilizers and pesticides. The impossibility of observing even the most elementary rules of hygiene means that diseases are widespread, especially dysentery, diarrhoea, malaria, and all kinds of infections. The camps are a filthy habitat that leaves no room for human dignity. From a short but continuous stay in two camps—of 10 days and a week, respectively—it was chiefly the tiredness and dreariness of the Khandeshis' existence that impressed me most strongly. People live packed very close to one another in extremely primitive conditions, often outside the regular family attachments and with an over-representation of young men and women. All sorts of social conventions and control mechanisms that apply back in their own village lose their significance and efficacy in this alien and harsh milieu. The mood in the camp is often tetchy, and small and unimportant differences of opinion easily blow up into fierce fights. The inhuman treatment that the cane cutters meet is unloosened between them in rancour and aggression (Breman 1994: 163).

The working day starts early and the men leave the camp first. The women come a little later, as they first have to prepare the food they take to the fields. The gang boss assigns each cutting team several rows of cane, which the men have to cut off close to the ground. The women follow on behind, cutting the cane stalks into smaller pieces and removing the leaves on the sides. If there is a child in the team, he or she makes the cut cane into bundles, tying it together with leaves. The work is heavy and has to be done quickly, with no protection for the feet against the stubble and no covering on arms and hands to prevent cuts from the sharp leaves. The midday break is short, just long enough to eat the meal. Water is fetched from an irrigation channel to drink and to wash the sweat off. The average daily yield is between 600 and 800 kilograms of cane, the equivalent of a 10-hour working day. Some teams finish before others, depending on their experience or the number of helpers for each cutter. The faster teams will sometimes help the slower ones, but if they are not closely related, they will come to some compensatory arrangement. At the end of the day, the gang members return to the camp. They walk back in a long, straggling procession, all arriving by the time darkness has fallen. My daily presence in both the camps and the fields made me realize the burden that the women have to bear. I quote from my field notes:

Although the cutting-knife is wielded mostly by the men, their helpers, usually the women, sometimes take over so that the men may rest. The cleaning, breaking and bundling of the canestalks, all very demanding tasks, are handled by the women. While the men drink some water or lie down exhausted during the short break, the women have to attend to infants they may have brought to the fields with them, the youngest not yet weaned. On returning to the camp at the end of the day, it is the women again who carry a bundle of wood for the cooking fire on their head, and back in the camp they have many chores to attend to. (Breman 1994: 259)

The working day continues through the night. Milling the cane is an industrial process that continues without interruption, and the same applies to the transport of the cane cut during the day. The transport has to be spread out so that the roads to the factory and the site itself do not become congested with lorries, tractors, and ox carts unable to unload their cargo. The daily processing of large quantities of cane is a logistical operation that is worked out in great detail far in advance. The planning starts with the planting of the seed and goes through to the end of the growth cycles, 14–18 months later. On the phased harvest timetable, the fields in which the cane is ripe for cutting are grouped in clusters. The members of the cooperative therefore know when the cutters will be working on their land. Until that time, they have to follow the instructions of management to the letter. The cut cane has to be milled within eight hours or the sugar content will fall. This means that the koytavalas are picked up during the evening or at night to be taken by tractor or lorry from the camp to the field in which they were working during the day. The men never know when this is going to be, but they have to be ready to leave immediately to drag the bundles of cane to the roadside and load them onto the vehicles. That takes an hour to an hour-and-a-half, after which they return to the camp, only to start the new working day a few hours later. The gadavalas are no better off. They take the cane to the factory themselves but have to wait their turn when they get there. Tractors and lorries have priority, and the ox carts have to wait for hours before they are unloaded. They form a buffer the factory can use to compensate for the uneven rhythm of the motorized vehicles, which may experience delays as the result of problems with loading or holdups en route. The frenzy not only continues throughout the day and night but also there is no weekly free day, not even for religious festivals.

The mukadam tolerates absence only in the event of illness. Leave to return home for a short time is only granted on very rare occasions, for example, the death of a close relative. If the cane cutters do not turn up for work, they do not get paid, and that is the last thing they can afford. On the other hand, the cutters are not paid if production comes to a standstill because a machine at the mill needs to be repaired for the fortnightly cleaning operation. And if the factory compound is too congested to continue unloading, or if a lorry has broken down on the road, this is radioed to the supervisors in the fields, and cutting is suspended for a few hours. Sometimes, teams are instructed to cut more cane and to keep working for longer hours. In such cases, the factory management is not prepared to accept responsibility for any risk whatsoever, or to pay the extra costs. I concluded from all this that the army of cutters is entirely at the mercy of the sugar factory for around seven months, without even a minimum of labour rights. This means that the workers have no set times for eating, sleeping, or resting. These and other activities can only be managed if they are not on duty. But they are always expected to be so. For work, everything else must give way. Even several basic social habits in their way of life— for instance, that women eat after their husbands, that baths are taken or at least the mouth is rinsed early in the morning on rising—cannot be followed. For the duration of the harvest, everything turns on keeping the factory constantly supplied; yet, this does not imply that there is any fixed rhythm. Every change that occurs—stoppage of the cutting, changes in the transport schedule, sudden orders (also) to cut double the quantity—has to be endured by the workers. The working day is long, knows no specific hours, and moreover, is in part not paid for (Breman 1994: 166).

Labour is a factor of production without human value. That became clear to me when I tried to calculate how many workers were involved in the cutting, how long they worked, and what they earned. My questions remained unanswered by the factory administration. Only the mukadam knew how many members each gang contained and how the work was divided up among them. His job was to make sure the migrants did what they had been contracted to do: cut enough cane and make sure it got to the factory on time. I summarized this complete subordination of the army of harvesters to the labour regime in the title I gave to my report: 'The Crushing of Cane and of Labour by the Co-operative Sugar Industry of Bardoli'.[3]

What wages do the cane cutters receive, and when are they paid out? Each cutting team consisting of at least two members is required to harvest around a ton of cane a day, but the average throughout the campaign is around two-thirds to three-quarters of that, from 600 to 750 kilograms per day. One indicator of the level of productivity is that the size of the army of harvesters is 30 per cent to 40 per cent larger than the volume of cane produced by the factory in tons per day. Wages are fixed on the basis of piecework. The rate of pay per ton is set every year, but the cutters are only told what it is at the end of the campaign and not beforehand. The factory management wants to know first what price it can get for the sugar. The financial administration draws up an account twice a month of how much cane each gang has cut on the basis of the slips written out by the slip-boys for each load of cane transported from the field. On arrival at the mill, the load is weighed and the exact quantity recorded. The mukadam comes to the mill every fortnight but does not receive the full pay his gang has earned. First, the advance he paid to the teams when they were recruited is deducted. Until the debt is paid off, the gang members receive only a grain allowance to meet their basic needs. The sacks of millet are delivered to the camp every fortnight. In addition to the allowance, the mukadam gives the head of each team a small amount of money to buy vegetables, dried fish, red pepper, and salt. Most of the men, however, use this pocket money to play dice or to buy tobacco and drink. Alongside the formal accounts, the mukadam keeps his own accounts to keep track of the money he has paid to the cutters, both the earnest money paid out at the start and anything else he has given them before departure or during the campaign. Once the cutters have worked off their debt, the mill still does not start to pay their full wages. Payment is postponed until the end of the campaign on the pretext that this is in the best interest of the workers themselves. On the last payday, the factory cashiers give the mukadams the balance of what their teams have earned. How the money is then distributed in the camps is no longer the responsibility of the mill management. And, of course, these intermediaries between the cooperative and the cutters find all kinds of ways to cheat the migrants. The latter have neither the knowledge nor the power to claim the amount they are actually due. The only weapon they have against fraudulent practices is to go and work for another mukadam the following season. But that is no guarantee that they will not be cheated again.

I have used the term neo-bondage to describe this labour contract, which commits the cane cutters to the regime imposed by the sugar factory from the start to the end of the harvest campaign. By accepting the advance, the migrants commit themselves to work to pay off the debt. But the state of bondage continues after the debt has been paid off because they only receive the wages they are due after they have harvested all the fields. In this way, the factory makes sure the migrants do not just pack up and go home. Their bondage is therefore founded not only in the fact that they receive a payment in advance but also by the holding back of their wages until the work has been completed. This 'custom', as the employers call it, is an effective means of pre-empting opposition to the abominable working conditions. The workers withhold protest against the long working days, the pace of the work, the great distance to the fields, the continual moving from place to place, the low grain ration, and so on, for fear of incurring the displeasure of the employer.

I was actually staying in a koytavala camp on an important Maratha feast day that normally would have been celebrated. However, the order came down from the field manager that work had to go on as usual. Nevertheless, some of the gangs in a nearby camp did not turn up that day. The grain allowance to the cutters involved was immediately stopped for a week as punishment, and a work ban was put on them for the same period. The mukadams of the gangs concerned hurried to the factory to apologize—initially in vain. A day or two later, they presented the managing director with a written statement in his office. In the most abject manner and words, they again acknowledged their disobedience, requested forgiveness, and promised never again to transgress the regulations. With ill grace and many stern words, the manager finally relented. He made a great show of filing their petition, gave permission

for the ration of grain to be handed out, and rescinded the work ban
(Breman 1994: 175).

In addition, the combination of advanced and postponed payment
means that the labourers are at the mercy of the untrustworthy practices
of the intermediaries, who provide credit at an exorbitant rate of interest.
It would be incorrect to calculate the wages the labourers actually receive
on the basis of the mill records. Although these show how little the
cane cutters are paid for the heavy work they perform—much less than
the minimum wage—the real extent to which they are underpaid is
concealed by the machinations of the mukadam.

The nature of the seasonal migrants' bondage is different from that
between hali and master. First, the cane cutters only commit themselves
for a limited period of time, which in theory does not exceed the duration
of the harvest campaign. It also lacks any of the elements of patronage
that committed master and servant to an all-embracing relationship with
each other and that was automatically passed down from generation to
generation. The mukadam stakes a claim to the labour power of the
members of his gang and pays them a wage in return. The agreement is
more specific by nature, is purely economic, and has nothing to do with
the acquisition of power and status as an aim in itself. The middleman
is after all a broker who works on commission and at his own risk and
expense. He acts as an agent in finding workers, setting them to work,
and paying them off at the end of the campaign. In theory, the migrants
are free to offer their services to a different gang boss every year. In
reality, however, they have learned that it often pays to stay with the
same one. His gang consists of a fixed core of workers who remain loyal
to him and who can rely on a wide range of favours. And they can ask
him for credit for exceptional expenses, like a wedding or paying for a
house. Such loans often take longer than one campaign to repay, which
means that the contract is automatically extended for the following
year. Jobbers with a bad name find it more difficult to recruit enough
workers, but it also happens that they refuse to employ candidates
who cannot work to full capacity or who have a reputation for being
difficult. The gang boss supervises the daily work and is an indispensable
link between the management and the workers. The company's office
and field staff have no direct contact with the cane cutters, and the
cutters fall completely under the authority of the gang boss. His word
is law in the camp. He takes charge of setting up and dismantling the
tents, collects the fortnightly ration from the factory and divides it up
among the teams (they all receive the same amount, irrespective of

the number of members in each team, and with deductions for days they have not worked through illness or for other reasons), and settles arguments between or even within teams. There is a small shop in the camp where the migrants can buy small items for their daily use. This is often run by the gang boss's wife or another family member, and customers can buy on credit, but up to a limit set by the gang boss. The far-reaching authority of the jobber-cum-gang-boss-cum-camp-leader becomes apparent when he is absent. Outsiders who speak directly to the cane cutters receive no answers to their questions but are referred to the mukadam. His authority expresses itself in his resolute treatment of those who are dependent on him, while his attitude to his superiors is typified by a moderated servitude and an ability to interact with them. Mukadams normally have little trouble in disciplining their workers, and even when this is done with the use of some force, they know that they can depend on the covert or even overt support of factory management. Intimidation can give rise to heated reaction, however, particularly when physical rather than verbal force is used. It would be quite inaccurate to picture the cane-cutting army as a docile mass of people whose spirit has been broken. Mukadams who handle their workers too drastically are likely to encounter some who are not afraid to show forcible resistance (Breman 1994: 246).

The low profile that the cane cutters adopt is not founded on a natural docility but on their awareness that they are in an alien environment and the fear of getting into trouble through ignorance of the appropriate code of conduct. The migrants rarely or never have contact with the local people in the area in which they spend more than half the year. This marginality is only part of the story. Their tendency to hide behind the mukadam for protection, and their dependence on him, reinforces the impression that the large army of harvest workers do not live in freedom. The final clause of the contract that the mukadam is made to sign with the mill commits him to leave the region with his gang as soon as the campaign is over.

The case studies reported above are based on practices I found in earlier rounds of my fieldwork. Is neo-bondage a phenomenon of the past that does not exist any longer or at least has gone down in magnitude? No. At the bottom of the informalized economy of India, neo-bondage is indeed rampant because the workforce suffers from lack of sufficient employment. Workers are hired and fired according to the need of the moment and receive for their labour power wages that are too low to live on. Consequently, the members of this huge reserve army have no alternative but to sell their labour power in advance and are thus entrapped in a state of indebtedness that takes away their freedom of movement. In a recent report, the International Labour Organization (ILO) identified debt bondage as a form of unfree labour to which poor peasants and indigenous peoples in Asia and Latin America fall victim. In an edited volume, Isabelle Guerin, Aseem Prakash, and I have highlighted the linkage between past and present forms of labour bondage in the Indian subcontinent (see Breman *et al.* 2009 and ILO 2009) and in a recent report, the ILO identified debt bondage as a form of unfree labor to which poor peasants and indigenous peoples in Asia and Latin America fall victim.

## NOTES

1. My PhD thesis, written in Dutch and published as *Meester en Knecht* (*Master and Servant*) came out in an English edition (Breman 1974a). An Indian edition was published by Manohar, New Delhi in 1979.

2. *Koytas* were the long knives used to cut the cane. The knives were owned by the factory, issued at the start of the campaign and collected again at the end. If one broke, the user had to pay for a replacement.

3. The original version was published in 1978, *Economic and Political Weekly*, vol. 13, nos 31, 32, and 33, pp. 1307–60.

# 7

# Proletarian Life and Social Consciousness*

## ADRIFT?

For rural workers in the central plain of south Gujarat, the home village is no longer the only or even the most important arena of employment. The moral economy which formerly kept the land-poor and the landless proletariat tied to the village and, conversely, obliged the owners of land or of other means of existence to rely exclusively on labour from the village or, at least to give priority to 'our people' whenever help had to be hired, is now only a memory. Even in the past tense, it is an idealized construction that is exaggerated, by both parties in opposite directions, in order to show up the contrast with the present situation more sharply. This does not alter the fact that mutual involvement which was so natural in the past has made way for an external orientation which has strengthened internal lines of division. In this respect, I would note that the breaking-up of local patron–client relationships preceded the outflow/inflow of labour in the countryside and did not result from it. It is certainly a fact that, once this trend had started, the moral economy continued irreversibly and more quickly to decline under the influence of large-scale labour circulation. In the modern economy, wage hunters and gatherers circulate along a wide variety of workplaces in differing branches of industry, whether or not in agriculture, or in the home village. The occupational multiplicity that characterizes the annual cycle of the rural proletariat is not only affected by seasonal fluctuations but is connected to the peaks and dips that also

* Originally published as 'Proletarian Life and Social Consciousness', in Jan Breman, *Footloose Labour: Working in India's Informal Economy*, Chapter 8, Contemporary South Asia 2, Cambridge: Cambridge University Press, 1996, pp. 222–64.

continue to determine the pattern of non-agricultural production. The succession of short-term activities, coupled with changes of worksite and frequently also of work sphere, gives this sizeable and loosely structured reservoir the same character which, in the urban economy, has lately become known as the informal sector.

It would be incorrect to give the impression that a drastic turnaround in the structure of economic production occurred recently or more or less overnight. The social history of Chikhligam, situated further into the interior, shows that for some generations now, members of households with little if any land have been accustomed to migrate for part of the year in order to supplement their income from agricultural labour. This trend has accelerated during the past quarter century. Development of physical infrastructure, that is, construction of roads and subsequent building-up of a network of bus connections, has certainly played a part in this. In course of time, distance has become easier to bridge. Widening of horizon is also expressed in greater familiarity with the outside world. This varies greatly, of course, but even the social space in which the rural underclass moves around has undergone scale enlargement. Orientation towards situations and events away from the village is contrasted by penetration of external influences into that habitat. One aspect of this two-way traffic in terms of employment is that the growing number of inhabitants who leave home for a shorter or longer period in order to seek a living elsewhere is countered by a variable stream of migrants coming into the village. Conventional modernization studies tend to praise labour migration as a step forward in the development process. This is based on the unsubstantiated assumption that migrants leave their homes because work is not available locally, while elsewhere their presence is needed to meet the lack of labour power. According to this fairly naive interpretation, wage differences form the principal if not the only motivation for mobility. Members of the National Commission on Rural Labour (NCRL) also seem to have succumbed to this actor-biased explanation based on rational choice which, in my opinion, underestimates the extra-economic forces that operate both on the departure and arrival side.

The prevailing big differential in wages between different regions has induced the migration of labour from the poorer regions to the areas of Green Revolution. Large-scale migration of labour from Bihar to Punjab is a classic case in point. There are now more than 10 million rural migrant labourers in the country. Interregional migration of labour in the process of development is inevitable and also desirable from the point of view of raising agricultural productivity as well as improving the income of labour. (GoI 1991, Vol. 1: vi–vii)

This point of view is difficult to harmonize with the synchronic in and outflow of massive armies of workers to and from south Gujarat.

What seems at first sight to be a turbulent spectacle of ebb and flow, an amorphous mass which flows back and forth without much sense of direction, proves on further examination to consist of workers who leave, stay away, or return with a definite objective in mind. Their nomadism varies according to length of time and distance, is not restricted to a single sector of the economy, involves both old and young people, individuals and households. The step outward is not a step in the dark. The mobilized workers follow existing routes and make use of earlier experience and contacts along the way or at the place of destination. Primordial loyalties, that is, the intervention or recommendation of fellow residents of village or *taluka*, members of the same caste or kin group, play a very important role and determine the access to or exclusion from the various migration circuits. Foremen and jobbers act as professional intermediaries, the latter particularly in mobilizing gangs of workers for all sorts of seasonal industry.

The majority of men and women who leave the village to do unskilled work return there again after a varying period of time. The nomads from elsewhere who flow in large numbers into the countryside of south Gujarat, particularly during the dry season, usually disappear when the monsoon approaches. In the same period, many workers in the textile mills and other industries of Surat, and other urban centres, return home on leave for one or two months. In their case, 'home' is in villages far away in other states of the country. The disruption of employment has been explained by suggesting that long and irregulars hours of work together with bad living conditions create a state of physical and mental agony from which the army of migrants can only recover by retreating every now and then to their place of origin. According to another type of interpretation, it is not the need for recuperation but ongoing involvement in agricultural operations of these alien workers that is a major reason for going home and coming back again after some time in a never-ending cycle. In line with debates which already started during colonial rule, an underlying argument of the latter view is to blame migrants for refusing to commit themselves unconditionally to an urban–industrial way of life (see Thompson 1993: 398).

A common factor among the heterogeneous mass of migrant workers rotating around this area is the lack of permanent jobs with protective employment conditions such as those that apply in the formal sector of the economy. The durability, regularity, and security that mark working life in the dignified circuit of employment are given shape in the combination of at least some of the following contractual features: work which requires formal education; payment based on time; complete and standardized payment immediately or shortly after the actual performance; regular and not excessively long working hours; organized protection of the workers' interests; and institutionalized bargaining procedures for consolidation and expanding acknowledged rights. Informal sector employment is distinguished by low scores on all these points, individually and collectively. However, as I have stated elsewhere (Breman 1980), a sharp dichotomy does not exist. Holmström has adopted the continuum that I outlined but has altered it into a sloping plane divided into various zones of different degrees of steepness. His typology, based primarily on an analysis of urban labour markets, those of Bombay and Ahmedabad in particular, describes a landscape which I also found in south Gujarat. In his richly documented social morphology of Indian labour, Holmström retracts the sharp dichotomy that he had supported in an earlier publication:

My image of the 'citadel' was too simple. The organized/unorganized boundary is not a wall but a steep slope. Indian society is like a mountain, with the very rich at the top, lush Alpine pastures where skilled workers in the biggest modern industries graze, a gradual slope down through smaller firms where pay and conditions are worse and the legal security of employment means less, a steep slope around the area where the Factories Act ceases to apply (where my wall stood), a plateau where custom and the market give poorly paid unorganized sector workers some minimal security, then a long slope through casual migrant labour and petty services to destitution. (Holmström 1984: 319)

My own interest is directed principally towards the broad-based foot of the slope, the bottom zones in which a very large proportion of the total working population is to be found. From this milieu of a complete or almost complete lack of assets that I have taken as the starting point of my study, only a rather small portion succeeds in finding and climbing the path that leads straight to the top of the slope, to the protected citadel of employment. The massive underclass lacks the equipment necessary to undertake such an uphill march. But those who try to fight their way up even a small part of the slope encounter all sorts of obstacles that prevent them from reaching their target or ensure that they do so only temporarily. The larger proportion have to stay at the bottom and have no choice but to go out hunting and gathering a wage.

Instead of speaking about one long extended slope, as Holmström does, I am inclined to argue that the landscape of labour has the appearance of a vast plain broken by many larger and smaller hills. These hills are zones of industrial activities whose top is made up of workplaces that are related to, or which even completely satisfy, the criteria just listed as characteristic of formal sector employment, while from lower down, attempts are made to gain access to the secure but fenced-off positions. Seen from this point of view, the social complexity cannot be reduced to a unilinear labour hierarchy. The configuration that I have in mind is that employers in every branch of economic business encircle themselves with a fairly small core of permanent workers through whom a reserve of casual workers can be drawn in and dismissed, in accordance with the need of the moment. Great mobility and fluidity prevail at the foot of the hills. There are many candidates for whatever chance that is made available. Those who qualify in the first instance are then interested in prolonging their employment for an indefinite period in the hope of, finally, gaining access to the privileged corps that enjoys more permanent tenure with all the advantages that this entails. Such a nucleus–periphery configuration may also be found in the early morning casual labour markets, prime examples of clearing houses in the demand and supply of manual labour. Regular employers here, however, are surrounded by a crowd of favourites who are rewarded with privileges in terms of recurrent employment.

There are a few workers who due to sheer grit and good luck have been able to strike good relations with some *mukadams* and contractors. These few are able to get 'regular' work with one or two contractors throughout the year. They have slightly different status than others. They are called 'permanent' workers by the *mukadams* as well as fellow workers. To please them, alongside provision of regular work, the contractors give them 'bonus' during Diwali. (Punalekar and Patel 1990: 133)

The chance of occupational advancement, in the sense of changing from casual labour to owning a job, is limited, with the result that such labour is forced to maintain its floating character in a horizontal direction. The strategy based on upward mobility within one branch of industry is thus under constant pressure from the necessity to seek or accept a temporary opening in an entirely different sector of the economy in the hope that it will lead to more durable employment.

Vertical mobility, and particularly promotion to employment in the formal sector of economy, is a rare phenomenon. Members of the bottom castes and classes in the rural hinterland also find it difficult to get access to informal sector jobs which are better paid, higher skilled, and more regular. The large majority of diamond cutters and power-loom operators, who stand at the top of Surat's urban informal workforce, belong to low-to-intermediate castes in their place of origin and come from households owning at least some land. Existing socio-economic inequalities in the milieu of departure are thus perpetuated and further sharpened by differential incorporation on arrival in the informal sector arena.

Even more than men, women find it difficult to get access to more attractive job opportunities. Agrawal concluded in her study of textile workers in Surat that while males increasingly seek and find entry to traditionally female jobs, the reverse is out of the question (Agrawal 1992: 258). Would that trend imply a growing gender imbalance in the composition of the workforce, not only between the formal and informal sectors but ultimately, also within the informal sector? This is what another researcher on the same subject seems to suggest in a long-term macro-analysis, showing how in various organized branches of industry which used to be dominated by women, their participation in the work process has declined drastically over the past 30 years due to rationalization, mechanization, and automation. According to Patel, factory management in collusion with trade union leadership opted for a patriarchal ideology—arguing that women were 'supplementary workers', that they 'work for pin money', that their 'primary role is domestic duties', etc.—which resulted in progressive replacement of females by males (Patel 1990: 3; for conflicting evidence, see Papola *et al.* 1993: 51–2). Omvedt, in another contribution to the same seminar, restated the marginalization thesis by pointing out that the main problem of women's work is that it has remained so highly invisible in census reports and other official statistics:

We should conclude that in agriculture and in almost all of the unorganized sector, women work harder than men—particularly when all forms of 'subsistence production' are included—whether or not this is reflected in the census data. Above all, we cannot at this point accept *any* generalizations regarding women's 'declining participation' as a result of overall economic trends. (Omvedt 1990: 63)

Like Omvedt and many other researchers, I am inclined to argue that households living in poverty operate on the assumption that they can only survive by selling the labour power of female members unconditionally, that is, to the extent possible and for prices which are generally much lower than paid to men. Because of the readiness of women to do any kind of work to maintain the survival level of the family, they constitute, in Omvedt's terminology, 'the ultimate reserve army of labour' (Omvedt 1990: 70).

The informal sector in the urban economy is terrain which is hostile to family life. Even those who have been in town or city for many years usually do not earn sufficient to allow their spouse and offspring to join them. The fact that dependent members of the household remain behind in the home village means that a large part of the mass of workers in the informal sector do not live with their families for long periods. It is separation which exacerbates the miserable life at this level of material deprivation. The prohibitively high cost of setting up a household in relation to income, keeps the circulation going. Moreover, these workers, so far from home, are only required to take part temporarily in the labour process at the place of arrival. This lasts no longer than the moment when their physical ability and mental resistance become subject to permanent wastage. The horde of workers needed to keep 250,000 or more power looms in Surat alone in operation are so fagged out after 10–15 years that they have to make way for fresh blood, brought in over long distances from various parts of the hinterland. The rejected workers have no choice but to return to their home village. Longitudinal research into the cycle of these working lives would throw more light on the costs and benefits for the victims who are exposed to such nomadism.

During the past 30 years, the economy of south Gujarat has undergone rapid growth, reflected in steady expansion of urban population. However, only a small proportion of new residents originate in the countryside of the state. This also applies to the inflow into the informal sector with which such a large part of the total economic space in cities is filled. As remarked, the landless or semi-landless milieu is the principal supplier of this mass of workers. In my fieldwork area, these are predominantly members of the de-tribalized castes, listed by government as 'Scheduled Tribes'. In 1961, they represented 50 per cent of the total population of Surat and Valsad districts, but no more than 14.5 per cent of the urban inhabitants. On that occasion, Halpatis were counted separately as a subcategory. Numerically, they included 11 per cent of the district's population, but only 6 per cent of the urban population. Between 1961 and 1971, the urban contingent among Halpatis grew only marginally, from 12.6 to 13.2 per cent. These caste-wise data (more recent ones are not available) agree with the results of my fieldwork in Gandevigam and Chikhligam. Dhodhiyas and Halpatis' from these two villages, who have settled in one of the urban centres of south Gujarat during the last 30 years, are few in number. The majority of Halpatis whom I encountered in the course of my research in Surat, Navsari, Bilimora, and Valsad, all situated along the north–south railway line in the western part of the plain, proved to have lived in the towns from a young age or even to have been born there. Does this mean that rural landless have stayed away from the urban employment arena? Such a conclusion would be incorrect. I have pointed out that many unskilled workers from villages commute daily to and from the towns. In addition to those who have found more or less permanent employment for an indefinite period in factories, workshops, shops, etc., these commuters also include daily paid workers from the intermediate zone between town and countryside. In the bazar, they hire themselves out early in the morning to any employer who needs their services immediately and usually for a short period varying from a few hours to a week. Finally, there are the seasonal migrants who leave home under the command of jobbers. They journey to diverse destinations, including workplaces nearby or in cities, where they stay for months. On a number of occasions, I have visited Halpatis and Dhodhiyas from Chikhligam in Bombay or Surat where they were employed in brickworks. Even those who made this journey for many years consecutively did not succeed in escaping to other and more permanent kinds of urban employment. They continued to be sojourners, forced to come and to depart again. The work rhythm during the annual cycle expresses the fact that, even outside agriculture, significant activity of economic life takes place in the open air and is marked by interchange of heat and cold, rain and drought. On the other hand, this does not necessarily mean that work in closed spaces is carried out by labour that is specialized and which works on a basis of continuity. Men and women who literally have a roof over their heads while working, for example, in factories and other walled-in locations, are by no means always more protected in their conditions of employment than are those who work under the open sky.

Circulation of unskilled labour in particular, I would conclude, applies not only to the change from one branch of industry to another. The fluidity that this continual movement of one of the major factors of production gives to the economic system as a whole is further augmented by the spatial mobility with which it is accompanied. In the debate on the concept, the 'informal sector' is taken to mean the unregulated segment of the urban economy. I have pointed out in earlier publications that it is impossible to distinguish in terms of employment between the rural and urban economy. Based on research reported upon in the preceding chapters, there is good reason to reconsider the frequently made distinction between urban and rural labour markets. As regards the mass of workers who have been the subject of my attention, there is no reason why they should be divided into two more or less closed circuits, urban and rural. On the contrary, I am much more inclined to emphasize the linkage between them in terms of labour circulation. The horizontal mobility which dominates the rural–urban market for unskilled labour is connected to a mode of production that is minimally capital intensive and which does not put a premium on establishing a stable work climate. Considered according to standards of efficiency, the continual trek of massive armies of temporary workers over long distances seems to be an enormous waste of time and money. It should be remembered, however, that the costs of that movement, that is, the long journey time and the outlay needed to reach the worksite or the home village, are passed on to the migrants themselves. This overhead charge is included in the price of labour in such a manner that the employers benefit, while on the other hand, the already scant resources of the workers are further depleted. The rationality of taking circulators away from their own habitat and employing them in an inferior capacity in distant enclaves, detached from the households to which they belong and deprived of all facilities that form part of a minimally acceptable social life, is connected, above all, to the disinclination to treat these people in any other way than as a commodity. That commoditization is accompanied by the refusal to contribute to the costs that are consequential to the reproduction of this underclass. Urban slum habitats do not enhance the social status of people who have managed to escape from the rural hinterland. Living in conditions of squalor and misery reflects negatively on the dignity of migrants who have come to seek refuge in informal sector employment which is more easily available here than in their village of origin. Gender bias in access to jobs is a main reason for females of rural households to stay back even if male members have secured a foothold in the city. More is at stake than just differential economic opportunities. On the one hand, there is the urge to live jointly and earn collectively, but on the other hand, the risk of tainting the reputation of the whole household remains an overriding concern. A strict code of conduct is required, as one slum dweller in Surat explains: 'Living physically so close to each other and having sexual infringements is not very unusual. What we do is to marry off our girls fairly young or send them off to the village and find a boy there. A girl who gets spoiled is also bundled off to the village' (Lobo 1994b: 100).

I consider the strongly increased size of the footloose proletariat, transported to regions that have their own surplus labour, to be an expression of economic dynamics along capitalist lines. Labour circulation connects various sectors and locations of the economy. To differentiate them in terms of capitalist and non-capitalist, as McGee (1982: 56; see also Armstrong and McGee 1985) suggests, for example, in my opinion would be to introduce artificial dividing lines. Such a segmentation does not acknowledge that the economy is integrated and controlled by rules and regulations that destroy the contrast between town and countryside.

## CONTROL AND ESCAPE

The various compartments into which the unregulated part of the economy is dispersed are filled with segments of workers whose social identity is highly diverse. This segmentation along lines of regional origins and caste membership emphasizes the heterogeneous composition of the labouring landscape that I have mapped out above. Brickwork owners in Bombay, for example, prefer to use Surthi gangs, with which they roughly mean to indicate the home area of Halpatis. The cane cutters who harvest the fields in south Gujarat are mostly Khandeshis from the similarly named region of western Maharashtra. Throughout Gujarat, road workers are primarily tribals from the hills of Panch Mahals. It so happens that the tyre repair workshops along the highway of south Gujarat are all manned by young males from Kerala. Kathiawadis have an unrivalled reputation as navvies. Finally, large construction projects seem to be manned mostly by Rajasthanis. The manner of recruitment provides an obvious explanation for this segmentation according to branch of industry. In most of these cases, it concerns seasonal workers recruited by contractors who have the same background as members of their gangs. Without thus being rooted in the milieu of origin, jobbers would have no chance of securing the workforce for which the employer has a temporary need. Primordial ties also play a role in employment for an indefinite period. Diamond cutters and textile workers are taken on through the mediation of their kinsmen, caste mates, or co-villagers already employed in the ateliers and workshops. I have earlier referred to the presence, in industrial enterprises, of a small core of permanent workers surrounded by a reserve labour force of fluctuating size. In this configuration, the former act as agents of their employers and are responsible for bringing in *badlis*, the temporary workers. Those who have secured a more or less protected position are under pressure from family and caste members, and people from the same village or district, to open the way to the bridgeheads that they occupy in this arena of employment as early arrivals.

Entrepreneurs in different branches of industry have no problem in admitting that their labour originates in particular regions, belong to specific castes, or have some other collective characteristic. The way in which they explain this fact gives little if any significance to recruitment mechanisms. Their reasons are that Halpatis have a special skill in brick making, Khandeshis are particularly suitable for the harvesting of sugarcane, Rajasthanis are the best construction workers, etc. These words of praise are supported with statements suggesting that present practices are based on long-standing tradition. Even at first sight, such explanations carry little conviction. These stereotyped opinions, which gain a certain social validity through constant repetition, are often accompanied by denigration of local labour which is abundantly available for the same work. Acute need sometimes compels employers to radically change their recruitment strategies, as threatened for a time at the end of 1992 in Surat. After the destruction of the Babri Masjid in Ayodhya on 6 December 1992, a pogrom broke out in the city during which some hundreds of Muslims lost their lives (see Breman 1993a). The spiralling terror and counter-terror also involved migrant workers, as both hunters and hunted, who reacted by leaving the city wholesale. The departure of some hundreds of thousands, principally single males, took place within one or two days. The harrowing events that they had witnessed, or of which they had been victim, caused many to swear that they would never return to Surat. The escalation of violence resulted in enormous economic damage. Production was brought to a halt, and the textile magnates in particular feared that, in future, they would have to manage without migrant workers from Orissa, Uttar Pradesh (UP), Andhra Pradesh, and other far distant places. While the pogrom was still in progress, the organization of textile employers turned to the district development officer to ask that a plan be drawn up for the large-scale recruitment of young males from lower castes in the nearby countryside. From one day to the next, these men thus lost the stigma of being 'unsuitable material'. What had always been said to be impossible, that is, a paid three-month apprenticeship, overnight gained approbation among employers. The energetic pioneers of this operation were not able to put it into effect, however. Within two months of the nightmarish events, the majority of those who had fled had returned to their looms, undoubtedly forced to do so by sheer economic necessity. Business as usual, was how the industrialists waved away my queries about the future. Nevertheless, the presence of a labour reservoir in the immediate vicinity is reassuring, a few of them were prepared to admit.

In my analyses, I have indicated the exercise of control through primordial connections as the most important motive for providing access to employment on the basis of regional or social segmentation. Halpatis, who until the middle of the twentieth century cut sugarcane in south Gujarat as bonded farm servants, are now disqualified as seasonal harvesters by the agro-industry. According to present employers in the area of my research, Halpatis are too lazy even to earn the meagre wage that is paid to agricultural workers. That exclusion apparently contradicts the refusal by brickwork owners in Bombay to change from 'alien' to local workers, when requested to do so by a government committee. They made it known that replacement of the Surthi gangs would be injurious to industrial interest since everyone knew that the migrants, that is, Halpatis, worked much harder than people from nearby. The general preference for outsiders is usually explained with the aid of such qualifications as diligence, reliability, amenability, and other virtues which workers from their own region seem systematically to lack. However, the procedure followed in recruitment of industrial workers shows that positive group labels are tested on the personal characteristics of the candidates in question. The persistent preference shown by textile mill owners in Surat for workers from Orissa is connected by one author with the specific characteristics that are attributed to this category as a whole: 'Oriya labourers are by nature hardworking, docile, sincere and submissive' (Barik 1987: 177). According to another source on the same type of employment, however, the status of 'alien' in itself is not a sufficient recommendation for admission. The employer tries to sift out undesirable elements in advance by making enquiries.

It is reported that the workers who show some militancy at the workplace or express their desire to form unions are blacklisted and scrupulously kept out of the selection process. Such a caution is exercised by the contractors also. They too insist on recruiting docile, submissive and abiding teams of workers. (South Gujarat University 1984: 65)

When the embroidery market faced the downward trend, the traders carefully weeded out the 'new' or 'militant' workers. They discontinued the former and punished the latter for their upright and 'defiant' nature. (Punalekar 1988: 126)

While casual workers, who form part of the reserve workforce of every enterprise, regularly change their employers, a transfer to another branch of industry is less common. The circular migrants are entrapped in corridors running from their homes to the workplace and back again. Movements sideways are hindered by the same primordial ties that helped the newcomers in finding 'their' destination: the bringing-in of fellows and rejection of outsiders. In my fieldwork, I have rarely come across a case of a textile worker who has become a diamond cutter, or vice versa. Even more than other circular migrants, seasonal workers are entering circuits that are intended to remain closed. They are tethered both by the provision of a cash advance and by months-long deferment of wage payment. The annually recurring mobilization of these armies of men, women, and often children, in conditions of immobility, would be inconceivable without the mediation of jobbers. These agents in the large-scale 'hire and fire' operations ensure not only that necessary numbers of workers reach their destination but that they also leave it when the time for departure has come.

The protected trajectories that have been drawn across the labouring landscape differ from one another in the rapidity with which migrants are supplied and taken away again, varying from a few weeks to an entire season to many years. Variation is large, and so too is the difference in wage levels. Among these diverse categories, all concerned with employment in the unregulated sector of the economy, the return to labour differs enormously. These wage differences in themselves are a sign of the friability of the structure of the labour market. They concern reservoirs of labour at a short distance from one another and which may be reached from my fieldwork villages immediately or within a few hours. Non-qualified outsiders are well acquainted with the existence of various circuits of better-paid employment, realize that they could double their current wage if they were allowed to join, but even in their own opinion, do not meet the criteria necessary to get access. This attitude does not necessarily imply internalization of the group opinions maintained in social exchange, but arises from a pragmatic view of the trouble, expressed in time and money, that it would cost to venture into unknown territory in combination with the factual incapability to attune economic behaviour to a long-term strategy. Landless workers and marginal peasants, whose life is already made vulnerable by underpayment of their labour, can seldom permit themselves the luxury of leaving niches of employment into which they have been confined more or less by accident.

The existence of dividing walls between branches of industry should not cause one to think that a completely homogeneous labour force exists behind those walls. The majority of employers prove to be well aware of the risks involved in any one-sided selection from one particular region or caste. The cooperative sugar factories of south Gujarat, which originally brought in their fieldworkers for the campaign exclusively from Khandesh, have changed to recruiting part of the annually increasing army of cane cutters from tribal regions in their own state. I attribute this trend to diversification to management's fear that labour unrest would be more difficult to manage if the inflowing horde of migrants had the same origins (Breman 1990: 558–9). I have observed the same phenomenon on a smaller scale in brickworks, whose owners prefer to do business with more than one mukadam in different parts of Gujarat. In this way, they limit the damage if brick-making gangs do not turn up at the start of the season, while, in their opinion, the mixed composition of gangs also lessens the chance of labour unrest. This seems to be a successful strategy. Migrants feel themselves not only to be strangers in the region to which they are brought, but behave as such towards one another.

When I asked the Halpatis from Chikhligam who offered me hospitality for a few-days in such a seasonal workplace near Navsari about the other workers, I did not become much wiser. They had no contact with other brick-making gangs, neither with the donkey drivers from north Gujarat nor the coal sifters from the Dangs, although for some months now they had worked at a distance of 10 or 20 metres from one another. 'We don't know those people and have nothing to say to them or to ask. The work takes all our energy. Why should we interfere with others when we hardly have the opportunity to sit down with our own kin?' (Fieldwork notes)

I have remarked above that informal sector employers, notwithstanding assertions to the contrary, are not interested in establishing stable labour relations. Workers who are brought in from elsewhere and who, after intensive and exhaustive use, are replaced by fresh blood, have only superficial contacts with the social milieu in which they are branded as outsiders. And that has to remain so. The reticent behaviour that is expected and even demanded of them as 'aliens' impairs their scant scope for manoeuvre. I have personally ascertained that the majority of Oriya textile workers, even those who have been in Surat for several years, speak only a few words of Gujarati. To attribute their few contacts with local people entirely to their obvious lack of interest in getting to feel 'at home' in their employment milieu is to ignore the fact that their employers have no wish for their isolation to be discontinued. In fact, this is why employers prefer to employ alien workers, even when an abundant reservoir of local labour is available. The migrant workers in Surat's textile industry have no bargaining power whatsoever.

> There is no paid holiday, sick leave or leave of any type—except forced unpaid weekly holidays due to power cuts—bonus, P.F., gratuity, first aid, ESJ, safety measures, accident benefit and workmen's compensation. Ninety per cent of the Oriya workers have no appointment letter, identity card or pay slip. Medical help is a luxury. The seriously injured is sometimes paid a few hundred rupees. At least 15 per cent of the workers are forced to do extra unpaid labour at some or other times. Potential recalcitrant workers are often forced to sign blank papers, scolded and even assaulted and retrenched without any notice or compensation. Many units maintain paid musclemen to 'discipline' the workers. (Pathy 1993: 12–13)

The possibility to retreat into a social space of their own, at least at the end of the workday, and to create a sphere of privacy, which negates the power of the bosses, explains why so many sources of informal sector employment in the city are declared to be out of bounds for Halpatis and other segments of the proletariat in the countryside of south Gujarat.

I have argued that in the landscape of my research, a wide variety of wage labour modalities dominate. There is a strong tendency to define informal sector work in terms of self-employment. This label is taken to mean that the initiative rests with a huge but diffuse body of workers acting on their own account and at their own risk in their struggle for subsistence. According to this point of view, the unregulated sector of the economy is populated by a mass of small manufacturers, homeworkers, service producers, and other petty entrepreneurs who ingeniously, though with varying degrees of success, keep their heads above water by operating more or less independently. However, one should not overlook the fact that in most cases, this concerns employment of the last resort to which men and women, adults and children take refuge by sheer necessity, because of non-availability of wage labour. The essence of self-employment is, moreover, strongly determined by the predominant practice of paying labour not according to time but for a standardized quantum (number, weight, or any other measure rates). Such piecework, combined with subcontracting of work, arouses the suggestion that self-employment is the common modality for earning a livelihood. This interpretation negates the fact, however, that in daily practice, wages are paid to workers who have no means of production of their own and are paid merely for their own labour power pure and simple. What is called self-employment is nothing other than a method of payment which forces the wage-dependent worker towards self-exploitation and subjects him, in the work process, to the dictate laid down by the employer or his agent. Underpayment inherent in this form of employment compels the workers, for example, the operators of power looms, to work an exceptionally long day. Frequently, however, as in road construction, brickworks, or sugarcane harvesting, underpayment is a way of forcing the involvement of women and children in team operation. In such cases, self-exploitation is not of an individual character but is extended to other members of the working household, usually via the family head.

Contract labour on an individual or gang basis puts a premium on the income of those who are capable of maximum effort. Such an employment pattern almost automatically leads to the exclusion, as full-time workers, of men and women of less than 15-years old or older than 40 years. My fieldwork findings are comparable to those of Kapadia who reports on her research among female agricultural labourers in a south Indian locality:

I had asked if women preferred to recruit their own kin. She replied, 'No, we don't. What's important is that the woman should be a good worker—she must be fast, because if she's slow she'll delay us all. So we don't take anyone who's old—because the old women have become slow—and we don't allow anyone very young because they don't know how to do it'.... Another factor, proximate residence, is of great importance as well. Rajalakshmi explained why: 'You've got to rush off for work early in the morning and can't spend time going to houses further away. So you call the other women for work very discreetly. If you wake the others they'll want to come too and when you refuse them they'll get angry and abuse you. So we take close neighbours: we wake them quickly and go off, with no fuss.' The discretion required in calling others for work is important, and for this reason, the recruiter usually keeps the job secret, telling only those women whom she wants on her team. (Kapadia 1995: 227)

This does not mean that those who fall below or above these limits are freed from taking part in the labour process. However, they do not yet, or no longer, meet the heavy demands made on physical strength and stamina, and therefore are not the first to be considered for work on a contract basis. The wastage that is an inevitable part of the work process causes people to be transferred to the less able-bodied part of the army of wage hunters and gatherers. Apart from older men and women who have literally been used up in the labour process, these include single women with small children and those who, even while still young, suffer from ailments or chronic diseases that invalidate them for full-time work. As a result of the little open visibility of such desperate cases, who keep a low profile also in the home milieu of the landless, not only the intense misery but also the numerical size of this category is not sufficiently known.

The contractualization of labour relations has created a harsh climate of competition in the milieu of the working poor. Incompetent, slow, feeble, handicapped, and other sorts of inferior workers tend to remain excluded from participation in joint work arrangements. The members of a self-constituted gang, for example, have a shared interest in not only recruiting the most qualified but also as small a number as possible in order to maximize their income. Emergent practices of exclusionary labour arrangements are not only noticeable in south Gujarat, but have also been observed in south India (Athreya *et al.* 1990: 145; Kapadia 1995: 226) and on Java in Indonesia (Breman 1995a: 27–9; Hart 1986: 681–96).

A permanent job such that makes working life more bearable and dignified, that is, gaining access to the formal sector of the economy, is a far distant ideal for the great majority of the workers who find themselves at the broad floor of the labour hierarchy. However, lack of regularity which characterizes their daily rhythm does not only have disadvantages. The term casual labour, *chhuta majuri*, also connotes an existence that is not conditioned by attachment to and dependency on a permanent employer. Wage hunters and gatherers are free. To be sure, they are free, in the first place, of the means of production and of other capital (skills, money with which to buy a secure job) needed to reach the higher zones of labour. Second, however, they are also free of the subjugation to a master that was formerly the fate of a farm servant. The landless proletariat try, as far as possible, to avoid modes of employment that infringe upon their gained freedom. That is possible only to a certain degree. The need to accept a cash advance on wages entails the obligation to subject oneself to the orders of an employer for the direct future. Back payment has a similar binding effect. The loss of independence that adheres to such a labour contract explains why it is only entered into through lack of a better alternative. That so many, nevertheless, have recourse to this last resort of employment indicates the enormous pressure on sources of livelihood in the bottom echelons of the economy. Even that disenfranchisement is subjected to restrictions of durability, range, and intensity. The work agreement is not entered into and continued for an indefinite time, as was the case with the *hali* of former times. The neo-bondage is further strongly economic in nature and restricts the imposition of the employer's will and his claims of superiority per se. The behaviour of wage hunters and gatherers not only expresses their longing for material improvement but also manifests their basic unwillingness to seek security in bondage. Theirs is a type of social consciousness that might be expected from the proletarian class.

The footloose proletariat reacts to the control over them exercised by employers by attempts to escape it. This is done in various ways. In my fieldwork villages, Halpatis show little interest in entering into permanent employment with a landowner belonging to the dominant Anaval Brahman caste. The status of bondage that is still associated with farm servants has an avoidance effect on the younger members of this landless caste in particular. They choose the more risky but freer life of a day worker. The new generation of Halpatis seems to grasp every opportunity to escape the agrarian regime. Away from the village and from agriculture, they earn a few extra rupees, mostly countered by greater effort besides the longer journey and work times. Their motivation for migrating is the anonymity which accompanies them in the outside world:

Hired for the day as loader–unloader, these young men and women stand in the back of the truck and together with their mates enjoy a freedom that is denied them when working in the fields. For them, that is also the attraction of the urban casual labour markets. They are certainly treated there as commodities, but at least they are not immediately identified and stigmatized as *sala Dubra*. (Fieldwork notes)

Their economic behaviour displays great flexibility in the sense that they work in and out of the village and combine agricultural labour with many other jobs, usually of short durability. Their strategy to constantly search for alternative sources of income is oriented towards preventing an employer securing their labour for a price that is far below the current daily rate for casual work. In addition to helping them to keep their heads above water in difficult circumstances, their occupational multiplicity is also a form of resistance to the pressure brought to bear on them to shut themselves into a more permanent dependency relationship. That they do not object to steady work is shown by the eagerness with which day workers seize the opportunity to hire themselves out to an employer who is prepared to take them on for an indefinite period at a reasonable wage. The scarcity of such jobs forces landless men and women to enter into contract with a mukadam with whom many of them will leave the village at the end of the monsoon. This is undoubtedly accompanied, for the length of their absence, with loss of autonomy. However, that restriction on their freedom of movement lasts no longer than a few months and is over when they return to the village.

In the effort to increase their manoeuvrability and independence, casual workers not only do not object but have a definite preference for piecework. I have earlier called such modes of subcontracting self-exploitation, and I have no reason to rescind that view. This does not alter the fact that to work for one's own account and risk has another and more emancipatory aspect. Piecework enables men and women in the prime of their working lives to free themselves of a direct tie to an employer which is felt as galling. The tendency to explain self-employment as a regrettable example of petit bourgeois behaviour ignores the possibility that employment on the basis of such contracts might benefit the dignity of labour.

When there is need for their labour power, payment based on piece rates and subcontracting of work in general offer the young and able-bodied in particular the chance to increase their earnings, often to more than the current day rate for unskilled or semi-skilled labour. Lack of regularity, however, is a noticeable characteristic of the disorderly lives of wage hunters and gatherers. Periods of top demand are interchanged, often unexpectedly, with days or weeks of little activity. Peaks and slacks are not restricted to agriculture and other sources of open-air employment, but also occur in the urban–industrial sector of the economy. This can be illustrated by the underutilization of labour power of textile workers and diamond cutters amounting to 25 per cent or even more of their availability on an annual basis. The cycle of production and stagnation also follows a fickle course in the informal sector, entirely consistent with the hunting and gathering reality.

Employers, individually and collectively, blame labourers for their lack of discipline. What do they mean by that? Pre-capitalist work regimes are considered to know of no haste or punctuality and do not accept the idea that time is money. All this changes, as Thompson has explained, in the transition to industrial capitalism which calls for a new type of labour discipline marked by the clock. 'Time is now currency: it is not passed but spent' (Thompson 1993: 359). He adds that the new valuation of time came about gradually, and even in the heartland of the industrial world, irregular labour rhythms were perpetuated right into the present century. The compulsion of clock time took much longer to get established in the peripheral zones of capitalism, such as the Bombay cotton mills in India, resulting in a factory proletariat only partially and temporarily 'committed' to the industrial way of life (ibid.: 398).

As observed in Chapter 5, landowners in Gandevigam and Chikhligam are of the opinion that the land-poor and landless fall short of the self-discipline which is a precondition for getting access to steady employment outside the village and agriculture. Nowadays, however, labour-thrift is not merely claimed for urban–industrial work but has also become a trait required of labour engaged in the rural economy. A workday of eight hours is the yardstick chosen by the government for the fixation of minimum wages in agriculture. By way of excuse for non-payment of this legal rate, farmers insist that labourers report for duty much later than 8 a.m., do not keep working until noon, take a meal break which is longer than two hours, and leave the fields again much earlier than six in the evening. *Kam chor—dam chor*, thiefs of work and (therefore) thiefs of our money, is the bitter complaint directed against local labour in general, and the Halpatis in particular. In an effort to check this sort of evasive, non-committal behaviour, agrarian employers feel that they have to exercise tight and constant surveillance. The rigorous discipline which they demand is, however, in striking contrast with the highly insecure terms offered by them: casual instead of regular employment and wage payment not based on time but on piece rate. By switching to piece-rate payment modalities, employers seem to have found an adequate response to their increasing lack of control over the quality and quantity of labour time about which they never stop complaining. Giving out work on contract is certainly of major importance in the internalization of self-discipline among a reluctant labour force (see also Kapadia 1995: 232).

In comparison with the agrarian cycle of the past, the workload has definitely increased. Indeed, labourers then had to work from dawn to dusk or even after nightfall. The bonded farm servants of south Gujarat were at the beck and call of their master and other members of his household at all hours of the day and night. However, their service conditions used to be less contractual and labour intensive. These halis received a daily allowance for which they had to work but at a lower intensity than nowadays or, in the slack season, were tolerated to just hang around without doing much (Breman 1974a). Such pre-capitalist work styles are not condoned anymore. The mukadam and other agents who assist informal sector employers in patrolling the worksites can be recognized by paraphernalia needed to measure output and adequate performance, such as a notebook and pencil in their breast pocket together with a wristwatch. In the landscape of my contemporary research, a clear demarcation between 'work' and 'life', which Thompson points out is a hallmark of mature industrial societies, continues to remain absent. It is therefore anything but surprising that the new schedule of capitalist employment that has emerged, characterized by less control over labour's person but more rigorous control over labour time, although thoroughly commoditized, is still not regulated by the clock. I want to emphasize, however, that clock time is not what informal sector employers have in mind when they talk about workers' lack of discipline. Their blame concerns, first and foremost, the 'irrational' refusal of a massive army, which is periodically redundant and chronically vulnerable, to surrender unconditionally; that is, the reluctance or even outright unwillingness of both males and females to make themselves available for the lowest possible price and to the maximal extent whenever or wherever required. To the immense chagrin of the owners of both agrarian and non-agrarian capital, that dictate for unrestrained extraction is flatly rejected.

There can be no doubt that employers' endless complaints about the thriftlessness of the workforce form a little convincing exoneration for their refusal to pay a reasonable price for labour. Rather than interpreting the defects of which they accuse their subordinates as expressions of economic irrationality, I have pointed out that those subordinates often have no choice but to stay away. That absence may be due to the necessity, now and again, to work somewhere else in order to repay a loan by providing labour, or to the need to allow one's body to recover at least minimally from the overuse to which it has been subjected. However, indiscipline is a correct term insofar as the described laziness, irregularity, and lack of responsibility result directly from the refusal of the workers to submit themselves completely to the yoke laid on them by the employer. Lethargy, intractability, and fickleness hide an attitude of resistance caused by the longing to keep the adversary at arm's length, even when self-interest is apparently not served or may even be impaired by such deeds of open or hidden sabotage. After all, why should men and women who are underutilized and underpaid purposely renounce an income which, in view of their poverty, they cannot really do without? Simply because uninhibited continuation of the effort does not provide such a wage that it is possible to escape the chronic state of poverty. In this respect, I would remind the reader that a number of budget enquiries in the milieu of unskilled labour to which I have devoted my attention, that is, agricultural labourers, brick makers, cane cutters, etc., have shown that they have to spend around 70–80 per cent of their income on food. This high percentage notwithstanding, many of them suffer from malnutrition. The idea that continual work would enable them to improve their lot substantially is completely implausible. In my opinion, it is essential to consider their 'fugitive behaviour' against this background, not as a sign of economic irrationality but as a demonstration of protest.

Subsistence needs demand that landless enter into commitments that will restrict their freedom of movement for some time. This takes the form of accepting cash advances in exchange for making one's labour power available if and when the employer has need of it. But those who receive such an advance show little scruple in withdrawing from the obligation to adapt to the wishes of the sponsor. Halpatis from Chikhligam who had deserted from brickworks grinned as they told me how the jobber who had contracted them made fruitless attempts to catch them. They clearly did not think of returning the earnest money they had received from him. It had long been expended on necessities. Accusations of bad faith would leave them cold. Their only worry seemed to be that on the following occasion, it might be difficult to find someone willing to give them an advance in exchange for the pledge to work. Without their intending it, something always happened that hindered them from complying with the contract in full and on time. Such a reflection indicates concern for the future but no remorse at having infringed a code of conduct that had been imposed upon them. Members of the rural proletariat would certainly not hesitate to grasp any opportunity that might occur to evade their existing bonds.

In the strategy followed by the massive workforce that stems from the rural underclass, marginal landowners have an advantage over their landless fellows. Other than the Halpatis, increasing numbers of Dhodhiya households have succeeded during the last two decades in withdrawing from the annual trek to the brickworks. This is due to the small piece of cultivable land that they own, even though its yield is not sufficient to ensure a livelihood. Work for a wage elsewhere is unavoidable, but the possibility of supplementing those earnings with food crops harvested on their own plot of land, however small, has given these mini-farmers a better starting point than that of the completely landless Halpatis. Dhodhiyas have always preferred to leave their wives at home, both to look after a bullock or cow and to enable the children to go to school, and perhaps also to spare the women the heavy labour in the brickworks. Landowning Dhodhiyas are able to take a ration of grain with them when they leave their homes at the end of the rainy season; this means they require less money during their stay outside the village for daily needs and are thus able to take more with them when they return home at the end of the season. Investing these savings in the farm by digging a well or buying an oil pump and in education for children, Dhodhiya males ultimately managed to avoid the brickworks (see also Veen 1979: 51–2). The little that they owned was sufficient at first to distinguish them from landless households in the village, and later, to increase their distance from those who were economically more vulnerable.

The state of affairs in Chikhligam has shown me how misleading it is to suggest that a small plot of land is like a millstone around the neck of its owner. According to this spurious argument, the pseudo-farmer is worse off than the true proletarian who, it is assumed, can go and stand where he will in an expanding economy. This notion also played a role in the idea of excluding landless workers from the policy of redistribution of agrarian resources that was half-heartedly implemented during the first few decades after independence. The example of Dhodhiyas in my fieldwork village, and of other tribal castes of marginal landowners in south Gujarat, shows that if Halpatis had each been given a small plot of land, this would have strengthened their resistance in a development process in which the demand for labour has increased less slowly than its supply. This is also Bharadwaj's conclusion in her study of India's rural labour market:

... the access to land appears to be a very important need for gaining livelihood in the rural areas and the dependency relations in exchange which the poorer land-operating and landless households are compelled into, arise due to the essential insecurity of this access. Since the perverse effects of exchange involvements act through such dependency relations the social power structure and the hegemony of the strong over the weaker party's livelihood derives from the same insecurity. Land and tenurial reforms could work as a first step in breaking this hegemony. (Bharadwaj 1990: 72)

Still, the social advance that the almost landless might have over the landless should not be exaggerated. The limited autonomy enjoyed by marginal landowners among the Dhodhiyas, even in the past, has been consolidated by using part of the yield of that land to gain access to resources away from agriculture and the village. In view of the continual increase of population, this strategy seems to have provided no more than a breathing space. It is almost impossible to subdivide family land any further, and the simultaneous growth of the literate part of the population entails that an ever-increasing level of education is needed to buy a protected position in the non-agricultural labour hierarchy that has emerged. Nevertheless, younger Dhodhiyas have a better chance of escaping a threatened existence than do the new generation of Halpatis who have to seek their way upwards from a situation of total landlessness and thus greater dependency.

## SOCIAL STRUGGLE

The footloose proletariat is made up of an enormous mass of men and women, adults and children, who possess little if any means of production of their own and who lead a circulatory existence in the lowest regions of the labour system. It is a conglomerate of diverse categories distinct from the social class of employees in formal employment, who usually carry out skilled and better-paid work, and whose conditions of employment have gained recognition and protection through the organized promotion of their interests. In fact, lack of collectively organized resistance is the principal reason why working life in the echelons of economy that I have researched continues to be so unbearably heavy and miserable. The meagre countervailing power of labour vis-à-vis capital is surprising in view of the greater volume of the former as against the latter factor of production. There are numerous reasons that prevent or hinder the creation of mutual solidarity that must precede any common efforts to improve the lot of workers.

The initial and most important obstacle is undoubtedly that by far the majority of economic sectors, almost all year round, experience such an overwhelming supply of unskilled labour that employers have little difficulty in satisfying their demand for it. Structural overcrowding creates an imbalance which has a crippling effect on attempts to achieve social progress at the bottom of society. There are quite alarming reports that the expansion rate of total employment hardly keeps pace with the growth of the working population (GoI 1991, vol. 1: 33–4). Intense competition for the limited work available creates a lot of tension among those who desperately seek ways to ensure their own immediate livelihood. The dissension which this can cause among workers is illustrated by the state of affairs in the urban casual labour markets:

Some labourers in Vadodara casual labour markets told us that if they do not get work continuously for 2–3 days they become restless and impatient. They try desperately to avail of the first opportunity to secure job, whatever the terms of work and wages. This infuriates others who witness the sliding down of the wage rates in such circumstances. Arguments and counter-arguments ensue, and occasionally it bursts out in open scuffles and physical fights. The contractors and *mukadams* keep their cool and watch the scene discreetly without much of an intervention. Of course, the labourers would not like to admit that such a thing happens. Most of them (83 per cent) said that there was never any quarrel, or cut-throat competition among them. (Punalekar and Patel 1990: 120)

Another obstacle is created by the transience, multiplicity, and unspecified nature of the jobs available. Working experience is undirected and contacts with employers are much too brief to provide the initial impetus to a collective stand. Moreover, modes of payment within the same enterprise and even for an identical job can lead to considerable differences in income. The bringing-in of women and children by means of male workers also has an obfuscating effect. These forms of indirect employment contribute to a multilayered subjugation to exploitative regimes and are coupled with interest conflicts that can extend into the household sphere. Circulation along various sectors and sites of employment is given a further accent by the inclination employers demonstrate to give preference not to local but to imported labour. Migrants who have little if any contact with the social milieu at the place of arrival are forced as 'aliens' to keep a low profile. The vulnerability of their position prevents them from taking a militant attitude. On the other hand, temporary employment and an alien background may help to strengthen bargaining power. Outsiders often show an indifference and even impertinence which local workers would not dare to manifest. Recruitment of workers along lines of primary group identities also hinders the development of solidarity in a wider circle. The feelings of loyalty that accompany this segmentation are of a different kind to those that are rooted in class contradictions. The immobilizing effect caused by horizontal division is increased by the pressure emanating from the need to invest in vertical dependency relationships. To rise in the labour hierarchy is only possible to a certain degree, but favoured treatment such as change from casual to permanent employment requires obediency towards the employer and the agents who surround him. Conversely, attachment of labour by means of cash advance or post-payment hinders the development of organized counteraction. Fixing in bondage is sometimes direct but also occurs with the aid of intermediaries such as jobbers and labour contractors. A summing-up of the many obstacles that explain the absence of any collective struggle to improve the workers' lot has, as common denominator, the enormous social heterogeneity of the army of workers, the unregulated rhythm of employment in large parts of the rural and urban economy, and the strongly fragmented nature of the market for unskilled labour. Thus, these three aspects have to be understood in their mutual interrelationships.

Markedly different is the more institutionalized promotion of interests by the much smaller force of wage workers who have managed to gain a permanent footing in the regulated, formalized, and protected sector of the economy. The greater bargaining power in the higher zones of the labour regime is given shape in the presence of trade unions, among other things. Leadership of these social movements, in which the self-organizing capacity of better-educated labour in permanent employment shows itself, exhibits little or no interest in the army of casual workers who roam around in the foothills of the economy. Would it not be attractive for the established trade unions to extend their mandate and care for the interests of this unorganized mass of workers? Apparently not, because one of the few common characteristics of the type of industries that I have researched is the lack of any trade union activities. This is due, in the first place, to disinclination of employers to countenance intervention of third parties in their supreme control over their workforce. It is a form of hegemony that is concealed behind the assertion, which I have frequently had to listen to, that unsolicited intervention of outsiders only disrupts the direct and cordial relationship between owner and worker. According to this line of thought, trade union activists are nothing but killjoys in the peaceful coexistence that has traditionally existed between capital and labour. It is a doctrine of harmony which has been propagated far over the state borders as a hallmark of economic and social life in Gujarat. The following statement, taken from a study of industrial entrepreneurship in the city of Surat, is a fine example of this wishful thinking:

Surat has remained since long, a city inhabited by people with a cosmopolitan outlook. Peace loving people of different castes, creeds and communities like Hindus, Parsis, Jains, Muslims etc. have lived together peacefully in Surat. People of this area are generous, broad-minded, and peace loving and easy going. They have broad humanitarian outlook, mutual fellow-feeling and love, dislike towards frictions and disputes, which have favourably influenced the climate of employer–employee relationship in the industries of Surat comparatively. Surat has therefore enjoyed comparatively a very peaceful environment in its industrial life. (Bhatt 1979: 37)

After having set the tone in this manner, the author then reports on his research among a wide sample of entrepreneurs in various branches of industrial production. Trade unions were largely inactive and were entirely lacking in 87 per cent of the industries examined. Summarizing the extremely negative opinions of trade unions held by his informants, the author concludes in a measured tone that: 'entrepreneurs generally did not like trade union activity and they did not hesitate to express their views' (Bhatt 1979: 172). Such opinions are easily recognizable for anyone who is to some degree familiar with the social Darwinistic mentality of the new middle class of employers. Their preference for a non-formalized style of management is connected, above all, to their refusal to comply with labour legislation and to their attempts to prevent employees from joining in a closed front. It is important to remember in this connection that the construct of the informal sector as an unorganized branch of industry does not apply as far as employers are concerned. Owners of salt pans and brickworks, quarry manufacturers, and diamond shop owners, have all set up their own associations to promote their professional interests. High on their list of priorities is to make sure, in concerted action, that their workforce does not achieve any organized countervailing power.

Moreover, government also shows little inclination to promote self-organization of the economic down-and-outs. This is evidenced by the irresolute labour legislation and even more, by its extremely defective implementation. While official pronouncements emphasize the role of government as neutral arbiter above the two parties in the social conflict, in reality, the interests of state and capital are interwoven. In day-to-day practice, their collective orientation easily causes a common front against the fragmented and defenceless proletariat. The editors of a recent national report on the deplorable situation of rural labour commissioned by the government state that they would already be well satisfied with only a mild opposition by the powerful coalition of state and capital to the slowly advancing process of social emancipation: 'Whenever the rural labour organizations are started, first comes the resistance from the vested interests and the Govt, machinery. The rural workers will gain strength if the resistance is not harsh and strong' (GoI 1991, vol. 1: 242).

That class-based alignment is clearly noticeable and helps to explain why trade unions are unable to get a foot on the ground in zones outside the formal sector of the economy. In addition to all the obstacles mentioned, this is the principal argument with which labour leaders try to explain their absence in the lower echelons of employment. Although defensively formulated, it is a plausible explanation of the limits encountered by organized action on the part of labour. But this is not the whole story. The attitude of established trade unions towards the class of casual labour and unprotected workers amounts to a combination of indifference rising almost to enmity. Trade union leaders are, in fact, convinced that the mass of workers at the bottom is too numerous to be accommodated within the formal sector system. They fear that pressure from below would lead to gradual erosion of the rights gained during a long struggle by protected labour. In this opinion, trade union leadership is assured of the support of the majority of its members. It is almost impossible to persuade the rank and file to show solidarity with workers who are less favoured in all respects. This is the classical statement going back to Marx, maintaining that the interests of formal and informal sector workers are antithetical.

It was in the interests of the formal workers to restrict the entry of informal workers to the labour market, which could lower their wages; and conversely, informal workers saw their chances of joining the formal labour market restricted by the high wages that organized formal sector workers managed to extract from their employers. The employers, Marx argued, would opt for labour-saving production processes as a result of such higher wages. (Sanyal 1991: 49–50)

By suggesting a dichotomy in the world of labour, consisting of a fairly small top and a broad basis, and reaching the conclusion that the two are separated from one another by an almost unbridgeable rift, it is made easier for the privileged to keep their distance from those who are deprived of their rights. However, this construction fails to appreciate that the zones of employment are indeed fluid and merge into one another to some extent. To see the heterogeneous horde of circular migrants at the bottom of the ladder merely as a reserve labour force that is ready to be brought in when the time demands and to be dismissed afterwards, is to show too mechanical an interpretation of the dynamics that characterize the labour system. These are undoubtedly tendencies that indicate a process of informalization of formal sector industry. The social forces underlying these dynamics cannot simply be reduced to the replacement of protected by unprotected labour, but are also connected to a reorganization of capital. This can be illustrated by the dismantling of textile factories in Bombay and Ahmedabad and the simultaneous installation of mechanical looms in small-scale workshops in Surat which operate in a work climate controlled by little more than the law of the jungle. A trade union strategy which is content to do little more than attempt to prevent the deformalization of enclave production, and which does not bother itself about the fate of the many more men and women who work in the 'unregulated' part of the economy, is doomed to failure before it even starts. 'Industrial unions cannot be organized when factories cease to exist; proletarian mobilization becomes more difficult when the formal proletariat represents a shrinking component of the labor force and its remaining members fear for their privileges; employers cannot be easily confronted when they remain well-concealed under multiple layers of subcontracting' (Portes *et al.* 1989: 258).

In opposition to this trend, much could be learned from experiences in Kerala during the last 20–30 years. In this southern state of India, informal sector workers in many branches of industry have been able to consolidate their bargaining position built up over many years of social struggle by organizing themselves into trade unions (Kannan 1988, 1990, 1992). However, the policy line currently favoured in India is to rectify such 'distortions' in the labour market as part of a more comprehensive process of structural readjustment. Actively promoted by national and international economic agencies, the trend is to do away with provisions and institutions regulating conditions of employment and job security, and to neutralize trade union pressure identified as both cause and effect of legally protected labour statuses.

Does it follow from the above that there is no form of collective struggle in the absence of trade unions? Not at all. In various branches of industry, informal workers have now and again been involved in forms of agitation whose purpose was to improve their situation. It is actually remarkable that all cases with which I became familiar in the course of my research are concerned with seasonal migrants, a category that has the name of being the last to undertake acts of resistance. The labour unrest during the mid-1940s in the salt pans along the coast near Bombay, in fact, confirms that opinion. The initiative was taken by labour rooted in the locality. Only in the second instance, and even then only marginally, did the Kharwas from south Gujarat become involved.

Practically all the local labour is organized, but there are many obstacles in organizing the imported workers. The Kharwas are very illiterate and ignorant and are rarely aware of their rights or interests. Moreover, the Kharwas move from centre to centre for employment practically every season and consequently the same set of workers are not often found with the same employer or at the same centre every year. This comparatively high labour turnover renders organization very difficult. It was also reported that employers prefer not to recruit Kharwas who happen to be active Union workers. The Kharwas thus are mostly inactive and efforts at organizing them have of necessity to be through the Khatedars. (*Report of the Salt Pan Industry in Bombay Province for the Year 1947–48* 1950: 29)

*Khatedars* are the gang bosses who accompany the migrants to salt pans for the duration of the season. The strikes called by the local unions ended in the formalization of employment in this industry. By only registering the gang bosses as members of trade unions, however, the spoils that materialized have been monopolized by them. The initiative for action in agro-industry in south Gujarat was taken by an urban trade union by whom the semi-permanent factory hands of the cooperative sugar enterprises were called out on strike for improvement of their working conditions, first in 1973, and again in 1981 (Breman 1978: 1358, 1985: 431). On the first occasion, an appeal was made to cane cutters in the fields to down their *koytas* in a show of solidarity, but their appalling working conditions did not even come up for discussion. In 1981, the set of demands did include an increase of cane-cutting rates and employers were thus faced by a closed front of factory and fieldworkers. The first of these were employed on formal terms and the latter on informal conditions. However, negotiations were concerned exclusively with concessions to the factory hands, while the much larger force of fieldworkers were ignored. That marginalization did not remain unchallenged, however. On the last payday at the end of the season, some thousands of harvest workers gathered in the factory grounds to protest about the low price paid per ton of cane. The disorders that arose ended with the arrest of some of the agitators, while factory management arranged for the harvesters to be immediately transported back to their place of origin. In 1989, unrest was again stirred by social activists who were concerned with the fate of the cane cutters. They forced government to intervene and managed to persuade a number of harvest gangs to demand a better wage, but in vain, because managements of the cooperative sugar factories gave short shrift to those who had dared to stick their necks out. An important factor is that both trade unions and social activists directed their action strategy towards the gang bosses, while on the other hand, employers exerted themselves to defuse the commotion by ensuring themselves of the loyalty of these key figures. In an earlier publication, I described the pressure from above to which the latter were subjected:

… managements convened a meeting to which all *mukadams* were summoned and said that they would not concede to the demands, attributed to irresponsible agitators. The labour contractors were then made to sign a blank sheet of paper, thereby enrolling themselves as members of a fake *mukadam* trade union, used as a legal fence by factory managements to cover up their shady labour practices. Gang bosses who refused to sign or who had a record showing that they did not put allegiance to the industry above all else, were told that they need not return for the next campaign. (Breman 1990: 593)

The history of the labour movement shows that the role of labour contractors and gang bosses is highly ambivalent. In situations with which I am familiar, they usually act as agents of the employers. But that the loyalty of these professional middlemen can take another direction is shown by the fact that they belonged to the vanguard of trade unions which came up early in the present century, for example, in Bombay's textile industry. The changes in methods of management which preceded that movement and by which the gang bosses in their advanced position felt themselves to be threatened, do not fall within the scope of this study.

The last example of collective action to which seasonal migrants sometimes resort concerns labourers in brickworks near Vadodara. In 1983, at the initiative of social activists, a trade union was set up which pressed employers and government to comply with existing labour legislation. That the gang bosses managed to retain their key position is shown by the strike demand that these *thekedar*s should be given a commission of 20 per cent on the total wages of their gang members. In this case too, employers tried to break the collective protest with the use of force (Randeria and Yagnik 1990: 85). The course taken by the protest has been discussed in the preceding chapter. Ultimately, thanks primarily to the attention given to the affair by the local press, a compromise was reached, but one which individual brickworks owners did not heed. The season, after all, was coming to an end. As was customary every year, the owners cut off the water supply and removed the corrugated iron sheets with which the migrants had built their temporary shelters. These brick makers had no alternative but to undertake the journey back to UP and accept the amount of money to which they still had a right, according to the patron who settled the final accounts. Had this disappointing outcome brought a definite halt to the willingness of this vulnerable labour force to take action? Not in the least. When I visited Ahmedabad in January 1993, work in the brickyards was once again at a standstill.

Between Ahmedabad and Gandhinagar lie the worksites of numerous brickyards which adjoin one another in this open plain. This proximity makes it easier for workers to adopt a common stand and to ensure that everyone adheres to it. Their demands are considerable. Firstly, cash advances paid during the monsoon must not be deducted from earnings during the season. Second, deductions from the rate per 1,000 bricks for breakages, supply of firewood, etc., must immediately be abolished. Third, the introduction of a new standard brick larger than the former *deshi* type means more work and should therefore be accompanied by an increase in the piece-rate. The owners show little haste to put an end to the strike. Production has now been in progress for some months and they will not be prepared to make any concessions until the piled-up stocks have been sold. So far, they have continued to pay the weekly allowances, indicating that they do not intend to force the conflict. Today (25 January 1993), the strike leaders are meeting to discuss the state of affairs. Their meeting place is in an open field somewhere along the main road between Ahmedabad and Gandhinagar. About 20 men are present and talking together. After about an hour the decision is unanimous: continue. They disappear again in various directions over the open plain. (Fieldwork notes)

In none of these cases has militancy by the workforce been crowned with any success. There has been no actual improvement to their situation, let alone achieving the higher goal of formalization of their employment. The value of their actions has been primarily in bringing pressure to bear on bureaucrats and politicians to put their paper promises into effect. Even after the outburst of such agitations, however, these third parties are reluctant to do so. The trouble involved in shifting the balance even an iota in favour of the underdogs is sufficiently illustrative of their weak bargaining power and the lack of outside support. The scale enlargement that has come about in the market for unskilled labour makes it possible for employers immediately to replace their workers by new ones, whether or not by tapping new sources of recruitment.

It has been possible to describe these labour conflicts in the branches of industry in which I am particularly interested, thanks to the availability of documents, statements by informers, and other source material. This does not mean that the social struggle which is waged has been restricted to those industries. Similar forms of collective action involving no more than some tens or hundreds of men and women are frequent occurrences, without even becoming widely known. This can be illustrated by considering the manner in which agricultural labourers' wages are increased in the villages. Although this concerns a working class that is the largest in the land, we are poorly informed about the course of events that precede such wage increases. In general, there is no case of any formal negotiations. I have found no evidence, however, for the suggestion made by Rudra that wage rises in agriculture are invariably the result of unilateral action taken by the employers (Rudra 1984: 260–1). Representatives of landowners and landless ultimately reach agreement on the introduction of new rates after a lengthy and loosely structured dialogue. This can be coupled with separate meetings among themselves involving varying numbers of farmers or labourers respectively. I further disagree with Drèze and Mukherjee who argue that no wage bargaining ensues when labourers are 'called to work', a colloquial expression often used. As they themselves have pointed out in their UP-based fieldwork report, both farmers and labourers agreed that a wage hike had to be extracted from the employers. Both parties 'show a fair degree of agreement on the circumstances when the wage standard changes: it increases when a farmer cannot find labourers at the going wage and is desperate to complete an urgent task' (Drèze and Mukherjee 1989: 260; see also Kapadia 1995: 223). The two parties are well acquainted with the other's spokesmen, and leave them to come to an arrangement. Sometimes, the wage increase is introduced immediately for all, but on other occasions, some of the landowners stick to the old rate for some time before accepting the new arrangement. In negotiations for a new round, existing differences in payment are not necessarily standardized in a common tariff.

Outsiders find such a course of events ambiguous. Even with hindsight, it is not easy to ascertain who has taken the initiative, who has taken part in the negotiations, and what reactions were shown by the two sides. This changes, however, if agreement is not reached and the parties see themselves forced to find more emphatic support for their point of view within their own milieu. While local agricultural labourers show signs of unwillingness to work, the landowners check whether replacements are available in the near vicinity or let it be known that they will make do with the labour power of their own households. The escalation can increase into a frontal stand, led by the hard nucleus on each side. If it comes to strike action, this is mostly taken by the agricultural workers at the start of harvesting. Such action seems to signal the existence of a kind of proto-union (Athreya *et al.* 1990: 158).

Such labour conflicts, which also occur in other sectors of rural employment, have three elements in common: spontaneity, local containment, and brevity. The first of these has already been discussed. The strike may be preceded by a long process of 'negotiations' but leadership is informal and the decision to strike can be taken on the spur of the moment. Lack of organization is further shown by the limited reach of the action. Only exceptionally does this extend beyond the village where the workers live. Finally, a strike seldom lasts longer than a week. Landless households simply do not have the reserves available to allow them to manage for more than a few days without income. Rudra has made the following comment on the highly localized character of the negotiating process: 'The labourers belonging to the same village do share some kind of community feeling; they do move as a group with the local employers. It is this group behaviour that explains the uniform wage rate of casual labourers within the same village' (Rudra 1990: 499).

The strategy followed by both parties in promoting their own interests has entered a new phase as a result of the temporary inflow of migrant labour into the countryside of south Gujarat on the one hand, and the easier access to employment away from agriculture and the village for the local landless, on the other hand. In that respect, my views differ from that of Rudra, according to whom the social consciousness of the landless class does not extend beyond the borders of the village. Nor do I agree with him that, within the village, landowners and agricultural workers are linked as in the past by vertical solidarity (ibid.: 499–500). Rudra's model of village-wide complementarity and consensus, overriding contradictions based on caste as well as class, is ill-conceived. To express their relationship purely in the terminology of patronage would be to ignore the change that has occurred in south Gujarat and, one would guess, not only there. I further disagree with Dasgupta who, following up on Rudra's argumentation, not only over-states the immobility of labour between villages but also assumes that the wage for casual labour is uniform within one and the same village (Dasgupta 1993: 235). Different terms of employment are actually a major source of conflict between landowners and agricultural workers giving rise to strikes, lockouts, and other industrial disputes at the local level. The willingness to resort to action in order to enforce wage demands has undoubtedly increased, but this does not signify that the landless proletariat manages to transform its growing militancy into supra-local solidarity. This precondition for the effective improvement of their situation is not satisfied. Commenting on the segmentation of labour, Kapadia noticed in her village of fieldwork in Tamil Nadu, a very strong mutuality between workers of the same caste–street but a much weaker mutuality between same caste workers in different villages (Kapadia 1995: 236). Her conclusions are similar to my findings in rural south Gujarat.

Men and women who try to sell their labour power on the urban casual labour markets with varying degrees of success, know all too well that open access to this arena seriously weakens their negotiating position versus employers. In the realization of their own isolation against the far greater social reach of the opposition, who would dare openly stick his or her neck out? Employers are able to collect and disseminate information on the workers with sometimes dreaded results. 'Their [that is, contractors'] contacts are wider. Their influence is greater. They are capable of spreading the news that such and such person is mobilising the workers against the contractors; and thus stall any further move on our part ... said one female worker from Surat casual labour market' (Punalekar and Patel 1990: 168). In view of the risk involved, it is understandable that resistance usually takes on a more veiled form. At a casual labour market in Bharuch, a regular attender who remained anonymous, had written with chalk on the wall of a building: labourers wanted: men Rs 25, women Rs 15. This advertising of the going wage rate was apparently an effort on the part of the workforce to close ranks. The researcher who reported this incident also noted the following complaint voiced by one of the women:

'Too many labourers in the market and lack of unity among them defeats our purpose of any collective action against the contractors and *mukadams*. They are few and we are many. They have the choice to pick and choose, while we have to silently agree to their terms of employment. They can dictate terms to us, and we are helpless. Some control over the entry of "new" labourers will exercise check over these tendencies', one labourer said in an agitated voice. (Punalekar and Patel 1990: 157)

Their ambition, it appears from discussions with workers, is that work be allocated through a registration system. New workers would then only be added to the list when vacancies arise. In fact, this would be similar to the rules regarding porters at railway stations and to that introduced many years ago by the Government of Maharashtra for various categories of casual workers.

## INCLUSION AND EXCLUSION: WIDENING CIRCLES OF IDENTIFICATION

In the present economic and general social climate, clear limitations are set on collective action initiated from below. To conclude from this that the rural proletariat has little choice but to submit itself passively to the labour regime imposed from above would not do justice to numerous other individualized forms of protest to which this vulnerable army of workers resorts. For the sake of brevity, I refer to Scott (1985) for a discussion of the arsenal of 'weapons of the weak', while noting that his micro-level report on the course of the anonymous everyday encounter between landowning and landless classes in the Asian countryside no longer occurs solely or even principally within the sphere of agriculture and the arena of the village.

As we have seen, employers prefer to bypass local labour, among other reasons for their lack of 'discipline'. However, the asserted adaptability and amenability of the aliens are largely a mirage, a type of behaviour caused by their lack of roots in the milieu to which they have come. Rotation of wage hunters and gatherers along various sites of employment is due not only to sectoral and seasonal fluctuations in the demand for labour, but also to the unconcealed disinclination of members of this footloose proletariat to enter into a labour contract considered by them as oppressive. That rejection can be expressed by refusing to set out with a gang boss who has the reputation of intimidating and disfranchising members of his gang, and more generally, by tending to withdraw from any employment that infringes their freedom of movement. I consider the avoidance of vertical dependency, and of subordinate behaviour with which that is linked, as the manifestation of a proletarian consciousness. In that sense, the circulation of labour must, in my opinion, also be explained as a deed of protest. Evasive behaviour certainly, but caused by the desire to keep one's own dignity intact. Put in rather different words, this was the essence of what workers told me in several ways during the course of my fieldwork. That escape from pressure exercised by superiors is indeed a frequent reason for leaving home, or returning to it, is shown by the report on the investigation among workers in Surat's textile industry.

Whenever conditions at workplace become unbearable, the popular response of the workers is to seek jobs in other factory units. This is the mode of response that involves no confrontation with the immediate supervisors or contractors or factory owners. The dissatisfied workers quietly leave that factory, and join some other factory. We found that as many as 583 workers (36 per cent) left a factory unit at least once due to some dissatisfaction with their working conditions. (South Gujarat University 1984: 71–2)

If they find the behaviour of the contractor objectionable, they change their employer. They very much resent the arbitrary role of the contractors and *mukadams*. They dislike if they are scolded for slight delay in reaching the workplace or if they are not provided tea at the work sites or if they are abused in foul language. They do not accept such insults meekly. (Punalekar and Patel 1990: 176–7)

For the same reason, gangs of seasonal labourers who search for work in the countryside during harvesting, will sometimes abscond in the middle of the night without finishing their work, to the rage of the farmer by whom they were employed. Landowners then speak of desertion, blaming the 'impulsiveness' of the alien workers. They never admit that it could be due to their own improper behaviour: a combination of too many curses, too long working hours, too low wages, and late or non-payment.

The vulnerability of unskilled labour at the bottom of the economy does not mean that this mass of workers shows restrained or even submissive behaviour. Their ability for active and prolonged struggle is limited, but that does not mean that they accept the yoke laid upon them as unresisting victims. As employment becomes less regular and wages lower, the intrepidity of the underdog seems to increase. 'Even dogs have a better life', one cane cutter stated before a committee set up by the High Court of Gujarat (Breman 1990: 582). In the open field, before this company of notables, the man made this unvarnished statement, not at all deterred by the presence of the manager of the factory for which he worked. What had he to lose? Nevertheless, such outbursts are rare expressions of anger which has to be kept pent up. That this weapon usually has little effect when used by the weak is shown by the story of a Halpati woman who works as a domestic servant in Surat.

Very often I ask the family where I serve to increase my wages. But my request falls on deaf ears. Sometimes, I disclose my protest by absenting from work or reaching their place late, and sometimes making a sullen and gloomy face. But nothing of this works. When I see the same family spending money freely on cloth, ornaments and Sunday parties, my heart burns with indignation. They have no money to increase my wage, but they have money to spend in ice-cream parlour. My children, Sunita and Balwant who sometimes accompany me to help me in my work often ask me unsettling questions. What answer should I give them?' (Punalekar 1992: 246)

Reservedness, lack of communicativeness, apparent docility, and other risk-avoiding behaviour certainly form an element of the working climate that I encountered in various branches of industry. But to describe such behaviour would be incomplete without emphasizing characteristics that suggest the exact opposite: bouts of open anger and flashes of defiance, a crude showing of bitterness and resentment. The inability to give free rein to this gamut of feelings vis-à-vis the opposite party causes the silenced protest to be turned inwards or to be vented against those who are even more vulnerable, particularly women and children. According to information received from women attending the urban morning markets for casual labour, more than a quarter of them are occasionally beaten by men of the household (Punalekar and Patel 1990: 142). Based on my own findings gained in this milieu, cases of child abuse are probably even more frequent. Moreover, it is a regular occurrence that local workers use extra-economic methods, that is, violence, to oppose the ingress of 'aliens' into their arena of employment. What begins as ordinary fisticuffs frequently results in destruction of property, theft, rape, and even murder. It will be clear that the discharge of frustration and aggression on others victimized by the same regime detracts from any feelings of solidarity among fellow sufferers and gives rise to a 'domination within domination' (Scott 1990: 26).

Early discussions of informal sector workers living in urban slums implied that, once roused to political consciousness, these people would foment radical movements and eventually join hands with the rural poor in a frontal attack on the established social order (Sanyal 1991: 43). I have found no evidence to back up such a scenario. The closed-shop character of most sources of employment in the segments of the rural and urban economy which were the focus of my research prevents proletarian consciousness from being transformed into class solidarity and its manifestation in class struggle.

In various recent publications, it has been argued that neighbourhood bonds more than class action give meaning and direction to individual choices as well as social action in the informal sector. In seeking openings in the labour market, there is no doubt evidence of change from a more vertical to a more horizontal orientation. For the time being, that change in direction is accompanied by an investment in primordial loyalties along lines of caste, religion, regional origin, etc. The Halpatis in the villages of my research do have a common identity articulated in a lifestyle which, in their eyes and those of others, emphasizes their communality and reproduces it for the next generation. To suggest that the social culture inherent to it is an expression of false consciousness does not do justice to the protection and security which is sought and partly found in such particularistic collectivities.

In south Gujarat, the village quarters, segregated according to caste, are the bases to which work migrants return at the end of the day, after a few weeks or an entire season, or for an occasional visit. Within that familiar domain, the wage hunters and gatherers find the opportunity to exchange their experiences and discuss the contacts that they have made 'outside'. What should not be overlooked is that caste consciousness can undergo scale enlargement in such a way that it approaches class consciousness: recognizing members of other sub-castes as fellow sufferers and feeling solidarity with them. To describe the mass mobilization of men and women, whether individually or in families, for far distant destinations as indicating a high degree of subjugation of labour to capital, is to ignore the tenaciousness with which the army of workers, at least temporarily, withdraws into its own sphere of privacy. However fragmented and heterogeneous their 'home' arenas may be, the forming of such *cordons sanitaires* restricts the reach of their work bosses. To the latter, their incomplete grip on the almost inexhaustible supply remains a source of immeasurable irritation. It also augments their inclination to depict this lack of control as a defect on the part of labour.

The great majority of Halpatis lead a segregated existence. In the countryside, members of this bottom caste are housed in neighbourhoods that have been built for them during the last two to three decades. In towns and cities too, the proletariat prefers to live in caste concentrations, although more intermingling does occur with other categories of similar social-economic status. When such living quarters are built at the initiative of Congress politicians, they usually carry names that refer to patrons from the Nehru–Gandhi dynasty: Indira Vasahat, Jawahar Lines, Rajiv Colony, Sanjay Nagar, etc. Almost always they are slums which, nevertheless, provide their inhabitants with a clearly marked territory of their own. The cohesive quality of such localities is made manifest when ranks have to be closed against outside attacks. Time and again, 'mobs' tend to resist municipal authorities when they try to demolish slums and deport their inhabitants. Other official agencies such as police, representative of and mainly catering to formal sector interests, similarly meet in this milieu with a united stand based on physical proximity. However, slum habitats only become arenas of solidarity in order to deal with hostile forces from outside. Internal divisions create strong tensions, and fears of unsocial elements from within are quite acute. Illustrative for that other side of the story is Lobo's narrative about a Surat slum:

Madhubhai even though residing in central part of the slum says that he sleeps just at the entrance of his hut with his family inside. Till about 12 at night the door is kept open as it is very warm inside. However, he is alert even if a cat or dog were to enter. If someone passes by he or she is asked to declare his or her name. If the name is familiar the person is allowed to pass. Many neighbours pass by humming a tune and from it people know who they are. The reasons for suspecting robbers from inside is mainly because they know who is at home and who is not at a particular time. One way of coping with the threat of robbery is to remain at home and find some means of earning while watching one's hut. 'My work of preparing boxes is done in the house itself', said a man. 'When we

slum. Among Muslims the group affinities are along kinship, e.g., Khans and Sheikhs. Among Bhaiyas there are caste groups. Oriya men though less in number consider relatives and villagers residing in one room or adjoining rooms as a group. The residents of Gujarat region do not appear as a group in their activities. Yet they interact locationally among themselves. I identified sixteen groups over a period of time. (d'Souza 1993: 12)

In accordance with the bifurcation of economy in a formal and an informal sector, a similar dichotomy is applied to society. This parallel duality is supposed to rest on two separate legal systems, each with its own logic and its own sanctions: the civil order and the social justice of the formal sector, vis-à-vis the tacit anarchy which is the destiny of the larger part of mankind coping with life in the backstreet (Kruyt 1994: 5–9). In earlier critical appraisals of the informal sector concept, I have consistently challenged the notion that the complexities of economy and society can be reduced to two distinct segments (Breman 1976b). For basically the same reasons, I want to express strong reservations about the new inclusion–exclusion contrast that has, in recent years, rapidly gained popularity. Splitting up work and life in south Gujarat, the arena of my empirical research for more than three decades, in a simple two-part division of which the segmented halves stand in hard and fast opposition to each other would do insufficient justice to a much more intricate reality. The inclusion–exclusion terms can be quite useful, but as dynamic instead of static mechanisms. Moreover, as all dual concepts, they require contextualization in specified temporal as well as situational settings and should not necessarily be understood in total and closed separation from each other.

As for the widening circle of identification, Shah (1993, 1994) has recently written several interesting essays, essentially arguing that traditional jati sentiments have been transcended to more encompassing bonds among a broader social spectre for which *qaum* (in Gujarati pronounced as 'kom')—still understood as caste or cluster of castes— has become the operative word. His point of departure is the wave of communalism reflecting the changing social fabric and, thus, politics of Gujarat.

Politicians whose primary support base is the *qaum* and who endorse communal politics as a legitimate form for mobilization, invoke or articulate the identity of the members, emphasizing their common interests and the need for unity and organization. For them, the *qaum* is a basic category for social division. It is argued that internal differences—if they exist—within the *qaum* are artificial, false and the result of the degeneration of the social system. The *qaum* leaders—traditional as well as modern—repeatedly induce this ideology with periodic emotional and sentimental reminders of the need to preserve *abru* i.e. prestige and status, and/or *dharma* of the *qaum* for development. These idioms are not alien to the members as they are inculcated in them from childhood. And their day-to-day experiences to a large extent confirm what is told to them by the ideologues of the *qaum*. Jobs or information about new opportunities are often obtained through linkages of caste and kinship. The members of the *jati* provide them security and help during small and big crises. And they realize that if a person from their *qaum* is in government office, it is easier to get their work done. Feelings of 'we' and 'they' are therefore reinforced. At another level, the notion of *qaum* gets extended to include all those who claim to be followers of the same religion. Though religious beliefs and value systems vary, the perceived commonality of symbols, rituals and beliefs tends to persuade the followers to believe in the 'we'. (Shah: 1993: 36–7)

Qaum is an advance towards vagueness, an imagined community between, on the one hand, the jati, the group consisting of 'real' caste mates to whom lines of kinship can be traced, and on the other hand, the amorphous body of believers to which in principle all practitioners of the same religion belong. In this highly fluid field of various and variable social clusters, people move around, aligning themselves in terms of inclusion versus exclusion according to the need to assert their identity in a specific context or at a particular moment. Underlying the search for affinity and solidarity in loosely structured, caste-like collectivities is a must for the floating mass of urban and rural slum dwellers to maximize their security. Discussing the modus operandi of the labour nomads employed in Surat's main industry, Pathy has this to say:

In an alien place, hard, stressful and insecure working and living environment, recurrent problems of health and language of communication, day to day humiliation in and around, and the fear of indiscriminate police implications in petty crimes, it is not surprising that the Oriya migrant workers tend to revalidate and consolidate their sense of community, caste, language, region and religion. (Pathy 1993: 15–16)

It would be wrong to conclude that informal sector workers only invest in communal bonds stretching on a diffuse continuum from jati to religion in order to safeguard their material interests. Qaum has also become an agent for articulating aspirations of emancipation in concerted action. Stigmatized social categories increasingly tend to seek redemption from a status of inferiority and dependency which are major features of the adverse circumstances under which they are compelled to live and work. New claims for dignity can be heard in the localities where the downtrodden reside. In Chikhligam, it became a major reason for Dhodhiya men to leave their women and children at home when they depart on the arduous trek to the brick kilns each year at the end of the monsoon. Earlier, I have explained the absence of regular family life among the migrant population of urban slums by referring to bad and costly housing conditions. However, it should be added now that many migrants also try to avoid exposing other members of their household, whom they consider to be particularly vulnerable, as long as possible, to the multiform sources of pollution and denigration associated with these habitats. On the inhabitants of such a locality in Surat, Lobo reports:

The future of their children and insecurity of their women and girls constantly worry the slum dwellers. Many of them don't bring their wives and children to the slum but leave them at their native villages. Because they have to put up with dirt, bad behaviour and they will get spoilt in the slum. They will be brought later when they grow up for jobs. One of the U.P. wallas said, 'We are staying in the slum because of our *majburi* (helplessness). Given a chance we would like to quit this slum and stay in a room in a dignified manner.' (Lobo 1994b: 93)

It is an aim difficult to realize in daily practice. Still, in a fundamental way, the ideology of inequality, presumably the hallmark of Hindu civilization, to a large extent seems to have lost social legitimacy. I consider this observation to be the most significant recapitulation of my research findings over a period of more than 30 years in south Gujarat. As noted earlier, there is a definite shift from a more vertical towards a more horizontal orientation in the principles of social organization. Of course, if need be, people are willing to openly acknowledge their dependency on patrons who are in a position to distribute favours and benefits, but the blatant sycophancy which used to mark their private and public behaviour as clients is a thing of the past. Qaum consciousness is rooted in communal and not hierarchical sentiments. At least at the ideological level, the emphasis is on shared instead of differentially ranked identities of all included in the same walk of life. Outsiders are defined as the excluded who supposedly have their own *sanskar* (culture) on which to base their fraternity. To the extent that these categories are better off and have more political power, their elevated status does not give them the ingrained right to social hegemony. Claims for domination and superiority from above are not easily conceded nowadays, and may even be actively resisted by those at the bottom of society.

In my scheme of analysis, duality is not a key concept. Social life and economic activity are multilayered and not segmented in only two circuits of formality and informality, separating people in just two broad categories: insiders or outsiders. Although rejecting the existence in theory and practice of a comprehensive and consistent bifurcation, it cannot be denied that wilful neglect of the misery imposed on the proletarianized rural and urban masses, floating around in a state of flux, cannot continue for much longer without creating the conditions for such a dialectical opposition. Segregation coming close to a system of apartheid is the ultimate result of the policy to make 'the informal sector' a no-go zone for policymakers. However, a planned and constructed duality is ultimately also bound to end in failure. A state which only accepts the market as a regulatory mechanism for dictating the terms under which labour has to work and live is not able to maintain a regime of law and order restricted to privileged citizens in their formal sector enclaves. The explosion of violence which Surat witnessed at the end of 1991 and beginning of 1992, or for that matter, the so-called plague which broke out in August 1994, should be read as signals that the informal sector outcasts cannot be kept in isolation and in a state of exclusion.

I shall make no attempts to generalize. Let me just reiterate, by way of conclusion, that the description and analysis presented focus on a region in India which has shown rapid and sustained economic growth. During the last 30 years, these dynamics have provided great benefit to owners of capital but without fundamentally reducing the degree of exploitation of labour. In the total production costs, the proportion of wages paid has declined rather than risen during this period. The force with which the process of social transformation is continuing manifests a brutal and predatory type of capitalism. Does it mean that this mode of production is still in a formative stage in India? I am inclined to disagree with authors representing that school of thought. What has been going on in south Gujarat during the last half century suggests a pattern of capitalist development that, in terms of industrial relations, is not characterized by gradual but progressive expansion of formalized employment conditions. On the contrary, after having been made mobile, the workforce at the massive bottom of the economy is kept in circulation, does not become stabilized but finds itself entrapped in an ongoing state of casualization, is not fully free in labour market negotiations but remains neo-bonded in some critical aspects, and is paid not constant (time) but flexible (piece) wage rates.

The trajectory of capitalist development which has come to dominate the South Asian landscape seems to be significantly different, on the one hand, from the earlier factorized production characteristic for the process of industrialization and urbanization during the nineteenth century in the North Atlantic part of the world and, on the other hand, from the brand of industrial capitalism that has emerged more recently and so forcefully in parts of East Asia (Taiwan, South Korea). More comparative work is required to trace the linkages between these various patterns of development at the global level and to analyse their separate but also their joint dynamics in a historical perspective. That comparison in both time and space is beyond the scope of this monograph. The case study presented remains confined to south Gujarat economy and society during the last few decades of the twentieth century. The findings reported will have to be contextualized in a wider national and international setting. This book has been written to throw light on the mechanisms of exclusion from life and from work in dignity of poor people in a region of high economic growth. Their plight, subsistence not far above the level of survival, is shared by a considerable part of mankind.

# 8

# Informality as a Regime of Exploitation and Marginalization*

## A RESERVE ARMY

In the preceding chapter, I concluded that the distinction between employment and unemployment is grounded in an analysis which has no validity beyond the formal sector of the economy. Within the setting of the informal sector, reality is far too complex to be considered in terms of this simple duality. The assertion in various publications that, despite the collapse of the large-scale textile industry in Ahmedabad, the percentage of open unemployment[1] remained unchanged at the low level of 2–3 per cent, denies the perception of the great majority of informal sector workers, based on their daily experience, that there is a severe and sustained shortage of work. The popular claim that the poor are too poor to allow themselves to be unemployed testifies to a very superficial understanding of the sometimes intermittent and sometimes sustained shortage of work confronting these people. The concept of underemployment can, of course, help to fill the twilight zone in quantitative terms between searching for and finding subsidiary work. Yet, this contrast too falls short in the attempt to apply methods used in the formal sector to the situation in the informal sector. Ghose, who appears to recognize this problem, notes that:

... many people, particularly women, are reluctant to admit to seeking paid work when they know such work to be unavailable: but they would in fact be quite willing to accept such work if and when available. For this reason, it is appropriate

* Originally published as 'Informality as a Regime of Exploitation and Marginalization', in Jan Breman, *The Making and Unmaking of an Industrial Working Class: Sliding down the Labour Hierarchy in Ahmedabad, India*, Chapter 9, New Delhi: Oxford University Press, 2004, pp. 259–93.

(though not strictly accurate) to regard subsidiary workers as discouraged workers rather than as non-workers; *it is wrong to regard them either as employed or as being outside the labour force.* (Ghose 1999: 2599; emphasis added)

Ghose goes on to conclude that many people who are counted as employed are actually substantially underemployed. In his opinion, this is a characteristic feature of an economy in which self-employment and casual wage employment are of disproportionate importance. Backed up by the anthropological part of my empirical studies in Ahmedabad, I am in complete agreement with this point of view. The previously mentioned claim by Dutta and Batley, based on comparison of data from successive National Sample Survey (NSS) rounds, that the rate of underemployment in Ahmedabad significantly declined between 1987–8 and 1993–4, seems to be grounded more in wishful thinking than careful investigation. The quantitative evidence for making this claim is in any case extremely disputable (Dutta and Batley 1999: 24–5) and there is no shortage of case studies to support a trend to the contrary. Homeworkers, for example, complain about a considerable decrease in the number of working days as a direct result of the influx of large numbers of women onto the labour market since the mill closures. Ghose believes that this is a more general trend, explicitly contradicting economists with more optimistic views (see Ghose 1999: 2600).

In addition to workers in regular paid jobs, the self-employed and casual day labourers also fail to exploit their labour power to its full potential. Few of them succeed in working more than 20 days a month. This led me to ask them about their monthly income, as opposed to what they earned on a daily basis. Street vendors seem to be the most susceptible to seasonal fluctuations, which prevent them from achieving a fixed rhythm of work. On days when it is raining, cold, or very hot, there is less demand for their services and they have to take account of a considerable drop in income. Daily-wage workers are similarly affected. On such days, they will go to the various labour markets in the city where workers are hired early in the morning, only to be turned away. It is the same story at the building sites, where they seek work as unskilled hands. It would, however, be incorrect to attribute the unpredictable nature of work in the open air purely to inclement weather. It may also be interrupted by holidays, or by disturbances of the public order, such as riots or political turmoil. Seasonal swings in the city's economy, caused by the complex configuration of industrial and commercial capital flows in the informal sector, have a greater impact on the mass of workers in this sector than on their counterparts in the better-regulated formal sector. There is, however, little detailed research into the nature and effects of these cyclical and erratic trends. This also affects homeworkers, whose way of earning a living is completely concealed from public view. The fact that they are apparently available for work at all times does not mean that they have work all the time. The delivery of raw materials is irregular, the power supply is unreliable, and (sub)contractors pass on fluctuations in demand for the end product without the slightest scruples.

To escape the harmful consequences of working in the informal sector, most of those exposed to this regime adopt a variety of strategies designed to increase the yield of their labour power. The first option is to work longer hours. Contrary to the provisions of the minimum wage legislation, those who earn a living in the manufacturing workshops have to work for much longer than eight hours a day. With hardly a break, they are made to work an extra half a day or longer. This is, of course, because the employer demands it. But it is also a form of self-exploitation resulting from the work being paid on piecemeal basis. The workers force themselves to work more and more and jump at the chance to work the following shift too if someone in that batch does not turn up. Street vendors and daily-wage labourers also alternate between days when they have nothing or very little to do and days when they work ceaselessly from early in the morning to late at night, and sometimes deep into the night. Others work longer hours in an attempt to supplement what they consider their main occupation with a secondary source of income which involves fewer hours or is irregular. Reports suggesting that subsidiary activities are uncommon in the informal sector—according to Unni, occupational multiplicity was limited to less than 3 per cent of her sample population, drawn from the economically active population in Ahmedabad (Unni 2000: 28)—testify to a serious underestimation of the need for workers to seek additional sources of income to ensure that they earn the minimum required to meet the costs of daily subsistence.

Yet another way of alleviating the pressure to earn enough to survive is to involve dependent members of the household in the labour process. These are, in the first instance, the women.[2] This is the real reason—rather than the supposed favourable effect of the informalization policy on employment in the informal sector—for their increased workforce participation rate after the mass redundancies of mostly men from the textile mills. In other words, the workforce expansion is supply rather than demand driven. The fact that women and children are forced to make use of their as yet unpaid labour power, both in and outside the home, increases the economic support base of the household as the primary social formation. The difference between women and children is that, whereas the former can take on a full workload, the children tend to be used as reserve labour. In this way, in terms of the nature of the work, the modality of employment, and the method of payment, the trend towards informalization has penetrated into the sphere of the family.

Those who believe that the increased workforce participation rate is the result of expansion of employment opportunities present as evidence not only the low level of unemployment but also the rise in the level of real wages of flexibilized labour. The inaccuracy of the first argument has already been discussed. In opposition to those who argue, on the basis of the NSS data already criticized above, that the labour of informal sector workers increased in value after the introduction of the new economic policy (Dutta and Batley 1999: 26; see also Sundaram 2001: 940), there are others who hold that the real wages of informal sector workers in Gujarat and in Ahmedabad have stagnated at extremely low levels (Mahadevia 2001: 156; Unni 2001: 2373).

Those who advocate that dismantling of the dualistic structure of the labour market was a necessary precondition for improving the position of informal sector workers support their argument with statistics which provide an incomplete and distorted view of the work and life of a large part of the population of Ahmedabad at the end of twentieth century. My own analysis can be summarized in a number of main points.

First, the informalization process has not fostered the growth of employment in the sense that supporters of this policy suggest. For the large majority of households which no longer enjoy the protection of formal sector employment—now restricted to approximately one-fifth to one-sixth of the total workforce—living standards have deteriorated in a real sense since they were forced into the informal sector. Their arrival only exacerbated the already vulnerable situation of the much greater part of the working population who were already active in the informal sector. The owners of capital are encouraged to make use of labour in a way that reduces its quality to the lowest possible level.

Second, this heterogeneous mass—divided into a number of main categories (own-account workers and regular or casual labourers)—at the base of the urban economy is underemployed in a way that remains underexposed in conventional statistics. The large majority is unable to make full use of its labour power for more than 20 full days a month on average, with extremes that extend far below this figure.

Third, what the majority of them have in common is the extremely low pay they receive for the work they do, and for a form of employment that takes no account of the time it entails and in which a significant part of the employers' risk is borne by the workers.

Fourth, to an even greater extent than before the introduction of the new economic policy, the government has decided not to monitor compliance with the minimum wage legislation. This legislation was introduced several decades ago for many branches of informal economic activity, albeit at a level that was invariably fixed below the poverty line.

Lastly, underemployment combined with underpayment results in an unpredictable pattern of curtailed or, conversely, prolonged working hours, in which the involvement of dependent members of the household in paid work also has to be taken into account. To explain these phenomena as indications of a growth in employment displays a manifest denial of the misery that underlies this economic strategy.

In my account, the flexibilized working population which dominates the city economy has the characteristics of a floating reserve army. Whole contingents are hired and fired by industrial and commercial capital according to the dictates of the moment. As a result, in the daily struggle to survive, this marginalized mass is condemned to perpetual mobility in the search for work, both within and between sectors and between modes of employment. Confined in their status of reserve labour, it is inevitable that this most vulnerable segment of the economically active population maintains its own reserve—the dependent members of their households. Out of public view, it is usually the weakest and smallest shoulders that have to bear the heaviest burdens of informalization. The image of shared poverty does not do justice to the inequality with which this form of existence, too, is permeated within the sphere of the household.

## IMMISERIZATION OF THE LABOURING POOR

Due to the lack of reliable workforce censuses, I am still unable to figure out with any accuracy the scale and intensity of poverty in Ahmedabad. It will come as no surprise that, in my opinion, the percentage of the population living below the poverty line is much greater than that assumed by researchers who base their calculations on the figures from the National Sample Surveys. Unni has calculated how much an informal sector worker would earn with a daily wage of 52 rupees and at 26 working days a month shortly before the turn of the century. This is taken as the amount required to enable the worker concerned and two dependent members of the household to remain above the poverty line as officially determined in 1998. On the basis of two working members of the household and accepting that the yield from child labour is often included in the income of the adults, this would amount to a little over 100 rupees a day for an average household. Assuming 312 working days a year (12 full working months of 26 days), it would mean an annual income of around 32,500 rupees. This is indeed above the 25,000 rupee level considered by Dutta and Batley as the upper limit for the lowest-income group. However, with Unni's much more realistic estimate of 250 (12 × 20) working days a year, the annual household income falls much closer to or actually within this lowest-income bracket. And that is not the end of the story. Unni's research shows that, in 1998, the real daily wage for informal sector workers lay at least 10 per cent (for men) and 33 per cent (for women) below the poverty line. The annual income that this lower figure produces for a household with two working members (a man and a woman), based on 20 working days a month, amounted to some 16,800 rupees, two-thirds of the amount established by Dutta and Batley as the poverty line. When calculated in this way, the claim based on the NSS statistics that less than a tenth of the population falls into the lowest-income group can no longer be accepted. The wage of 47 rupees for men and 37 rupees for women, which Unni refers to for 1998 (and which is confirmed by my own findings), applied to the average informal sector worker, that is, to the large majority of the working population. Even more alarming are the figures quoted by Joshi for the inhabitants of a slum on the banks of the river that divides the city in two. Of the 7,512 households he studied in 1998, the monthly income of around 57 per cent was below 1,000 rupees, and of 35 per cent between 1,000 and 2,000 rupees. Only 6 per cent had an income of between 2,000 and 3,000 rupees (Joshi 1998).

My findings refute the position that, since (and as a result of) the reforms in the labour market, poverty in Ahmedabad has been reduced to not more than a residual category. I tend towards the opposite conclusion—that the flexibilization of employment has worsened rather than improved the economic situation of a substantial part of the working population. The National Centre for Labour (NCL) calculated for 1996 that, for a reasonable level of subsistence and based on a normal working week, a worker would have to earn a daily wage of 125 rupees. At that time, the greatest part of the informal sector workers came nowhere near this level of income, even if they mobilized all the potential labour power in the household.

By no means do I wish to argue that poverty remained at a constantly high level over a long period of time. Repeated fieldwork-based studies which I have carried out from the early 1960s onwards in rural south Gujarat lead me to the conclusion that, especially in the 1970s and the 1980s, there was a reduction in the incidence of poverty in the state's rural economy. Improvements in communications and transport played a prominent role in the progress in which the land-poor and landless segments of the population also shared during this period. The trend towards technological modernization facilitated the escape of the rural underclass from the system of agrarian bondage that characterized the *ancien regime*. The widening and deepening of the labour market made it easier to leave the villages and the urban economy came within reach for many more people than before (see, for example, Breman 1996). Schemes in those years introduced by the state government, largely for electoral reasons, to tackle poverty helped to widen the socio-economic space and created more room for manoeuvre. In the course of my rural fieldwork in this period, I was able to observe the beneficial effects of some of these programmes. Infrastructural works increased the demand for labour and the resulting diversification of employment led to an increase in real wages for rural labourers. Credit enabled small landowners to raise their productivity, as a result of which the members of self-cultivating households no longer or less frequently had to hire themselves out as labourers and dependent members of these households increasingly opted out from the hunt for paid work. Cheap grain through the public food distribution programme ensured that the higher levels of income were not completely offset by an immediate increase in the cost of basic necessities. The noon meal schemes, which were introduced to encourage children from illiterate households to go to school, had the same effect. The criticism aimed at these initiatives at the time was undoubtedly justified, but their favourable impact on the material and non-material condition of the land-poor and the landless classes must not be underestimated.

The transition to the policy of structural adjustment from the late 1980s onwards meant that funds for most of these programmes were no longer available or were considerably reduced. Attempts to improve the relative position of deprived groups through additional support measures were abandoned. The new strategy was based on the belief that the advancement of economic growth offered a less costly, more effective, and faster way of reducing the incidence of poverty. The leap forward in its net state domestic product made by Gujarat during the last decade of the twentieth century is above the average for the country as a whole, and applies particularly to the industrial–urban sector of the economy. The accelerated decrease in the incidence of poverty between 1987–8 and 1993–4, already mentioned above, may also seem to contradict my conclusion that the income of most households in Ahmedabad depending on employment in the informal sector is far below the level needed for a standard of living above the poverty line. This contradiction in interpretation acquires even more significance if other aspects relating to the quality of life are taken into account. The measurement of poverty should not remain limited to the quantification of income but needs to be defined in qualitative terms as well. One important observation is that the reforms in economic policy, as in many other Indian states, resulted in considerable cutbacks in expenditure in the social sector (including on education and health care). Hirway and Mahadevia point out that the conversion of economic growth into human development has received scant attention from the Gujarat government. The percentage of the budget allocated to basic education, public health care, sanitation, nutrition, and drinking water supply remains below the national average. The implementation of the structural adjustment programme did not lead to any real improvement in this unfavourable track record and the authors speak of a lack of political will to alleviate the accumulated deprivation (Hirway and Mahadevia 2000: 203).

The picture that emerges from this is confirmed, as far as Ahmedabad is concerned, by the sprawling slums. A major segment of the city's population lives cramped together in these deprived neighbourhoods, exposed to extreme pollution and excluded from the most elementary civic amenities. The situation in the slum described by Joshi in 1998 is certainly not exceptional and is confirmed by other reports.

About 55 per cent of the households lived in *kachha* or tin shed houses and the remaining 45 per cent in *pucca* houses. Their water supply and sanitation position made pathetic reading in so far as 80 per cent of the households had no water connection and 93 per cent were without toilet facility of their own. About 50 per cent had electricity connection but with regard to proximity to civic amenities, 60–68 per cent had to travel 1–2 km to the nearest school, bus stop, post-office and dispensary facilities. (Joshi 1998)

... another primary survey carried out among the slums in Ahmedabad found that out of 28 settlements surveyed, only 17 had latrines, and that too were community ones. Also, though all the areas had access to water from some source, the quantity was so inadequate that residents were unable to bathe every day. The slum dwellers stated that the quality of the water was a big problem that led to skin diseases and stomach ailments. (VIKAS 1996)

Various studies link living in a slum to working in informal sector conditions. The lack of access to public services, which the better-off segments of the population take for granted, is closely related to an employment regime that offers little or no protection against the power of capital. This can be illustrated by an interesting study conducted in the early 1990s as part of an investigation by local non-governmental agencies to determine the effects of structural adjustment on the urban poor. The commissioned report compared the level of education and health care of households in a neighbourhood inhabited by potters on the outskirts of Ahmedabad with that of workers in the textile mills residing in the industrial localities. The mill workers had a regular job in the formal sector and enjoyed all the privileges of the legal protection and security provided by this form of employment. One important difference was that, although the average family size was almost the same, the number of dependent household members was much smaller in the milieu of the potters. In the households of the textile workers, the women and children were usually relieved of the obligation to do paid work. The mill workers earned four times as much as the potters were individually able to make, a difference that reflected the much higher level of training and the more regular mode of payment in the textile industry. The striking disparity in literacy between the two groups repeated itself in the younger generation. While the children of the mill workers, both girls and boys, usually went on to secondary school, this was uncommon among the potters because the children had to contribute to the household income from an early age. There was a similar contrast in the area of health. The families of the mill workers had a higher life expectancy and were covered against ill health by their membership of the public health insurance scheme. At the end of her case study, the researcher concluded that creating low-pay employment without social services was an insufficient method of tackling poverty (Mahadevia *et al.* 1994: 389). I would add here that the former mill workers now find themselves in the same position as potters were at the time of Mahadevia's study.

Does this imply that life in the informal sector always and inevitably means a life of poverty? Excluded from this state of deprivation are, in the first place, all those who do not belong to the subaltern classes in the urban economy. Own-account workers may very well be highly trained professionals such as chartered accountants, lawyers, and doctors with high incomes. Also white-collar employees in private business are often appointed to staff positions without being protected by tenured work contracts. Both their educational qualifications and their salary level exempt them from the kind of precarious livelihood associated with the large majority of the informal sector workforce. Focusing on this fragmented mass embedded in the lower economic echelons, I tend to agree with Mahadevia's estimate that two-thirds of the families which constitute this enormous reserve army of Ahmedabad are living in poverty (Mahadevia 2001: 156). Who, then, succeed in extricating themselves from the generally prevailing misery? Among this more fortunate minority, I certainly include the bosses, contractors and subcontractors, supervisors, jobbers, moneylenders and pawnbrokers, commission agents, and other brokers who exploit the cheap labour power of the informal sector workers for their own gain. All these figures too are embedded in this milieu, and they act as intermediaries in the flow of profits realized from the sale of aggregated labour power (for example, by contracting work gangs) or from putting-out work performed (for example, to homeworkers). Their mediation extends— broken up in various steps—to the formal sector economy. Positioned close to the source, they claim for themselves a significant part of the surplus value generated by exploiting the army of casualized labour. It is difficult for outsiders to ascertain exactly how much they earn, but it is usually far more than the wages earned by the lowest category of formal sector workers.

Other households in a relatively favourable position are those where there are no longer young children to be cared for, but where the adults have not yet reached the age at which they can no longer work. The heterogeneity of the informal sector milieu applies not only between categories but is also expressed through strong fluctuations in time within categories. During the most productive period for a household which—as long as those involved remain in reasonable health and are neither too young nor too old—may last for a cycle lasting 10–15 years, the labour power of most if not all members is used to the maximum. In 1998, the total income from employment in such households could amount to 3,000 or even 4,000 rupees a month. In such cases, income poverty may no longer be the most pressing problem, but this does not change the fact that deprivation in all other respects remains a major feature of the lifestyle of these households.

Among those who manage to survive above the poverty line are also those who do not have to rely solely on the sale of their low or unskilled labour power. These include the owners of petty means of production— such as motorized rickshaws, handcarts, or street stalls—or parcels of land or small buildings in the slum areas, who not only use this property themselves but rent or lease it out. In his recent study, so highly praised by politicians and policymakers, de Soto paints a glorious picture both of the volume of capital in the informal sector and the extent to which it is distributed among the masses at the base of the economy (de Soto 2000).[3] This does not change the fact that the informal sector segment that has access to such forms of minor property, particularly in the context of South Asia, happens to be in a more favourable position than the much higher percentage of households that are completely or largely excluded from owning means of production themselves.

Lastly, there is another source of income for people in the informal sector milieu which gives a small percentage of the households a larger budget than would appear in any survey-based studies: a wide range of extra-legal or out-and-out criminal activities. Such activities are obviously not restricted to the informal sector, but are also the order in the higher economic circuit. The lack of quantitative study of such activities is naturally related to the fact that responses may not be reliable and that there is insufficient knowledge to determine the extent to which they might be unreliable or incomplete. This is unfortunate, but there are many widely varying phenomena whose level of reality cannot be determined only in the accuracy with which they can be measured.

The well-known paper dating back to 1971 with which Hart focused attention on the informal sector problem, made a primary distinction between legitimate and illegitimate activities (Hart 1973: 67). During my fieldwork in Ahmedabad, I kept an account of all the different sources of income he included in the latter category. They can be clustered into a number of activities: theft (burglary and pickpocketing) and fencing; robbery and extortion (ranging from the threat of physical violence to less serious forms of intimidation); informal moneylending and pawnbroking; fraud and bribery (or being an accessory to bribery, including the selling of real or false permits, diplomas or driving licences, evading the payment of fines for unauthorized use of, for instance, the electricity supply or preventing the confiscation of means of production or merchandise); distilling and smuggling liquor; trading in weapons or drugs; gambling and banned games of chance; the prostitution of women and children as well as touting for them; and finally, the use of violence against persons for payment (d'Costa 2002: 351, 364). The distinction made between self-employment and casual or regular wage labour also applies to all these activities. Those working on their own account and at their own risk may combine this with membership of gangs hired on a regular or incidental basis by landlords and slum bosses to drive out squatters, by politicians to intimidate opponents or to persecute minorities, or to even settle scores between criminals themselves. The scale of the work provided and the income generated in this way should not be underestimated in an economy where more than half the total money circulation takes place outside the legal–administrative purview. The revenue from criminal activities permits the more professional practitioners to enjoy a lifestyle that may not be very comfortable, given the risks involved, but is certainly better than living on or below the poverty line. Fired mill workers expressed fears, and for good reason, that their sons—who, like them, are forced to live at a much lower level of subsistence—would succumb to the temptation of the easy pickings offered by a life of crime (Engineer 1985a, 1985b).

The link between illegality and informality has been made before. This applies not only to the way crime exploits labour but equally, or perhaps even more so, to the way in which non-legal financial transactions are used in an attempt to evade legal permits and bans. One-sided admiration for the power of the entrepreneurial capacity that functions as the motor of the renewed urban economy denies the criminal nature of a not insignificant part of it. Spodek passes clear judgement on the practices that have become common with the informalization of capital in Ahmedabad:

Crime, particularly economic crime, had become a way of life in Ahmedabad. Economic pressures were such that honest compliance with the law had become difficult. The consequences for the city both in lack of funds and in extraordinary cynicism were devastating. So great was the shortfall in collection that before 1994 Ahmedabad was almost insolvent. Social capital declined in tandem. (Spodek 2001: 1632)

Land speculators and slumlords have added to the criminalization of local-level politics. While surveying the large range of illegitimate activities, it should not be forgotten that informal sector workers are not only the hunters but also the hunted. The fact that, for most households, their total earned income remains below the poverty line does not mean that they are exempt from all kinds of illegal levies. These include raids from the formal sector to relieve such easy prey of a part of their income. Here, too, numbers and figures are mere guesswork and cannot really express the nature and scale of these levies. And this is by no means the only facet of the 'hidden economy' which is underexposed in statistics on which viewpoints are based which testify to an explicit formal sector bias.

## THE MEASUREMENT OF POVERTY

The much greater incidence, intensity, and heterogeneity in the poverty situation of the army of informal sector workers in Ahmedabad which I perceive can partly be attributed to methodological differences between studies with a more quantitative approach and those that are more qualitative in nature. This same distinction also occurs in a slightly different manner in the contradictory views often expressed in macro as against micro-studies. I participated in a conference on this theme in 1985 at which economists and statisticians engaged in debate with anthropologists and sociologists on disciplinary similarities and differences in the measurement of rural poverty in India.[4] The meeting was organized in response to the striking contrast between the picture presented in the early 1980s by the NSS data suggesting wide-scale rural impoverishment and the comparatively much more hopeful case studies of the economic dynamics produced by local-level researchers, including those engaged in anthropological fieldwork. As convenor, Bardhan expressed his satisfaction that the interaction had helped to increase understanding in both camps of the limitations of standard research methods in the respective disciplines. His appeal not only to focus on each other's substantive findings but also to become better acquainted with different research techniques for trying to unravel reality deserves to be endorsed but does not seem to have enjoyed much follow-up. The same division appears to be emerging once again, only this time the economists are interpreting the NSS figures to show an acceleration in the reduction of poverty, especially in the urban economy, while on the other hand, most anthropological reports do not share that optimistic judgement. Case studies and return visits to the same locations of research over time like those I conducted in south Gujarat, with a strong local focus and not primarily aimed at generating large databases to be processed in statistical form, provide no confirmation of what macro-studies see as an encouraging development in the right direction. In line with what one of the participants at the above-mentioned workshop called 'the ideology of measurement', I am sceptical about a method of quantification based on registration techniques with a formal sector bias and which are insufficiently adapted to the concrete situation we are addressing: life and work in a state of poverty. Unni had the following to say on this matter in a recent publication: 'The current methods of data collection and concepts used in the population census and labour force surveys are inadequate to track the growing informalisation of the labour force. Work, which is increasingly being pushed into informal work situations, requires more innovative methods to capture in official data collection efforts' (Unni 2000: 63).

Hirway has raised similar criticisms and concludes that NSS concepts and methods are not able to capture satisfactorily informal sector work (Hirway 2002: 85–6). The modus operandi of these two economists, who have long-standing experience with empirical and quantified research in the lower echelons of the urban and rural economy in various regional settings, testify to a level of detail and nuance that is far superior to the rather mechanistic approach followed by NSS field rapporteurs.

One aspect of the measurement of poverty that requires further discussion is the share of their income that people have to spend on other things than just food, such as housing, clothing, health care, and education. The convenient assumption that non-food expenses accounts for about 20–30 per cent of income is rarely tested on the basis of a thorough and long-term analysis of the budgets of a relatively large group of households which are sufficiently different in composition. Statistics are usually aimed at establishing what people require to stay above the poverty line, and insufficient account is taken of the real, often widely fluctuating and opaque patterns of expenditure of the significant part of the population that live beneath it. In addition, all kinds of overhead costs related to such a situation of deprivation are not taken into consideration.

What must also not be negated is the pressure to suggest that, because certain forms of data are not collected, that the scale, nature, and dynamics of poverty are not as bad as postulated. In contrast to the equally biased tendency to claim that poverty persists unabated or is even getting worse—with the all too simple slogan 'the rich get richer and the poor get poorer'—there is the converse distortion of reality that demonstrates a conscious or unconscious blindness regarding the exposure of certain facets of poverty. Drèze and Sen's comments are relevant in this respect:

... the justification for focusing on outputs and incomes lies ultimately in the impact that their augmentation may have on the freedoms that people actually enjoy to lead the kind of lives they have reason to value. The analysis of economic development must take note of both the causal connections, and also of other policies and institutional changes that contribute to the enhancement of human capabilities. The success of development programmes cannot be judged merely in terms of their effects on incomes and outputs, and must, at a basic level, focus on the lives that people can lead. (1995: 12–13)

This comment leads, in the first instance, to a critical reappraisal of the conclusion that the labour market reforms resulted in a substantial decrease in that part of the working population in Ahmedabad that belongs to the lowest-income class. On the basis of surveys conducted by the National Council of Applied Economic Research, it is maintained that the policy of informalization has fulfilled its promise to reduce poverty and improve the distribution of income (Dutta and Batley 1999: 22–4). The presented statistics also showed that there was no change in the percentage of households with an income of less than 36,000 rupees a year between 1990 and 1993. On both counts, however, two-thirds of the population surveyed remained below this level. In households with an average number of five to six members, there was therefore only $150–$180 available for the subsistence of each member. This is not yet half the amount set by the World Bank as the international minimum (a dollar a day, recently doubled to 2 dollars a day) for a decent standard of living. The authors could defend their standpoint by claiming that the amount used as a yardstick for urban poverty at the time, according to official government records, was only one dollar a day for the entire household (that is, 11,800 rupees per year). Instead of accepting this, I conclude that lowering the yardstick for poverty indicates a deliberate and persistent underexposure of the problem, in the same way that the unequal distribution of economic growth is not taken into account.

Another aspect that receives little or no attention in quantitative poverty studies is that, by retaining a constant definition of the deprivation situation, to facilitate comparison, no account is taken of people's changing perceptions of the insufficiency of their level of subsistence. The perception of poverty depends partly on shifts in the balance of social distribution which are made manifest in different lifestyles. The suggestion that income inequality in Ahmedabad has been reduced as a result of the liberalization of capital and the informalization of labour is wishful thinking and can be maintained only if, during the collection of data, no attention is devoted to many aspects of either pauperization at the base of the urban economy or clearly visible signals of enrichment at the top. In this connection, I see the tendency to idealize self-employment in the many policy studies on the informal sector as an extension of the desire on the part of the authorities concerned to avoid or minimize involvement with flexibilized labour. The obstinacy with which this form of employment is defined as microenterprise, while it is, in fact, often little more than barely concealed wage labour, creates the impression that this multitude of petty independents are quite able to meet their own basic needs and are, moreover, perfectly capable to make their own arrangements in protecting themselves against the adversities of life. It is an ideological statement which suggests that working on one's own account and at one's own risk is the best social safety net, with self-help as the guiding principle.

There is much more at stake than the measurement of poverty, and the problem that arises cannot be explained only by referring to different research methods between disciplines—in concrete terms, the contrast between quantification and qualification or a micro versus a macro approach. The poverty line approach, which has been so prominent in the continuous debate waged on the percentage of the rural and urban population remaining below or moving above it, is deeply flawed. Instead of trying to figure out where the demarcation should be fixed (close to the bottom of the human condition it seems), the more fundamental question is how poverty should be conceptualized. In spelling out the uneven distribution of progress versus degradation, dimensions such as quality standards of housing and schooling, rise in infant mortality, loss of hope for a better life in the next generation, and exposure to pollution cannot be overlooked. Criteria other than purely economic growth indicators would bring out the destructive consequences of the predatory nature of Gujarat's path to capitalism.

From a sociological or anthropological standpoint, it is important not only to measure phenomena in isolation from each other but also to explore the effects of their interaction by placing them in their social context. In the study of poverty, relational aspects such as marginality, discrimination, and dependency are of significance. I have examined these aspects in detail in preceding chapters dealing with the situation in which the former textile mill workers now find themselves. Their alienation from mainstream society is expressed in their reduced access to public services and institutions, including those that are in theory intended for each and every citizen of Ahmedabad. This is accompanied by a loss of control over the conditions that determine the quality of their lives now and in the future. Market discrimination in how they live and work reinforces the acute sense of deprivation and ensures that they do not enjoy equal opportunities to improve their situation. Members of stigmatized groups naturally seek contact with their own kind—Muslims, Dalits, and other social minorities exposed to discriminatory practices, both individually and collectively—for mutual support and protection. A life of dependency, however, goes hand in hand with restricted choice and lack of mobility. Indebtedness forces the ex-mill workers to sell their labour power and that of other working members of the household and, in exchange for an advance payment, had to settle for a lower wage. Such ties of dependency restrict the room for manoeuvre and erode the already fragile powers of resistance. The incapacity to escape the power of the employer or his agents, to always be at their beck and call, is a fate that not only befalls agricultural labourers in rural areas. The pressure to take extra risks and to perform dirty or hazardous work can lead to permanent health damage. Any conceptualization of poverty which fails to take the physical and mental ability to work into consideration seems to be ill-defined. Still, these and other aspects are completely ignored in poverty assessments that focused exclusively on levels of either income or expenditure.

The various dimensions of vulnerability can occur independently from each other and this differentiation contributes to the heterogeneity of deprivation. There can also be a cumulative effect, however, a general state of misery in which these dimensions coincide. This extreme state of vulnerability makes it necessary to consider the ultra-poor as a separate category. At a conservative estimate, around one-fifth of the households in Ahmedabad living beneath the poverty line belong to this pauperized residual category. As in other states, Gujarat has introduced a number of measures to alleviate the dire need of these people, including a modest old age pension scheme for agricultural labourers, a monthly allowance for needy widows and those with a physical handicap, and maternity benefits for landless women. But these entitlements are not honoured because of a lack of funds and the necessary administrative capacity, and therefore remain inaccessible to the majority of the target group. This is why I am in complete agreement with Jhabvala's observation that in the informal sector milieu, there is an enormous and as yet unfulfilled need for work-related social security (Jhabvala 1998; see also Dayal 2001; Unni and Bali 2001: 30–1).

It should no longer be necessary to observe that development is more than just growth of the gross national product. Yet, this is the conventional yardstick employed by the Indian government, urged on by the leading transnational organizations, to measure the progress made in reducing poverty. There has been much support for calls to use the much broader concept of capability to assess the dynamics of economic, political, and social well-being which find articulation in the Human Development Index. But translating good intentions into a different development strategy, in which efforts to achieve growth are accompanied by both a just distribution of wealth and the participation rather than marginalization of informal sector labour, is a different matter. On the basis of my own research and with reference to a large number of studies with a similar approach, I have endeavoured to demonstrate the untenable and unjust nature of current economic policies in the case of the majority of the people living and working at the bottom of Ahmedabad's economy. Persistence with the doctrine of neoliberalism with its almost social Darwinist mindset, will lead here too to further widening of the gap between rich and poor.[5] Gujarat could be understood as an experiment for trying out what will happen to state and society under a policy regime which does not attempt to mitigate the most brutal consequences of a market-led mode of capitalist production. The total eclipse of the kind of Gandhian values which, for the better part of the last century, were so important in the promotion of a public image both within and outside the country has also led to the shrinking of social space needed for humanizing economic growth. The disappearance of a climate leaning towards social democracy and tolerance has been accompanied by an increase of communal hate politics. The labouring poor have suffered in manifold ways from this unfortunate trend, but they are by no means the only victims.

In acknowledgement of the urgent need to establish a social safety net for the footloose proletariat stuck at the bottom of the urban and rural economy, the Government of India has now signalled its willingness to introduce umbrella legislation to promote the welfare of unorganized and unprotected labourers. In its recent report, the National Commission on Labour recommends the establishment of a special (Employment and Welfare) Board. All workers belonging to this huge segment of the labouring poor would have to be registered, either by employers or themselves, at facilitation centres to procure an identity card. This document should provide them basic protection and welfare.

Measures for protection have to include a policy framework that ensures the generation and protection of jobs, and access to jobs; protection against the exploitation of their poverty and lack of organisation: protection against arbitrary and whimsical dismissals; denial of minimum wages; and delay in the payment of wages; protection against unauthorised deductions; and safety and dignity at places of work. The system of Welfare should include access to compensation for injuries sustained while engaged in work; provident fund; medical care; pensionary benefits; maternity benefits and child care in the case of women workers. (GoI 2002, vol. 1: 752)

For various reasons, these wide-ranging proposals should not be taken very seriously. The huge labour bureaucracy needed to implement this policy would not be able to deliver what it has on offer, because of the lack of countervailing power among the targeted clientele.

The way the labour inspectorates have operated in Gujarat clearly demonstrate how and why these state agencies fall short of what their major task is: to protect labour against exploitative and repressive practices (see Breman 1994: 291–331). Another reason for the failure that can easily be predicted is the clause which says that the worker must make a commensurate contribution to the cost of the scheme. The assumption that most, if not all, of these underprivileged workers do have the financial capacity needed to overcome their current and future vulnerability is hardly realistic.

## THE ONGOING STRUGGLE FOR A BETTER LIFE

In searching for an answer to the question why poverty reduction has proceeded so slowly in south Asia, Drèze and Sen pointed to the traditional significance of inequality as an organizing principle of the social system. 'Successive governments in India have had reason enough to rely on the unending patience of the neglected and deprived millions in India who have not risen in fury about illiteracy, hunger, illness, or economic insecurity. The stubborn persistence of these deprivations has much to do with that lack of fury' (Drèze and Sen 1995: 87). Is endless patience, the apparent capacity to endure immense poverty in silence, indeed the state of mind with which a large part of the working population responds to its exclusion from a better existence? I myself encountered more anger and resentment than patience during my fieldwork in Ahmedabad. But then, too, it becomes necessary to explore why these anxieties have not successfully been converted into a force for emancipation. In my view, the low glow of this spark has less to do with the power of tradition than with the impact of the new economic regime.

The countervailing power of the poor to rise up in protest is allayed by pre-empting any opportunity to express it. One way of doing this is to remove these underclasses, as much as possible, from the public eye. Instead of a policy aimed at improving the misery of the subaltern classes, the emphasis lies on measures designed to frustrate acts of resistance to the established order. The propagation of an image of '*la classe dangereuse*' runs parallel with the message that they can only be prevented from causing social disruption by being kept firmly in their place. In this view, poverty is seen as an existence on the margins of legality. The way in which the men, women, and children who make up the huge pool of informal workers in Ahmedabad benefit from extra-legal practices which they encounter in their daily lives has already been discussed. But more frequently, they themselves are the victims of such practices. Their very existence is, by definition, a violation of countless formal provisions relating to the use of city space. Lower-ranking civil servants and street-level officials responsible for the preservation of public order and authority demand tribute for tolerating informal sector activities in locations where they are not permitted and the sale of perishable goods under conditions that do not comply with the hygiene regulations.

Amidst the situation of increasing informalisation of labour market and thus increasing vulnerability of the labour at the lower end of the market, the city government has become stringent on the urban development issues. Because there has been an increase in the number of hawkers in the city, an activity to which many displaced workers had resorted to, the city government has started a major anti-encroachment drive in the city. This has brought hawkers' ire, pushing them to resort to agitation. (Mahadevia 1998: 528)

This comment suggests that economic, political, and social vulnerability does not appear to stop informal sector workers from resisting prosecution. A significant factor is that, unlike the large owners of formal and informal riches, they lack both the social capital and the money power to buy the services—legally or illegally—of politicians or bureaucrats to defend their interests in the formal sector of the economy. People living on the margin of survival are an easy prey for slumlords and land speculators.

As is often observed, in the landscape of informal sector labour, the struggle to improve living conditions is hampered by the weak articulation of collective action. Although strikes and other forms of militancy are not rare, they are usually sudden, fragmented, and more or less spontaneous eruptions of protest. Such recurrent acts of resistance are restricted to disconnected local disputes, flaring up and dissipating again in a short time. The incapacity to express power and solidarity systematically rather than sporadically is, in the first instance, a consequence of the segmented and highly volatile nature of the informal labour regime. The small scale and fragmented arenas that dominate this pattern of employment present an obstacle to the emergence of organized structures to represent interests within, let alone across branches of industry. This is further hindered by the lack of security regarding the continuation (or not) of work contracts that are intentionally vague. The widely varying modalities of employment in the informal sector—ranging from self-employment to casual or semi-regular wage labour paid

412 At Work in the Informal Economy of India

on a piecemeal basis—force workers to adopt different and sometimes mutually conflicting survival strategies. In addition, those who provide work tend to respond extremely negatively to any attempts on the part of workers to form a common front. Bargaining for favours on an individual basis is considered preferable to acting as a spokesman for others in claiming alleged rights. Such expressions of joint assertiveness can be enough to qualify for instant dismissal. Other than the quality of the work performed, the extent to which an employer sees an employee as obedient and essentially docile is an important criterion in hiring, promotion, and firing.

Clearly, too, besides the way in which they are employed, the state of dire poverty in which the majority of those who work in the informal sector live presents an obstacle to collective action. In such deprived circumstances, they do not have the time, space, or reserves necessary to make demands together with those who share their fate. The dismissed mill workers have not only been forced into greater deprivation in material terms. Having to agree to a regime of exploitation and subordination as a result of their loss of job security is an extremely heavy burden to bear. And it means having to leave behind the self-respect that was such a significant part of their social consciousness as mill workers and trade union members.

The riots in the past revolved around the promise held out to the subaltern castes (both Dalits and Other Backward Castes [OBCs]) for a larger share in the public cake. The solemn pledge to the lower classes for a better deal in the spoils of development was very much a product of Congress politics, but also in that party, rather lightly made to a segmented vote bank clubbed together on the basis of their underprivileged status. That electoral strategy has been overtaken by systematic efforts since the early 1980s to split the ranks of the labouring poor on the basis of their diverse social identities. In the campaign led by the Bharatiya Janata Party (BJP) party and her front organizations, religious loyalties were articulated and became fault lines in the sharpened struggle for access to scarce resources at the lower end of the urban economy. The earlier antagonism between Patels, Dalits, and OBCs was invalidated in a new political agenda which urged all of them, as Hindus, to confront the 'enemy in our midst', the Muslim minority. These new alignments should, moreover, be understood as a consequence of the vacuum left by the now practically defunct Textile Labour Association (TLA).

Unable to comprehend why they were expelled from the formal sector of the economy, the former mill workers in Ahmedabad feel disillusioned and alienated. Some of the victims of the policy of informalization have been unable to accept their fate and have sought 'early retirement'. But the awareness still exists that their former assertiveness was a product of the social struggle they had fought. The memory of this time explains why their anger at the inactivity of the TLA at the time of the closures is mixed with nostalgia for the way in which, in better times, the union had assured them a better quality of work and life. The downfall of this once so mighty representative of the power of labour seems imminent. In the old city centre, the imposing union building in the city's centre—completed in 1950 and voluntarily funded by members' contributions—wears a deserted look. Gone are the glory days of mass meetings and union power located here that confronted the city's captains of industry. A bronze sculpture above the entrance to the *Gandhi Majoor Sevalaya* depicts the way in which the 'righteous struggle' was fought: two mill workers, a man and a woman, look up with adoration at the Mahatma as he points the way to a shining industrial future. Women had been made to leave the mills long ago and have been followed more recently—with the exception of a small rearguard—by the men.

Notwithstanding my major reservations about the analysis given by Varshney for the outbreak of communal violence in Ahmedabad, which I will discuss in more detail later, I have no problem in accepting his indictment of the TLA leadership in their failure to put up a fight in the last round of the righteous struggle.

As the first generation of truly committed leadership passed away, the TLA became the victim of its own success. Its new leaders did not have to work as hard, and the bureaucratised top and middle of the organisation increasingly lost touch with the base. By the 1960s, much against the Gandhian principles, some of its leaders had started living lavish lives; in the name of conciliation they had also developed collusive relations with mill owners; and they were no longer responsive to workers' interests. (Varshney 2002: 273)

The harsh conclusion, however, suggests a break in style between past and present union bosses which, at least in my opinion, should be moderated in favour of the leaders still around.[6]

The few aged union leaders who have remained semi-active argue among themselves who bears the greatest responsibility for the decline and fall of their life's work. Everyday, they still come for a couple of hours to the office to meet workers who have not yet given up hope of receiving the compensation to which they are entitled but which has not yet been paid out. In my interviews with the elderly directorate, I asked what was going to happen now, but received no answer. Obstinately, I probed further and asked whether it might not have been possible for the sacked workers to remain members of the TLA. No, I am assured by the general secretary, a man well into his eighties, because without factories there is no need for trade unions.

But is this true? The Self Employed Women's Association (SEWA) tells a different story. Ela Bhatt, the founder of this organization for working women at the base of the urban economy, started her long career when she joined the TLA staff in 1955. She helped devise the gratuity scheme which gave members the right to a bonus payment for every year they had worked in the mill. As head of the department responsible for providing the wives of the mill workers with information on child care and housekeeping, she became aware of how women were accustomed to work at home to help earn income for the family. This experience made her critical of her role within the union—educating her clients to be good mothers and housewives. In 1972, she was given permission to set up a union for women within the TLA and took the office of secretary. At her initiative, a bank was established to meet the desperate need for credit among the members, either self-employed or working for wages. In her daily activity, Elaben Bhatt encountered practices of discrimination against mill workers from the lowest caste. This reinforced her belief in the value and necessity of the reservation policy, which included a package of measures intended for the protection and the promotion of upward mobility of members belonging to the scheduled and backward castes. Her forceful opinions were not shared by many of the TLA leaders and in 1981, after she had expressed her support for continuation of this public policy in a mass meeting, she fell into disfavour. Subsequently, the union leaders broke all ties with her and SEWA. Now, although the TLA is on the verge of folding up, SEWA is thriving. In Ahmedabad alone, the membership has gone up to more than 150,000 women, who make use of the services it provides, such as credit, health facilities, life insurance, and legal aid. The women who were expelled from the mills in the previous generations can rightly be seen as the present-day torchbearers of the 'righteous struggle' that Gandhi launched in the early years of the last century to improve the lot of the industrial workers. SEWA is, for instance, also responsible for organizing the protests of street vendors against their eviction from public space. A few years ago, Ela Bhatt and her staff achieved one of their greatest successes when the International Labour Organization (ILO) adopted a convention for the protection of homeworkers.

Hopefully, the recommendations she has made to the Second National Commission of Labour on informal sector labour will have an equally favourable effect. There is no reason to have all too high expectations of this report, but the least that policymakers should be obliged to do is devote more attention to the position of women in the informalized labour market (National Commission on Labour 2002).

As part of the programme of economic liberalization, the flexibilization of labour has resulted in a dramatic weakening of the political position of the trade union movement. Yet, in forming an opinion on this decline, and the concomitant exodus of members, it should be realized that, even in the heyday of collective action, with a planned economy and a huge public sector, only a very small percentage of the working population ever belonged to one of the many organizations representing labour. In the post-colonial era, the large unions became used to protecting, almost exclusively, those employed under formal sector conditions. Also, among this vanguard—which never accounted for more than a tenth part of the working population—less than half have ever become union members.[7] This select group allowed itself to be led, both at and outside the workplace, by interests and loyalties which ran counter to more encompassing bonds of solidarity. The call to strengthen class consciousness and to define the stakes in the social struggle on the basis of shared interests, even when the ideology of some of the more radical unions considered the existence of such a consciousness self-evident, always had to compete with allegiance to social ties of a primordial nature. In the large textile industry in Ahmedabad, right up to the end, caste was a major factor, not only in the organization of work in the mills but also in the representation of the workers within the TLA. The increasing practices of discrimination to which the Muslim community has been exposed in the city in recent decades meant that the proportion of the working population in the mills that belonged to this minority had fallen considerably long before the closures. Muslims used to form a much larger group within the mill workforce. I spoke earlier of how Muslim leaders told me that they had taken no action to oppose this selective expulsion for fear of sparking off communal riots. The same information is also reported by Mahadevia and d'Costa (1997: 43).

The collapse of organized representation has made the army of ex-mill workers, and their male offspring in particular, vulnerable to invitations from communal forces to join them in various kinds of locality-based activities. The sustained policy of the Indian trade union movement not to mobilize informal sector workers should be judged as a historic blunder. Timely acknowledgement of the organic links between the formal and informal sectors of the economy would have made it possible to co-opt the labouring poor in the struggle to promote the rights of all segments of the working class in a balanced manner. A broader-based programme than the one which continued to focus only on a small and shrinking segment of the total workforce could have prevented the agents of organized labour from becoming helpless bystanders to the ongoing onslaught of informalization which has eroded whatever political strength they might have had in the past. There have been some remarkable exceptions, however, to the general decline of the formal labour movement. In Kerala in particular, social activists aligned to different political parties have successfully campaigned for a minimum of socio-economic security for men and women in the informal sector of the economy.[8] What at one stage seemed to be swimming against the tide may very well become a new model for facilitating the emancipation of fragmented and subaltern segments of the working population. In representing the interests of the labouring poor, the new organizations have to draw up an agenda which distinguish them from conventional trade unions catering to members higher up in the employment hierarchy.

## THE LAST ROUND

Social ties based on principles other than class solidarity play a leading role in the articulation of identities in the informal sector milieu. Caste and creed operate as signposts in seeking and finding work. Entitlement to favours and protection or support in the event of misfortune are also channelled along these lines. Such forms of social inclusion take on the character of networks based on primordial bonds without necessarily always emerging as neatly structured associations. This explains why they remain often invisible to outsiders. The suggestion that these are forms of false consciousness overemphasizes their ideological aspect, whilst denying the practical significance of caste and religion to the way in which people try to reduce their vulnerability in daily life. Such identities also permit collective action, especially in situations where class-based assertiveness might be subject to all kinds of social restrictions. This is how we should also understand the strength of sectarian movements which call on their followers to free themselves from a situation of repression and deprivation. But, in contrast to the emancipatory èlan that these segmentary movements may display, there is also the fact that mobilizing such formations for political, economic, and cultural objectives occurs at the expense of breaking through horizontal dividing lines, or indeed even tend to reinforce them. Strengthening identities within a closed group can shift the focus of attention away from solidarity with 'others'. Short-range engagement prevents the search for bonding with those who share the same fate on the basis of a social perspective inspired by the struggle for a better existence for all those who live in poverty.

It is not, in the last instance, for this reason that the strategic choices made by SEWA in Ahmedabad merit attention. The union is aware of the diverse identities of its membership, the large majority of whom come from the lower and lowest Hindu castes and the Muslim minority. But the starting point for the programme of activities is not their differences but the interests they share: their position as working women; and as residents of deprived neighbourhoods or slums. In the informal sector landscape, loyalties based on restricted associational networks retain their power because of their clear benefits to those who belong to them. Next to work, gender and locality can be seen as examples of identities which are appropriate catalysts for collective action. Adopting these as guiding principles for mobilization at grassroots level encourages a feeling of solidarity that helps to break through more restrictive social barriers. In the final analysis, the success of this formula depends on the ability of the SEWA leadership to upgrade its grassroots cadre to senior staff positions and on the understanding, both at the top and among the rank and file, that their struggle is not only for economic gains but also to build up political power in the fight for justice and equity. That endeavour, ambitious but highly commendable, is endangered if the established order goes on to encourage division along vertical lines and propagates hatred and the elimination of people who are reconstructed as a new class of 'untouchables'.

In a recent study on the socio-political context of communal violence in India, Varshney has focused on the importance of civic networks for binding Hindus and Muslims together (Varshney 2002). He argues that in the case of Ahmedabad, a truly impressive level of civic activity was built up during the national movement, to a large extent initiated by Gandhi. The main pillars of civil engagement that emerged were: (*a*) the Congress party, which brought people of all communities together; (*b*) a wide variety of social and educational agencies, set up by Gandhi and his associates, which later became known as non-governmental organizations (NGOs); (*c*) business associations (such as the Ahmedabad Management Association [AMA]) which had a long tradition of inter-communal interaction in the framework of artisan and mercantile guilds; and (*d*) last but not least, the TLA as a working-class organization which had both Hindu and Muslim mill hands in its fold and a programme that preached unity. In Varshney's opinion, these institutions were together crucial for producing a social climate characterized by harmony. Once these pillars started to crumble, and the collapse of the textile industry happened to be a major turning point, communal violence became ferocious. The author himself modifies his thesis of a strong Hindu–Muslim engagement which prevailed until a few decades ago. Congress leaders were never able, nor did they aim to, mobilize a large number of Muslims in the city during the anti-colonial struggle; only few Gandhian institutions reached out to either urban or rural segments of the main religious minority, the business associations in the city had an in-group character and did not promote civic interaction. As for the TLA, Varshney concedes that a large proportion of Muslim mill workers decided to stay away from this union. Following up on the substance of earlier chapters, I beg to differ from his main argument suggesting that political Hinduism is an altogether new phenomenon in Ahmedabad which has brought to an end the climate of tolerance and harmony built up by Gandhi and his disciples. A.M. Shah, amongst others, has critically questioned the suggestion that Gandhi's message of non-violence had penetrated deeply in Gujarati society and culture during his lifetime. Whatever social relevance it then had, it certainly did not survive him (A.M. Shah 2002: 58). My own opinion is that the communal divide which already existed in the past was strengthened by the segmentary, though not confrontational, politics adopted by Congress before and after independence. This parochial strategy, the KHAM coalition consisting of Kshatriyas, Harijans, Adivasis, and Muslims, contained the underclasses in their own and separate identities as convenient vote banks. This electoral design was successful for a short span of time only because it provoked a vigorous and vicious backlash from those higher up in society. Their pent up resentment was the momentum which the Hindutva forces capitalized to come to power.

My historical perspective on social transformation in Gujarat differs from the one presented by Varshney. His analysis lacks empirical substantiation and, moreover, falls short in discussing the changing political economy of the state and its ramifications for the social fabric in which the people are enmeshed. In my opinion, the forces of communalism need to be understood by taking into account the fierce competition for the shrinking or expanding economic space in which the various social classes constituting urban society are involved. As I have argued in previous chapters also, the recurrent riots in Ahmedabad towards the end of the twentieth century cannot be understood merely as an upsurge of Hindu nationalism under high-caste leadership, planned and organized from a Hindutva perspective. The high tide of communalism is engineered by the promotion of a political economy which seeks to keep the working classes fragmented and in a state of dependency in order to reduce the price of their labour to the lowest possible level.

At the end of February and in early March 2002, violence once again erupted in Ahmedabad—on a scale and intensity that far surpassed that of previous years. As I have said before, it is much too facile to suggest a direct causation between the looting, burning, and killing, which reached its climax in the industrial localities of the city, and massive impoverishment due to the collapse of the textile mills in the preceding quarter of a century. A major difference with the earlier communal riots was that this time, the search and destroy operation was not a spontaneous outburst of discontent and rivalry among people living at the bottom of the urban economy but well planned in advance and carried out with brutal precision. In an article, written when the violence in the streets of Ahmedabad was still going on, G. Shah identified four types of actors.

The organizers, who meticulously prepare plan and evolve strategies. Many of them are not on the site. They also chart out the route for the attacks in different localities. VHP leaders had admitted, the list identifying Muslims was prepared on the 28th morning [note: February 2002]. The organizers are primarily the top rank leaders. The majority of them happen to be Brahmins. And more important, they subscribe to the brahmanical ideology of the caste system. The second set of actors are the skilled and experienced personnel constituting the core. They have mastered the craft of breaking shutters and doors, pulling down ceilings and walls, using electrical devices for setting fire and burning people, using swords and other weapons. In the present riots, gas cylinders and other chemicals were used to destroy property. They function in a group of ten to twenty with all the necessary equipment. The leaders of the group (more than one) are committed 'Hindutvavadis', believing that they are performing their dharma, and are trained like all terrorists, be they Muslim or Christian fundamentalists. For them, their caste or other identity is not important, though it would seem that the majority of them belong to the upper and middle castes. The rest are professional goons routinely involved in criminal activities. They are called and mobilized by the organizers who provide patronage and political protection. (G. Shah 2002: 1391)

There is ample documentation for the conclusion that the escalation occurred largely because the BJP state government provided no protection for the victims of persecution, but gave its supporters a free hand—and even encouraged them—in their witch-hunt against members of the religious minority. The reconstruction of communal identities under the Sangh Parivar aegis has produced an all-Hindu platform from which the Muslims are targeted as outsiders. Dalits have lost their 'beyond the pale' classification and are supposed to pay for their social acceptance within the Hindutva fold by joining the hunt against the excluded minority made to live at the margins of society as a new category of untouchables.

Eyewitnesses like Kapilabehn, a SEWA grassroots worker, have given nightmarish descriptions of the recent violence and counter-violence.

What can I tell you? I have seen terrible scenes—everything happened in front of my eyes. I have seen mobs of 4,000 to 5,000 men stalking the city with guns and swords, burning and looting. I have seen one man's hands cut off, another's stomach ripped open and intestines hanging out. I have also seen the police actively participating in all of this. I have seen the dead and injured lying on the road with no first aid. I have seen death, blood, suffering, fear—I have seen things like never before. I can never forget what I witnessed. When I visited Ambikanagar, a Hindu community, there was nothing there; everything had been razed to the ground. It was the same for Mariam bibi ka Masjid, a Muslim area. Not a single hut was left. All we could see were the charred remains of the house and the belongings strewn about. I sat down and cried, how can we rebuild after such destruction? (Bhatt 2002)

Like many women who are members of this informal sector trade union, Kapilabehn lives in a part of the city where the textile mills used to be located which, until the recent past, provided their men with formal sector work. It is indicative of the scale of the violence that raged in the former textile neighbourhoods that, of the 155,000 women who in early 2002 were members of SEWA in Ahmedabad, 38,000 became victims to a greater or lesser extent of the wave of anger and hatred that lasted for several weeks. 21,900 were forced to flee to one of the 46 camps set up to provide emergency shelter (Bhatt 2002: 17). What needs to be highlighted is that on an earlier occasion, during the riots of December 1992, Hindu nationalists managed to intimidate SEWA's leaders into submission. The warning came, thus Varshney reports, that: 'If they organised for communal harmony on a large scale, they were told, the offices of SEWA and its workers might not be safe. It was obvious to SEWA that if it wanted to fight Hindu national militants, the union's infrastructure would inevitably become a larger of the militants' wrath' (Varshney 2002: 254).

The author adds that the SEWA sisters concluded that they would rather lie low and secure their own homes than organize for peace on a bigger scale. Varshney's preposterous comment on this episode is that a male union of such large membership would not have cowered under this threat. He seems to have lost sight of the brutal treatment with which the Sangh Parivar warriors, then and now again, have dealt with their opponents. Having said that, I agree that SEWA should make use of the public space it has created to take a political stand and to squarely confront Hindutva's agenda, because the underlying ideology is totally opposed to the interests of the working class, irrespective of women and men, Muslims or Hindus.

The residents of the slum localities were not only the victims of communal rage and hatred but also responded en masse to the call to eliminate the members of the opposing group. The main targets of the violence were Muslims, many hundreds of whom—men, women, and children—were killed, often in the most horrific ways. The pogrom made it clear that the Sangh Parivar organizations had succeeded in inciting the *lumpen* army of unemployed and semi-unemployed youth in the old industrial districts to murder, looting, and arson. In an early report on these events, I made a link between the mass redundancies that accompanied the closure of the mills, the impoverishment and degradation of the industrial neighbourhoods, and the pogroms which took place largely in this milieu. The social cohesion that once existed has gone. Although even when the mills were open, the adjoining workers' colonies were divided according to caste and faith, these were small-scale concentrations no larger than a few chawls or blocks of houses. The other was not at a distance but highly visible and touchable as a workmate, a customer, a neighbour, or a friend with whom close contact was maintained both within and outside the mill. I already had occasion to refer to Jivan Thakore's recollections in the preceding chapters about 'the good old days' before the mills started to close down. There is no denying that working in the mill together created feelings of inter-communal friendship and solidarity that have since faded away.

Our Monogram mill housed an equal number of Muslims and Christians along with Hindu workers. There was a small setup of Hindu's *Meldi* goddess in the spinning division of our mill. Mechanic department had a bigger temple of *Mahadev* (Lord Shankar), and Shaal department had a mosque near it. All freely visited these places without any hindrances. Muslim leaders used to be present for any events in temples of *Meldi* and *Mahadev* and Hindu leaders would participate in *Vayaj* (religious discourse) at mosque. Such emotional interaction kept communal harmony in our mill intact....

Ismail, a resident of juni chawl in Bapunagar was of my age and operated a doffet machine in the shift next to mine (he undertook *Haj* pilgrimage in 1999). He is a brother-in-law of Rasul, my friend from Rajpur. So, I consider him coworker as well as friend. Ismail had retained a Brahmin cook at his son's marriage for cooking for fifty of us Hindus. We participated happily in their marriage ceremonies as Muslims also attended ours. We visited each other's house in the event of any sickness in their family. Such were the emotional bonds we shared. We went to mourn death in Muslim household and they visited Hindus in such circumstances. They also joined in the last journey and stayed with us through the entire cremation ceremony. Such feelings of love and brotherhood died with the death of the mills. Ahmedabad's industrialists not only slaughtered the mills but also wrecked the Hindu–Muslim brotherhood. This is the whole truth. (Thakore 2002)

This close-knit community feeling which used to exist, lives on in the narratives about what has been lost. They are memories of visits to one's neighbours, to take part in the joys and sorrows of family life, to pay their respects or to show each other hospitality on festive occasions, to share the burden of everyday problems. This mesh of social cohesion that transcended the separate identity niches broke down once the mill had closed, the TLA started to fade away, and municipal agencies, due to lack of funding, ceased or drastically curtailed their welfare activities, which were also meeting points. The climate of social Darwinism that replaced it not only established the right of the survival of the fittest, but meant that the weakest at the base of society are forced to compete with each other as hunter and hunted. In the course of my own stay in Ahmedabad during these fateful days in March 2002, I met with the secretary general of the TLA. He told me about his despair when he failed to get through to the police commissioner or to politicians of the ruling party once the pogrom had started. The lack of response to his incessant calls from his office on 28 February 2002 made him realize that the state machinery deliberately refused to end the rampage and that his union now really had become a spent force (Breman 2003: 1486). In the wake of the communal riots which swept through the mill localities in 1969, the TLA leadership had invited Khan Abdul Badshah Khan, better known as the 'Frontier Gandhi', to visit Ahmedabad. In the Jumma Masjid, he called for reconciliation and criticized those who used their own faith to persecute others who thought differently and blamed them of practising a false social consciousness. His speech was reprinted in *Majoor Sandesh* in March 2002. When I left Ahmedabad at the end of that month, order and peace had not yet been restored in the city. The curfew was lifted in some parts of the city, only to be re-imposed the next day in the same or other localities because of new incidents. There has been hardly any discussion of what all this meant for the large number of working-class households who fully depend on the erratic and meagre yield of their labour power. Even under so-called normal circumstances, steady employment is difficult to come by, but for more than three weeks at a stretch, they had not able to move around in their cumbersome search for gainful work. For many of them, the regular state of deprivation in which they live has further deteriorated into destitution. Without any food left and bereft of all creditworthiness, they have to survive on whatever private charities are willing to dole out to them (Breman 2003: 1487). What does deserve attention is that, with a few exceptions, the institutions that represent civil society took no action at all when the communal riots and the horrific violence that accompanied them broke out. Ahmedabad is proud of the large number of non-governmental agencies located in the city. In the past, commentators have widely praised their role in tackling poverty. This generated a hugely exaggerated picture, which included the glorification of NGO initiatives to which the private sector and the local government also contributed (see Dutta 2002 and others). These efforts have, however, reaped few benefits for the poorer sections of the population, and for the large number of Muslims among them in particular. For collective action, the city's excluded minority has always been, and remains, dependent on charity from their own community. In the pauperized industrial districts of Ahmedabad, 'the righteous struggle', which did succeed in generating a certain amount of inter-communal solidarity, lives on only in the memory of a better past.

Collective action is a necessary condition for the achievement of a better life. In the 1930s, the inhabitants of Marienthal in Austria were able to alleviate the poverty resulting from their dismissal from the factories because of the unemployment benefits they received. The state-funded allowances were extremely meagre but essential for their survival during the economic recession. A welfare state which provides ample social security from the cradle to the grave may have become a chapter in the social history of West European societies. This does not mean to say, however, that the social awareness that has been aroused through a long process of emancipation should inevitably be subordinated to the unbridled interplay of economic supply and demand. The price for that, expressed in the emergence of new inequalities in and outside the labour market, is too high. Social security schemes should be insisted upon if only to build up the countervailing power needed to mitigate the harmful consequences of employment insecurity. As I come to the end of my argument, I observe that regulation by the government and restriction of the workings of the free market are necessary to put an end to the exclusion from a decent standard of life of the huge and still growing army of labour in the informal sector, which is in many respects used as a reserve. To ensure that a coolie class of untouchables does not form at the broad base of the world economy, encompassing a considerable proportion of humanity, the formulation and implementation of an extensive programme of social welfare is urgently required.

## NOTES

1. Defined as usual as 'not working but seeking or available for work during the major part of the reference period'.

2. The progressive participation of women in paid work is well documented. See Hirway and Unni (1990); Jhabvala and Bali (n.d.); Jhabvala and Shaikh (n.d.); Mahadevia (1998: 522–5, 2001: 151–5); Mahadevia and d'Costa (1997: 34–5); Unni (2000: 22–3); Unni and Bali (2001); and elsewhere.

3. For a critical review, see Breman (2001b).

4. The workshop, sponsored by the Social Science Research Council in New York in collaboration with the Indian Statistical Institute, was entitled 'Rural Economic Change in South Asia: Differences in Approach and in Results between Large-scale Surveys and Intensive Micro Studies'. For a summary of the discussion, see the introduction to the published proceedings, edited by Bardhan (1989), which include contributions by most of the participants.

5. For recent arguments in a similar vein, see Harriss–White and Gooptu (2000); Hensman (2001).

6. Although some of these veterans are quite scrupulous in making decisions and adhere to a Gandhian lifestyle, I should add that other senior leaders would find it difficult to defend themselves against accusations of fraud and corruption. The leadership of the union has started selling off assets and property in a manner which is anything but transparent. Transactions are also not accounted for but remain hidden from public scrutiny. Members were never kept closely informed about the union's business and nowadays, less than ever before.

7. The trend is not towards increase but further decline in organizational strength. According to the *World Labour Report 1997–8*, published by the 1LO, union membership as a percentage of non-agricultural labour dropped from the already low level of 6.6 per cent in 1985 to 5.5 per cent in 1995 (ILO 1998).

8. For an early report of these struggles, see Kannan (1988).

# 9
# Myths of the Global Safety Net*

Media reports on the economic meltdown have mainly concentrated on the impact of the crisis on the rich nations, with little concern for the mass of the population living in what used to be called the Third World. The current view seems to be that the setbacks in these 'emerging economies' may be less severe than expected. China's and India's high growth rates have slackened, but the predicted slump has not materialized. This line of thought, however, analyses only the effects of the crisis on countries as a whole, masking its differential impact across social classes. If one considers income distribution, and not just macro-calculations of gross domestic product (GDP), the global downturn has taken a disproportionately higher toll on the most vulnerable sectors: the huge armies of the poorly paid, undereducated, resourceless workers that constitute the overcrowded lower depths of the world economy.

To the extent that these many hundreds of millions are incorporated into the production process, it is as informal labour, characterized by casualized and fluctuating employment and piece rates, whether working at home, in sweatshops, or on their own account in the open air; and in the absence of any contractual or labour rights, or collective organization. In a haphazard fashion, still little understood, work of this nature has come to predominate within the global labour force at large. The International Labour Organization (ILO 2002) estimates that informal workers comprise over half the workforce in Latin America, over 70 per cent in Sub-Saharan Africa, and over 80 per cent in India; an Indian government report suggests a figure of more than 90 per cent

* Originally published as 'Myths of the Global Safety Net', in Jan Breman, *Outcast Labour in Asia: Circulation and Informalization of the Workforce at the Bottom of the Economy*, Chapter 12, New Delhi: Oxford University Press, 2010, pp. 361–8.

(Government of India 2008). Cut loose from their original social moorings, the majority remain stuck in the vast shanty towns ringing city outskirts across the global South. Recently, however, the life of street hawkers in Cairo, tortilla vendors in Mexico City, rickshaw drivers in Calcutta, or scrap mongers in Jakarta has been cast in a much rosier light. The informal sector, according to the *Wall Street Journal* (*WSJ*), is 'one of the last safe havens in a darkening financial climate' and 'a critical safety net as the economic crisis spreads' (Barta 2009). Thanks to these jobs, former International Monetary Fund (IMF) Chief Economist, Simon Johnson, is quoted as saying, 'the situation in desperately poor countries isn't as bad as you'd think'. On this view, an admirable spirit of self-reliance enables people to survive in the underground circuits of the economy, unencumbered by the tax and benefit systems of the 'formal sector'. These streetwise operators are able to get by without expensive social provisions or unemployment benefit. World Bank economist, W.F. Maloney, assures the *WSJ* that the informal sector 'will absorb a lot of people and offer them a source of income' over the next year.

The *WSJ* draws its examples from Ahmedabad, the former mill city in Gujarat where I conducted fieldwork in the 1990s. Here, in the Manek Chowk market—'a row of derelict stalls', where 'vendors peddle everything from beans to brass pots as monkeys scramble overhead'—Surajben 'Babubhai' Patni sells tomatoes, corn, and nuts from a makeshift shelter: 'She makes as much as 250 rupees a day, or about $5, but it's enough to feed her household of nine, including her son, who recently lost his job as a diamond polisher'. Enough: really? Five dollars for nine people is less than half the amount the World Bank sets as the benchmark above extreme poverty: 1 dollar per capita per day. Landless households in villages to the south of Ahmedabad have to make do with even less than that—on the days they manage to find work (Breman 2007b).

Earlier this year, I returned to the former mill districts of the city to see how the economic crisis was affecting people there. By 2000, these former working-class neighbourhoods had already degenerated into pauperized quarters. But the situation has deteriorated markedly even since then. Take the condition of the garbage pickers—all of them women, since this is not considered to be man's work. They are now paid half what they used to get for the harvest of paper, rags, and plastic gleaned from the waste dumps on their daily rounds. To make up the loss, they now begin their work at 3 a.m. instead of at 5 a.m., bringing along their children to provide more hands. The Self Employed Women's Association (SEWA), which organizes informal sector workers in the city, reports that 'incomes have declined, days of work decreased, prices have fallen and livelihoods disappeared'.[1] Their recent newsletter presents Table 9.1, testifying to the crash in prices for the 'goods' collected on the dumps.

TABLE 9.1    Prices Paid to Ahmedabad Waste Collectors

Price in Rs/km

| Items | April 2008 | January 2009 | Percentage Change |
|---|---|---|---|
| Waste steel | 6 | 3 | −50 |
| Steel sheets | 10 | 5 | −50 |
| Plastic bags | 8 | 5 | −37.5 |
| Newspaper | 8 | 4 | −50 |
| Hard plastic | 15 | 7 | −53 |
| Soft plastic | 10 | 4 | −60 |
| Dry bones | 4 | 2 | −50 |
| Waste hair | 1,000 | 300 | −70 |

*Source*: SEWA newsletter, 15 May 2009.

A SEWA activist based in Ahmedabad reports on the anguish she met when visiting local members. One of these, Ranjanben Ashokbhai Parmar, started to cry: 'Who sent this recession! Why did they send it?'

I was speechless. Her situation is very bad, her husband is sick, she has 5 children, she stays in a rented house, she has to spend on the treatment of her husband and she is the sole earner in the family, how can she meet her ends? When she goes to collect scrap she takes along her little daughter, while her husband sits at home and makes wooden ice-cream spoons, from which he can earn not more than 10 rupees a day.

In the industrial city of Surat, 120 miles south of Ahmedabad, half the informal labour force of the diamond workshops was laid off overnight at the end of 2008, with the collapse of worldwide demand for jewels. Some 200,000 diamond cutters and polishers found themselves jobless, while the rest had to contend with drastic reductions in hours and piece rates. A wave of suicides swept the dismissed workers, who—with a monthly income of little more than $140—were reputed to belong to the most skilled and highest paid ranks of the informal economy. These bitter experiences of the recession-struck informal economy in Gujarat can be repeated for region after region across India, Africa, and much of Latin America. Confronted with such misery, it is impossible to concur with the World Bank's and *WSJ*'s optimism about the sector's absorptive powers. As for their praise for the 'self-reliance' of those struggling to get by in these conditions: living in a state of constant emergency saps the energy to cope and erodes the strength to endure. To suggest that these workers constitute a 'vibrant' new class of self-employed entrepreneurs, ready to fight their way upward, is as misleading as portraying children from the chawls of Mumbai as slumdog millionaires.

## RURAL ROPE'S END

The second option currently being touted by the Western media as a 'cushion for hard times' is a return to the countryside. As an Asian Development Bank official in Thailand recently informed the *International Herald Tribune* (IHT), 'returning to one's traditional village in the countryside is a sort of "social safety net"'. The complacent assumption is that large numbers of rural migrants made redundant in the cities can retreat to their families' farms and be absorbed in agricultural work, until they are recalled to their urban jobs by the next uptick of the economy. The IHT evokes a paradisial rural hinterland in northeast Thailand. Even in the dry season, 'there are still plenty of year-round crops—gourds, beans, coconuts and bananas among them—that thrive with little rainwater. Farmers raise chickens and cows, and dig fish ponds behind their homes.... Thailand's king, Bhumibol Adulyadej, has long encouraged such self-sufficiency' (Fuller 2009).

Similar views were published at the time of the Asian financial crisis in 1997. Then, World Bank consultants assumed that agriculture could act as a catchment reservoir for labour made redundant in other sectors, based on the notion that the army of migrants moving back and forth between the country and urban growth poles had never ceased their primary occupation. The myth persisted that Southeast Asian countries were still essentially peasant societies. These tillers of the land might go to the city to earn extra wages for cash expenditure, but if they lost their jobs, they were expected to reintegrate into the peasant economy with no difficulty. This was far from the case, as I wrote then.

Returning to the localities of my fieldwork in Java this summer, I listened to the latest stories of men and women who had come back to the village, having lost their informal-sector jobs elsewhere, and find no work here, either. Of course not: they were driven out of the village economy in the first place because of lack of land or other forms of capital. There is no family farm to fall back on.

The departure of the landless and the land-poor was a flight, part of a coping strategy. Now that the members of this rural proletariat have become redundant in Jakarta or Bangkok, or as contract workers in Taiwan or Korea for that matter, they are back to square one, due to an acute and sustained lack of demand for their labour power in their place of origin. A comparable drama is taking place in China. Out of the 120 to 150 million migrants who made the trek from the rural interior to the rapidly growing coastal cities during the last twenty-five years, official sources report that about 10 to 15 million are now unemployed. For these victims of the new economy, there is no alternative but to go back 'home' to a deeply impoverished countryside.[2]

The Asian village economy is not capable of accommodating all those who possess no means of production; nor has the urban informal sector the elasticity to absorb all those eager to drift into it. According to policymakers' notions of cross-sectoral mobility, the informal economy should swallow up the labour surplus pushed out of higher-paid jobs, enabling the displaced workforce to stick it out through income-sharing arrangements until the economic tide turned again. I have never found any evidence that such a horizontal drift has taken place. Street vendors do not turn into *becak* drivers, domestic servants, or construction workers overnight. The labour market of the informal sector is highly fragmented; those who are laid off in their branch of activity have no alternative but to go back 'home', because staying on in the city without earnings is next to impossible. But returning to their place of origin is not a straightforward option, given the lack of space in the rural economy. Nevertheless, my informants do not simply lay the blame for their predicament on the economic meltdown. From the perspective of the world's underclasses, what looks like a conjunctural crisis is actually a structural one, the absence of regular and decent employment. The massive army of reserve labour at the bottom of the informal economy is entrapped in a permanent state of crisis which will not be lifted when the Dow Jones Index goes up again.

## NEW ECONOMIC ORDER

The transformation that took place in nineteenth-century Western Europe, as land-poor and landless peasants migrated to the towns, is now being repeated on a truly global scale. But the restructuring that would create an industrial–urban order, of the sort which vastly improved the lot of the former peasants of the Northern hemisphere, has not materialized. The ex-peasants of the South have failed to find secure jobs and housing on their arrival in the cities. Struggling to gain a foothold there, they have become mired, for successive generations, in the deprivation of the shanties, a vast reserve army of informal labour.

In the 1960s and the 1970s, Western policymakers viewed the informal sector as a waiting room, or temporary transit zone: newcomers could find their feet there and learn the ways of the urban labour market. Once savvy to these, they would increasingly be able to qualify for higher wages and more respectable working conditions. In fact, the trend went in the opposite direction due, in large part, to the onslaught of market-driven policies, the retreat of the state in the domain of employment, and the decisive weakening of organized labour. The small fraction that made their way to the formal sector was now accused of being a labour aristocracy, selfishly laying claim to privileges of protection and security. At the same time, the informal sector began to be heralded by the World Bank and other transnational agencies as a motor of economic growth. Flexibilization became the order of the day—in other words, dismantling of job security and a crackdown on collective bargaining. The process of informalization that has taken shape over the last 20 years saw, among other things, the end of the large-scale textile industry in South Asia. In Ahmedabad itself, more than 125.000 mill workers were laid off at a stroke. This did not mean the end of textile production in the city. Cloth is now produced in power-loom workshops by operators who work 12-hour days, instead of eight, and at less than half the wages they received in the mill; garment manufacture has become home-based work, in which the whole family is engaged day and night. The textile workers' union has all but disappeared. Sliding down the labour hierarchy has plunged these households into a permanent social and economic crisis.

It is not only that the cost of labour at the bottom of the world economy has been scaled down to the lowest possible level; fragmentation also keeps the underemployed masses internally compartmentalized. These people are competitors in a labour market in which the supply side is now structurally larger than the—constantly fluctuating—demand for labour power. They react to this disequilibrium by trying to strengthen their ties along lines of family, region, tribe, caste, religion, or other primordial identities which preclude collective bargaining on the basis of work status and occupation. Their vulnerability is exacerbated by their enforced rootlessness: they are pushed off the land, but then pushed back onto it again, roaming around in an endless search for work and shelter.

The emergence of the early welfare state in the Western hemisphere at the end of the nineteenth century has been attributed to the bourgeoisie's fear that the policy of excluding the lower ranks of society could end in the collapse of the established order (de Swaan 1988). The propertied part of mankind today does not seem to be frightened by the presence of a much more voluminous *classe dangereuse*. Their appropriation of ever-more wealth is the other side of the trend towards informalization, which has resulted in the growing imbalance between capital and labour. There are no signs of a change of direction in this economic course. Promises of poverty reduction by global leaders are mere lip service, or photo-opportunities. During his campaign, Obama would once in a while air his appreciation for Roosevelt's New Deal. Since his election, the idea of a broad-based social welfare scheme has been shelved without further ado. The global crisis is being tackled by a massive transfer of wealth from poor to rich. The logic suggests a return to nineteenth-century beliefs in the principle and practice of natural inequality. On this view, it is not poverty that needs to be eradicated. The problem is the poor people themselves, who lack the ability to pull themselves up out of their misery. Handicapped by all kinds of defects, they constitute a useless residue and an unnecessary burden. How to get rid of this ballast?

## NOTES

1. SEWA newsletter, *We the Self-employed*, no. 18, 15 May 2009. SEWA began organizing informal sector workers in Ahmedabad in the 1970s, and has subsequently expanded its activities across India, and even beyond.
2. See 'Prologue' in Breman and Wiradi (2002: 1–38).

# 10

# The Eventual Return of Social Darwinism*

The universal disregard of the poverty condition in which a sizable part of mankind continues to live, and the inadequacy of strategies selected to tackle this prime social question, is connected to the return of inequality as a fashionable doctrine both at the national and global level. Elaborating on the ideological push in favour of more and not less inequality, my point of departure is a recent study outlining the main tenets of social Darwinism (Hermans 2003).[1] The central proposition of Darwin's *The Origin of Species* was that the development of organisms must be seen as a struggle to survive over a period of millions of years (Darwin 1983 [1859]). The principle of natural selection implied continual adaptation to the surrounding environment in a way that ensured that superior species would emerge, succeeding where those which lacked the necessary qualities to survive had not. The ultimate appearance of man was proof of this progressive biological selection process. Darwin's theory represented a break in the static interpretation of nature according to which all forms of life were ranked in a hierarchy in which man had occupied the highest position since 'the beginning'. The application of Darwin's ideas to social and political theory became known as social Darwinism.

One of the leading pioneers of this school of thought was Herbert Spencer who had already vented ideas similar to those of the British biologist. Darwin adopted his expression of 'the survival of the fittest' as a more expressive formulation of the mechanism of natural selection for

* Originally published as 'The Eventual Return of Social Darwinism', in Jan Breman, *Outcast Labour in Asia: Circulation and Informalization of the Workforce at the Bottom of the Economy*, Chapter 13, New Delhi: Oxford University Press, 2010, pp. 369–78.

social development. Initially, this process was closely linked to the laissez-faire doctrine, which suggested that the struggle to survive would produce the best results if left to its own devices. Such a formula precluded any form of interference with what was considered to be a natural process. Very quickly, however, this hands-off approach became replaced by more pessimistic views which no longer automatically associated evolution with progress. The last phase of development of the theory towards the end of the nineteenth century was marked by the socio-biological programmes of Ernst Haeckel and others, who were preoccupied by the dangers of degeneration. Despite their many differences, the ideas on human and social development that laid the foundations for the emergence of social Darwinism were logically connected and came about over a period of a few decades only. They spread surprisingly fast in the international arena, Europe and North America in particular. The first to actually use the term 'social Darwinism' was the French anarchist, Emile Gautier, in 1879.

The initial conceptualization subsequently acquired strongly negative connotations. It was seen as extremely individualistic, denying any form of state intervention and overemphasizing the importance of competition as opposed to solidarity as the driving force of social interaction. This viewpoint does not do justice to a completely different interpretation of Darwinism which, rather than sing the praises of unbridled individualism, actually criticizes it fundamentally. From the latter perspective, it formed the basis of calls for public intervention to harness the free play of social forces. Here, the emphasis lay on the possibility for people, in the struggle for survival, not to fight against each other, but to work together and towards the well-being of all. The aim to put an end to unfettered self-interest through cooperation and solidarity also denied the evangelism of inequality, which would countenance no concession to the principle of 'every man for himself'. What attracted radical reformers to Darwinism was the way it broke through the hierarchic order which still prevailed. The egalitarian traits these critical minds identified in the theory did not glorify atomistic individualism, but promoted collectivism. This was at the root of the emancipatory interpretation that both Marxists and Fabians gave social Darwinism. But collectivism also had a conservative if not reactionary variant. In the theory of eugenics, which was rapidly gaining ground, the survival of the fittest was presented as the right of the strongest, and led to calls to liberate society and mankind as a whole from undesirable elements, who were a burden to themselves as well as to the world at large.

The conservative–progressive dichotomy is not useful as a means of clarifying social Darwinist thought. The proponents of industrial capitalism, founded on harshness and inequality, were reformist in the sense that they rejected the religious–aristocratic social order and sought refuge and support in modern science. The original laissez-faire approach was definitely anti-authoritarian and anti-traditionalist, radical in its individualism and its resistance to the supremacy of the pre-industrial alliance of church and state. This does not change the fact that the reversal in the social interpretation of Darwinism—from a predominantly optimistic–liberal individualism to a pessimistic and socially conservative collectivism—had a strong influence on the triumph of the latter in the later discussion on human and social development. Darwin was convinced that his theory of evolution had brought about a sea change in thinking on society and civilization. Yet, the mechanism of natural selection he described cannot be seen in isolation from ideas on political economy which had been around for much longer. The biologist was strongly influenced by Thomas Malthus, who had warned half a century earlier, of the disruption of the natural order resulting from the unbalanced growth of food supply and population. According to Malthus, it was necessary to allow all forms of social misery—pestilence, hunger, and war—to continue unhampered, regrettable as this may be, to avoid an unsustainable demographic explosion.

The conclusion quickly followed that the mechanism of natural selection was not active—or at least, not active enough—in civilized society. While Darwin was still working on his sensational publication, a fierce debate raged in British Parliament inspired by the long drawn-out struggle to introduce the first piece of industrial labour legislation. In the well-to-do circles to which Darwin belonged, there was widespread and sharp criticism of the intolerable generosity of the Poor Laws. Government support must not and could not be used to halt the ongoing process of pauperization. One solution to the problem of what to do with the inferior and redundant elements in the population was to ship them off to the colonies. In what he called his 'Malthusian views', Darwin endorsed the prevailing belief that hunger and a high mortality rate had a positive impact. The bourgeois economic ethos on which this viewpoint was based gave priority to relentless hard work, individual achievement, and reward according to merit, and had no time for misfits and lazy layabouts. Darwin retained his belief in progress, but recognized that since the dawn of civilization, it had acted as an obstacle to the mechanism of natural selection. Progress was therefore not a law of evolutionary regularity.

In the social–political debate, natural selection opened the door to standpoints in which norms and values were subordinated to the biological health of individual, people, and race. Advocates of a form of social Darwinism, which would tolerate no contamination of the principle of the survival of the fittest, were convinced that the lower classes were inferior. Nature and society were cruel only to those who did not possess the vitality and quality required to survive. The poor led incomplete and inadequate lives because they were incapable of taking control of the circumstances in which they were forced to maintain themselves. But the instinct among civilized people to sympathize with these helpless wretches offered them unwarranted support and protection. By tempering the natural play of social forces instead of allowing them free rein, modern society had burdened itself with a parasitical underclass. In the civilized part of the world, the lower classes—who reproduced the fastest—were seen as 'modern savages'. To reverse the threat of degeneration, these paupers should be forbidden from having children. For the better element of the labouring poor, there was still the possibility of being uplifted at some time in the future. But for the riff-raff below them, the only real remedy was social exclusion. These *Untermenschen* were a threat to the might and health of the nation. In 1904, the British government instigated a Royal Commission on the Care and Control of the Feeble-Minded. Winston Churchill was among those who advocated enforced sterilization. The mechanism of laissez-faire could no longer be relied upon to deal with those weak in mind and body. To do nothing would just exacerbate the evil. Supporters of what amounted to social cleansing wished to replace the invisible hand of the market with the hard hand of the state. This variant of social Darwinism was founded not on the principle of equality but of inequality. Where Darwin had seen the key to evolution as the survival of the fittest, in the sense of the most favoured species, this view reversed the mechanism of natural selection to mean the right of the strongest in a hierarchically structured and explicitly interventionist social order.

The struggle to survive had produced a modern society structured in terms of superiority and inferiority. Such a duality was even better illustrated in the distinction between more and less civilized peoples. Although Darwin was not one of the architects of this form of social Darwinism, he can be seen as one of its proponents. This is evident not so much in his first book as in its sequel, *The Descent of Man* (Darwin 1981 [1871]). His views on the differences among the human species make this very clear. He had no scruples about repeating the sentiments of one of his allies, who stated that the Irish were careless, dirty, and without zeal, and 'bred like rabbits'. The Scots, on the other hand, were shown as thrifty, foresighted, and ambitious. Darwin had great admiration for the United States of America (USA), where the population was the result of natural selection. The most energetic and bravest people from Europe had departed for America and their success in the New World was clear evidence of the qualities they possessed. From civilized humanity, there was a direct line back to the primitive savages who inhabited the margins of the earth and who were seen as 'our living ancestors'. And then, there were the static Oriental civilizations, which, stubbornly and for no good reason, held on to their centuries-old cultural heritage and demanded a degree of conformity from their people that precluded behavioural variation and therefore, prevented them from taking the great leap forwards.

Social Darwinism was explicitly racist in character. The concept of progress on which it was founded reinforced the belief that the white race were the Chosen People. Savagery and civilization were not just a matter of individuality but also of the societies constructed around them. The lack of adequate clothing, arms, and tools meant that our living ancestors were simple 'children' who—lacking efficient protection against the selective working of hard external circumstances—could not pursue the further development of their physical and spiritual capabilities. Such expressions of the inequality between races were, of course, an apology for colonial expansion and domination. Intermarriage or interbreeding was out of the question, as this would bring the superior race down to the level of the inferior. The disregard in which Negroes in particular were held fuelled the view that they would not advance even if they came into contact with Western civilization. Their limitations were genetic. Black people were seen as children for whom growth to adulthood was excluded.

Herbert Spencer was a social Darwinist *avant la lettre*. The affinity between the ideas of the two men did not mean that they agreed with each other in all respects. One difference of opinion that remained irreconcilable was Spencer's belief in the self-regulating capacity of industrial society. Spencer took the stance of a prophet of liberalism that was, in fact, ultra-conservative, and his hyper-individualism, together with a virulent anti-statism, made him a favourite of Andrew Carnegie and other American captains of industry. By contrast, Darwin did not go beyond expressing his concern that the development of civilized society would cancel out the effect of natural selection. He feared that the spread of pauperism would have a detrimental effect on the biological strength of the British people. Without losing his faith—he retained the belief that humanity would continue to benefit, also in modern society, from the unhindered working of the process of natural selection—Darwin proved sensitive to the argument that some degree of government intervention was required to see to it that the 'favoured races' keep their privileged position. The ultimate consequence of this standpoint was the necessity of social engineering to ensure that the struggle to survive in a global society was decided in favour of those who had shown themselves to be the fittest and the strongest.

The ongoing confrontation with the weaker elements somehow surviving at the bottom of industrial society was, however, interrupted when increasing tensions abroad required closing the ranks at home. The creation of a strong state was increasingly seen as a necessity for national survival. The support of the lower classes was indispensable in the imperialist fight against other nations and races. This geopolitical realization was expressed in the award of basic rights to the working masses and was accompanied by an improvement in living standards at the base of industrial society. The principle of competition still prevailed but in the social Darwinist variant of imperialist ideology, the focus of the struggle to survive no longer lay in efforts to weed out the unworthy in our own midst. It was directed outwards, in the engagement resulting from the inequality between people and races. Their subjection was a matter of denigration and discrimination. In the racist practice of colonial statecraft, more than in Western societies themselves, social Darwinism came into its own. Such racist overtones can, again, be discerned in current debates on the ongoing process of globalization; more specifically, in the variant suggesting and promoting a clash between civilizations.

I would like to conclude with some additional comments which relate the past, dealt with by Hermans in fascinating detail, to the present. In the first place, how to explain the disappearance—or at least, the declining prominence—of social Darwinism from the early twentieth century onwards? The question is relevant because of a possible re-emergence of ideas on society and culture inspired by social Darwinism. The neoliberalism in vogue at the end of the twentieth century heralds, in some ways, a return to social Darwinism of the more extreme kind *à la* Spencer. The reason to go back to an earlier round is not because it provides a retrospective interpretation of a historical school of thought, but because it comes at a time when debates in the social sciences are contextualized in the setting of the turbulent and ever-advancing process of globalization.[2]

A number of the factors which contributed to the erosion of this heavily charged ideology at the beginning of the twentieth century were highlighted in the literature belonging to the first round of the debate on the merits and demerits of social Darwinism. First, there was the widely shared belief that sending the poor to the colonies, whether or not of their own volition, would solve the problem of pauperization at home. In this way, internal tension could be discharged by external expansion. Mass migration to what were seen as empty regions—which often resulted in the enforced evacuation or elimination of the 'natives' and alienation from their right to dispose of the means of production they owned—is no longer an option in the current structure of the global economy for societies wishing to rid themselves of those they consider counterproductive because of their apparent incapacity to help increase the national surplus. Whereas Darwin explained the flow of emigrants to America as the process of natural selection at work, people who nowadays seek to escape poverty at home and find a better existence in the more highly developed parts of the world are stigmatized as economic refugees. In the past, however, migration to the city or overseas was the traditional escape valve in Europe for the people from the rural hinterlands who suffered worst in the fight to survive.

The eclipse of social Darwinism at the end of the nineteenth and the beginning of the twentieth centuries must, however, be seen primarily in the light of the burgeoning resistance to the cruelties of the industrial society. The working masses proved to be militant and forced improvements in their situation. What were initially little more than the weapons of the weak and desperate—recalcitrance, sabotage, and other forms of subversive behaviour—were gradually replaced by emancipatory activities organized collectively and on the basis of solidarity which resulted in the alleviation of poverty. This change for the better was partly prompted by an increasing fear among the bourgeoisie that continued exclusion would result in the propertyless hordes rising in revolt. The problems associated with including what was seen as *les classes dangereuses* were considered to weigh less heavily than the unrest that would eventually erupt into open hostility if this expanding segment at the base of society continued to be refused access to civil life and respectability.[3]

But whether the declining popularity of social Darwinism at that moment in time can be explained by the increasing pressure from below or the enlightened self-interest of the better-off, the fact that the social and economic value attached to labour—and consequently, the price that had to be paid for it—increased was a significant factor in the change that occurred. This slow but steady trend towards embetterment, empowerment, and growing respectability can be traced back to an early pattern of industrialization and a production system which was still heavily labour intensive. For the masses in Western societies, who had been expelled from their rural–agrarian existence during the nineteenth century, the cities and other sectors of the economy appeared, at first, to offer insufficient employment opportunities. The inevitable consequence of this was impoverishment and eventual pauperization. However, the relatively low level of technology that characterized this phase of industrialization ultimately enabled a mass of people, until then written off as superfluous and of no use, to be employed gainfully in moving the process forward. The industrial reserve army turned out to be much more than useless ballast. Skilling and schooling put an end to the combination of underemployment and too low wages. Around the turn of the century and in the early years of the twentieth century, the poor succeeded in becoming fully fledged participants in the labour process of Western societies and contributed to the growth in prosperity. The increasing dignity of the working classes led to greater political representation and was a logical outcome of this trend towards equality.

I have sketched this process briefly to suggest that the rebirth of social Darwinism is caused by the absence of the factors which, in the first round, helped temper or even dissipate an ideology which held a substantial part of the world's population themselves responsible for the defects of their existence. Social theories prevailing in an earlier round of globalization considered improvement impossible for these people because they lacked the required qualities for improvement; at the same time, any claim by or on behalf of the underprivileged masses to a reallocation of the resources needed to survive was considered illegitimate.

In the beginning of the twenty-first century, awareness seems to grow that continuation of the current economic and social policies at global level will make it impossible to solve the problem of mass poverty. This agonizing reappraisal also applies to the post-industrial societies where despite—or perhaps because of—rapidly expanding wealth, resistance to a more even spread of property, power, and status has grown in recent decades. The recent trend towards greater inequality affects all of those who live down below, at the bottom of society, but in particular the segment of the unskilled and unqualified whose origins lie 'elsewhere'—those with different skin colour, ethnicity, or religion. After their arrival, supposedly 'temporarily', in the prosperous zones of the world, they are not given permission to settle permanently, or have great difficulty in receiving that permission. In an incomparably harsher way, a much higher percentage of people are exposed to destitution in countries where the triumph of capitalism is a more recent phenomenon. The circumstances which eventually allowed their predecessors in the early industrialized countries access to the mainstream society do not apply to these latecomers. The once 'empty' regions of the world are considered 'full' and their resources have been appropriated by earlier waves of settlers. Moreover, technological advances have made production much less labour intensive.

Finally, the informalization of gainful employment which has become a major trend, especially in developing countries, in this late phase of capitalism hampers steady increase in the wretchedly low wages and replaces regular employment with casual, irregular, and spasmodic work arrangements, paid not in time-based wages but on piece rates. An economic regime of this kind discourages militancy and obstructs the mobilization of the labouring poor into unions and other mass-based organizations.[4] The countervailing power of the working masses to resist is extremely weak. The agendas of the transnational institutions with a mandate to steer the global economy pay lip service to combating poverty, but in the neoclassical policies that lie behind them, the increasingly vocal message is that the poor masses mainly have themselves to blame for their plight. What other explanation is there for the fact that they do not possess a greater proportion of the world's wealth? Deprivation and subordination has not yet been transformed into a policy-systematic exclusion. But the idea seems to have been revived that it is not poverty itself, but the degenerated human material suffering from it, that represents an unacceptable burden for the better-off of the world. In that reactionary perspective, rather than poverty, the poor themselves constitute an intolerable nuisance.

## NOTES

1. The study originated as a PhD thesis at the University of Amsterdam. The author discusses in rich detail the history and variety of social Darwinist thinking from the middle of the nineteenth century until the end of the second decade of the twentieth century. In my chapter, I have summarized the main features of his work and line of argumentation.

2. I pointed out the parallels between past and present in a collection of essays. See Introduction and Chapter 1 in Breman (2003: 1–14, 17–50).

3. For arguing along these lines, see de Swaan (1988).

4. I have devoted a number of publications to this development, including 'A Question of Poverty', my valedictory address at the Institute of Social Studies, reprinted in Breman (2003: Chapter 6, pp. 194–220).

# Bibliography

Agrawal, S. (1992), 'Women, Work and Industry: A Case Study of Surat Art Silk Industry', Unpublished PhD thesis, South Gujarat University, Surat.

Armstrong, W. and T.G. McGee (eds) (1985), *Theatres of Accumulation: Studies in Asian and Latin American Urbanization.* London: Methuen Augel.

Athreya, V., G. Djurfeldt, and S. Lindberg (1990), *Barriers Broken: Production Relations and Agrarian Changes in Tamil Nadu.* New Delhi: Sage Publications.

Awachat, A. (1988), 'The Warp and the Weft', *Economic and Political Weekly,* vol. 23, nos 1 and 2, pp. 1732–6 and 1786–90.

Bardhan, P. (ed.) (1989), *Conversations between Economists and Anthropologists: Methodological Issues in Measuring Economic Change in Rural India.* New Delhi: Oxford University Press.

Barik, B.C. (1987), 'Unorganized Migrant Labour in the Textile Industry of Surat', in V. Joshi (ed.), *Migrant Labour and Related Issues,* pp. 165–78. Ahmedabad: Gandhi Labour Institute.

Barta, Patrick (2009), 'The Rise of the Underground', *Wall Street Journal,* 14 March 2009.

Bharadwaj, K. (1990), *On the Formation of the Rural Labour Market in Rural Asia.* New Delhi: Centre for Economic Studies and Planning, School of Social Sciences, Jawaharlal Nehru University.

Bhatt, E. (2002), *Shantipath: Our Road to Restoring Peace.* Ahmedabad: SEWA.

Bhatt, P.K. (1979), 'Growth of Entrepreneurship in South Gujarat', Unpublished PhD thesis, South Gujarat University, Surat.

Boeke, J.H., W.F. Wertheim, and G.H. van der Kolff (eds) (1966), *Indonensian Economics: The Concept of Dualism in Theory and Policy.* The Hague: Van Hoeve.

Breman, Jan (1974a), *Patronage and Exploitation: Changing Agrarian Relations in South Gujarat, India*. Berkeley, CA: University of California Press.

———— (1974b), 'Mobilization of Landless Labourers: Halpatis of South Gujarat', *Economic and Political Weekly*, vol. 9, vol. 12, pp. 489–96.

———— (1976a), *Een Dualistisch Arbeidsbestel? Een Kritische Beschouwing van het Begrip 'De Informele Sector'*. Rotterdam: Van Gennep.

———— (1976b), 'A Dualistic Labour System? A Critique of the "Informal Sector" Concept', *Economic and Political Weekly*, vol. 11, nos 48, 49, and 50, pp. 1870–6, 1905–8, and 1939–43.

———— (1978), 'Seasonal Migration and Cooperative Capitalism: The Crushing of Cane and of Labour by the Sugar Factories of Bardoli, South Gujarat', *Economic and Political Weekly*, Special nos 31–33, vol. 13, pp. 1317–60.

———— (1978/1979), 'Seasonal Migration and Cooperative Capitalism: The Crushing of Cane and of Labour by the Sugar Factories of Bardoli, South Gujarat', *Journal of Peasant Studies*, Part 1, vol. 6, no. 1, 1978, pp. 1–40; Part 2, vol. 6, no. 2 ,1979, pp. 168–209.

———— (1980), *The Informal Sector in Research: Theory and Practice*. Comparative Asian Studies Programme no. 3. Rotterdam: Erasmus University.

———— (1985), *Of Peasants, Migrants and Paupers: Rural Labour Circulation and Capitalist Production in West India*. New Delhi: Oxford University Press; and Oxford: Clarendon Press.

———— (1990), '"Even Dogs are Better-off": The Ongoing Battle between Capital and Labour in the Cane Fields of Gujarat', *The Journal of Peasant Studies*, vol. 17, no. 4, pp. 546–608.

———— (1993a), 'The Anti-Muslim Pogrom in Surat', *Economic and Political Weekly*, vol. 28, no. 10, pp. 737–41.

———— (1993b), *Beyond Patronage and Exploitation: Changing Agrarian Relations in South Gujarat*. New Delhi: Oxford University Press.

———— (1994), *Wage Hunters and Gatherers: Search for Work in the Urban and Rural Economy of South Gujarat*. New Delhi: Oxford University Press.

———— (1995a), 'Work and Life of the Rural Proletariat in Java's Coastal Plain', *Modern Asian Studies*, vol. 29, no. 1, pp. 1–44.

———— (1995b), 'Labour Get Lost: A Late-capitalist Manifesto', *Economic and Political Weekly*, vol. 30, no. 37, pp. 2294–9.

Breman, Jan (1996), *Footloose Labour: Working in India's Informal Economy*. Cambridge: Cambridge University Press.

———— (1999), 'The Study of Industrial Labour in Post-colonial India: The Formal Sector—An Introductory Review', in J.P. Parry, J. Breman, and K. Kapadia (eds), *The Worlds of Industrial Labour: Contributions to Indian Sociology. Occasional Studies 9,* pp. 1–41. New Delhi: Sage Publications.

———— (2000), 'The Impact of the Asian Economic Crisis on Work and Welfare in Village Java', Dies Natalis Address delivered on 12 October, Institute of Social Studies, The Hague.

———— (2001a), 'A Turn for the Worse: The Closure of the Ahmedabad Textile Mills and the Retrenchment of the Workforce', Wertheim Lecture 12, Centre for Asian Studies, Amsterdam School of Social Science Research, Amsterdam.

———— (2001b), 'A Question of Poverty', Valedictory Address Institute of Social Studies, The Hague.

———— (2003), *The Labouring Poor in India: Patterns of Exploitation, Subordination and Exclusion*. New Delhi: Oxford University Press.

———— (2007a), *Labour Bondage in West India: From Past to Present*. New Delhi: Oxford University Press.

———— (2007b), *The Poverty Regime in Village India*. New Delhi: Oxford University Press.

Breman, Jan and Arvind Das (photographs by Ravi Agarwal) (2000), *Down and Out: Labouring under Global Capitalism*. New Delhi: Oxford University Press.

Breman, Jan, Isabelle Guerin, and Aseem Prakash (eds) (2009), *India's Unfree Workforce: Of Bondage Old and New*. New Delhi: Oxford University Press.

Breman, J. and G. Wiradi (2002), *Good Times and Bad Times in Rural Java: Socio-economic Dynamics in Two Villages towards the End of the Twentieth Century*. Leiden: KITLV Pers.

Bromley, R. (1990), 'A New Path to Development? The Significance and Impact of Hernando de Soto's Ideas on Underdevelopment, Production and Reproduction', *Economic Geography*, vol. 66, no. 1, pp. 328–48.

Buchanan, D.H. (1934), *The Development of Capitalist Enterprise in India*. New York: Macmillan.

Chakrabarty, D. (1989). *Rethinking Working Class History: Bengal 1890–1940*. New Delhi: Oxford University Press.

Chandra, B. (1966). *The Rise and Growth of Economic Nationalism in India: Economic Policies of Indian National Leadership, 1880–1905*. New Delhi: People's Publishing House.

Chattopadhyay, G. and A.K. Sengupta (1969), 'Growth of a Disciplined Labour Force: A Case Study of Social Impediments', *Economic and Political Weekly*, vol. 4, no. 28, pp. 1209–16.

Chowdhury, S.R. (1996), 'Industrial Restructuring, Union and the State: Textile Mill Workers in Ahmedabad', *Economic and Political Weekly*, vol. 31, no. 8, pp. L7–13.

Costa, W. d' (2002), 'In the Cauldron of Communal Conflicts: Shrinking Political Space and Vulnerability of Minorities', in A. Kundu and D. Mahadevia (eds), *Poverty and Vulnerability in a Globalising Metropole: Ahmedabad*, pp. 349–72. New Delhi: Manak.

Crouch, H.A. (1979), *Indian Working Class*. Ajmer: Sachin.

Darwin, Charles (1981 [1871]), *The Descent of Man, and Selection in Relation to Sex*, republished by J. Tyler Bonner and R.M. May. Princeton: Princeton University Press.

————— (1983 [1859]), *The Origin of Species by Means of Natural Selection, or the Preservation of Favoured Races in the Struggle for Life*, ed. J.W. Burrow. London and Harmondsworth: John Murray and Penguin Books.

Das, A.N. (1984), 'The Indian Working Class: Relations of Production and Reproduction', in A.N. Das, V. Nilkant, and P.S. Dubey (eds), *The Worker and the Working Class: A Labour Studies Anthology*, pp. 161–80. New Delhi: Public Enterprises Centre for Continuing Education.

Das, A.N., V. Nilkant, and P.S. Dubey (eds) (1984), *The Worker and the Working Class: A Labour Studies Anthology*. New Delhi: Public Enterprises Centre for Continuing Education.

Dasgupta, B. (1973), 'Calcutta's "Informal Sector"', *Institute of Development Studies Bulletin*, vol. 5, no. 2, October, pp. 53–75.

Dasgupta, P. (1993), *An Inquiry into Well-being and Destitution*. Oxford: Clarendon Press.

Dayal, M. (ed.) (2001), *Towards Secure Lives—SEWA's Social Security Programme*. London: Sangam Books.

Desai, J.L. (1981), 'Art Silk Processing Industry in Surat', Unpublished PhD thesis. South Gujarat University, Surat.

Desai, K.M. (1985), 'Artisans of Diamond Industry', Seminar on *Industrial Workers and Social Change*, Centre for Social Studies, Surat.

Drèze, J. and A. Mukherjee (1989), 'Labour Contracts in Rural India: Theories and Evidence', in S. Chakravarty (ed.), *The Balance between Industry and Agriculture in Economic Development*, Proceedings of the Eighth World Congress of the International Economic Association, Delhi, India. Vol. 3: *Manpower and Transfers*. Basingstoke: Macmillan Press, pp. 233–65.

Drèze, J. and A. Sen (1995), *India: Economic Development and Social Opportunity*. New Delhi: Oxford University Press.

Dutta, S.S. (2002), 'Partnership for Urban Poverty Reduction: A Review Experience', in A. Kundu and D. Mahadevia (eds), *Poverty and Vulnerability in a Globalising Metropolis*. New Delhi: Manak, pp. 237–67.

Dutta, S. and R. Batley (1999), 'Urban Governance, Partnership and Poverty: Ahmedabad', Working Paper 16, International Development Department, School of Public Policy, University of Birmingham.

Engineer, A.A. (1985a), 'From Caste to Communal Violence', *Economic and Political Weekly*, vol. 20, no. 15, pp. 628–30.

————— (1985b), 'Communal Violence Engulfs Ahmedabad', *Economic and Political Weekly*, vol. 20, no. 27, pp. 1116–20.

Fuller, Thomas (2009), 'In Southeast Asia, Unemployed Abandon Cities for Their Villages', *International Herald Tribune*, 28 February.

Ghose, A.K. (1999), 'Current Issues of Employment Policy in India', *Economic and Political Weekly*, vol. 34, no. 36, pp. 2592–608.

Gillion, K.L. (1968), *Ahmedabad: A Study in Urban History*. Berkeley and Ahmedabad: University of California Press and New Order Book Company.

Goode, W.J. (1963), 'Industrialisation and Family Change', in B.F. Hoselitz and W.E. Moore (eds), *Industrialisation and Society: Proceedings of the Chicago Conference on Social Implications of Industrialisation and Technical Change*, pp. 237–55. Paris: UNESCO.

Government of Gujarat (1975), *Report of the Advisory Committee for Minimum Wages of Workers in Brick Manufacturing Industry*. Ahmedabad: Office of the Labour Commissioner, Gujarat.

GoI (Government of India) (1931), *Report of the Royal Commission on Labour in India*. London: HMSO.

————— (1969), *Report of the National Commission on Labour*. New Delhi: Ministry of Labour, Employment and Rehabilitation, GoI.

————— (1991), *Report of the National Commission on Rural Labour* (2 vols) (Reports of Study Groups). New Delhi: Ministry of Labour, GoI.

GoI (Government of India) (2002), *Report of the National Commission on Rural Labour, Vol. 1.* New Delhi: Ministry of Labour, GoI.

———— (2008), *Report on the Conditions of Work and Promotion of Livelihoods in the Unorganised Sector.* New Delhi: National Commission for Enterprises in the Unorganised Sector, GoI.

Government of Maharashtra (1976), *Report of the Minimum Wages Committee for Employment in the Salt Pan Industry in the State of Maharashtra.* Bombay: Government of Maharashtra.

Groenou, W.W. van (1976), 'Sociology of Work in India', in G.R. Gupta (ed.), *Contemporary India: Some Sociological Perspectives.* New Delhi: Vikas, pp. 169–99.

Harriss, J. (1982), 'Character of an Urban Economy: "Small-scale" Production and Labour Markets in Coimbatore', *Economic and Political Weekly,* vol. 17, nos 23 and 24, pp. 945–54 and 993–1002.

Harriss–White, B. and N. Gooptu (2000), 'Mapping India's World of Unorganized Labour', in L. Panitch and C. Leys (eds), *The Socialist Register 2001: Working Classes, Global Realities,* pp. 89–119. London: Merlin Press.

Hart, G. (1986), 'Exclusionary Labour Arrangements: Interpreting Evidence on Employment Trends in Rural Java', *Journal of Development Studies,* vol. 22, no. 4, pp. 681–96.

Hart, K. (1973), 'Informal Income Opportunities and Urban Employment in Ghana', in R. Jolly, E. de Kadt, H. Singer, and F. Wilson (eds), *Third World Employment: Problems and Strategy,* pp. 66–70. Harmondsworth: Penguin.

Hensman, R. (2001), 'The Impact of Globalisation on Employment in India and Responses from the Formal and Informal Sector'. Clara Working Paper No. 15, Amsterdam.

Hermans, Cor (2003), *De Dwaaltocht van het Sociaal-Darwinisme: Vroege Interpretaties van Charles Darwins Theorie van Natuurlijke Selectie, 1859–1918* (The Quest of Social-Darwinism: Early Interpretations of Charles Darwin's Theory of Natural Selection, 1859–1918). Amsterdam: Uitgeverij Nieuwezijds.

Heuzé, G. (1990), 'Workers' Struggles and Indigenous Fordism in India', in M. Holmstrom (ed.), *Work for Wages in South Asia.* New Delhi: Manohar, pp. 173–89.

Hirway, I. (1995), 'Safety Net of Renewal Fund', *The Indian Journal of Labour Economics,* vol. 38, no. 2, pp. 185–200.

———— (2002), 'Employment and Unemployment Situation in the Nineties: How Good are the NSS Data?', *The Indian Journal of Labour Economics,* vol. 45, no. 1, pp. 69–87.

Hirway, I. and D. Mahadevia (2000), *Gujarat Human Development Report 1999*. Ahmedabad: Mahatma Gandhi Labour Institute.

Hirway, I. and J. Unni (1990), 'Employment and Occupational Diversification of Women in India', ILO–ARTEP Working Paper, New Delhi.

Holmström, M. (1976), *South Indian Factory Workers: Their Life and Their World*. Cambridge: Cambridge University Press.

————— (1984), *Industry and Inequality: The Social Anthropology of Indian Labour*. Cambridge: Cambridge University Press.

Howell, J. and U. Kambhampati (1997), *Liberalisation and Labour Markets in India: A Socioeconomic Study*. Research Report, Department for International Development (DFID), UK.

ILO (International Labour Organization) (1972), *Employment, Incomes and Equality: A Strategy for Increasing Productive Employment in Kenya*. Geneva: ILO.

————— (1998), *World Labour Report 1997/1998: Industrial Relations, Democracy and Social Stability*. Geneva: ILO.

————— (2002), *Decent Work and the Informal Economy*. Geneva: ILO.

————— (2009), *The Cost of Coercion: Global Report under the Follow-up to the ILO Declaration on Fundamental Principles and Rights at Work*. Geneva: ILO.

James, R.C. (1960), 'The Casual Labour Problem in Indian Manufacturing', *The Quarterly Journal of Economics*, vol. 74, no. 1, pp. 100–16.

Jani, M. (1984), *Textile Workers: Jobless and Miserable*. Ahmedabad: SETU.

Jhabvala, R. (1985), *Closing Doors: A Study on the Decline of Women in the Textile Mills of Ahmedabad*. Ahmedabad: SETU.

————— (1998), 'Social Security for Unorganised Sector', *Economic and Political Weekly*, vol. 33, no. 22, pp. L7–12.

Jhabvala, R. and N. Bali (n.d.), *My Life, My Work*. Ahmedabad: SEWA Academy.

Jhabvala, R., R. Dhawan, and K. Mahajan (1985), *Women Who Roll Bidis: Two Studies of Gujarat*. Ahmedabad: SEWA.

Jhabvala, R. and R. Shaikh (n.d.), *Wage Fixation for Home-based Piece Rate Workers: Technical Study Based on Survey of Workers in Gujarat, India*. Ahmedabad: SEWA Academy.

Jolly, R., E. de Kadt, H. Singer, and F. Wilson (eds) (1973), *Third World Employment: Problems and Strategy*. Harmondsworth: Penguin.

Joseph, C. (1978). 'Workers' Participation in Industry: A Comparative Study and Critique', in E.A. Ramaswamy (ed.), *Industrial Relations in India: A Sociological Perspective*. New Delhi: Macmillan, pp. 108–41.

Joshi, S. (1998), *Socio-economic Study of Slums on Sabarmati River Banks in Ahmedabad City*. Surat: Centre for Social Studies.

Joshi, V. (1987), 'Casualisation of Labour in Textile Industry', in S.S. Mehta (ed.), *Indian Textiles: An Intersectoral Perspective*. Ahmedabad: Oxford & IBH Publishing Co., pp. 144–58.

Kalathil, M. (1978), 'Industrial Relations in a Small-scale Industry', in E.A. Ramaswamy (ed.), *Industrial Relations in India: A Sociological Perspective*, pp. 89–107. Delhi: MacMillan.

Kanappan, S. (1970), 'Labour Force Commitment in Early Stages of Industrialisation', *Indian Journal of Industrial Relations*, vol. 5, no. 3, pp. 290–349.

Kannan, K.P. (1988), *Of Rural Proletarian Struggles: Mobilization and Organization of Rural Workers in Southwest India*. New Delhi: Oxford University Press.

———— (1990), 'State and Union Intervention in Rural Labour: A Study of Kerala', ARTEP Working Papers, New Delhi.

———— (1992), 'Labour Institutions and the Development Process in India', in T.S. Papola and G. Rodgers (eds), *Labour Institutions and Economic Development in India*, Research Series No. 97. Geneva: International Institute of Labour Studies, ILO.

Kapadia, K. (1995), *Siva and Her Sisters: Gender, Caste and Class in Rural South India*. Boulder, CO: Westview Press.

Karnik, V.B. (1967), *Strikers in India*. Bombay: Manaktalas.

Kerr, C. (1960), 'Changing Social Structures', in W.E. Moore and A.S. Feldman (eds), *Labor Commitment and Social Change in Developing Areas*, pp. 348–59. New York: Social Science Research Council.

Koelen, J.H. (1985), 'Stenen: Arbeidsmobiliteit in Zuid Gujarat. Een Onderzoek naar de Werkgelegenheid van de Tribale Bevolking in Diamantslijperijen en een Steengroeve' (Stones: Labour Mobility in South Gujarat. An Investigation of Employment of the Tribal Population in Diamond Workshops and a Stone Quarry), Unpublished MA thesis, Anthropological-Sociological Centre, Department South- and Southeast-Asia, University of Amsterdam.

Kruyt, D. (1994), *Informal Sector Economy and Informal Society: Poverty and Social Change in Latin America*. The Hague: Directorate General Ministry of Foreign Affairs.

Kumar, D. (1965), *Land and Caste in South India: Agricultural Labour in the Madras Presidency during the Nineteenth Century*. Cambridge: Cambridge University Press.

Kundu, A. (2000), 'Globalising Gujarat: Urbanization, Employment and Poverty', *Economic and Political Weekly*, vol. 35, nos 35 and 36, August–September, pp. 3172–82.

Kundu, A. and D. Mahadevia (eds) (2002), *Poverty and Vulnerability in a Globalising Metropole: Ahmedabad*. New Delhi: Manak.

Kundu, A. and A.N. Sharma (eds) (2001), *Informal Sector in India: Perspectives and Policies*. New Delhi: Institute for Human Development and Institute of Applied Manpower Research.

Lakha, S. (1988), *Capitalism and Class in Colonial India: The Case of Ahmedabad*. New Delhi: Sterling.

Lal, R.B. (1982), 'From Farm to Factory', *Adivasi Gujarat*, vol. 4, pp. 24–93.

Lambert, R.D. (1963), *Workers, Factories and Social Change in India*. Princeton, NJ: Princeton University Press.

Leadbeater, S.R.B. (1993), *The Politics of Textiles: Indian Cotton-mill Industry and the Legacy of Swadeshi, 1900–1985*. New Delhi: Sage Publications.

Llosa, M.V. (1994), *De vis in het Water, een Autobiografie* (Original title, *El pez en el agua*, 1993). Amsterdam: Meulenhoff.

Lobo, L. (1994a), 'Problems and Coping Mechanisms of People in a Surat Slum', Paper presented at the seminar on 'Urban Poor in India', Centre for Social Studies, Surat.

———. (1994b), *Encounter with Urbanism: Coping Mechanisms in a Slum*. Surat: Centre for Social Studies.

Loknathan, P. (1993), 'Employment and Wages in Indian Economy', in T.S. Papola, P.P. Ghosh, and A.N. Sharma (eds), *Labour, Employment and Industrial Relations in India*, pp. 43–64. Presidential Addresses, The Indian Society of Labour Economics. Delhi: BR. Publishing Corporation.

Lorenzo, A.M. (1943), *Agricultural Labour Conditions in Northern India*. Bombay: New Book Co.

Lubell, H. (1991), *The Informal Sector in the 1980s and 1990s*. Paris: Development Centre of the Organization for Economic Cooperation and Development.

Mahadevia, D. (1998), 'Informalisation of Employment and Incidence of Poverty in Ahmedabad', *The Indian Journal of Labour Economics*, vol. 41, no. 3, pp. 515–30.

——— (2001), 'Informalisation of Employment and Poverty in Ahmedabad', in A. Kundu and A.N. Sharma (eds), *Informal Sector in India: Perspectives and Policies*, pp. 142–59. New Delhi: Institute for Human Development and Institute of Applied Manpower Research.

Mahadevia, D. (2002), 'Interventions in Development: A Shift towards a Model of Exclusion', in A. Kundu and D. Mahadevia (eds), *Poverty and Vulnerability in a Globalising Metropole: Ahmedabad*, pp. 80–132. New Delhi: Manak.

Mahadevia, D. and W. d'Costa (1997), *Poverty and Vulnerability in Ahmedabad*. Ahmedabad: Oxfam Trust.

Mahadevia, D., T. Jain, and B. Acharya (1994), 'Informal Sector and Social Well-Being under Structural Adjustment Programme', *The Indian Journal of Labour Economics*, vol. 37, no. 3, pp. 379–90.

Mamkoottam, K. (1982), *Trade Unionism: Myth and Reality; Unionism in the Tata Iron and Steel Company*. New Delhi: Oxford University Press.

Masihi, E.J. (1985), *Trade Union Leadership in India: A Sociological Perspective*. Delhi: Ajanta.

——— (1993), 'Workers of Closed Textile Mills of Ahmedabad', School of Social Science, Gujarat University, Ahmedabad, mimeograph.

McGee, T.G. (1982), 'Labour Mobility in Fragmented Labour Markets: The Role of Circulatory Migration in Rural–Urban Relations in Asia', in H.I. Safa (ed.), *Towards a Political Economy of Urbanization in Third World Countries*, pp. 17–66. New Delhi: Oxford University Press.

Mehta. B.E. (n.d.), *Urban Rejuvenation through Property Redevelopment: Reusing Lands of Textile Mills under Liquidation in Ahmedabad*. Ahmedabad: Centre for Environmental Planning and Technology, School of Planning.

Mehta, B.V. and P.G. Pathak (1975), *The Art Silk Industry of Surat*. Surat: Centre for Regional Development Studies.

Mehta, M. (1985), 'Urban Informal Sector: Concept, Indian Evidence and Policy Implications', *Economic and Political Weekly*, vol. 20, no. 8, pp. 326–32.

Mehta, P.C. and R.S. Gandhi (n.d.), *Man-made Textile Industry of Surat*. Surat: Mantra.

Mehta, S. (n.d.), 'Request for Assistance from the National Renewal Fund for Ahmedabad's Textile Mills', Unpublished paper, Ahmedabad.

Mehta, S.S. (1995), 'Exit Policy and Social Safety Net', *The Indian Journal of Labour Economics*, vol. 38, no. 4, pp. 603–9.

Mehta, S.S. and D. Harode (1998), 'Industrial Sickness and Workers: Case of Gujarat Textile Industry', *Economic and Political Weekly*, vol. 33, no. 52, December, pp. L71–84.

Mookherjee, S. (1987), 'Union Response to Textiles Restructuring: Experience in Gujarat', in S.S. Mehta (ed.), *Indian Textiles: An Intersectoral Perspective*. Ahmedabad: Oxford & IBH Publishing Co., pp. 132–44.

Moore, W.E. (1951), *Industrialisation and Labour*. Ithaca: Cornell University Press.

Moore, W.E. and A.S. Feldman (eds) (1960), *Labor Commitment and Social Change in Developing Areas*. New York: Social Science Research Council.

Morris, M.D. (1960), 'The Labour Market in India', in W.E. Moore and A.S. Feldman (eds), *Labor Commitment and Social Change in Developing Areas*, pp. 173–200. New York: Social Science Research Council.

———— (1965), *The Emergence of an Industrial Labour Force in India: A Study of the Bombay Cotton Mills, 1854–1947*. Berkeley: University of California Press.

Mukherjee, R.K. (1945), *The Indian Working Class*. Bombay: Hind Kitab.

———— (1993), 'The Role of Labour in Democratic Socialism', in T.S. Papola, P.P. Ghosh, and A.N. Sharma (eds), *Labour, Employment and Industrial Relations in India*, pp. 103–13. Presidential Addresses, The Indian Society of Labour Economics. Delhi: B.R. Publishing Corporation.

Munshi, S. (1977), 'Industrial Labour in Developing Economies: A Critique of Labour Commitment Theory'. *Economic and Political Weekly*, vol. 12, no. 35, pp. 74–87.

Myers, C.A. (1958), *Labour Problems in the Industrialisation of India*. Cambridge, MA: Harvard University Press.

National Commission on Labour (2002), *Report of the Study Group on Umbrella Legislation for the Workers in the Unorganised Sector*. New Delhi: Ministry of Labour, Government of India.

National Planning Committee (1940), 'Minutes', May, Collection of papers in Nehru Memorial Museum, New Delhi.

Noronha, E. (1996), 'Liberalisation and Industrial Relations', *Economic and Political Weekly*, vol. 31, no. 10, pp. L14–20.

———— (1999), 'Duration of Unemployment and Re-employment, I and II', *Management and Labour Studies*, vol. 24, nos 2 and 3, pp. 96–112 and 150–61.

Noronha, E. and R.N. Sharma (1999), 'Displaced Workers and Withering Welfare State', *Economic and Political Weekly*, vol. 34, no. 23, pp. 1454–60.

Omvedt, G. (1990), 'The "Unorganized Sector" and Women Workers',
Paper presented at the Seminar on 'Women and Work', Centre for
Social Studies, Surat.

Ornati, O.A. (1955), *Jobs and Workers in India*. Institute of International
Industrial and Labour Relations. Ithaca: Cornell University Press.

Panitch, L. and C. Leys (eds) (2001), *The Socialist Register 2001: Working
Classes, Global Realities*. London: Merlin Press.

Pant, S.C. (1965), *Indian Labour Problems*. Allahabad: Chaitanya
Publishing House.

Papola, T.S. (1970), 'Economics of Labour Market', in V.B. Singh
(ed.), *Labour Research in India*, pp. 170–87. Bombay: Popular
Prakashan.

Papola, T.S. and G. Rodgers (1989), 'Restructuring in Indian Industry',
in G. Edgren (ed.), *Restructuring, Employment and Industrial
Relations: Adjustment Issues in Asian Industries*, pp. 29–79.
New Delhi: World Employment Programme, ILO.

———— (1992), 'Labour Institutions and Economic Development in
India', Research Series No. 97, International Institute for Labour
Studies, Geneva.

———— (1993), 'Employment of Women in South Asian Countries',
*The Indian Journal of Labour Economics*, vol. 36, pp. 48–56.

Papola, T.S. and K.K. Subrahmanian (1975), *Wage Structure and
Labour Mobility in a Local Labour Market: A Study in Ahmedabad*.
Monograph Series No. 4. Ahmedabad: Sardar Patel Institute of
Economic and Social Research.

Papola, T.S., P.P. Ghosh, and A.N. Sharma (eds) (1993), *Labour,
Employment and Industrial Relations in India*. Presidential Addresses,
The Indian Society of Labour Economics. Delhi: B.R. Publishing
Corporation.

Parmar, R. (1989), *A Worker's Struggle for Fundamental Reform: Life
and Times of Mr. Vasuntlal Chauhan*, translated from Gujarati by
K. Nanavati. Ahmedabad.

Parry, J.P., J. Breman, and K. Kapadia (eds) (1999), *The Worlds of
Industrial Labour: Contributions to Indian Sociology*, Occasional
Studies 9. New Delhi: Sage Publications.

Patel, B.B. (1988), *Workers of Closed Textile Mills: Patterns and Problems
of their Absorption in a Metropolitan Labour Market*. Ahmedabad:
Oxford & IBH Publishing Co.

———— (1997), 'Informalisation of Industrial Labour: Displaced
Textile Workers in Gujarat and their Struggle for Alternatives'.

Paper presented in the workshop on 'The Worlds of Indian Industrial Labour', Centre for Asian Studies, Amsterdam.

Patel, S.J. (1952), *Agricultural Labourers in Modern India and Pakistan.* Bombay: Current Book House.

Patel, V. (1990), 'Perspective on Women's Work and Status', Paper presented at the seminar on 'Women and Work', Centre for Social Studies, Surat.

Pathy, J. (1993), *The Dreary December and the Oriya Textile Workers in Surat.* Surat: Centre for Social Studies.

Perlin, E. (1979), 'Ragi, Roti and Four-yard Dhoties: Indian Mill Workers as Historical Sources', in M. Gaborieau and A. Thorner (eds), *Asie du sud: Traditions et Changements*, pp. 451–57. Paris: Editions du CRNS.

Portes, A., M. Castells, and L.A. Benton (1989), *The Informal Economy: Studies in Advanced and Less Developed Countries.* Baltimore: Johns Hopkins.

Prakash, Gyan (1990), *Bonded Histories: Genealogies of Labor Servitude in Colonial India.* Cambridge: Cambridge University Press.

Punalekar, D.S. (1992), 'Urbanization and Social Change: A Case Study of a Fringe Village', Unpublished PhD thesis, Sardar Patel University, Vallabh Vidyanagar.

Punalekar, S.P. (1988), *Informalization and Dependency: A Study of Jari and Embroidery Workers in South Gujarat.* Surat: Centre for Social Studies.

——— (1993), *Seeds of Marginalization and Instability: A Study of Street Children in Gujarat Cities.* Surat: Centre for Social Studies.

Punalekar, S.P. and A. Patel (1990), *Survival Strategies of Female Casual Labourers in Gujarat: A Study of Female Workers of Casual Labour Markets (Chakla Bazars) in South and Central Gujarat Cities.* Surat: Centre for Social Studies.

Raj, K.N. (1993), 'Unemployment and Structural Changes in Indian Rural Society', in T.S. Papola, P.P. Ghosh, and A.N. Sharma (eds), *Labour, Employment and Industrial Relations in India.* New Delhi: The Indian Society of Labour Economics and B.R. Publishing Corporation.

Ram, K. (1984), 'The Indian Working Class and the Peasantry: A Review of Current Evidence on Interlinks between the Two Classes', in A.N. Das, V. Nilkant, and P.S. Dubey (eds), *The Worker and the Working Class: A Labour Studies Anthology*, pp. 181–6. New Delhi: Public Enterprises Centre for Continuing Education.

Ramachandran, V.K. (1990), *Wage Labour and Unfreedom in Indian Agriculture: An Indian Case Study.* Oxford: Clarendon Press.

Ramaswamy, E.A. (1977), *The Worker and His Union: A Study in South India*. Bombay: Allied Publishers.

———— (1988), *Worker Consciousness and Trade Union Response*. London: Oxford University Press.

———— (1990), 'Indian Trade Unionism: The Crisis of Leadership', in M. Holmstrom (ed.), *Work for Wages in South Asia*, pp. 160–72. New Delhi: Manohar.

Ramaswamy, U. (1983), *Work, Union and Community: Industrial Man in South India*. New Delhi: Oxford University Press.

Randeria, S. and A. Yagnik (1990), 'Holiday from Labour Laws', in A.R. Desai (ed.), *Repression and Resistance in India: Violation of Democratic Rights of the Working Class, Rural Poor, Adivasis and Dalits*. Bombay: Popular Prakashan, pp. 82–8.

Ray, R.K. (1979), *Industrialisation in India: Growth and Conflict in the Private Corporate Sector, 1914–47*. New Delhi: Oxford University Press.

Report of a Survey (1978). 'Working Class Women and Working Class Families in Bombay', *Economic and Political Weekly*, vol. 13, no. 29, pp. 1169–73.

*Report of the Salt Pan Industry in Bombay Province for the Year 1947–48* (1950). Bombay: Government Central Press.

Robb, P. (1993), *Dalit Movements and the Meanings of Labour in India*. New Delhi: Oxford University Press.

Rudra, A. (1984), 'Local Power and Farm Level Decision-making', in M. Desai, S. Rudolph, and A. Rudra (eds), *Agrarian Power and Agricultural Productivity in South Asia*, pp. 250–80. New Delhi: Oxford University Press.

———— (1990), 'Class Relations in Agriculture', in U. Patnaik (ed.), *Agrarian Relations and Accumulation: The Mode of Production Debate in India*. New Delhi: Oxford University Press.

Sanyal, B. (1991), 'Organizing the Self-Employed', *International Labour Review*, vol. 130, pp. 39–56.

Scott, J.C. (1985), *Weapons of the Weak: Everyday Forms of Peasant Resistance*. New Haven: Yale University Press.

———— (1990), *Domination and the Arts of Resistance: Hidden Transcripts*. New Haven: Yale University Press.

Sen, S. (1977), *Working Class of India: History of Emergence and Movement 1830–1970*. Calcutta: K.P. Bagchi & Co.

Shah, A.M. (2002), 'For a More Humane Society', *Seminar*, no. 513, pp. 58–60.

Shah, G. (1993), 'Surat 1993', *Seminar*, no. 411, pp. 34–7.

———— (1994), 'Identity, Communal Consciousness and Politics', *Economic and Political Weekly*, vol. 29, no. 19, pp. 1133–40.

———— (2002), 'Caste, Hindutva and Hideousness', *Economic and Political Weekly*, vol. 37, no. 15, pp. 1391–3.

Sharma, B.R. (1970), 'The Industrial Workers: Some Myths and Realities', *Economic and Political Weekly*, vol. 5, no. 22, pp. 875–8.

———— (1974), *The Indian Industrial Worker: Issues in Perspective*. New Delhi: Vikas.

———— (1978), 'Union Involvement Revisited', *Economic and Political Weekly*, vol. 13, no. 30, pp. 1233–9.

Sharma, P.D. (1980), *Textile Labour Association: Role Effectiveness and Workers' Perception*. New Delhi: Indian Council of Social Science Research.

Sheth, N.R. (1968), *The Social Framework of an Indian Factory*. Manchester: Manchester University Press.

Singer, M. (1968), 'The Indian Joint Family in Modern Industry', in M. Singer and B.C. Cohn (eds), *Structure and Change in Indian Society*, pp. 423–52. Chicago: Aldine Publishing Co.

Singh, R.R. (1971), *Labour Economics*. Agra: Sri Ram Mehra & Co.

Sinha, G.P. (1993), 'Crisis in Industrial Relations Policy', in T.S. Papola, P.P. Ghosh, and A.N. Sharma (eds), *Labour, Employment and Industrial Relations in India*. Presidential Addresses, The Indian Society of Labour Economics. Delhi: B.R. Publishing Corporation, pp. 259–73.

Soni, J. (1990), 'Jari Industry and Women Workers', Paper presented at the seminar on 'Women and Work', Centre for Social Studies, Surat.

South Gujarat University (1984), *Working and Living Conditions of the Surat Textile Workers: A Survey*. Submitted to the Honourable Chief Justice of the Gujarat High Court (17 December). Surat: Department of Sociology, South Gujarat University.

Soto, H. de (1989), *The Other Path: The Invisible Revolution in the Third World*. New York: Harper & Row.

———— (2000), *The Mystery of Capital: Why Capitalism Triumphs in the West and Fails Everywhere Else*. London: Bantam Press.

Souza, P. d' (1993), 'Coping with Problems of Investigating Conditions of Slum Dwellers', Paper presented in the seminar on 'Urban Poor in India', Centre for Social Studies, Surat.

Spodek, H. (2001), 'Crises and Response: Ahmedabad 2000', *Economic and Political Weekly*, vol. 36, no. 29, pp. 1627–39.

Sundaram, K. (2001), 'Employment–Unemployment Situation in the Nineties: Some Results from NSS 55th Round Survey', *Economic and Political Weekly*, vol. 36, no. 11, pp. 931–40.

Swaan, A. de (1988), *In Care of the State: Health Care, Education and Welfare in Europe and the USA in the Modern Era*. Cambridge: Polity Press.

Thakore, J. (2002), 'Me and My Mill' (Hum ane mari mill), *Naya Marg*, 1 and 16 September.

Thompson, E.P. (1967), 'Time, Work-Discipline and Industrial Capitalism', *Past and Present*, vol. 38, December, pp. 56–97.

————— (1993), *Customs in Common*. Harmondsworth: Penguin Books.

Thorbecke, E. (1973), 'The Employment Problem: A Critical Evaluation of Four ILO Comprehensive Country Reports', *International Labour Review*, vol. 107, no. 5, May, pp. 393–423.

Thorner, D. and A. Thorner (1962), *Land and Labour in India*. Bombay: Asia Publishing House.

Unni, J. (2000), *Urban Informal Sector: Size and Income Generation Processes in Gujarat, Part I*. SEWA–GIDR–ISST–NCAER Report No. 2, National Council of Applied Economic Research, New Delhi.

————— (2001), 'Gender and Informality in Labour Market in South Asia', *Economic and Political Weekly*, vol. 36, no. 26, pp. 2366–77.

Unni, J. and N. Bali (2001), 'Subcontracted Workers in the Garment Industry in India', Working Paper No. 123, Gujarat Institute of Development Research, Ahmedabad.

Varshney, A. (2002), *Ethnic Conflict and Civic Life: Hindus and Muslims in India*. New Delhi: Oxford University Press.

Veen, K.W. van der (1979), 'Urbanization, Migration and Primordial Attachments', in S.D. Pillai and C. Baks (eds), *Winners and Losers: Styles of Development and Change in an Indian Region*. Bombay: Popular Prakashan, pp. 43–80.

Versluys, J.D.N., P.H. Prabhu, and C.N. Vakil (1961), *Social and Cultural Factors affecting Productivity of Industrial Workers in India*. New Delhi: UNESCO.

VIKAS (1996), *Life and Living of Urban Poor. Participatory Research and Training Workshops Series, Part II: Urban Poor and Environment*. Ahmedabad: Vikas Centre for Development.

Vyas, K.I. (1979), 'Tribals in a Non-tribal Setting: A Sociological Study of Tribals in an Urban Community', Unpublished PhD thesis, South Gujarat University, Surat.

World Bank (1995), *World Development Report—Workers in an Integrating World*. Washington, DC: The World Bank.

———— (2000), *World Development Report, 2000–1: Attacking Poverty*. Washington, DC: World Bank.

# About the Author

**Jan Breman** is Emeritus Professor of Comparative Sociology at the University of Amsterdam and Honorary Fellow with the International Institute of Social History in Amsterdam. The themes of his research are past and present labour relations, and work and employment in rural and urban South and Southeast Asia. Most of his publications are empirical studies in which he contextualizes his fieldwork-based findings in macro settings. Among various others, he has authored *Outcast Labour in Asia: Circulation and Informalization of the Workforce at the Bottom of the Economy* (Oxford University Press, 2009; paperback edition in 2012) and *The Poverty Regime in Village India: Half a Century of Work and Life at the Bottom of the Rural Economy in South Gujarat* (Oxford University Press, 2007), and co-authored (with Arvind Das; photographs by Ravi Agarwal) *Down and Out: Labouring under Global Capitalism* (Oxford University Press, 2000). He has also co-edited (with Isabelle Guérin and Aseem Prakash) *India's Unfree Workforce: Of Bondage Old and New* (Oxford University Press, 2009), and (with K.P. Kannan) *The Long Road to Social Security* (Oxford University Press, 2013).